INSPIRED to TEACH

*The Story of the College of Sarum St Michael
(Salisbury Training College)*

1841-1978

by
Jenny Head
and Anne Johns

ELSP

Published by ELSP
in 2015

www.ex-librisbooks.co.uk

Origination by Ex Libris Press
Bradford on Avon, Wiltshire

Printed by Gomer Press
Llandysul Enterprise Park
Llandysul
Ceredigion   Wales
SA44 4JL

ISBN 978-1-906641-79-5

CONTENTS

'I like to think that what has been attempted here since 1841 will live on. In the schools, in the parishes and in the hearts and minds of the children taught by our students will be enshrined the very purpose for which the College was set up'.

Christian Wilson, College Principal, 1978

Foreword

by

The Rt Revd Nicholas Holtam, The Bishop of Salisbury

The College of Sarum St Michael/Salisbury Training College made a great contribution to education. Established in 1841, it was the Diocesan Training College to supply women teachers to National (Church of England) schools in the Dioceses of Salisbury and Winchester, to complement that for men in Winchester. In 1905 an HMI report said: "The teachers it sends out are hardworking, high minded and intelligent". That suggests a certain standard of those who were 'Inspired to Teach.'

Former members of the College still gather every year in extraordinary number. Very nearly everyone is now retired, but what a contribution they have made to education and to the lives of countless young people! At reunions it is easy to be nostalgic, but that is not the spirit of the occasion. Nor is it the spirit of this History of the College. There are stories and it was fun. It has been well worthwhile setting down an orderly account whilst there are still people able to do so, and others to read and enjoy it. Yet, what is striking about the people who trained at Sarum is that they are still passionate about education and young people, and they still feel they have a contribution to make from their training, experience and wisdom. This is to do with the spirit and spirituality of the place, of a College set in the Cathedral Close.

The College motto was 'In quietness and in confidence shall be your strength'. It sounds practical: don't fuss, get on with it and do the job for which you were trained. The prophet Isaiah was addressing a rebellious people and telling them how to behave. In this, Sarum St Michael might still have a contribution to make through its former students to the rapidly changing educational landscape.

This is a rich History for which much gratitude to Anne Johns and Jenny Head. It is to be cherished and enjoyed and wherever possible its lessons are still to be deployed in quiet confidence.

+Nicholas Sarum

We dedicate 'Inspired to Teach' to Chris and Henry, our boyfriends of the 1960s, our husbands for 45 years. We thank them for their support, encouragement and patience, which has meant everything to us.

Introduction

In 2011, at the Annual Reunion of the College of Sarum St Michael Old Students' Association, exactly 170 years since Salisbury Diocesan Training College opened, around 500 past students gathered in the Cathedral to celebrate their College years. It is remarkable that although the College closed in 1978, there are still around 500 members of the Old Students' Association. We all share memories of a special college, of a unique place and time, and of living and learning in The Close. Founded in 1841, the College was the first Church of England Training College for women teachers.

Under the Cathedral spire we were 'inspired to teach'.

Many people have expressed a desire that the College memories and experiences be recorded in a book. We hope that this varied and lively collection of photos, reflections, letters, memoirs and illustrations will bring its special ethos to life.

Situated in The Close, the College absorbed the atmosphere and spirituality of the Cathedral, leaving a deep and lasting impression on students and their teaching, and influencing the lives of many. It made a significant contribution to the development of education, and is, of course, deeply embedded in the history of Salisbury.

Jenny Head & Anne Johns
February 2015

The Cathedral from the west
painted by Sue Finniss from
A Walk in The Close

Acknowledgements

We are extremely grateful to Adrian Green, Director of The Salisbury Museum for allowing us to work in our old College library – nowhere could have been better! We have greatly appreciated the support and encouragement shown to us by the staff and volunteers. King's House Café provided us with delicious sustenance in what was the College 'Quiet Room'.

We are indebted to former students, friends and all who have shared their memories and photographs and everyone who has given a financial donation and/or pre-ordered the book. There are too many to mention individually but our heartfelt thanks to them all! The College of Sarum St Michael OSA helped us to begin by giving us a generous loan.

Roger Jones, our publisher and graphic designer, has entered into the project with such enthusiasm and commitment. We appreciate his patience with two novice authors and his expertise and skill in presenting the material. We are indebted to Kevin Sanders for setting up our website and for his valuable ongoing IT support and Michael Marshman for putting us on the right road with a clear business plan.

We are fortunate in having talented friends whose artistic skills have contributed so much to the book: Sue Finniss, Pat Jones, Kate Sykes, Austin Thorp and Jean Watts. We thank Alan Clarke for generously sharing his photographs, Dr Ian Smith for use of his photographs from 'A photographic essay of College Life 1883-1978' and Robert Poole for the use of his mother's photographs.

We are grateful to The Right Revd. Nicholas Holtam, Bishop of Salisbury, for his interest and belief in our project and for writing the Foreword. We value the sponsorship by The Chalke Valley History Trust and being given a pitch at their exciting History Festival.

Our thanks to the *Salisbury Journal*, Revd Dr John Gay, Helen Gibson at the Dorset County Museum, Tracy Godden and the Fern Street Settlement , Cedric Rees Johns, Caroline Rippier, Katharine Shearing and Ruth Newman for their advice and encouragement. We have appreciated the help of Joan Aiwerioghene, Eric Hart, Richard Maidment, and John Waddington (for information about the Old Deanery and Medieval Hall). The Wiltshire and Swindon History Centre, Sevington Victorian School, the Male family, Gerald and Sue Shergold re Skylark Coaches and numerous archivists have also contributed to the book. We are grateful to Judith Nicholls for allowing us to include her poems. Our thanks to Geraldine Beare for her skilful editing and to Diana Davies for her thorough final proof read. 'Diolch' to Pît Dafis of Gomer Press.

We value the support from 'Fitting Tribute' of Edington Station Yard for their help with storage.

This book could not have been written without the thorough research of Miss Lucy Sanderson Taylor, former lecturer in Education and author of College in the Close. Her admirable work is the backbone of so much of our own writing. Our thanks go to Miss Joan Hughes who put together *The Last Ten Years*.

Sheila Higgins and John Say lectured in English at the College in the 1960 and 1970s. We were delighted when they agreed to be our proof readers and it has been a privilege and a joy to work with them. As we recorded the story, John and Sheila 'lived it' with us, immersing themselves in our writing and putting in long hours of thoughtful work. Even more, they shared our enthusiasm, provided listening ears and kept us going when we were flagging. We always felt better after meeting them! Thank you, John and Sheila, for your wonderful contributions to *Inspired to Teach*.

Chapter 1

In the Beginning

1841 - 1891

In the beginning

children require schools, schools require teachers, teachers require training ...

In the beginning, there was no state involvement in education. In the early 19th century education was seen as a philanthropic enterprise in which the children of the poor could be provided with rudimentary schooling, as well as religious and moral instruction. Society was based on a rigid social structure and the quality of life that a person could expect depended on whether he or she was born into poverty or plenty. This is illustrated in the hymn *All things bright and beautiful* which was written by Mrs Cecil Alexander in 1848:

> 'The rich man in his castle,
> The poor man at his gate,
> God made them, high and lowly,
> And order'd their estate'

There was, however, growing recognition of the plight of poor children. A series of Factory Acts introduced legislation to protect children in factories and cotton mills, and to reduce their working hours. The need for a disciplined and obedient labour force that would meet the increasing demands of industry was also recognised. Charles Dickens, in writing about impoverished children who turned to crime in order to survive, succeeded in awakening a sense of responsibility in people. He felt that education would surely lead the way to a better life.

Education was becoming a topical subject, but concern, even hostility, was expressed about the possible consequences of giving poor children any more than 'general instruction in reading that they may read the Scriptures'.

It was against this background that two religious societies finally brought education to the fore.

The National Society for the Education of the Poor in the Principles of the Established Church was founded in 1811 by the Church of England. It was financed by private charity and set out to plant a National (Church of England) School in every parish in England and Wales. Children would receive secular instruction 'sufficient to guide them through life in their proper station'.

> 'The inclusion of the fourth 'R' of Religion alongside the other three (reading, writing and 'rithmetic) was assumed as right. It took the form of the Bible, Catechism and prayer book services'.
> Derek Gillard, *Education in England*

The British and Foreign School Society, founded in 1814, had trained male and female teachers since 1806. The society, which was non-denominational, set up British Schools as well as teacher training institutions.

Elementary schools founded by both societies began to spread across the country, aided by annual government grants from 1833.

In 1839 Dr James Kay became the Secretary of the Committee of Council on Education, which was the first central government agency to be concerned with public elementary education. Recognising the need for trained teachers, Dr Kay succeeded in extending the government grants to include the building of Training Schools. By 1860 the National Society owned about 90 per cent of elementary schools.

The National Society remains true to its roots today, two hundred and four years after it was founded:

> 'It was through The National Society that the first universal education in England and Wales was established. Although the state later joined us, we have maintained our deep commitment to distinctive Christian education for the whole community. Today nearly one million pupils are educated in nearly 5,000 Church of England and Church of Wales schools. The church-school family is a national treasure that is greatly appreciated by parents across the country'.
> *Celebrating 200 Years of the National Society*, 2012

Joshua Watson, a principal founder of the National Society
© National Portrait Gallery

The Salisbury story begins

The National Society encouraged each diocese to form a Board of Education. The Bishop of Salisbury, Edward Denison, was a great supporter of education, fearing that the lack of schooling contributed to the restlessness of the poor. A meeting of interested clergy and laity was held on 13th December 1838. One of the resolutions arising from it was to 'take into consideration the expediency of founding an Institution for the training of Masters and Mistresses'.

In January 1840 the Revd William Hony, Secretary of the Salisbury Diocesan Board of Education, received a letter from the Revd John Sinclair, Secretary of the National Society, saying that the newly founded schools required trained staff. The concept of teacher training was growing.

The Winchester and Salisbury Diocesan Boards of Education met in March 1840 to confer about the possibility of setting up Training Schools in both cities. The proposed premises in Winchester had previously been used by the School of Choristers, and were deemed more suitable for men. Salisbury did not argue the point and agreed that 'the establishment of a Training School in Salisbury for Mistresses was most desirable'.

Urgency was in the air. The Training Schools were to be opened as soon as possible and Salisbury was quick to respond. Advice was received from the Principal of the National Society Central School as to the organisation of boarding houses, the daily timetable, staffing and salaries and the furnishing and provision of a house.

'It was felt strongly that the style of living in the establishment should be such as not to raise the ideas of the pupils above the station of village schoolmistresses; nor on the other hand so low as to deter persons above the rank of the poor from becoming inmates'.

Regulations for the Management of the Training School, Salisbury Diocesan Board of Education (SDBE)

Salisbury Training School was founded in 1841. Our research leads us to believe that, amidst a flurry of activity to train teachers, Salisbury was the first college to be founded specifically for women. The institution owed much to the vision and commitment of its founders, especially Bishop Denison and Canon (later Bishop) Hamilton.

Having embarked on the process of finding a 'person of superior attainments' to lead the Training School, members of the Salisbury Diocesan Board of Education were confident in their final choice. This is reflected in the report of the *Salisbury and Winchester Journal*:

Salisbury and Winchester Journal, 1839

Salisbury and Winchester Journal, 1840

Mrs Duncan: the first Lady Superintendent

Margaret Duncan was born in 1791 in Methlick, Aberdeenshire. She was a well-educated Scots woman who taught in Edinburgh for some years and became well known for her excellent work and enlightened views on education. Initially this was in the 'Sessional School' that opened in 1813. The school had one teacher and many children and the Monitorial System of teaching was successfully used. Mrs Duncan went on to use the same system in a boarding school for 30 girls in her home in Edinburgh.

> 'We had recently the pleasure of witnessing a most beautiful specimen of the adaptation of this system to the instruction of young ladies at the school of Mrs Duncan in this city. The correctness of her pupils' answers to every question put to them, relative to what they read, we have never seen surpassed'.
>
> *Account of the Edinburgh Sessional School, 1830*

At this time Mrs Duncan was a member of the Revd John Sinclair's Episcopal Church and was grateful for his support when 'circumstances of domestic difficulties' befell her. This friendship with John Sinclair was to prove significant in later years.

Mrs Duncan, the first Lady Superintendent 1841-1862
Courtesy of The Salisbury Museum

In about 1838 Mrs Duncan came to London to be near to her now married daughter. Although continuing to board and instruct several pupils from Edinburgh, her own future was uncertain. She had become painfully aware that governesses were not respected members of London society, many being almost as ignorant as their pupils and overworked and underpaid. Shocked by this situation and concerned about her own circumstances, Mrs Duncan wondered how she would find respectable and remunerative employment.

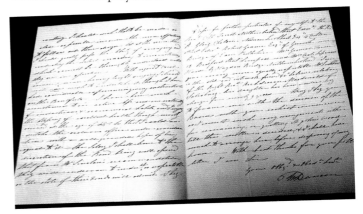

Mrs Duncan's acceptance letter
Courtesy of Wiltshire & Swindon History Centre

On November 6th 1840 she received a letter from the newly established Salisbury Diocesan Board of Education, inviting her to become Governess of the Training School. This letter did not come as a complete surprise, for her friend the Revd John Sinclair was by now Secretary of the National Society and had already discussed the interesting proposition with her. Put in modern terminology, it can be seen that Mrs Duncan was 'head-hunted'. She was then approximately 48 years old and an experienced, dedicated and innovative teacher, but she was used to instructing 'young ladies from good families'. Pupils at the Training School would be coming from working class homes and from National Schools where they would have had only an elementary education.

Mrs Duncan had, however, found pleasure and intellectual fulfilment in running her boarding school, and could envisage that this residential role might provide similar satisfaction, as well as some status and security. She could see, too, that her own religious commitment, grounded in the Scottish Episcopal Church, a church that was in full communion with the Church of England, would be acceptable to her employers, the Diocesan Board of Education. Perhaps, too, we may imagine that this keen teacher was excited by the challenge of teaching others to teach.

Mrs Duncan's letter to the Salisbury Diocesan Board of Education tells us more about her. Lucy Sanderson Taylor (LST) commented on this in *College in the Close*:

'The vocabulary is competent; there is exactness of composition and elegance in style, in keeping with a well-educated person of those times. They show dignity and firmness of character and a clear-headed, business-like handling of affairs, together with a depth of earnestness in her approach to her work'.

As a professional woman with exemplary high moral and intellectual standards, Mrs Duncan was perfectly capable of organising her own affairs. Her excellent work in Edinburgh, the backing of the National Society and an impressive array of referees convinced the Salisbury Diocesan Board of Education that she had the requisite skills to lead the fledgling Training School.

Mrs Duncan was duly appointed Lady Superintendent of The Training School which opened at Number 8/9, Bishop's Walk, The Close on January 15th 1841.

Having arranged for the sale of her London house and the purchase by the Salisbury Diocesan Board of Education of some of its furnishings, Mrs Duncan duly arrived in Salisbury on Monday January 11th 1841. This certainly didn't leave much time to prepare for the opening but, as she explained in a letter, her daughter was 'having an increase to her family' and she wished to spend a few days with her - a comment that suggests humanity and warmth of character. Mrs Duncan also expressed her appreciation to the Board for their thoughtfulness in arranging for someone to be in the house to greet her when she arrived. The weather, however, was less welcoming, with The Close being inundated with flood-water.

By the time that Mrs Duncan retired in 1862, there were more than sixty pupils and the Training School had moved into King's House. During her time as Lady Superintendent she had won the affection of pupils, showing patience, kindness, concern and consideration, but also setting exacting standards and being very strict in requiring attention to every one of her rules and regulations. She did, however, have a lighter side to her character.

'What a profound influence she had over us and in what awe she kept us, but when she chose to unbend, with what quaint, racy speeches she would delight us'.

Letter from C Teviot
Courtesy of Wiltshire & Swindon History Centre

Bishop Hamilton's words express admiration, respect and gratitude to the person who had, from the beginning, nurtured and steered the Training School.

'That excellent Lady who has conducted the Institution with such wisdom – such devotedness – such gentleness – such a single eye to duty – such consideration and patience, as to have drawn around her the affections not only of her pupils, but of all who have been conversant with her work, has had in the change of heart and character in some of her pupils, and the growth in Christian steadfastness of others, good cause to rejoice'.

Terminology

For reasons of consistency the following terminology will be used throughout 'In the Beginning', which covers the first 50 years of the College:

Lady Superintendent (Principal)

Pupils (Students)

Governesses/Mistresses (Teachers)

Training School (College)

Pupil teacher (trainee teacher in school)

The Monitorial System

The Monitorial System, devised by Joseph Lancaster, provided schooling for large numbers of children at a low cost. Teachers were in short supply, and with this method one person could control many children. The system relied on child monitors who were recruited from amongst the older and more advanced pupils. The monitors were then instructed by the teacher before passing on what they had learnt to the other pupils.

Lancaster's methods were discredited by the 1840s but, in getting children off the streets and into schools, he had helped to sway public opinion in favour of a basic, moral education that might result in an obedient, trained work force.

Mr Biddlecombe I presume?
Courtesy of The Salisbury Museum

Mr Biddlecombe Music Master

Mrs Duncan had explained in her letter of acceptance that she did not wish to undertake the teaching of singing. Mr James Biddlecombe was therefore employed as Music Master to give pupils twice weekly singing lessons. He also taught Arithmetic from 1848.

> 'Mr Biddlecombe was besides being one of the singing men, also church pricker, or copier of music for the choir, overseer of The Close and collector of taxes and rates in The Close, in addition to running a small school and having the charge of about half a dozen boys whom he undertook to educate'.
> Peter L. Smith, *In the Shadow of Salisbury Spire*

Disciplining the boys was a challenge. Mr Biddlecombe resorted to corporal punishment and was given vociferous encouragement by his daughter from the kitchen window.

Instructing docile and amenable young ladies at the Training School was probably more congenial. Mr Biddlecombe certainly appears to have been a great favourite in the Training School and a pupil from the 1840s remembered that he was often 'the only gentleman present' on enjoyable occasions such as Mrs Duncan's birthday evenings.

Mr Biddlecombe retired in 1859. Martha Gibson, writing in 1891, mentioned in her reminiscences that 'he attended three times a week. He was getting on in years then and of course is now at rest'.

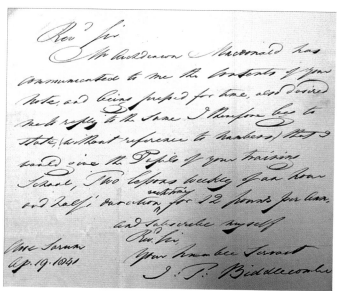

Letter from Mr Biddlecombe agreeing to be Music Master
Courtesy of The Salisbury Museum

Pupil Teachers and Queen's Scholars

In 1846 the Committee of the Council on Education issued minutes on the arrangements regarding pupil teachers. Bright pupils aged thirteen or over could remain at school to become assistant teachers. They were apprenticed to teachers who had been approved by HMI and they stayed until they were eighteen years old. During this time they received seven and a half hours of tuition per week from the teacher, in order to improve their own knowledge and skills. They taught the younger pupils each day to gain practice in teaching. At the age of eighteen, at the end of their apprenticeship, they were eligible to enter an examination leading to a Queen's Scholarship which would finance their attendance at a Training School. Successful candidates were known as 'Queen's Scholars' because they were supported by money from the Queen's Government. In 1856 these scholars were required to pledge to teach for a certain number of years at a recognised school, or had to repay the grant.

At Salisbury Training School the number of Queen's Scholars gradually increased. In 1871, when there were 67 pupils in residence, all but one were Queen's Scholars.

A pupil recalling The Training School in the 1850s wrote:

'As yet pupil teachers were a novelty – I think there were about two in our number, and these excellent of their kind – but as they began to pour in, in great numbers, in the following year, we regarded their coming rather as an intrusion into our family party, and we did not readily take to each other. While they despised us for the want of knowledge of technicalities which they were familiar with, we, on our part thought them one-idea'd, wanting in general knowledge, and in some cases pedantic and conceited'.

Entry Requirements 1841

'Previously to admission they will be examined in reading, writing, and spelling – in the first four rules of arithmetic, simple and compound, in the history of the Old and New Testaments, and in the Church Catechism. Without a competent knowledge of these they will not be admissible'.

From the first book issued by the Diocesan Education Committee

Reference for Jane Simmonds, 1842

Jane Simmonds, whom I wish to recommend to the Salisbury Training School for Mistresses, is a young woman who has attended my Sunday School for some time to teach the younger children. She was never a scholar in my school and I find her having by no means a perfect acquaintance with Scripture and with History. She can read and write, it being in the first person only, and she can do Arithmetic both simple and compound. She wishes much to learn, has a good understanding and a very good character. I trust that she will be accepted. She is ready to go at any time in the next week you may fix.

Courtesy of Wiltshire and Swindon History Centre

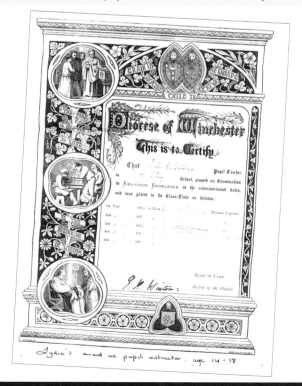

Lydia Steven's Pupil Teacher Certificate
Courtesy of Wiltshire and Swindon History Centre

The early houses of the Training School

On January 15th 1841 Salisbury Training School opened; there are different views as to whether this was at No 8 or No 9, The Close. The two houses were originally one house, slightly different in date. Canon Steward stated:

> 'The house, lately occupied by Mrs Fawson, in the Close on the east side of the Bishop's Walk, was opened for Training School Mistresses by The Diocesan Board of Education, with Mrs Duncan as the Lady Superintendent'.
>
> *Our Training College, Salisbury 1841-1908* Canon Steward (known as 'The Red Book')

Number 9 The Close

In her book *The College in the Close*, Lucy Sanderson Taylor described a survey on the house in February 1841 by Mr J. M. Peniston, which indicated that the house was in reasonable repair, with some plastering and pointing needing to be done. There were fireplaces in all the rooms, clothes-closets in bedrooms and shutters to some of the windows. The kitchen floor was stone, partly repaired with white brick and very rough in parts. The pantry and washhouse required attention. There was a privy adjoining the coalhouse and an ash hole under the large dining-room.

Mary Ann Bolland was a pupil who arrived in 1843. She remained at the Training School as an assistant until 1848. She recalled the household arrangements as being unsatisfactory, with burnt and unappetising food.

Canon Steward wrote: 'In 1843 The Board purchased the lease of the Registrar's House, the house now occupied by Mr Broderick, for £1293'. Dora Robertson, writing in her book 'The History of Number 11, The Close', believes that Number 11 was where the Training School moved. It is currently part of Bishop Wordsworth's School.

In March 1849 a pupil arriving at the Training School related how she felt homesick:

> 'But time and work proved speedy healers. The College then was really a private residence, the rooms being fitted up for 33 students. We left the old house for good when we broke up for the Midsummer Vacation. We used to think the rooms in that house were cosier than in the present one. The evergreens were peeping in at the windows and made them very pleasant. A lawn stretched at the back of the house, and on it grew a large mulberry tree, which tempted us sorely, as it was forbidden fruit'.

By 1850 the Board was feeling pleased with an increase in pupils due to the Training School's reputation for achievements, and felt this justified moving to larger premises. The Training School moved into its new home 'The King's House' in July 1851, with 33 pupils in residence.

Number 11 The Close

Martha Gibson: The first student

Sharing the wintry reception of January 1841 came a young woman aged sixteen years, eleven months, by stage coach from the Parish of Chelsham, near Croydon in Surrey'. Her father's 'station in life' was recorded in the first Admission Register as 'day labourer'.

Martha Gibson had been educated at the National School in Chelsham. It is likely that the stage coach referred to in the quotation above, was in fact a mail coach, as there were regular daily services between Salisbury and London in the early 1840s. Martha, as a young woman travelling alone, was chaperoned on her journey by her vicar. Mail coaches travelled faster than stage coaches, but still at a speed of no more than 10mph. Her journey from Croydon would have been a long and tiring adventure into the unknown.

Martha's ability, character and desire to teach had been noted at her school. Her standard of 'acquirements' on entering college was, however, recorded in the Admissions Register as 'very low indeed'. She was the only pupil at the Training School for the first six weeks and her memories, recorded in 1891, reveal how she felt:

'I left my home about 15th January in the year 1841, my own Minister accompanying me to the School where I met Mrs Duncan and the servant. I remained alone for about six weeks. Of course I felt very lonely having no other companion. After that time a Young Person came by the name of Whicher whose parents were Managers of the Wilton Union. As time went on we increased in number and soon got into School

Order. Our time for rising was soon after six; we were early to lessons as we had to attend the Cathedral every day, and had our walks with Mrs Duncan. We also took our turn in keeping the school-rooms clean and in order. I can only say we were all very happy and joyful together'.

Martha's health and conduct were very good. She clearly made progress and in her first year was described as being an able pupil and of being 'tolerable in the industrial department'. Alas, by Christmas 1842 she had become less than diligent and her behaviour was described as 'trifling and flippant'. Leaving this momentary lapse behind, the following year showed marked improvement and she was praised for 'diligence in studies and very good work with young children' and for 'being active and neat in needlework and housework, with steady conduct since Christmas'.

The 1841 Census was taken in June and records Martha Gibson as living at the Training School with Mrs Duncan, Alice Lander (Mrs Duncan's three year old granddaughter) and four other pupils aged between fifteen and twenty-five years. By the end of 1841 there was a total of twelve pupils.

Martha left the Training School on April 17th 1843, by which time there were 23 pupils, and took charge of the National School at Haslemere. She taught there for eleven years, earning an annual salary of approximately £30, before marrying George Stenning, a carpenter, in 1853. Martha and George had three children and the 1881 census records the family as living at 79, The High Street.

Martha Gibson on her journey to Salisbury Training School January 1841
Painted by Kate Sykes

By 1891 Martha was widowed. This was the year of the Training School's 50th Jubilee and Canon Edward Steward (Principal), having been in touch with her vicar, invited her to come to stay for the reunion, paying her travelling expenses as she was living in straitened circumstances. Martha's reply to Canon Steward ends with the words:

'I now close with the hope of seeing dear old Salisbury once more'.

Why did Martha end her life in the Workhouse? When Martha Gibson arrived in Salisbury in 1841 she must have been full of hope and optimism about her life ahead. After her husband, George Stenning, had died, Martha fell on hard times and her family was unable to support her. Workhouse records no longer exist, but the 1901 Census records her as a pauper aged 77, living at the Union Workhouse, Hambledon. Conditions were tough and the daily routine in workhouses was often demeaning to the inmates. She died there in 1908 aged 84 years, following a stroke. It is possible that she may have been in the hospital attached to the workhouse, where conditions may have been a little better. She probably had a pauper's funeral. What a sad ending to a life once so full of spirit and endeavour.

St Bartholomew's School, Haslemere

Union Workhouse, Hambledon
Courtesy of Peter Higginbotham and workhouses.org.uk

No.	When and where died	Name and surname	Sex	Age	Occupation	Cause of death	Signature, description and residence of informant
68	Third August 1908 Union Workhouse Hambledon R.D	Martha Stenning	Female	84 years	widow of George Stenning a Carpenter of Haslemere R.D	Cerebral Haemorrhage Coma. Certified by C W Bookir F.R.C.S	E E Howard Master Union Workhouse Hambledon

CERTIFIED to be a true copy of an entry in the certified copy of a Register of Deaths in the District above mentioned.

Given at the GENERAL REGISTER OFFICE, under the Seal of the said Office, the   30th   day of

DYD 543275

Martha's Death Certificate
Courtesy of Somerset House

Setting Chapter 1 in context: A Table of some significant events

Date	Educational	National	Local
1811	Founding of the National Society by the Church of England	Jane Austen published 'Sense and Sensibility'	St Martin's School opened next to St Martin's Church. It was the first National Society School
1833	The State started to give annual grants to the National and British & Foreign Societies for building elementary schools	Factory Act made it illegal to employ children under nine years of age.	Over 1200 children attended Sunday Schools in Salisbury. Use of gas lamps growing (Salisbury Gas Company established 1832)
1837		William IV died. Queen Victoria came to the throne	Meeting in Salisbury about Anti-Corn Law activities. 4,000 attended.
1840	Statutory govt grants for education extended to Training Schools.	First use of anaesthetics. Start of Penny Post. Queen Victoria married Prince Albert	Free Trade demonstration against the Corn Laws on Harnham Hill
1841	Five Training Schools founded by the National Society for the Church of England	Following the Napoleonic Wars the British Empire had become the world's leading power. First UK Census	Salisbury Training School opened – the first designated college for women. Mrs Duncan Lady Superintendent. Martha Gibson was the first pupil but 12 pupils by end of first year
1843	The Factory Act introduced 'half-timer' system of education	Dickens published *'A Christmas Carol'*	
1844	Ragged School Union formed to cater for the poorest children unable to pay 'school pence' demanded by voluntary schools	Queen Victoria opened The Royal Exchange	
1846	Dr James-Kay-Shuttleworth's Pupil Teacher scheme adopted	Repeal of the Corn Laws.	
!847	New grants also extended to workhouse schools	Samuel Morse sent the first telegraph message	First train from London to Salisbury. Celebrations in the Market Square
1849	Dr James Kay-Shuttleworth retired and was made a baronet	Great Famine in Ireland and many people died	Outbreak of cholera in Salisbury-(the 'Venice of England') 192 died.
1850	1,000 schools receiving government grants		Piped water supply for Salisbury
1851		Great Exhibition in London	Population of Salisbury 9,455 Workhouse 'unsuitable' - open privy
1853		Start of the Crimean War	
1854		Battle of Balaclava-The Charge of the Light Brigade	Bishop Denison died and was succeeded by Bishop Hamilton
1855		Livingstone found the Victoria Falls	The last public hanging in Salisbury
1856	Department of Education established to administer grants	End of Crimean War. The Second Opium War began	A fully loaded cattle train from Bristol crashed at Salisbury
1859		Darwin published 'The Origin of the Species'	City growing fast – much building. Salisbury to Yeovil railway opened
1860	6,000 schools receiving grants	The Nightingale Training School for Nurses opened in London	Salisbury Museum & the Theological College were founded
1863	Payment by Results scheme (Revised Code 1862) reduced number of pupil teachers	First section of London Underground opened. Formation of International Red Cross	30 entrants to Training School, diminishing numbers beginning to reflect effects of Revised Code
1870	Forster's Education Act set the framework of education for all children between 5 and 13	British Red Cross established. Death of Charles Dickens	Sir George Gilbert Scott working on renovation of interior of Cathedral
1872		Thomas Hardy 'Under the Greenwood Tree'	Ragged School opened in Milford Street.
1879		Thomas Edison invented the light bulb	
1880	School compulsory from 5 to 10 years	First Boer War	Canon Steward appointed as Chaplain to The Training School
1888	The Cross Commission found Payment by Results and Pupil-Teacher systems unsatisfactory	Clara Grant (old student) doing pioneering work in the East End of London.	
1890	Payment by Results abandoned during the 1890s	The Forth Bridge was opened. It had taken 7 years to build and had cost the lives of 98 men.	Opening of Bishop Wordsworth's School. Canon Steward Principal of the Training School

New Sarum Liberty of The Close

Date	People recorded in the Census
June 1841	Margaret Duncan (45* – Teacher), Martha Gibson (15*), 4 other pupils and Alice Lander (3) Mrs Duncan's granddaughter
March 1851	Margaret Duncan (59 – Superintendent & Governess). Emma Steddy (34 - 2nd Mistress), 27 pupils and 1 servant
April 1861	Margaret Duncan (70 – Superintendent) 1st Governess, 2nd Governess, Model School Mistress, Teacher, 71 pupils, 3 servants
April 1891	Constance Mary Hill (42 – Lady Superintendent and Matron) Barbara Forth (30 – Governess), 4 other governesses, 73 pupils, 3 Laundresses, a Cook, 2 Kitchen Maids and 2 Housemaids

*In the 1841 Census, ages of people over 15 were usually rounded to the nearest five years.

The Census returns reflect the growth of the Training School. By 1851 Emma Steddy had been appointed as Second Mistress. Shortly afterwards the Training School moved to King's House and by 1861 resident staff included Mrs Duncan, a First Governess (Miss Barrett) and a second Governess (Miss Jackson). The Mistress of the Model School and her Pupil Teacher also lived there. The number of domestic staff had increased noticeably by 1891.

Mrs Duncan in later years
Courtesy of Wiltshire and Swindon History Centre

Miss Hill
Courtesy of Wiltshire and Swindon History Centre

The College Authorities & Members of the Staff

Presidents

THE RIGHT REV. THE LORD BISHOPS OF THE DIOCESE

Bishop DENISON, 1841 – 1854. Bishop MOBERLY, 1869 – 1885
Bishop HAMILTON, 1854 – 1869. Bishop WORDSWORTH, 1885

Secretaries

Rev. W.E. HONY, 1841

Rev.Canon HAMILTON, 1841 – 56

Rev. Chancellor FRASER, 1856 – 60

Rev. Canon MORRICE, 1860 – 1884

MEMBERS OF THE STAFF

Lady Superintendents
Mrs DUNCAN, 1841 – 1862
Miss AUSTIN, 1863
Miss PONTET, 1863 – 4
Miss GREENLAW, 1865 – 1882
Miss RODWELL, 1883 – 6
Miss HILL, 1887

Chaplains
Rev. E.C. COLLARD, 1856 – 1864
Rev. RICHARD PHILLIPS, 1864 – 1876
Rev. EDWIN COOMBES, 1876 – 9
Rev. EDWARD STEWARD, 1880

Governesses
Miss SIMMONDS, 1843 – 4
Miss BOLLAND, 1845
Miss JARVIS, 2nd Gov. 1848 – 9
Miss STEDDY, 2nd Gov. 1849 – 1851
Miss BARRETT, 3rd Gov. 1851 – 2nd Gov. 1852,
  1st Gov. to 1863
Miss BRAITHWAITE, 2nd Gov. 1851
Miss MAYNE, 3rd Gov. 1852
Miss BALDWIN, 3rd Gov. 1853 – 4
Miss GODDARD, 3rd Gov. 1854 – 6
Miss JACKSON, 3rd Gov. 1856, 1st Gov. 1863 –1889
Miss WATTS, 2nd Gov. 1863 – 5
Miss MOORE, 3rd Gov. 1863 – 5
Miss YELF, 2nd Gov. 1865 – 1876
Miss STEVENS, 3rd Gov. 1865
Miss JOYNSON, 3rd Gov. 1866
Miss GREENSLADE, 4th Gov. 1873 – 6
Miss READ, 3rd Gov. 1868 – 74
Miss JENNINGS, 4th Gov. 1874, 2nd Gov. 1876 – 9
Miss A. PEPPERELL, 3rd Gov. 1876 – 1881
Miss l. GILL, 4th Gov. 1876 – 9
Miss RHODES, 1879 – 1884
Miss F.A. LEWIS, 2nd Gov. 1880 – 86
Miss M.A. LIPSCOMB, 1880 – 86

Lecturers
Mr BIDDLECOMBE (Music) 1841 – 53
  (Arithmetic) 1848 – 53
Mr COLLARD, 1853
Mr RICHARDSON (Music), 1859
Mr HAYDEN (Music), 1879
Mr TIFFIN (Drawing) 1858 –1876
Mr HARRIS (Drawing), 1883
Mr WHEELER (Arithmetic) 1886

Miss F. SMALL, 1884 – 9
Miss MANNING, 1886
Miss WHATLEY, 1888
Miss CROOK, 1889
Miss FORTH, Head Governess, 1890
Miss NEWMAN, 5th Gov. 1890

Practising Schools, - (Mistresses of Method)
Miss LUCAS   Model School
Miss FORD   Model School
Mrs WHEATON St Edmunds
Miss WHEATON
Miss WARD, 1881
Miss BIANCHI
Miss SMITH
Miss FANNER, 1883

Medical Officers
Dr COX, 1841
Dr. GROVE, 1842
Dr TATUM, 1875
W.D. WILKES, Esq. 1875 – 88
E. KINGSCOTE, Esq. 1889

Source: Edward Steward, *Our Training College*

Rules to be observed in the Dormitories

1   Students to rise at six o'clock and be in the school-room at quarter to seven for Prayers.

2   To turn down the bedding and to open the windows before they leave their bedroom.

3   Not to enter each other's room without permission.

4   Not to take anything to the sick without leave.

5   Hats, Books, Jackets etc not to be kept in the Dormitory cupboards.

6   No eatables of any kind, save biscuits, to be kept in boxes and no tea, cocoa to be made in bedrooms.

7   Dresses for Sunday use are to be fetched from the Dress Cupboard before dark on Saturday afternoons and taken back before nine on Monday morning.

8   Students not to be in bedrooms during the day except Saturday afternoon.

9   Gas not to be lighted without permission.

10   At quarter to ten HS to see that silence is enforced for prayers.

11   Any case of sickness or things for repair to be reported to the Lady Superintendent.

12   No books except books of Devotion to be read in the Dormitories.

13   Cleanliness and tidiness to be observed and care taken of furniture etc.

14   The Head Student to be held responsible for observance of rules.

Governesses, Instructors and Pupils

Mrs Duncan, the Lady Superintendent, was at first the only instructor, apart from Canon Hamilton, whose Sunday evening lectures were 'thoroughly appreciated' as were Mr Biddlecombe's Singing Classes and Arithmetic lessons. A Second Mistress, Miss Jarvis, was appointed by 1849. She taught the second class, took her meals with the pupils and accompanied them to the Cathedral and on their walks.

Pupils in the 1850s were still doing three hours of washing and six hours of mangling or ironing in the laundry each week. 'The life was hard, too exhausting for many a girl, almost hateful to a few'.

Nineteenth century lecture room
Courtesy of The Salisbury Museum

After listening to complaints about the food, Canon Hamilton directed the pupils' minds to Keble's hymn, and the need for self-denial in the Christian life. The hungry pupils felt that they had already had more than enough 'room' to deny themselves, but Canon Hamilton did, however, direct more money into the provision of food, and from then on it improved.

> The trivial round, the common task,
> Will furnish all we ought to ask
> Room to deny ourselves, a road
> To bring us daily nearer God.
> *John Keble*

'If possible, we loved him (Canon Hamilton) more than before' wrote a pupil in her reminiscences of the 1850s.

It is likely that Thomas Hardy used his sisters' experiences at the Training School in Salisbury (Melchester) in his novel *Jude the Obscure*.

'The seventy young women, of ages varying in the main from nineteen to one-and-twenty, though several were older, who at this date filled the species of nunnery known as the Training School at Melchester, formed a very mixed community, which included the daughters of mechanics, curates, surgeons, shopkeepers, farmers, dairymen, soldiers and villagers'.

'She told him about the school as it was at that date, and the rough living, and the mixed character of her fellow-students, gathered together from all parts of the diocese, and how she had to get up and work by gas light in the early morning'.

Clara Grant, a pupil in the 1880s, recorded that the 'Original Ideal of Industrial Work was too much in evidence. Only four servants were kept and practically all the sweeping, dusting and laying of tables was done by weekly Pantry Parties of six pupils'.

During the 1880s pupil numbers were between 70 and 76, in two years, with four resident staff, including the Mistress of the Model School and her pupil teacher.

Many governesses were recruited from the best ex-pupils and became friends, as well as teachers to the pupils. The Head Governess, Miss Jackson, was an 'imperishable memory' to those who knew her, remaining on the staff for thirty-three years of ungrudging service and being succeeded in 1890 by Miss Barbara Forth. Mary Whatley, who headed the Certificate List in 1887, was appointed to the staff within a few weeks of leaving the Training School. Clara Grant described her as 'the best brain of our year, with her broad outlook, deep insight and gentle humour'.

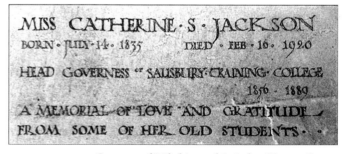

MISS CATHERINE S JACKSON
BORN JULY 14 1835   DIED FEB 16 1920
HEAD GOVERNESS OF SALISBURY TRAINING COLLEGE
1856 - 1889
A MEMORIAL OF LOVE AND GRATITUDE
FROM SOME OF HER OLD STUDENTS

Courtesy of Wiltshire and Swindon History Centre

Canon Edward Steward was appointed Principal in 1890, following the reorganisation of the internal management of the Training School by the Diocesan Board of Education. Miss Hill, who had been appointed Lady Superintendent in 1887, kept the title, though some of her many duties were transferred.

Canon Steward, together with Miss Hill, whom he later described as the 'Lady Abbess of King's House', then set about the task of transforming a Training School of no more than eighty pupils into a collegiate group of buildings that would house and train twice that number.

The Clergy

Bishop Denison	1841 - 1854
Bishop Hamilton	1854 - 1869
Bishop Moberly	1869 - 1885
Bishop Wordsworth	1885 - 1911

The newly founded Training School owed much to two distinguished men: Bishop Edward Denison, whose vision and determination led to its establishment, and Canon Hamilton who was made Clerical Superintendent and Secretary of the Training School until he succeeded Bishop Denison in 1854. Canon Hamilton visited the Training School frequently, getting to know the pupils and taking great care in allotting them to schools. It was said that he 'succeeded in raising its intellectual and religious standard most markedly'.

During the first fifty years Bishops Denison, Hamilton, Moberly and Wordsworth all took an 'unflagging interest in the work of the Board of Education and the Training School'. The support and nurture provided by members of the clergy cemented the relationship between Cathedral and College right from the start.

Dress

'The dress of the pupils is to be most plain and economical'

Miss Jackson with fellow students at the Training School, circa 1870s   Courtesy of Dorset County Museum

Neighbouring colleges delighted in calling the pupils at Salisbury Training School 'The Nuns of St Mary's. Prim round white caps, secluded lives, long hours spent in the 'Cathedral Church of the Blessed Virgin Mary'. It was an apt description and the name stuck!

Students at ease in the Common Room, circa 1880   Courtesy of The Salisbury Museum

In the beginning, a close watch was kept on the appearance of pupils and on the clothes that they wore, as befitted working class girls who were being prepared for teaching in elementary schools. Canon Hamilton insisted from the beginning that pupils should wear 'Caps of Service' when inside the house. A pupil from 1849 wrote:

> 'Our heads in the house were adorned with caps, which were particularly disliked, and out of doors with bonnets; parasols were forbidden, and umbrellas had to answer the purpose'.

Boots were likely to have been strong, serviceable and suitable for taking daily constitutionals with governesses. A pupil from 1888 remembered:

> 'I wonder how many ever forgot the chalk deposits which would so persistently cling to their shoes, which would have to be cleaned by their owners'.

Saturdays were spent on domestic duties, which meant laundry work that involved washing, using a heavy mangle and ironing, as well as repairing clothes and doing the housework. 'All frills on garments to be crimped, gophered, or "Italian ironed" was the order once given'.

In 1868 permission was given to wear hats instead of bonnets for the daily walks and by 1889 the 'round saucer-like caps' that had been worn indoors were laid aside. An act of liberation that must surely have been received with joy!

By 1885 charwomen and washing women were employed and in 1889 a Bradford Washing Machine was bought for £10.00, as well as galvanised tubs and props for clothes lines. Life was improving.

An Early View of the Training School

The Prince Henry Window

- In 1220 the Cathedral's foundation stones were laid. King's House dates back to this period.

- It is said that in 1483 King Richard the Third lodged at King's House.

- There are various accounts of a ghost known as 'The Grey Lady' appearing on the stair of what was known in college days as 'Red Cross Hall'. This name was due to the red glass on the door, traces of which may still be seen.

- Various windows in the house have writing scratched upon them and the initials of the craftsmen working on the glass.

- Improvements were made to the house between 1560 and 1580 including the magnificent cross-wing with mullioned windows. This was the first use of brick as a 'show material' in The Close.

- The great newel post was probably erected around 1598, taking the main staircase up to the top of the house.

- In 1610 and 1613 King James the First and his family were entertained here. The coat of arms of Henry, Prince of Wales, is in the mullioned window of a room overlooking the Cathedral. This room became the Principal's office for the Training College.

- In 1623 Thomas Sadler, the resident at this time, was knighted. His wife, Dame Elihonor Sadler lived in King's House for over 50 years.

- In the 1700s the house was converted into four tenements. During the latter part of this century two schools occupied part of the premises.

- An unusual resident was Lieutenant General Henry Shrapnel who invented the Shrapnel shell. He was resident in King's House from 1785 until 1836.

- In 1837 Godolphin School moved into the house, but later moved to Milford Hill as this was considered a healthier position.

- In 1850 T. H. Wyatt converted the building into The Training School and added the 'Model School'.

- In 1851 The Diocesan Training College was transferred to the King's House in July. It was known at this time as The Training School.

- After the Second World War the future of the College hung in the balance. The decision was taken that the College was to remain and restoration and improvement work began. Work was completed in 1963.

- In 1978, after 137 years, the College finally closed by decision of the Dept. of Education and Science and the Church authorities. Thousands of students had received excellent training at the College.

- King's House became the home of The Salisbury Museum in 1981.

- During 2013-2015 the authors of *Inspired to Teach* undertook their research in the old College Library in King's House, by the kind permission of Salisbury Museum, and enjoyed delicious food and drink in King's House Café!

King's House Porch

Canon Steward, *Our Training College*

Staff and students under mullioned windows Courtesy of The Salisbury Museum

King's House Staircase

King's House was leased to Hugh Powell of Great Durnford, a registrar to the Bishop from the 1560s-1580s. He made many alterations to the house, (including adding the attic windows) to give the impression of a more impressive building. He died in 1587 and his widow, Elihinor, continued to live in the house, marrying Thomas Sadler nine years later. They carried out more improvements during the late 16th and early 17th centuries. These included the great parlour and:

> 'Sadler's fine oak staircase of 1598 with its newel post extending the full height of the house'.
>
> (Excerpt from *The Buildings of King's House* a pamphlet published by The Salisbury Museum)

The staircase and post are still in place today. So many students over the years have climbed up and down the stairs, probably without appreciating the great age of the staircase and post.

King's House Staircase

The Cathedral and the Training School

'Melchester was a quiet and soothing place, almost entirely ecclesiastical in its tone … standing under the walls of the most graceful architectural pile in England, he paused and looked up. The lofty building was visible as far as the roof-ridge; above, the dwindling spire rose more and more remotely, till its apex was quite lost in the mist drifting across it'.

Thomas Hardy: *Jude the Obscure*

The Training School was founded on the principle that 'the work of Instruction is a Christian calling', and from the beginning the Cathedral and its worship was woven into the fabric of the pupils' lives. Daily attendance at Cathedral Matins is likely to have been a welcome respite from lessons and domestic work for those first pupils, cloistered in their small community.

Sundays in the 1850s began with Holy Communion in the Cathedral at 7am, followed by breakfast, then private reading in the schoolroom. Pupils attended the 10.15am service with dinner on their return. Collects and Keble's hymns were repeated to Mrs Duncan from 2-2.30pm, followed by a Cathedral service at 3pm. In the evening the pupils often listened to Mrs Duncan reading a sermon. The day ended with singing hymns and psalms, during which, as Clara Grant remembered, 'some of us wept copiously'. Prayers at 9pm, followed by bed, completed the day. A mistress wished each pupil 'good night', whilst carrying a lantern along her draughty route. One pupil wrote:

'To me Sunday was like a dreary November day, never to be forgotten – much more like a Lenten fast than a bright Easter feast'.

Others appreciated the Sunday services with their beautiful music, but the 'long daily weekday services on a spongy breakfast and in such a strenuous day involved serious strain and inroads on our time'.

A pupil from the 1860s had fond memories of Communion services in the Lady Chapel, but was less happy about having to sit in galleries (since removed) over the stalls at other services.

'We looked out on the accumulated dust of ages upon the carved canopies, and the only sounds, apart from the organ, were echoes. We often wondered why we were put out of the way there'.

Clara Grant, who entered College in 1886, remembered that 'not one of us could help loving the Cathedral, that rich part of our heritage'. She had vivid memories of the noisy clatter of the "Frills" (the choristers) and of 'good Bishop Wordsworth with his truly noble nose and balloon sleeves'.

Often tired and frequently hungry, the presence of the Cathedral comforted, strengthened and inspired the pupils, sustaining their work and the ethos of Christian service that was at the heart of the Training School.

> In thy house, great God, we offer
> of thine own to thee;
> and for thine acceptance proffer,
> all unworthily,
> hearts and minds and hands and voices,
> in our choicest psalmody.

Words from the hymn *Angel Voices*, written by Francis Pott in 1866 and adopted as the Training School hymn soon afterwards.

Salisbury Cathedral
Courtesy of Barrie Pictures

The Early Curriculum

For the first pupils, lessons and domestic work occupied the day from 7am to 9pm. Their only breaks were conducted walks and daily attendance at Cathedral Matins.

> 'In 1852 the School migrated to King's House. I found the discipline very strict, the fare Spartan and the amount of housework seemed appalling. Our entrance examination had required us to define a noun, verb and preposition, to simplify fractions, to give dates for the Deluge, the death of Abraham and the anointing of Saul'.
>
> *College Archives*

Mrs Duncan taught Scripture, Church History, Grammar and Reading. Miss Barrett taught English History, Geography, Music, Needlework and Map Drawing. The Chaplain taught Religious Studies, and visiting masters taught Arithmetic, Science and Music.

The effects of Robert Lowe's unpopular 'Payment by Results' scheme were felt throughout the country. Salisbury reflected what was happening nationally, with numbers of entrants dropping to a worrying 25 in 1865, but rising to 40 in 1891 as the demand for trained teachers began to rise.

The breadth of curriculum in the College was maintained as far as possible and Salisbury rode out the storm. The wisdom of this was shown in 1867 when, in the first step to lessen the strictures of The Revised Code, grants were offered for the teaching of History and Geography in schools. The Training School was admirably supported by the diocese and the Board of Education, which provided extra funds when needed. Private fee-paying pupils filled some of the vacancies.

In 1883 the subjects at College included English Literature, Grammar, Arithmetic, Drawing, Geography, History, Economy, Religious Studies, Botany, Needlework and School Management. By this time, the 'industrial work' required of earlier students was moving towards Domestic Economy, ensuring a better practical knowledge of Cookery.

> 'Oh what a contrast to day-dreams of College! Our sleeping and rising, our work and study, eating and walking – all were governed by rules'!

Clara Grant, an exceptional pupil who had a great desire to learn, felt frustrated by the ordered life, the monotony of the work and the lectures that were followed by dictated summaries that had to be written at lightning speed. She resented the many tests, the lack of freedom and the fact that there was no time for questions and discussion. 'There was no escape' was her wry comment! There were, however, some lighter moments.

> 'Pupils wore round white net bonnets in the house. When they rushed to the window to see an approaching visitor, they gave a misleading impression of a house with a splendid domestic staff!'!
>
> *Farthing Bundles* Clara Grant

Despite the harsh regime, Clara had warm memories of both Canon Steward and Miss Hill.

Salisbury Diocesan Training School.

Children with a College student, circa 1870   Courtesy of Dorset County Museum

Appointments to Schools, 1891

Courtesy of Wiltshire and Swindon History Centre

Victorian Exercise

The value of a daily walk was recognised right from the start. Early reminiscences record the monotony of those walks, which rarely varied from Harnham Hill and the Dean's Terrace (Bishop's Walk). In the summer, after the 3pm Cathedral service, there was invariably a 'walk around watery Harnham'. A memory from the 1870s describes: 'a procession of 70-80 young women walking out two by two for a constitutional and accompanied by governesses'. These chaperones were necessary as Salisbury was seen as being a dangerous place that was full of rough characters. Young women did not go around unescorted at this time and the Training School was responsible for the pupils.

In 1872 or 1873 'a covered space under the principal dormitory was fitted up for recreation'. There is no indication of the nature of this recreation, but the College accounts show that in 1881 a 'Set of Lawn Tennis' was purchased from Mr Beach for £3.00 and in 1883 expenses included 'repair of croquet mallets, as well as tennis racquets, nets and balls'. Tennis and croquet were probably both played on the lawns around King's House.

Callisthenics (rhythmic physical exercises designed to cultivate gracefulness of movement, as well as strength) were introduced and were in some ways a precursor of Music and Movement, but were discontinued in favour of Drill. Mr Ormesby was employed as Drill Instructor and accounts show that flags, staves, stars and medals were purchased, as formation marching had taken the place of graceful performances.

The game of Rounders started in 1887, with the purchase of a bat and balls. In 1888 a battledore and shuttlecock were bought for eleven shillings. This was a game that was played by two people using small rackets called battledores.

Salisbury Cycling Club was founded in 1885 and cycling soon became popular at the Training School. At the end of the first fifty years, opportunities for exercise were increasing, along with the growing national interest in sport.

"Crocodile Ladies Please"   Drawn by Pat Jones

Battledore racket

'Anyone for battledore?'
Christmas 1883

Courtesy of The Salisbury Museum

Inspections were a regular occurrence in The Training School and the pupils probably felt the same concern about them as students and teachers do today.

It was during the nineteenth century that Her Majesty's Inspectorate (HMI) developed a high reputation for encouraging standards. In 1891 Canon Steward wrote that 'Her Majesty's Inspectors may be said to have been the pioneers of education…indeed to them is in a large measure due the immense improvement of the science of teaching in both the higher grade as well as in Elementary Schools'.

On 31st July 1847, when there were 30 pupils at the Training School, a notice was received that the Revd FC Cook HMI, would arrive on November 8th and spend six days 'in examining all the candidates for certificates, and four days in inspecting the premises, the management, and the proficiency of the pupils in training'. There were four months in which to prepare for the forthcoming visit.

The report is extremely interesting:

'The pupils read with singular ease and good taste. Their intonation is perfectly free from vulgarity and affectation. Many of their papers in Religious Knowledge prove not only that the pupils are thoroughly instructed in the doctrines which the English Church maintains as the most sacred portion of her inheritance, but that they have really a most comprehensive knowledge of religious subjects…I have remarked in many, and more or less in nearly all, the presence of those qualities which are most essential to a teacher: good temper, shown under very trying circumstances; an unaffected yet self-possessed deportment, such as acts upon children both as an example and a governing principle; and lastly good sense in what they attempted and what they omitted. All the studies and employments of the pupils have been made subsidiary to the formation of a humble, contented and devout character'.

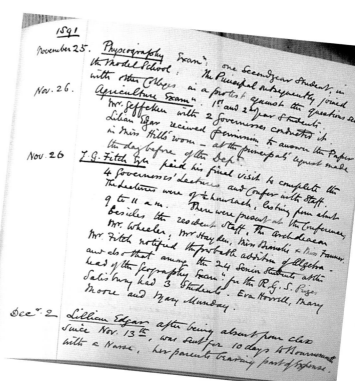

Inspection report
Courtesy of Wiltshire and Swindon History Centre

The inspector strongly advised an increase in numbers up to 60 pupils. This resulted in the Board eventually acquiring The King's House.

Regular inspections continued by HMI and by the Diocesan Board. After the HMI visit in 1852, Mrs Duncan was authorised to give cake and tea to the scholars at the Practising Schools. What a treat that must have been!

In 1861 Mr Cook HMI drew the attention of the Committee to the inadequacy of the staff and the need for a 'museum'. Various gifts were donated for the museum including an owl, an iguana and a mole!

Mr J G Fitch HMI revisited the Training School in 1890 and was pleased with 'the bearing of the students, the work of the staff, and the premises and their order'.

During the past 50 years, inspectors had encouraged not only higher standards and more contact with pupils, but also better living conditions for the pupils themselves. Inspection reports often mention the special quality of the students. Conditions were hard for them, but they were mostly devout and caring. Even in the early days their diligence and the impact of their environment shone through.

Requirements on entry to the Training School for an Exhibitioner in 1849 were:

'To read and write fairly, to write from dictation tolerably, to work accurately at sums in the four rules of arithmetic simple and compound, to have fair knowledge of Holy Scripture and of the Church catechism'.

Examinations were a regular feature of Training School life. A record was kept of each pupil's progress and conduct. In 1846 the Committee of Council on Education instituted the Teachers' Certificate, to be awarded to pupils who passed the examination at the end of the Training Course. This meant that the Government would contribute to the teachers' salaries. The minimum salary increased to £90 for a male teacher and £60 for a female teacher.

In 1847, the Revd FC Cook, HMI, conducted the Examination. Of the sixteen school mistresses and ten pupils who were examined, four schoolmistresses and five pupils received certificates. This was the first encounter with examinations and standards gradually improved.

A Queen's Scholar from 1853-54 wrote:

'Our examination was the same as for Certificates, but with the option of leaving out Domestic Economy and Music. It commenced on Monday evening at 6 pm and ended on Saturday at 1 pm'.

A circular issued in 1854 stated that pupils who failed their first year examinations were required to be re-examined. In 1871 the Diocesan Inspector's Examination in Religious Education was a written one, and a much higher standard was expected. In 1890, the results for the outgoing pupils were the best results ever obtained during the fifty years the Training School had existed. The committee was delighted!

Kate Hardy Archbishop's Certificate
Courtesy of Dorset County Museum

Typical questions set by the Education Department at the Certificate Examination:

English Grammar: Define the following parts of speech, and apply each definition to an example: - a noun, a verb, a preposition.

Geography: Explain the geographical allusion in Ps cxxvi.5; "Turn our captivity, O Lord, as the rivers in the South".

Scriptural Knowledge: Give dates for the following events – The Deluge; the Passage of the Jordan; the Death of Abraham; and the anointing of Saul.

Arithmetic questions included reducing fractions to their simplest form.

Prize Books

Prize medals

The First Prize-givings

Prize-givings started in 1855, by which time the Training School had moved to King's House. Mrs Hamilton, wife of the Dean, began to give an annual prize of five guineas for Needlework. This continued until 1891, by which time she also gave ten guineas towards the Religious Knowledge prize fund.

On December 7th 1883, 'before a goodly number of friends and former pupils,' the Dean of Salisbury gave an address and distributed the prizes. The prizes included a set of Shakespeare's plays, as well as books and lenses for:

> 'excellent collections of dried flowers that were given to four senior students. 'M J Ayres received the Chaplain's Prize for the "hardest worker" and visitors and students enjoyed tea in the prettily decorated dining room. A very pleasant evening was spent listening to part songs by the students and this ended with a loud expression of thanks to Miss Rodwell, the Lady Superintendent, for her 'self-denying efforts, not merely for the happiness of the students on that day alone, but for their highest interests throughout the past year – the first she had spent among them'.
>
> *College Archives*

Averil Taylor's grandmothers, Annie Beaumont and Elsie Farmer, were both at College from 1885 until 1887. Annie was awarded two prizes in 1886 – a Bible and a complete Shakespeare. They are impressive books that have the college badge on the front covers and labels inside giving the year of the award and Annie's name. The two medals are both for 'superior merit' and one has 'History' on it.

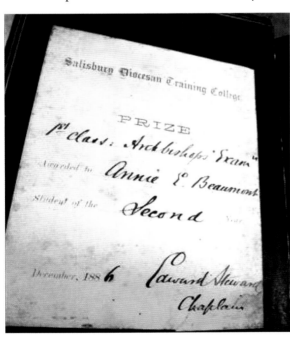

What was 'The Model School'?

> 'The cream of our school work lay in the Model School attached to the Training College. Such a gem of a school where we sat and watched the work in order to report the lessons we heard, and to pick up methods that were to guide us in our own teaching. Never did we see such a school before, nor such children! And if the week for the Model school followed a working week in the pantry it was the best boon that could be bestowed'.
>
> Extract from the reminiscences of a pupil at The Training School from 1862-63

In 1840, in the proposals for the organisation of The Training School, the Diocesan sub-committee had included the use of a 'good Model School' to be linked to the Training School.

The aim of the Model School, which opened in January 1852, was that it would be:

> 'Not so much a practising school, as to set before the eyes of the pupils (that is to say the students) a perfect village school, one maintaining a standard of excellence above what ordinary village schools can reach, but at which they should aim'.
>
> *Our Training College* by Edward Steward

A link was made with the Girls' Department at St Martin's, which included sharing an annual building grant and placing the Mistress of the Girls' School under the direction of a Training School Mistress.

Canon Steward stated that in 1857, 'The Practising Class that used to come from St Martin's School to the Model School was discontinued, students going instead to St Martin's.' This followed an HMI inspection, which had found that pupils from the Training School spent less time in schools than normal. Canon Steward reported that in one year this was only 70 hours in the year against 340 elsewhere. Following the report, the hours spent in schools were increased to about 180 per year.

Pupils from St Edmund's School attended the Model School until it closed in 1863. Traces of it can still be seen, including the site of the original door.

King's House showing the Model School

Sevington Victorian School exterior

Sevington School interior with teacher
Courtesy of Sevington Victorian School

Elizabeth Alice Gale, 1866–1940

A Suitcase full of Memories

In 1986 a suitcase was donated to the Dorset County Museum. It contained a wealth of fascinating information including documents and photographs recording the life of Elizabeth Gale. She was a student at Salisbury Training School from January 1885 until Christmas 1886.

As a child, Elizabeth attended Charminster School, Dorchester, where she was an excellent pupil. She became a pupil monitor and was so highly regarded that a subscription was raised in the village to pay towards her entrance fee to the Training School as a Queen's Scholar. A document sent to Charminster Vicarage indicates the payment of £10 admission fee.

A letter from The Master of Charminster School, dated November 1884, was written to Edward Steward, Principal of the Training School, requesting a list of books which Elizabeth would need. 'We are anxious to show our appreciation of her work and her exemplary conduct as well as the zeal and diligence with which she has discharged her duties in this school'.

Elizabeth worked hard at The Training School and was in The Second Division in both her years. On finishing her training she was appointed teacher at Melcombe Bingham School, ten miles from Dorchester. Unusually, Elizabeth carried on teaching after marrying the local blacksmith. The majority of female teachers during this period were not allowed to teach after they married, and so most female teachers were single. It is interesting that many children still tend to call their teacher 'Miss'.

Lydia Elizabeth Stevens

Lydia Stevens was the daughter of a dairy farmer, and from the age of fourteen was a pupil teacher at North Eling School near Lymington. She was admitted to Salisbury Training School in 1877 aged eighteen, having been recommended by her local vicar.

During an examination of her teaching by an HMI Lydia was judged to be 'an animated teacher and a very fair disciplinarian'. She obtained a post at Redlynch School in the New Forest, where she taught until marrying her husband Charles Newman. Lydia and Charles had nine children and remained in the area for the rest of their lives.

The 1870 Education Act

The 1870 Education Act established the foundations of our national system of state education, providing schools for all children between 5 and 13.

The Act declared that:

- The country would be divided into school districts.
- School Boards would be formed in areas that had insufficient provision to oversee and complete the provision of schools.
- Board Schools would be non-denominational and partially state funded.

Impact of the 1870 Act

Schools, scholars and teachers more than doubled in number from 1870 to 1880. Two thirds of the school places were provided by the Churches and one third by the School Boards.

1 The Church of England was determined to retain the existing system. In Salisbury the Diocesan Board of Education gave grants to 53 new church schools.

2 The increased demand for teachers led to more entrants to Salisbury Training School.

3 Religious Knowledge examinations were no longer required in Training Schools by the Department of Education. The Church of England appointed its own examiners.

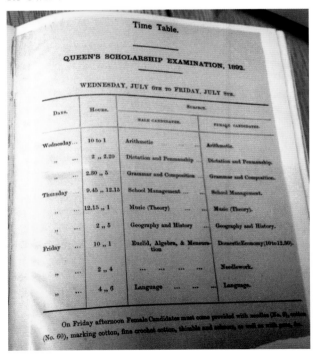

Courtesy of Wiltshire & Swindon History Centre

St Martin's School, Salisbury

The National Society established a school in St Martin's parish and 78 girls were admitted. This was the first National School in Salisbury. A sum of £630 was raised by public subscription and a building next to St Martin's Church was purchased. This building had been in use as a malt house and then as a prison for French soldiers captured in the Peninsular War.

St Martin's School had strong links with The Diocesan Training School. In the 1840s the Girls' School at St Martin's was under the direction of the Governess of the new Diocesan Training School so that she might give her pupils 'efficient instruction in teaching'.

The school was situated a short distance from the Training School. Pupils from the Girls' Department attended the Model School at the Training School until 1857. The school continued to be used for teaching practice until the College closed in 1978.

A school report for 1840 indicates that it was open to children over five years of age, who were recommended by subscribers. Attendance was at 8.45 am and 1.15 pm on weekdays and on Sundays at 9 am and 2 pm. Sickness was the only acceptable reason for absence. The children were expected to be clean and smart. On Mondays they were expected to bring one penny for the use of books, slates and as a contribution towards their instruction. The children were firmly expected to behave as Christians, 'that is be kind to each other and never lie, steal or use bad words'.

In 1859 there were two departments. On the upper floor around 200 boys were taught in two rooms by the master and five pupil teachers, whilst on the ground floor 80-90 girls were taught by the mistress and two pupil teachers. In 1890 two new classrooms were built, increasing the accommodation for 617 pupils.

A famous pupil who attended St Martin's was Tom Adlam VC, who was born in 1893. It was in 1916, at Thiepval, in France, that the deed for which he was awarded the Victoria Cross took place.

St Edmund's School

In 1815 a day school in union with the National Society existed in the Parish of St Edmund. By 1818 it had become a Sunday School. In 1835 it received a grant of £40 from the government and probably became a day school again. At that time it was attended by 69 boys and 49 girls.

In 1860 a new school was built to the west of the church. This was placed in union with the National Society and was used as a 'Practising School' for the Diocesan Training School.

Dora Hughes, a college student from 1910-1912, later became Headteacher of St Edmund's School, until her retirement in 1952.

St Martin's Church of England Infant School

The Hardy sisters

Thomas Hardy, the famous novelist and poet, was born in Higher Bockhampton, near Dorchester on the 2nd June, 1840. His sister Mary was born a year later on the 23rd December 1841. Several years later his brother Henry was born in 1851, followed by the younger sister Kate on 2nd September 1856. Mary and Kate were both pupils at Salisbury Training School and Hardy used their experiences in the writing of his novel *Jude the Obscure*.

Mary was Thomas's main childhood companion until he went to school at the age of eight. The pair maintained a warm and affectionate relationship throughout their lives. Mary shared Thomas's love of the arts and of peace and solitude, and remained single throughout her life.

Mary and Kate's parents paid for their education and later their Training School fees. Mary initially attended a local Dame School and later a private girls' school in Dorchester. The 1860 Training School entry records describe Mary as the daughter of a builder who was recommended by the Revd AG Shirley of Stinsford. She became a Queen's Scholar in her second year, which meant that her parents no longer had to pay.

Mary's conduct was 'good' throughout all her time at the Training School. As a pupil her abilities were described as 'diligent', 'improving slowly' or 'persevering'. On leaving her grading was 'moderate'. She received a Teacher's Certificate of the second class, which indicated that she had completed the course in two years rather than three years (third class) or one year (first class). Life was difficult for Mary at the Training School: rules were very strict and the food was meagre.

On leaving the Training School Mary, obtained a post, as a probationer, at Denchworth National School, near Wantage and then at North Waltham in Hampshire. She found the teaching difficult with 'hardly a trace of order or discipline'. She was happier teaching in her subsequent posts at Minterne Magna and Piddlehinton, only four miles from Bockhampton.

In 1875 Mary was appointed Headmistress at The Bell School for Girls in Dorchester.

By the time Kate arrived at the Training School in January 1877 many changes had taken place. Government funding had been reduced and pupils were expected to assist with cooking, cleaning and other domestic chores. On admission Kate was said to be 'strong and in good health'. She was very unhappy during her time at The Training School. The discipline was even sterner since her sister's time there.

Food was poor and Kate was often hungry. There were many restrictions on pupil behaviour both in and outside the Training School. In 1883 Kate made it clear that she did not 'mind if Tom publishes how badly we were used'.

On leaving the Training School Kate obtained a post at Sandford Orcas School near Sherborne. She made improvements and probably enjoyed her role in the village.

In June 1882 she wrote to the committee of the Dorchester National Schools with a request that she be given a job assisting her sister in Dorchester. Kate's application was successful and she went to work with Mary until they both retired in 1897. Mary died in 1915 aged 74 and Kate in 1940 aged 84.

Kate Hardy (far left) at the Training School with fellow students

Courtesy of Dorset County Museum

Kate Hardy Admission Register

Courtesy of Wiltshire and Swindon History Centre

Envelope from Thomas Hardy to Kate

Courtesy of Dorset County Museum

Letter from Thomas Hardy to Kate

Courtesy of Dorset County Museum

CLARA GRANT OBE 1867-1949: 'The Bundle Woman of Bow'

Clara Grant
Courtesy of Fern Street
Settlement

Clara Grant was born in Chapmanslade in Wiltshire, in 1867. When she was five years old a National School was opened in the village and she was one of the first pupils. She wrote that 'life was simple and natural, but it was narrow', and she yearned to be a teacher and to live in London. In later years Clara realised she owed much to her village childhood, particularly to the 'joy of meeting and greeting in our own streets,' and to the richness of friendships and relationships, starting with those around her and widening as the years rolled on.

Clara moved from Chapmanslade to Frome with her family when she was seven and became a pupil teacher there when she was thirteen. She gained a Queen's Scholarship, First Class, to Salisbury Training School in 1886 aged 19.

Students numbered 76 and there were four resident staff with visiting masters for Arithmetic and Music. She remembered the spartan regime, inadequate food and emphasis on Religious Instruction and monotonous academic work. Clara stated that the training was 'not perhaps the best preparation for the independent lives in large towns or lonely villages where many of us went, but it was the ideal of the day, and many of us fitted into it'.

Clara wrote:

> 'Salisbury students have left their mark in remote villages near home, and are doing pioneer missionary work in the distant outposts of our Empire, and the 'King's Daughters', living out the fine traditions of their King's House, can hope to be numbered among their country's 'honourable women'.
>
> *Farthing Bundles* by Clara Grant

At the age of twenty-one Clara became Headteacher of an infant school for about 120 children in Melksham, Wiltshire. It was in 1891, at the age of twenty-four, that she fulfilled her dream and moved to a school near Euston followed by six years in Wapping. She said 'I love Wapping and I was as happy as a queen there'. In 1905 she became Headteacher of Devons Road School, now known as 'The Clara Grant School.' She challenged the dull methods of teaching at that time. She used Christmas cards to make games for the children, and showed how it was possible to maintain interest and concentration without the severe discipline that was then widely imposed in schools.

Clara cared deeply for the welfare of the local people. She provided hot breakfasts for the children in her care, supplied them with clothes and shoes and, most famously, created and distributed 'Farthing Bundles'. Children could purchase for one farthing, a bundle of toys wrapped up in newspaper or tissue and string. The distribution ceremony was held every Saturday morning and Clara became known as 'The Bundle Woman of Bow'.

Clara wrote that Farthing Bundles were:

> 'Surprise packets of odd trifles for which our little East End neighbours lined up weekly, in all weathers, for twenty five years. With their wonderful instinct for simple things, they transmute the odd little contents into playthings not to be found in costly toyshops and wealthy nurseries'.

Devons Road School backed on to Fern Street and in 1907 she set up the famous Fern Street Settlement in three houses, which had been donated by a benefactor. At this time 2,000 bundles a year were given out. The Bundles were so popular that in 1913 Clara had a little wooden arch made. Only those who could pass under the arch could purchase a bundle.

Children queuing to go under the wooden arch
Courtesy of Fern Street Settlement

Children in 1970s with Farthing Bundles © Homer Sykes

The Funeral of Clara Grant

Her funeral was a triumphant procession, a royal progress indeed. It was impossible to get to the Settlement. All the Bow Common streets had sent their flowers, the schools, and others too. The Temporary Church of Old Hallows' was crammed, and Blackthorn Street had more in it than the Church could hold. The procession that led the simple coffin into and out of the Church must have rejoiced her heart, for here were Baptist minister, Mission leader, Wesleyan minister, and Church of England clergy of all shades. Clara Grant knew the need for a reunited Church. "Jesus lives," we sang, and heard of her courage, humour and humility. No wonder mothers with babies in arms, and old folks, too, stood at the doors all the way up Campbell Road; no wonder many had walked to the cemetery, and formed a great square around her grave! Her relatives, her staff, her many 'children and mothers of Bow Common', the Mayor and the Town Clerk, stood together in honour of the 'great little woman'.

An extract about Clara's funeral from an 'Appreciation of Miss Clara Grant' published in Bow after her death

On the top of the arch were the words,

**'Enter all ye Children Small,
None can come who are too tall'.**

In 1914 the total of Bundles which were distributed was 14,621(300 per week).

1n 1917 Queen Mary visited Fern Street Settlement. In 1929 Clara's book 'Farthing Bundles' was published and 6000 copies were printed. She was awarded the OBE by King George the Sixth in January 1949. Sadly Clara died in October of that year, only having given up running the Settlement in May. She was so popular that mourners blocked Fern Street on the day of her funeral.

Farthing Bundles
Drawn by Pat Jones

Clara's Funeral　　　　Courtesy of the Fern Street Settlement

The Revised Code of 1862

The Revised Code of 1862, known as 'Payment by Results', was introduced as a means of providing sound and cheap elementary instruction to all.

'If it is not cheap, it shall be efficient, if it is not efficient, it shall be cheap', were the words of Robert Lowe, Vice President of the Committee of Council on Education.

Government grants for education would be based on school attendance and on the success of pupils examined in 'the basic skills' by government inspectors.

- The Revised Code was deeply unpopular and had considerable impact.

- Teachers felt insecure as their salaries depended on their results.

- The number of pupil teachers declined. Salisbury admitted only 25 in 1865.

- The school curriculum was restricted to reading, writing and arithmetic.

- Training School grants were dependent on examination results.

Cover of the first Register

Courtesy of Wiltshire and Swindon History Centre

A Spartan Regime

In 1847 the Revd F. C. Cook HMI had drawn attention to the ill heath of the pupils. In a year and three quarters, two of the pupils had died, and five had shown such 'symptoms of weak constitutions as to give no reasonable hope that they could ever undertake the anxious and trying duties of Schoolmistresses'.

Food in the early days was sparse. A pupil who joined The Training School in 1843 explained how a parcel from home was much frowned upon: 'for if it contained a cake from mother, it would certainly be "so indigestible" that at the end of three months if a girl had a headache the cause would be "that heavy cake which had come from home". The cook at this time was described as 'a very slovenly and illiterate person, but she excelled in burnt pea soup and rice milk'.

Christmas in the early days was a meagre affair:

'The Christmas festivities consisted of roast beef and plum pudding; two puddings were made, and special orders left that only one was to be eaten at Christmas, the other on New Year's Day'.

'We never had any luxuries in the way of food, and for growing girls not always necessaries – two slices of bread and butter each for breakfast and tea; no more, hungry or not. One loaf was divided between us all when we came back from the Cathedral. No supper; but from 6 pm to 8 am was too long to fast, and so it led to us having things from home. We were allowed to have a hamper on our birthday. Our meat was good in quality. We had puddings on Friday and Saturdays only, either suet or rice; no other kind was ever given to us'.

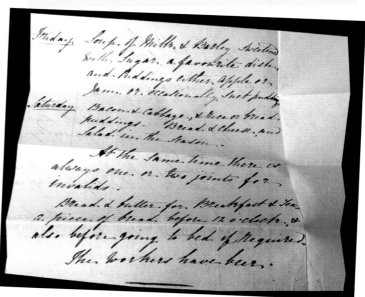

Training School Diet

Courtesy of Wiltshire and Swindon History Centre

A reminiscence by a Queen's Scholar in The Training School in 1853:

> 'On Good Friday the late Canon Fisher always sent a plain bun and orange for each student. One and a half pounds of butter was allowed at each meal, but it got to be a mere apology for butter towards the end of the last loaf. On Easter Sunday we commenced with fresh butter and an egg (the only one in the year)'.

Thomas Hardy probably used Kate Hardy's experiences when writing about Sue Bridehead in his novel *Jude the Obscure:*

> 'She confessed with something of shame, that she was dreadfully hungry. They were kept on very short allowances in the College, and a dinner, tea and supper all in one was the present she most desired in the world'.

In the 1860 and 70s budgets were tight and food remained sparse. In 1877 repairs to the bakehouse are recorded, which suggests that home made bread was produced. In 1885 beans, raspberries, cabbages and fruit trees were growing in the garden.

Clara Grant (1886-1888) recalled:

> 'When I entered college the regime was still spartan. Our fare had improved on that of our predecessors, for we had suppers of bread and cheese, with a mug of cold milk and beer. Cake was provided on Sundays'.

The accounts identify spending on medicines, for example in 1883, Sulphate of Quinine was purchased and an ear syringe. A nurse was hired when necessary. Occasional illnesses were treated with homely remedies, but there was also more serious ill health. In 1872 a student died from pleurisy and in 1890 an epidemic of influenza placed 30 students and 4 members of staff 'hors de combat'.

There were regular cases of illness. A Training School diary from 1890 recorded:

> 'We had our first case of influenza, followed by 33 other cases. The "eight room" was used as a sickroom in addition to the infirmary, and a trained nurse was engaged for a fortnight, as well as additional help in the house, the head housemaid herself being ill. The Lady Superintendent was incapacitated for three weeks. Attendance at the Practising Schools ceased for a fortnight'.

Health and food had improved but there was still a long way to go.

College dining room

Courtesy of The Salisbury Museum

Emma Cheesman: A pupil in the 1860s

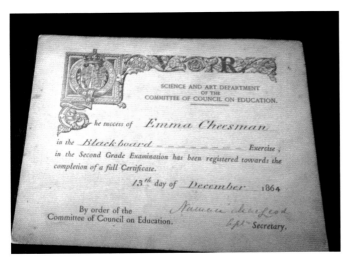

Emma's Certificate   Courtesy of The Salisbury Museum

Dress made in needlework
Courtesy of The Salisbury Museum

Emma Cheesman was born in October 1844. She was a pupil-teacher at Sherborne National School from February 1858 until she passed the Queen's Certificate (1st class) and entered The Training School in January 1863.

A lesson plan on the death of St Stephen has also been kept. It is dated October 15th 1863 and is meticulously written in ink in a neat copperplate style. It is likely that Emma taught this lesson in the Model School.

Needlework was an important part of the Victorian curriculum and the exquisite tiny garments that Emma made for her final examinations were looked after lovingly and handed down by her family. They survived air raids and floods and are a reminder of the painstaking toil of those early pupils.

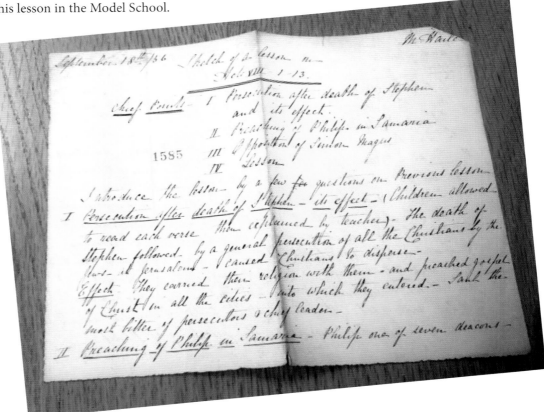

Emma's lesson plan   Courtesy of The Salisbury Museum

Little Williams

Drawing by
Pat Jones

By our day, the miniature shirts of 1862 had been replaced by four-inch knickers, with gussets and button holes retained. When completed, holes were made, and repaired with calico patches as an exercise in mending. The garment was never referred to by the correct name.

The story, handed on from year to year, was that as students were once completing a piece of work, 'Miss Newman gazed dreamily out of the window at Williams the gardener. She turned and said, "Now take out your little Williams" and the name remained for ever after'.

An extract from *Our College*
written by Violet Hayward, a student from 1908-1910

Williams the gardener

In lighter vein

Early life in The Training School was hard for the pupils, but thankfully there were occasional lighter moments. They had some fun playing practical jokes on each other. A pupil from the 1840s remembered:

> 'One night a harum-scarum student, who used to perambulate the stairs in a sheet and rattling a bunch of keys, stepped into a basin of cold water which we had set as a ghost trap'.

There was a grand dinner provided for the pupils by the Committee to celebrate the christening of the Prince of Wales in January 1842, when the city held a procession and a firework display. Other entertainments sadly passed them by, as they were 'kept close'.

Pupils enjoyed musical activities. There was an old piano in the classroom and a harmonium in the schoolroom, which was used to accompany the evening hymn. By 1862 there were the musical evenings, probably introduced by Mr Richardson, the assistant organist of the Cathedral, who was appointed to teach music in 1858.

A pupil from 1862 recalled:

> 'What could be merrier than our singing nights? Only the threat, "if you do not attend you must have single practice the next night," could keep down our spirits. Training, however, was not all work, even in those days, and good laughs some of us have in talking over our holiday evenings, Easter gatherings, Mrs Duncan's birthday party, our charades and musical evenings, our picnics at Stonehenge, our occasional long walks, blackberrying and watercress gathering'.

Connections with the outside world gradually increased. On July 7th, 1882 horse-drawn vehicles took pupils to the New Forest. *The Illustrated London News* (price sixpence) was taken in 1883. The Second Year visited the carpet factory at Wilton and a botanical exhibition. In 1885 the 'Salisbury Journal' was taken. In the summer there were excursions to Alderbury, Stonehenge and the local Flower Show. In October pupils enjoyed the visits by London Theatrical companies, who put on plays in the Assembly Rooms and other local venues. In November 1885, students attended Oxford University Extension Lectures and at least seventeen attended some astronomy lectures.

The pupils did have a little time to relax. In 1887, the old Model School was fitted up as a sitting room for them.

One can imagine the pupils, after a hard day's work, at last sitting down and enjoying a conversation with their friends.

In 1887, the City of Salisbury celebrated Queen Victoria's Golden Jubilee. The front of the college was decorated with roses and illuminated. The students had a day's holiday in the New Forest. A bonfire blazed on Harnham Hill; a procession passed through the city and 'rustic sports' took place to open Victoria Park. A dinner for nearly four thousand took place in the Market Square at which the Dean said grace and the Mayor proposed the Royal Health. In this year there was also the Choral Festival in the Cathedral and the Bath and West Show took place in Salisbury. The world of the pupils at the Training School was gradually becoming wider.

'Those were the Days'

In the *Salisbury Training College Chronicle* of 1958 Emma Shaw, (Jan 1888-Dec 1889) wrote a delightful picture of her life in college.

> 'I was 89 last October. Our College days were very happy, though much different from today. On Sundays we had to wear bonnets with ribbon strings and no flowers or feathers. Incidentally I wore it when I went to interview the School Managers of my first school at Southall. We were allowed to go into the town, on Saturdays only, about once in three or four weeks to do a little private shopping. Two mistresses took us every day, except Saturdays and Sundays, for walks, two and two, crocodile fashion. Our walk was usually along the Odstock Road or up to Harnham Hill. We provided our own sheets and teaspoon, pudding spoon and fork, and if they were left on the dining table we had to pay a halfpenny fine. On Sundays three of four of us were invited into the Lady Superintendent's room to tea, which was taken more or less in deadly silence, or we looked at books of fossils or fungi. Ah! Those were the days! Still, they were happy'.

The Old Students' Association and Magazine

The Church Teachers' Union was established in 1881 to 'band together Church Teachers throughout the land'. Two years later, Miss Rodwell, Lady Superintendent of Salisbury Training School, established the Sarum Branch of the Church Teachers' Union and her eloquent letter in the January 1884 edition of *Our Quarterly* asked for support from former pupils.

> 'In quietness and in confidence shall be your strength'
>
> 'It has not seemed either right or reasonable that there should be no general medium of communication between those who have left us and ourselves who work on still within the same walls, attend the same heartstirring Cathedral services, are moulded by the old influences and are animated with the same zeal and love that has moved teachers and taught for forty years past. As we write now on the eve of the departure from our midst of 35 girls in whose individual characters we have conceived an intimate and personal interest, the truth of the wise king's words strikes a sad chord, 'One generation passeth away and another cometh.' And it is in the hope that the passing away of this kind may be minimised, that by memories reawakened the friendships of old school days may burn bright once more, that the girl student's esprit de corps may not fade … we appeal to those mistresses who have gone before forth from us, not yesterday or today, but many years ago, to help us to link more closely the present with the past, to contribute their experience to our columns – to hold out the right hand of fellowship to those 'prentice hands who leave Salisbury year by year, because they too were Salisbury students'.
>
> *College archives*

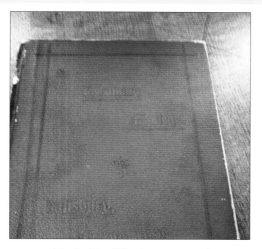

'The Red Book' by Canon Steward

Canon Edward Steward, Chaplain to the College, requested that several pages of *Our Quarterly* should be localised by training schools for the benefit of their outgoing pupils. '50 copies (of the 1884 magazine) printed with local matter were bespoken by Salisbury. A separate publication called *Our Magazine* first appeared in 1886.'

The Old Students' Association and the College Magazine had therefore both started before 1891, the 50th Anniversary.

Church times Union Prayer

Our Quarterly Cover

A Verse from the Training School Song

In quietness and confidence,
As students in a School
Where hearts are trained and minds are taught
By Church-appointed rule;
Beneath the old Cathedral's shade
We have a House that still
A King, we hope, will claim his own,
And order to His will.

The song was written by Miss Steward and set to music by Dr John Stainer. The words reflect the Training School Motto that appears above Miss Rodwell's letter in the 1884 magazine.

August 1891: The Jubilee Reunion

'After carefully weighing the pros and cons, we
have come to the conclusion that the time for
the Jubilee Reunion most generally convenient
for school mistresses will be during the summer
holidays. Therefore will our friends take out their
pocket books and note Wednesday August 19th.
The accommodation of the College is known to
most of our readers. At the most we can give beds to
seventy. Miss Hill will reserve these for Tuesday and
Wednesday nights in order of application; at the same
time she would be grateful if all who could do so with
convenience would arrange to stay with friends, or in
rooms in the town. Meals will be provided in College'.

Our Quarterly ,1891

Canon Steward
Courtesy of Wiltshire and Swindon History Centre

The Jubilee Reunion was so successful that a Triennial
Reunion was then proposed, the first taking place in
1894. At the end of the first fifty years there were growing
feelings of pride in the history of the College, and unity
amongst the generations of students.

Staff & Pupils 1880s

Courtesy of The Salisbury Museum

1841–1891
'In Quietness and in Confidence shall be your Strength'

In 1891 the Diocesan Committee recorded their pleasure and pride in the improved standards and accommodation at the Training School, as was noted in the HMI Inspection of that year. Canon Edward Steward recorded their words in his book, *Our Training College*.

'Nurtured and maintained by many wise heads and loving hearts, it has for 50 years pursued its holy work, which we believe has had God's blessing upon it. Its past history encourages the hope that in the years to come it may fulfil the desire of its founders, to maintain and uphold the work of Church education, especially in the dioceses of Salisbury and Winchester'.

Canon Steward also recorded in the Training School Annals 1891, some of the many recent changes that there had been in education:

'The annals of our elementary education do not contain any more eventful year as this, the fiftieth in the life of our Institution. It witnessed the most important modifications of the Code since 1870. Payment by Results, the Merit Grants and "percentages" were abolished; individual Examination was superseded by Examination by sample; teachers were allowed greater freedom in classifying their scholars and more liberty in the choice and treatment of class subjects'.

Great strides had been made in improving education during the first fifty years of The Training School, now to be known as Salisbury Diocesan Training College. Since Martha Gibson's arrival, 1,548 pupils had been trained to be schoolmistresses.

The hard work and devotion of staff and students ensured that the foundations of the college remained secure for the following eighty-seven years. What courage, stamina and determination the early students had demonstrated! They worked diligently and also forged firm and lasting friendships. Their close relationship with the Cathedral was an integral part of their lives, providing strength, security and sanctuary when times were hard, and an inner spirituality that shone through their work.

'As birds of passage on some mid-sea isle,
From divers lands and bound on divers ways,
In company assembled for awhile,
Then lose each other in the ocean haze,
So are we parted when are done the days
Of our brief brotherhood within this pile,
The world grows wider then; new hopes beguile;
And from new lips we wait the word of praise.
No lifeless page is this that bears enrolled
Names once familiar, and bids reappear
Forgotten faces. One has climbed to fame
One – it may be the most dear –
Just does his life's work well and is the same'.

Verse by F. Bourdillon, quoted in *The Red Book*

Birds of passage

Painted by Austin Thorp

Salisbury Diocesan Training School.

A. T. Osmond, del.

Chapter 2

In Quietness
and in Confidence

1891-1918

'When Britain really ruled the waves' wrote WS Gilbert in *Iolanthe*, the comic opera that he wrote with Arthur Sullivan in 1882. The words were satirical, but Britain in the last decade of the 19th century was a powerful nation with a large empire. Queen Victoria had been on the throne since 1837. The country, by now industrialised, had an ever growing population and was peaceful and prosperous.

Martha Gibson travelled to Salisbury by mail coach in 1841, but 50 years later, students probably travelled by train. There was a good rail network across the country. Travel had become easier and the seaside holiday was approaching its heyday.

Public money was spent on swimming baths, parks and libraries in order to provide opportunities for self-improvement. Salisbury was no exception.

> 'No doubt people in Salisbury had always swum in the rivers on a hot day, but in 1892 there was at last a purpose-built indoor pool'.
> Ruth Newman & Jane Howells, *Salisbury Past*

The City Library opened in 1890. Charles Dickens, HG Wells and Oscar Wilde were popular authors at this time. Thomas Hardy and Conan Doyle were writing their novels.

Salisbury had flourishing clubs for cycling and athletics, whilst activities such as photography, gardening, golf, skating and cricket were all growing in popularity. People went to the races, to football matches, music halls, theatres and concerts. Leisure was important!

House-building was gathering pace, gas cookers became common in the 1890s, and some people even had indoor bathrooms. There were technological, medical and scientific advances.

Despite the progress, there was still great social inequality and more than a quarter of the population was living at or below subsistence level. Workhouses were still feared and loathed. The status of women had improved, but it would be many years before students at the College in the Close could vote.

Staff and students before the First World War
Courtesy of The Salisbury Museum

Edward Steward, the first person to hold the title of Principal, had a profound influence on the College. It was largely through his leadership, guidance and vision that by 1913 Salisbury had become one of the leading Church Training Colleges. He inspired affection and great respect in those who knew him.

Canon Steward taught Mathematics, Religion and English Literature. Reminiscences from former students speak for themselves:

'Our beloved Principal – we can still see him sitting at his desk in the senior classroom, his eyes seemingly half-closed as though to ensure that nothing came between his listeners and the meditations forged in his mind and spirit. His class sat motionless, held by the magic of the interpretation of lines from Hamlet or the wonder of his revelation of the scriptures.'

Dora Hughes (1910-12)

'Lecturing on Divinity was Canon Steward who was certainly worth listening to. He was also worth watching. Whilst he talked, his blue eyes were tightly closed and his hands writhed ceaselessly with a bunch of keys or a small ball of string. His erudition was immense - on his death his books led to the foundation of the Steward Library at Church House'.

Evelyn Hart, *Before I Forget*

Canon Steward was a married man, whose home during his 'college' years was in Manor Road, Salisbury. His first wife sadly died in 1908. Four years later he married Mabel McIvor, who had been Head Student at King's House (1902-4), and a member of staff at Barnard's Cross from 1910 to 1912.

Canon Steward's work in the diocese was highly valued; he was deeply involved in the educational controversies of his day, successfully supporting Bishop Wordsworth in his bid to extend local church schools and to provide new ones by voluntary effort. Five new church schools were founded in the city, one of these being Bishop Wordsworth's School, which still flourishes today.

The Salisbury Club began in Canon Steward's day, as well as the College Magazine, which he ensured was kept at a high level of thought and literary style. He wrote *Our Training School*, recording the annals and register from 1841 until 1891. He loved the countryside and was the life and soul of the annual college picnics at Stonehenge. At the Reunion at Whitsuntide 1904, he was presented with £140 for a long fishing holiday in Norway, as an acknowledgement of his 'busy and devoted life'.

After retiring in 1913, Canon Steward maintained his interest in the College, watching every development, attending reunions and keeping alive old friendships. He died in 1930 and was mourned by many people.

A memorial tablet to Canon Steward was dedicated in the Chapel by the Archdeacon of Sarum on June 20th 1931.

In blessed memory of
The Chaplain and Principal of the College 1880-1913
EDWARD STEWARD. Magd. Coll: Oxon MA
Canon of Salisbury Cathedral
Founder of this Chapel of the Holy Angels 1899
At rest 11th April 1930
His Life an Inspiration; His Memory a Benediction

Canon Steward (Principal), speaking at a College Prize-Giving in 1912, made the following comment:

'In 1841 the number of men and women receiving professional training was "but a hundred or so," but now, in 1912, they number 11,000. Salisbury therefore might justly claim to be a pioneer in the great national movement of the training of elementary teachers'.

Canon Edward Steward: Principal, 1891-1913

The Salisbury Hostel

LADIES as ELEMENTARY SCHOOL TEACHERS.
A Hostel has been opened to prepare the DAUGHTERS of Clergy and other Professional Men for the Queen's Scholarship Examination, Christmas 1898.

The *Guardian* March 1898

This advertisement was the response, expressed by Canon Edward Steward, Principal of the Diocesan Training College, to a vexed question raised in national newspapers: 'What shall we do with our daughters?'

By the mid-1890s teaching was beginning to be seen as a desirable career for women. Apart from the small number who attended university the career was, however, only open to young women who had been to elementary schools and had followed the pupil teacher route to training college. It was felt that parents whose daughters had been educated privately and had possibly attended secondary schools, would welcome the opportunity for them to train as schoolmistresses. Canon Steward identified this need and acted on it.

The Salisbury Hostel opened in 1898 with three students. It was affiliated to The Training College and the fee was £50 a year for tuition, board and lodging. Students were prepared for the Queen's Scholarship, which they needed to pass in order to enter the College for their training.

During the next 10 years, 77 students were educated at the Hostel. It closed in 1908 as the specialised course that it offered had become unnecessary with advances in secondary education.

Audley House

In 1890 Canon Steward purchased the house adjoining King's House from Mrs Trollope, the mother of the novelist Anthony Trollope.

'Much comfort and accommodation has been gained during the past year by the addition of an adjoining house, which was purchased by the Principal at a cost of £900, and which the Committee have for the present resolved to rent. The house provides an excellent Cookery School, dormitories for 8 students, sitting rooms and bedrooms for 2 Governesses, and rooms for servants'.

College Annals 1890

In 1895 the adjoining house was rented, providing a museum and increasing the accommodation for students in that block to twenty six. The total number of students in training in 1895 had risen to eighty. In addition to The Cookery School and other rooms, a science room was built in the yard in 1903.

Audley House in the autumn

Miss Olga Blackburn was a College lecturer in English from 1951 until her retirement in 1970. She had fond memories of Audley House:

'To many the privilege of residing in Audley will remain a lasting memory; the gracious ambience had an effect upon all, an effect which strengthened with time and will not be easily erased.

Some would have stressed the fact that the house had many disadvantages: there were howling draughts, where doors did not fit, and in winter one often sat at one's desk, legs wrapped in a blanket, which at times ascended to the shoulders. Audley was reputed to have its ghosts. There were claims that a ghostly hand had been felt and seen. On the occasions when one slept in Audley guest-room, sleep was often broken, but that was because of the noise of the water pipes.

To those who legally held a key to the side door of Audley the little sheltered porch was a boon and a delight. During the summer one could take refuge there, with a pile of examination scripts or Special Essays, and work for long sunny hours undisturbed and, for the most part, unseen, though vaguely aware of the comings and goings of many and sustained by the scent of roses in King's House forecourt.

With restrained dignity Audley stands facing the west front of the Cathedral. Perhaps now that young life has gone from the house, the old ghosts have taken over. One hopes, however, that the echoes of the merry laughter of student coffee parties still lingers on to delight the benign, quizzical spirit of Anthony Trollope'. *CSSM Chronicle*, 1978

Garden view of King's House
Courtesy of The Salisbury Museum

Principal's sitting room (later the Quiet Room)
Courtesy of The Salisbury Museum

In 1895 the students returned to College to find improved 'quarters'.

> 'After a somewhat prolonged holiday we commenced our first term on Thursday September 5th. We owed the additional week to the carpenters and bricklayers, who could not make our new quarters habitable in time. 'The first and second floors above are devoted to dormitories, bathrooms, and some capital rooms for Sunday frocks'.
>
> *Our Quarterly,* 1895

In 1897 Sir Henry Oakley, HMI for Training Colleges, visited the College. He praised the work of staff and students but also commented that the Junior Classroom (for first years) was too small.

This was a dim room with low windows facing north. The use of the room changed and it became the 'drill room' also serving as a recreation room in wet weather. Beyond this room, and towards the garden, was built a new classroom, intended to accommodate 50 students with a dormitory above it. It was also used as an examination room. The dormitories above this room were constructed with single cubicles and all the old dormitories were also converted to single cubicles. What an improvement!

A corridor with a window seat and beautiful windows gave access to the drill room. In 1898 a new dining room was built to seat 120 persons, on the south side of King's House. It adjoined the kitchens, which made the serving of meals much easier. The old dining room became a large common room for the students. Outside the dining room a staircase led up to a vestibule from which there was access to the Servants' Hall with five bedrooms. The main staircase led

up to the main lecture room and dormitories. The senior classroom of the college was a beautiful room, looking east to the Cathedral and west to the river. In 1898-1899 the former Model School was fitted up as a Science Laboratory. The College could now accommodate 98 students.

At the north end of the main building of King's House, a door panelled with coloured glass on plain glass, suggesting a red cross, led into a small hall known as Red Cross Hall. The door was situated at right angles to the main building, opposite what was the old Model School. Immediately to the right of the door was a beautifully proportioned room with a low ceiling, which was initially used by the Principals as an office, but eventually had more general use and was known as 'The Quiet Room'. Today this delightful room is in use as the café attached to Salisbury Museum and happily, the Red Cross door is still in place.

> 'This room had its own atmosphere of ancient and longfelt peace, just as the splendid major classroom had its atmosphere of ancient courtly welcome and long exercised intellectual exchanges. Such was the maze of corridors, stairs and steps, which connected together the various rooms, but they gave character to the College as a building, and very few can have lived there without responding to a feeling of belonging and sense of inheritance'.
>
> *LST ibid*

THE ENLARGEMENT
OF THE
Training College for School Mistresses
SALISBURY.

A general account of the recently-erected New Buildings, by which 20 more teachers may be admitted for training for our Elementary Schools, will be found in the *Diocesan Gazette* for January, 1900.

The **Enlargement** falls under two heads, that of **New Buildings**, and of **Reconstruction**.

Of this the following is a summary :—

New Buildings : built in flint and cement, with mullions and dressings of Hamhill stone, in work and character entirely in keeping with the architecture of the old House.

A Chapel, seating 120 (Students and Staff).

A Dining Hall for 120 (now near the kitchen, &c.) (40 × 22 × 11).

Class Room for 50 Students (38 × 24 × 14).

Three Dormitories with 29 cubicles.

Laundry Room and three Bedrooms.

Larder and Servants' Hall. Staircase, Vestibule, &c.

Reconstruction : Dormitories entirely refitted with single cubicles.

Large Students' Common Room (out of former Dining Room).

Science Lecture Room and Laboratory (out of Students' Sitting Room).

The condemned Class Room has reverted to a Drill Hall and Recreation Room in wet weather, and for use as an occasional Examination Room.

A Bath Room (two baths) out of a bedroom.

Fittings (1) Two separate systems of hot water pipes throughout the whole house and new wings. (2) A new heating apparatus for five baths. (3) Electric light installed throughout.

Garden : The encroachment of the new building on the recreation ground has been met by laying out in lawn and gravel paths the strip of garden ground going down to the river.

All this has been accomplished without touching the picturesque front of "The King's House," in the Cathedral Close.

Courtesy of Wiltshire and Swindon History Centre

A Student's Memories of living in King's House 1896–1898

Mrs. Agnes Harris was a College student in 1896-98. In 1972 she wrote an interesting account of her life at that time. It was printed in the Chronicle of the College of Sarum St Michael in 1972, when Mrs Harris (who was then aged 97) lived in Canada.

'There were only 80 students and they lived a far more restricted life than the present generation. Special permission was required for coming and going and they might never go out of the college without a companion. Daily walks were taken in groups accompanied by a governess and clothes and general appearance were required to be less gay or 'neat not gaudy, for the apparel oft proclaims the man'. The day started with morning service at the Cathedral, because the chapel was not yet built, and went on with lectures, studies, tests and practice teachings. Saturday afternoons were given over to recreation, lawn tennis and other games. The ball was often lost over the old Deanery wall and when the Dean had collected a hatful, he would return them. The evenings were taken up with dances and concerts given by the students themselves'.

Building Improvements

It seemed a very unusual occurrence for us to reassemble for a new year's work in the middle of the week. But as painters and paperers who were employed in joining together properly the old house with the new, had not finished, we deferred the students until Wednesday, August 30. The house looked so clean and bright, with new brown linoleum carpeting the dormitories, which now give a comfortable separate cubicle to each student, and with the electric light, which has supplanted gas throughout the College. A new system of hot water pipes with radiators at points of vantage warm the corridors and some of the rooms. Miss Forth's sitting room has lost its partition, and now is the object of everyone's admiration, while Miss Hill is at last able to enjoy privacy and quiet, as the new staircase gives students access to their rooms without passing her door.

Our Quarterly, 1899

The Dining Room in 1910

'In 1910 there were nine tables, each with seating for not more than twelve. At that time students numbered 96. The staff had breakfast in an alcove. A hand bell was frequently rung for "less noise please" and occasionally for "silence", but it is surprising how much noise could be made by forks dropped onto a tiled floor, and pepper scattered strategically!

Violet Hayward, *Our College*

Electric Sparks

In 1917 two students wrote 'Electric Sparks' alongside their names in the Old Boathouse. By that time electricity had been installed for eighteen years. What a difference it must have made to the lives of the students! In 1899 Canon Steward recorded that as part of the King's House extensions there was the 'installation of electric light and heating apparatus throughout'. The students must have been delighted to have electric light in their dormitories.

Senior Classroom
Courtesy of The Salisbury Museum

KING'S HOUSE TRAINING COLLEGE,(SENIOR CLASS ROOM), SALISBURY.

The College Dining Room
Courtesy of The Salisbury Museum

The Chapel of the Holy Angels

The 1887 Inspection Report recommended that there should be a College Chapel. The inspectors felt that daily attendance at the Cathedral service 'crowded the work of the day into too limited time'. Canon Steward, the Principal, strongly believed that daily worship should continue to be at the very heart of College life.

By 1895, the suggestion of building a Chapel was being openly voiced in *Our Quarterly*:

> 'Dare we look on into the future? It is for you, Students of the present and the past to decide whether a Chapel shall be ever an accomplished fact. Will not some generous friend open a Chapel Fund at Messrs Pinckney's bank'?'

Canon Steward set out to enthuse Bishop Wordsworth. The Bishop, whilst valuing the presence of the students in the Cathedral, supported the scheme readily, as is shown in this extract from his letter to the Salisbury Diocesan Board of Education (SDBE) in 1898:

> 'Such a chapel will minister to the devotional life of our students. It will increase their sentiment of loyalty to the Church and of affection to the School when they leave it. It will also enable, I trust, the whole body to be gathered together for public worship, even on busy and stormy days when attendance at the daily services of the Cathedral would be difficult or impossible'.
>
> *Wiltshire & Swindon History Centre*

An appeal for money was widely circulated and donations came in from clergy, the National Society, Church Colleges, MPs and many other people. The results reflected support for the Church's involvement in education, and appreciation of the work of the College. The total cost of the Chapel was £900, of which a magnificent £400 was contributed by former students.

The foundation stone was laid on July 11th 1898, which was the 'Day of Thanksgiving for the Restoration of the Cathedral Spire'. Dr Frederick Temple, Archbishop of Canterbury, Bishop Wordsworth, five other bishops and eighty priests crossed The Close in procession for the service.

How was the dedication decided? Canon Steward and Bishop Wordsworth considered which saints there were whose lives would demonstrate to every student the holiness and significance of her calling. The Bishop paced up and down his study. Suddenly he stopped. 'Their Angels do alway behold the face of my Father which is in Heaven.'

'That's it, Steward, the dedication is 'The Chapel of the Holy Angels.''

On Whit-Monday 1899 the Chapel was dedicated by Bishop Wordsworth 'to the glory of God and in memory of William David Morrice'. Canon Morrice had been 'secretary and practically Principal of the College from 1861 to 1885'. At this time there had been a rapid changeover of Principals and it is likely that Canon Morrice took over much of the administration.

The reflections of Dora Hughes, who was a student from 1910 until 1912, portray the Chapel at the very heart of the College:

> 'Sundays grew to a close with Evening Prayer in the College Chapel. Voices were softer, footsteps lighter and movements slower than when we gathered on a weekday. Were we conscious of "Time's winged footsteps"? for indeed each Sunday marked the passing of time, as the flowers in the border of the garden marked the passing of the seasons. The deep Autumn weeks melted into the chill of October. The river mists and fog crept up as we walked through the dim light of late November evenings. Soon it was Spring, then Summer, the garden spiced and glowing. Always, in Chapel we seemed to be drawn together into a one-ness that was unlike any other experience of the week. Singing, we gave our praise and thanks; kneeling, we dedicated afresh "hearts and minds and voices". "In quietness and confidence shall be your strength" we meditated, not yet knowing how many times in the years to come we should call on those words for anchorage when times were dark and stormy'.

Chapel interior
Courtesy of the The Salisbury Museum

Laying the Foundation Stone of the Chapel
Courtesy of The Salisbury Museum

That the Church may be guided by the Holy Spirit to do the full will of God in the present crisis of education.

That our people may be trained in prayer and service.

For the War.

That the Holy Spirit may inspire the nations of the world to desire and attain to a just and enduring peace.

That the Lord Christ Himself would bless and comfort all who are in sorrow and suffering through the War.

That He would defend and bless all who command our armies; all who serve in battle under our King; and all our Allies; and lead them to victory in His own good time.

That He would keep our aims pure and true.

That He would grant to us true repentance for all our sins and shortcomings.

That He would make England faithful to her Lord in this great trial laid upon her.

Thanksgiving.

We thank Thee, O Lord

For Thy Spirit stirring in our Church and nation.

For the fresh union springing up amongst all classes.

For the great blessings vouchsafed in and through this War.

For " All Thy servants departed this life in Thy faith and fear."

Salisbury Training College.

——♦——

Guild of S. Mary the Virgin.

——♦——

EASTER, 1918.

——♦——

" In quietness and in confidence shall be your strength."

The Chapel of the Holy Angels

August 1901 – The College Diamond Jubilee

During the 60 years that the College had been in existence, 1,955 students had trained there as schoolmistresses. Salisbury-trained teachers from far and near returned for the Diamond Jubilee.

A service in the Cathedral was followed by a 'sumptuous lunch in a spacious tent. What a time it was of hearty greeting and renewed friendships. We were almost girls again!'   *College Archives*

At Bishop Wordsworth's kind invitation, former students visited the Palace. On returning to the College, they had tea on the lawn before 'dancing merrily to the strains of the Volunteer Band'.

Canon Steward spoke on the subject of 'change', saying that if there was to be progress, then change was inevitable. He felt that nearly all past students would agree with the abandonment of the white caps and the class walks! He also felt that 'the amount of heavy work formerly imposed on students had not been desirable and that the custom had therefore been abandoned, and a large staff of servants had been engaged'. Whilst there was regret that daily worship in the Cathedral was no longer part of College life, Canon Steward pointed out that they now had their own College Chapel, which was greatly valued by the students.

Salisbury Diocesan Training College

Reunion, Thursday, Aug. 22, 1901

(The Sixtieth Year of the College).

CELEBRATION OF HOLY COMMUNION IN THE CATHEDRAL AT 8 O'CLOCK.

Breakfast.

MATINS AND SERMON IN THE CATHEDRAL AT 11.

LUNCHEON AT 1 O'CLOCK.

Tea on the Lawn at 4.30.

EVENSONG IN THE CHAPEL AT 7.30.

Supper at 8.

We hope to be able to welcome a large number of former Students on this occasion, and that you will make every effort to come.

Kindly reply on the other half of this notice, which should be detached and returned to the Lady Superintendent.

EDWARD STEWARD, Principal.
C. HILL, Lady Superintendent.

Food Glorious Food – 'Joy Pellets' and 'Pavement'

King's House in 1900 by Ruth Spencer 1909-11

'We were due to go to Stonehenge for a picnic so Mr Eady, Clarice's father, a strawberry grower, sent us masses of strawberries for our tea which were most welcome. As you may imagine, fresh fruit was a joy as we had only one orange given to us after Saturday lunch. The food was pretty awful. My mother used to send me a huge fruitcake every week and at the beginning of each term I would take fruit out of our Abbotsbury School House garden.'

During the First World War, food was rationed, but the students were grateful to Florrie, the Head Cook, for her efforts. After the war she married a Canadian soldier in the Cathedral and the students 'filled the choir and sang for her'.

A student recorded that 'We had meat only three days a week; on alternate days there was thin soup and bread followed by a stodgy pudding; no tuck boxes from home was the rule'.

During 1917-1919 'Miss Adam had the difficult task of dealing with rations and we were sorry for her when she had to announce in the Dining Hall yet one more meatless day'.

A typical menu in 1917-1919 as recorded by a student:

Friday – kipper or bloater for breakfast, cheeses, watercress or other salad with round oat biscuits we called 'joy pellets' for lunch, and baked potato with beetroot, or pickles for supper. A Saturday night's supper was noted for very hard baked pastry with tasteless jam we called 'pavement'.

In the 1890s the students still maintained their 'industrial work' alongside their more formal studies, but gradually this began to move more towards Domestic Economy. In 1873, The National Training School of Cookery was established in London. Canon Steward believed it would be useful for the students, and for the reputation of Salisbury Training College, to develop a school attached to the college.

> 'He (Canon Steward) brought ardent joy into the setting up of a Cookery Kitchen in the college and into the details of its working. There in the simple kitchen of the little house, Audley, which he had bought personally for the College, were held the first Cookery Classes of the College and those of the Elementary School children in Salisbury.'
>
> *Everett Papers, Book Two*
> Courtesy of Salisbury Cathedral Library

The log books from St Martin's School show that teachers from the school regularly attended Cookery lessons at the College. Children from the school also attended the classes. How exciting it must have been for them!

Most students at this time would have been familiar with Mrs Beeton and her famous reference book first published in 1861. They would have relished the opportunity to develop their own skills and knowledge.

> 'The course included at least twenty lessons, in which all the principal methods of cooking should have been taught, e.g. roasting, baking, boiling, frying, stewing, soup making, cooking of vegetables, making and cooking of puddings, cakes, bread, soup making and invalid dishes'.
>
> *Canon Steward*

The course also aimed to provide 'knowledge of the management of ordinary stoves and ranges and the methods of cleaning the cooking utensils'.

Demonstration lessons were given and hearty and warming food was prepared.

A menu from a lesson on Pastry (Boiled and Baked) dated October 1891:

Rabbit Pie	Roly Poly Pudding
Cornish Pasties	Jam Puffs
Beef Steak Pudding	Tartlets
Sausage Rolls	Treacle Pudding
Meat Patties	Fruit Pie

The results of the first examination in Salisbury were published in 1890 and showed that eight candidates obtained a diploma. The success rate improved and the Cookery School continued until 1898.

Above: Typical Food as prepared in the Cookery School

Right: General Scheme of Lessons
Courtesy of Wiltshire and Swindon History Centre

General Scheme of Cookery Lessons proposed for the Salisbury Training College 1891 with details of the first Set.

The following scheme has been based on the principle that each Student and child shall receive;— first, instruction in theory;— secondly, demonstration by the Instructress;— and thirdly, actual practice in Cookery.

Scullery work is taught in each lesson instead of in a single lesson at the commencement, Students or children (as the case may be) being taught to clean and put away every utensil used.

Miss Mary Constance Hill: Lady Superintendent 1887–1917

Mary Constance Hill was a person of many talents. In 1887, under Bishop Wordsworth, she was appointed as Lady Superintendent. Her efficient household management and financial expertise were soon recognised. During her three decades at the College she brought about greater comfort and improved living conditions for both staff and students.

> 'At last Miss Hill has been able to give each Student what she was long wishing for - a roomy cubicle with a wardrobe to herself, and the floors of the dormitories have been laid with linoleum'.
>
> *Michaelmas 1898 Magazine*

Canon Steward, who worked with her and took on some of her duties when he became Principal in 1891, paid tribute to her unselfish, unending devotion to duty, referring to her as 'the Lady Abbess of King's House'.

An article in the College Magazine in 1912 focused on her kindness and concern for the students:

> 'For 25 years she has lovingly tended the many generations of Students who have passed under her care, giving a personal service which has called out a loving, loyal devotion from all our hearts, and won for our College the highest reputation in England for real care of its Students'.

Former students remembered with gratitude her 'numberless letters to ex Students in trouble, ill-health or loneliness, her fostering of our College Guild and Magazine, the excellence of her arrangements for our Great Re-unions. Her skill as an indoor architect and outdoor gardener have helped to make King's House what it is to so many of us, our most beautiful and best loved place on Earth'.

Miss Hill died in 1925. Former students subscribed to a memorial fund, part of which was set aside to form a fund from which help might be given to old students in need. Miss Hill's Fund was established before the development of the welfare state with its National Insurance, and at a time when teachers' salaries were low and pensions correspondingly inadequate. The Fund was still receiving donations in 1968. In 1984, six years after the College closed, the Newsletter included a request that former students should let the committee know of anyone who would benefit from a small donation.

Courtesy of The Salisbury Museum

Influenza epidemics were prevalent in the country from the 1890s until the 1920s. In 1890 thirty students and four members of staff became ill and there was a further outbreak in 1892. Miss Hill, writing in *Our Quarterly*, Michaelmas 1895, explained that 'when half a dozen girls were ill in different parts of the house the distribution of medicines and beef tea involved a walk upstairs and downstairs of miles'. A larger and more convenient Infirmary was prepared for use.

'At the further end is the dormitory with eight beds, next to this the nurse's room and bathroom, while as we enter we pass through a bright and lofty sitting room for convalescents. Out of what was the governess's room opens a door admitting us to an outside staircase, so that should a case of infection arise, the whole set of rooms can be completely isolated'.

The new Infirmary was ready in time for the extensive influenza epidemic in the winter of 1895.

'We had our Religious Knowledge examination. One student was absent, as ill with influenza, and five others were hardly fit to enter, though they struggled bravely through the six hours'.

Time to go home - a welcome rest for tired staff and students:

'Right gladly did everyone in the King's House depart for a ten days' vacation on Saturday April 6th. Throughout the term influenza had been claiming its victims amongst Governesses and Students alike; indeed, two Students actually retired to the Infirmary on the morning of our departure. There was no fear of their escaping before the Doctor pronounced them fit to travel. Woe betide the Student who dare creep back into class without Nurse's leave and knowledge!'

Accidents occasionally happened … Marjorie fell off her bicycle in September 1905 and was absent from class for over a month. Bad headaches continued to affect her ability to study and after further absences she was 'ordered home for rest by Doctor' in March 1906.

Health at the College during the First World War remained quite good, although there were, inevitably, times of low spirits alongside news of wartime disasters. There was, however, a measles epidemic in 1918 and 46 students also succumbed to the virulent influenza epidemic. For the first time for over 30 years a student died in the College. 'Fevers in the town' always caused concern. An epidemic of Scarlet Fever in 1905 led to a doctor at the Endless Street Surgery warning Canon Steward of the risks of students 'being infected and bringing the disease home to the College'.

Death announcements in the College Magazines were all too frequent:

Lilian Fletcher (1900 -1902), who was known to have 'delicate heart and lungs", contracted influenza and quietly breathed her last'.

Lucille Marrett 'passed away in her home at St Clement's Jersey in 1906, in her 20th year'.

Nellie Bate (1904 -1906) died six months after she had started teaching, following a 'serious attack of influenza.'

These untimely deaths of young women who had just started teaching are a poignant reminder of the fragility of life in pre-antibiotic and pre-National Health Service days.

SALISBURY TRAINING COLLEGE,
Nov. 28, 1901.

PRIVATE.

To King's Scholarship Candidates.

In case you may wish to be transferred to another Centre for the Examination, I have to inform you that on Nov. 20 a single case of Diphtheria occurred among the resident Students.

I would point out that all the 120 inmates of the College remained in residence and none have suffered; that the College Infirmary is thoroughly isolated; and that the Medical Officer considers that the Candidates who come up on Dec. 9 or 10 for Examination will run no risk of infection.

Unless I hear from you to the contrary, I shall conclude you desire to be accommodated here, and will make provision accordingly.

If you desire to be transferred to another Centre, you must apply *immediately* to the Board of Education, and at the same time inform me that you will not present yourself here for the Examination.

EDWARD STEWARD,
Principal.

Courtesy of the Wiltshire and Swindon History Centre

Miss Forth Courtesy of The Salisbury Museum

Miss Forth was appointed Head Governess in place of Miss Jackson in 1890. She was also Mistress of Method in the College, and became Vice-Principal in 1907. She succeeded Canon Steward as Principal in 1913 and served the college for 23 years. Miss Forth succeeded in maintaining Canon Steward's high standards of care and work.

As Mistress of Method, Miss Forth was responsible for the organisation of the practical work of the students in teaching in the schools, by demonstration and instruction. A teacher from each school worked in close liaison with the College lecturer.

During the First World War Miss Forth maintained a high level of stability in the College and strove to keep an atmosphere of calm. She took part in many Diocesan discussions related to education, and promoted a variety of religious and secular interests. She established the Old Deanery as a hall and library as well as a way of extending accommodation for students and staff.

Evelyn Hart was a student at the College in 1913. In her book 'Lest I Forget' she wrote a delightful account of college life and included a description of Miss Forth:

'I well remember many of the staff. The Principal Miss Barbara Forth, essentially Victorian, large, deeply religious, infallibly correct. Had she been a man I feel sure she would have been a Bishop'.

On retirement Miss Forth lived at 36 The Close and often attended services at The Cathedral. She maintained close links with the College through the OSA.

It is evident from autograph books and records that students remembered Miss Forth with great affection. Every year she devoted a whole day to writing an individual and very personal letter to each student, which she sent enclosed with the final examination result. Lucy Sanderson Taylor wrote a moving description of Miss Forth in her final days:

'It was characteristic that to the very last, bent and often in pain, she would cross The Close, even in the darkness and cold of winter to Communion Service in the Cathedral'.

Miss Forth was awarded an MBE in the New Year's Honours List in January 1936. She died on Lady Day in 1943.

Miss Forth's Sitting Room Courtesy of The Salisbury Museum

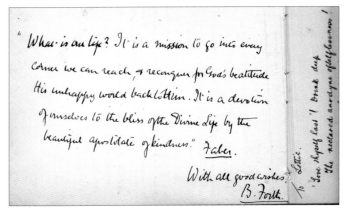

Henrietta Mabbott was 20 when she entered College at Christmas 1895. She was a Diocesan Exhibitioner and had been a pupil teacher at St Peter's School, Parkstone. The College Register describes her as 'not strong, but free from positive illness'. Her conduct was 'excellent' and she was described as being a 'very determined teacher who conquers difficulties, reliable and thorough, teaching clear and impressive'. Her discipline was 'very good.' Henrietta was awarded a prize for Needlework in July 1897 and also a First Class Certificate in the Archbishop's Examination.

She was appointed to Overton National School in Hampshire in 1897. By this time the school-leaving age was officially thirteen, but pupils were frequently removed for farm work from ten years onwards. The school log books show that the widening curriculum now included handwork and domestic economy (cookery and laundry) for girls and cottage gardening for boys.

Autograph Albums were very popular in Victorian times. Henrietta treasured her album, which includes exquisite coloured and painted sketches. Verses written by popular poets such as Thomas Moore were carefully penned. Miss Forth also contributed, quoting a few appropriate lines from Samuel Coleridge.

Henrietta left College in July 1897. A fellow student wrote about the influence that College services would surely have in the years to come:

'On the last Sunday evening of the term, the Staff and Students assembled in the Chapel of the Bishop's School at 8pm. The quiet walk across the Cathedral green, the solemn service, the farewell words of counsel from the Principal, will doubtless be among the things of the past which have entered into our lives and become, as it were, a part of ourselves. In the hours which we can secure for quiet reflection and heart-searching, or in the days when we are dragged down by weariness and depression will not some of these words come back to us? Shall we not remember that we were counselled to seek for strength in earnest prayer for ourselves and the children in our schools, in frequent Communions, and by taking advantage of any opportunity of spending a few minutes on our knees in the quiet and peace of God's House? We shall do well to cherish, as something very precious to us, the recollection of that Sunday evening and of that early morning when we knelt together in the Lady Chapel'.

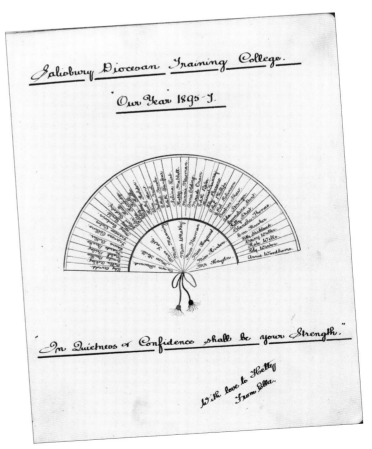

Violet Hayward recorded an amusing incident. One unfortunate student was required to take a large iron pill each morning. Making the excuse of needing a glass of water, she then went into the garden and threw the pills over the Deanery wall. Somehow the Dean discovered her name (Violet thought it must have been the College Nurse who gave the game away). In due course she received a small parcel containing a box of pills, with a note from the Dean to the effect that he had been watching her botanical experiment with great interest, but as the seeds were showing no sign of germination, he was returning them herewith!

Drawings by Pat Jones

LIST OF CLOTHES & ARTICLES REQUIRED.

2 pairs of Sheets; 2 Pillow Cases; 6 Towels; 2 white Toilet Covers.
Night-dress Case; 2 Clothes Bags; Comb Bag.
Woollen Dressing Gown (washable); Print Dressing Jacket.
Warm Slippers; Sponge; Tooth and Nail Brushes.

Of Underclothing—not less than 3 of each garment worn.
2 Washing Petticoats (coloured); 6 Handkerchiefs (or more).
2 Holland or Print Pinafores with sleeves.
1 Pinafore with sleeves—of very cheap material (for practice in Chemistry).
2 Table Napkins (Spoons, Forks and Napkin Ring are provided).

Waterproof; Umbrella; 2 pairs of Shoes or Boots, one of which *must be thick*; 1 pair of House
    Shoes; Tennis Shoes; Galoshes.

2 plain Print or Linen Shirt-blouses, without lining or trimming, and made with collar and cuffs
    of the same material, which should be such as will wash well (not a dark colour or large
    pattern).
1 Coat and Skirt.   1 Dress Skirt extra.
1 Dress or Skirt for best wear, made of useful material, quiet in colour, and as simple as possible.
1 White or Cream Blouse.
1 or 2 other Blouses.

1 Sailor Hat, white straw (broad brim preferred).
A special ribbon and badge for this are supplied at the College.
1 good Hat for Sunday wear, simple and quiet both in shape and trimming—no feathers.

Keeping up Appearances

Dora Hughes was a student in 1910. In an article written in the 1952 College magazine she described her arrival at college:

'On the afternoon of an early September day in 1910 I walked for the first time as a student into the entrance hall of King's House…I made my way up the first flight of the oak stairway, and turned into the slightly gloomy atmosphere of the dormitory, carrying my suitcase with me. I was rather proud of its contents, the new saxe-blue dressing gown (home-made), the new navy-blue coat and skirt (tailored), the high-necked white shirt blouses, accompanied by black and white silk ties, the best straw hat with the black band with narrow white stripes, the every-day straw, with the band in wide black and white stripes, and the white muslin dress for special occasions.

There was a special Hat Room in King's House at this time. It was at the corner of the corridor leading to the Junior Classroom. The outside wall was used for notice boards. The room was shelved inside in two layers, with each student having a place on each shelf for the everyday hat and the Sunday hat – one above the other. Hats were deemed to be very important in keeping up a smart outdoor appearance'.

Violet Hayward, in her book *Our College* described the fashion in 1909 regarding hair:

'By 1909 fashion was veering towards bobbed hair but we were forbidden to adopt it. As we had but recently attained to the dignity of using hairpins, Miss Hill, with a shocked gaze, had frequently to implore us to "go and tidy your hair". This was particularly if any visitors were expected, especially Bishops'.

She also described the required contents of the students' wardrobes:

'Our wardrobes had to contain a dark skirt, white dresses, white blouses and the college tie, but uniformity was only required on special occasions, visits of Bishops, death of a King, Prize Day etc. In Winter and Summer we wore straw boaters, with a black and white band and a college badge'.

In her 1916 diary Hilda Noyce described her return to College, following an interview for a teaching post in Warminster:

'When I arrived in Salisbury I fearfully and tremblingly walked towards College painfully aware of my "private hat". I tried Audley Passage Gate but alas! it was locked. I marched in boldly to find 'Raisins' reclining at ease on the front lawn and Miss F. planted in her sitting room window. I minutely expected the edict 'Send Hilda Noyce to me' but it never came and I am still alive to tell the tale'.

Gertrude, the Girl in the Hat

Gertrude Lucy Allen (known as Gertie) was at Salisbury Diocesan Training College from 1906 to 1908. Her daughter (Rosemary Browning) has a childhood memory of seeing her wear her College blazer. It had DTCS on it, along with a Tudor Rose. Rosemary followed her mother to College in 1938 and found that several of the staff (notably Miss Stevenson and Miss Grist), who had taught Gertie, were still there.

Sketch from an autograph book, 1916

The Old Boathouse

At the time of the closure of the College, the boathouse was a small, long-disused building situated at the end of the garden. Its use as a boathouse at some period was confirmed by the boat hooks which hung outside. There are no college records of students participating in any boating activities.

The names and remarks were written on all four walls, but mainly on the west wall around the window. The earliest year-group of students from which names are inscribed was the 1911-1913 group. On June 19th 1912 three students wrote:

'We are ye holy trio 1911-1913,' and then repeated the inscription:

'We are three, MMB, CEB, IMC-Ye holy trio.'

Further names were inscribed in 1912-14 and 1913-1915. A set from 1913-1915 gave the information that the students were resident in 'South Dorm.'

Another group designated themselves as 'the Goodest Juniors'. Two of these left the note: 'Mabel King and Mary Timpson tried to do Divinity here May 5th 1915. Wasn't a success! Divinity didn't appeal to us at that particular moment'.

A final record by two students in 1918-1920 declared '8.9.18 Both fed-up.' Perhaps they were feeling homesick, having just entered college.

One can easily imagine the chatter and fun the students must have had over the years in The Old Boathouse down by the river. It is quite hard to imagine them doing something so daring as writing on the walls, but it provides a very interesting insight into their lives. They left college and went on to teach, but it is sad to think that at least three of the young women were soon to die of influenza.

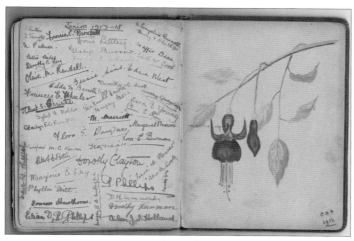

Autographs with nicknames

Nicknames

The Balfour Act of 1902

1 School Boards were abolished.

2 Responsibility for education was given to the newly formed Local Education Authorities.

3 LEAs were required to support education beyond the elementary stage and including teacher training.

In Salisbury, Canon Steward, fearing the secularisation of education, entered the many debates as successive governments attempted to change the legislation.

In 1900 Canon Steward had the foresight to realise that the growth of secondary education was likely to result in an increased number of applicants for training, some of whom would be non-conformists. As the foundation of King's House specified 'the principles of the Church of England' as admission criteria, he persuaded the Committee to purchase Barnard's Cross as a residence for non-Anglican students.

Two years later the Board of Education decreed that if Church Training Colleges wished to receive grants, they must forfeit the right to use denominational criteria when offering places. Following a protest by the Church of England, the government backed down and it was agreed that the Church Colleges could select up to 50 per cent of their students on the basis of their denominational allegiance. The way ahead was clear and Barnard's Cross could come into being.

> 'The old College is moving with the times. We are endeavouring to cope with the increasing demand for trained teachers by opening a class for fifty Day Students. The authorities have purchased a large residence about a quarter of a mile from the College in St Ann's Street. We propose to add a Dining Hall, Class-rooms and Dormitories, so that eventually all the fifty Students can be accommodated on the premises.'
>
> Canon Steward 1903

Miss Fitzgerald, Lady Superintendent, had the task of preparing Barnard's Cross for its first students, and, in the following year, of furnishing and opening the new building:

> 'In the pretty cubicles, the comfortable common room and the many details affecting the well-being of the Students, may we see her taste and thoughtfulness'.

Barnard's Cross, a fine old Salisbury house, was acquired in 1903 and 25 students were admitted that autumn. Building began and Canon Steward proudly pointed out that the modern extension would be 'heated by hot water and electrically lighted throughout'. He went on to say that 'we have hired a meadow of six acres, by the trees on Harnham Hill, whither parties of girls wend their way daily for hockey or rounders'.

At the College Prize-giving in July 1904, the committee of the Diocesan Board of Education was thanked for 'so readily and promptly enabling the College to be in advance of the times'. Canon Steward regretted that they could not receive the Barnard's Cross students into the College itself, but he was 'sure he was speaking on behalf of Staff and Students, when he said that they would extend to them their sisterly friendship and not regard them as in any way isolated from the corporate family life of the College'.

Barnard's Cross was formally opened by Bishop John Wordsworth on November 2nd 1905. A service was followed by 'a most happy evening party for the Staff and Students of the whole College, with many Salisbury Teachers and other friends'.

A memoir written after Canon Steward's death described this as 'a great day in the annals of the College ... the College came into its own and took a prominent place in the eyes of the educational world'. The College now had 160 students, 50 at Barnard's Cross, 100 at King's House, and about 10 others as day students at the Hostel.

Barnard's Cross soon developed into a flourishing community with events that included Fancy Dress parties, Morris and Country Dances, Folk Singing, Mission Sales, expeditions to Groveley Woods and the New Forest, and carol singing to children in the Workhouse. Tennis and hockey matches were played against King's House and there were topical debates between the houses. 'In 1908 "VOTES FOR WOMEN" smiled a welcome from a notice board'! The Local History Club had expeditions to Downton Moot, Breamore, Wilton, St Thomas's Church and Old Sarum. It seems probable that the 'Moonlight Walk through the Cloisters with Dr Baker' was very popular.

Plays were performed regularly: *Antigone* in 1908 and *The Cricket on the Hearth* in 1909. The 1905 production made use of the new stage and electric footlights.

Canon Bernard, speaking at the prize-giving in 1906, summed up the relationship between Barnard's Cross and King's House as 'healthy rivalry – there is nothing like a little competition to get the best out of people's work'.

The students particularly enjoyed entertaining their little neighbours from 'The House of Industry' in St Ann Street.

> 'Never had such a demure little band entered by the Garden gate! A casual remark on the extreme quietness of the children, made to the Matron, called forth the answer, "Indeed, I hope they will be, Miss," a remark well calculated to stir our most secret and determined opposition. We tried music, then games. It was games that did it! The excitement of musical chairs was not to be resisted. There was no longer quietness.

We seized our opportunity, and what was one Matron against sixty students? We played Donkey's Tail, Hunt the Slipper and Simon Says. The Matron thanked us for what was entirely our pleasure, but not one of us would have foregone the smiles and nods from a certain little window as we passed down St Ann Street to the Early Service at the Cathedral the next morning'.

[According to *Kelly's Directory* 1915 there were 20 'female inmates' in The House of Industry in 1915. Their ages ranged from 9 to 19 and they were probably all orphans.]

Miss Black, who had succeeded Miss Fitzgerald in 1906 as Lady Superintendent, made the house a 'home from home' and was especially remembered by the Channel Island students. Miss Simpson, the Housemistress during the First World War, was appreciated for her skill in housekeeping at a time when 'less than 50 per cent of the very economical ration to which we had reduced ourselves, was allowed.'

Life at Barnard's Cross during the war was sometimes disturbed by Zeppelin Drill, 'when, by the light of candles and electric torches, we find our way down to the cellar'.

The Chapel of All Saints

Ever since Barnard's Cross opened in 1903, the need for a Chapel within its precincts was felt by staff and students alike. A subscription list was started in Autumn 1908 and there was a ready response. The sum guaranteed was liberally supplemented by friends of the College. Donations were also received from former students, the Society for Promoting Christian Knowledge (SPCK), the National Society, the Church Building Society and the Diocesan Board of Education. Dr Baker, who was to be the Chaplain, put considerable energy and commitment into the project.

The site chosen was in the garden, near to the Love Lane wall. The Chapel was designed by GLW Blount to seat 80 worshippers and to be of Norman-French style. Local building materials included oak from the New Forest and flint from Wiltshire Downs. The Foundation Stone was laid on May 29th 1909 and the building rose rapidly, with the Dedication taking place five months later on October 23rd. The weather was wild and tempestuous and students were seated under an awning, but 'no weather could damp our happiness over the completion of our Chapel'.

'The Chapel looked beautiful in pure whiteness, against which the dark wood of the screen and the beams of the roof showed to the greatest advantage. All the flowers used for the Sanctuary were white, with green foliage to relieve them'.

Bishop Wordsworth pointed out in his address that 'the new Chapel pointed inwards, towards the College and that herein we might find a reminder that the spirit of the daily services should enter into and sanctify the whole life of the community'.

*The Chapel of All Saints
Barnard's Cross*
Courtesy of Salisbury Museum

Salisbury Diocesan Training College, Barnard's Cross
All Saints Chapel.
No 5.

'This severely chaste and beautiful building that we now call our own'.
Courtesy of The Salisbury Museum

Barnard's Cross

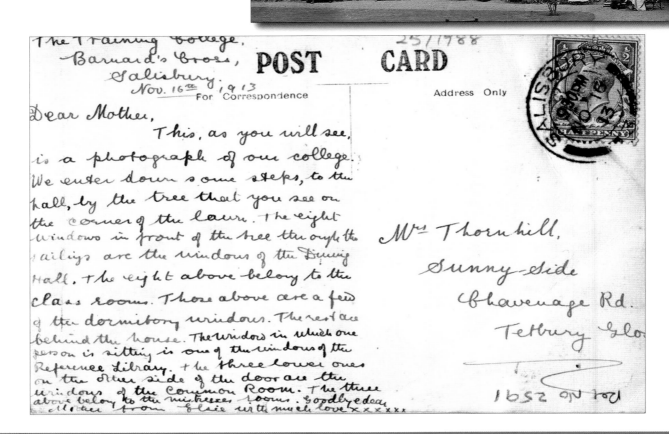

The Training College,
Barnard's Cross,
Salisbury,
Nov. 16th, 1913

POST   **CARD**

For Correspondence

Address Only

Dear Mother,
This, as you will see, is a photograph of our college. We enter down some steps, to the hall, by the tree that you see on the corner of the lawn. The eight windows in front of the tree through the railings are the windows of the Dining Hall. The eight above belong to the class rooms. Those above are a few of the dormitory windows. The rest are behind the house. The window in which one person is sitting is one of the windows of the Reference Library. The three lower ones on the other side of the door are the windows of the Common Room. The three above belong to the mistresses' rooms. Goodbye dear Mother from Elsie with much love xxxxx

Mrs Thornhill,
Sunny Side
Chavenage Rd.
Tetbury Glo.

Students from the Channel Islands first appear in records in the 1860s. Eugenia Bockhill from St Peter's, Jersey was recorded as a pupil at the Training School in the 1861 Census. During the next 40 years Channel Island students continued to come to Salisbury for their training, often returning to appointments at schools in their home islands.

The link between Jersey and the College was formalised in 1904. In 1905, Canon Steward reported that 'they had come to very fair terms with the States of Jersey, so that Jersey would send them every year a good number of students'. It was intended that students from Jersey would mostly, but not exclusively, join Barnard's Cross.

A reciprocal agreement was drawn up between the States of Jersey Education Committee and the College. Jersey paid £200 towards the extensions of the College in Barnard's Cross and the College agreed to place at the disposal of the Education Committee in Jersey two annual Exhibitions for admission into Barnard's Cross for board, lodging and training as King's Scholars'. The Agreement also stated:

'Students accepted from the island into Barnard's Cross would be paid £5 annually by the States of Jersey Education Committee and £2.50 by the College authorities. Students from the island who were accepted into King's House would not be entitled to this remuneration'.

(Wiltshire & Swindon History Centre)

In 1909 two students from Barnard's Cross and two from King's House were appointed to Jersey schools. Four more students accepted posts in Jersey in 1910. In July 1914, Barnard's Cross held a reunion of seven past, present and future Guernsey students.

A student from the Channel Islands remembered her arrival at Barnard's Cross in 1914:

'A chintzy, decorated sitting room gay with flowers. Against the fireplace stands a tall, gracious figure with an outstretched hand welcoming a group of very raw recruits to the halls of learning . The Islanders arrive to report to the Vice-Principal'.

The kindly figure who had greeted the Island students was Miss Rodgers, who subsequently became the Head of Barnard's Cross:

'A closed sitting room door labelled "Miss Rodgers." In the half light of passage and stairway lurk hesitant students with problems: illness of loved ones, "school prac" worries, misunderstandings in friendships … but the name on the door had come to mean understanding, sharing and halving of problems. The door would open to the slightest knock; there would be help'.

Margaret Montgomery was important to students from Jersey. She joined the staff at College in 1900, having been Head Student at King's House in 1899. In 1909 Miss Montgomery was appointed to the Headship of the Pupil-Teacher Centre in Jersey:

'When in 1909 the need of teacher training and of preparing Students for College life in England was recognised in Jersey, it was to Canon Steward that the Dean of Jersey and the Education Department of the States turned for help'.

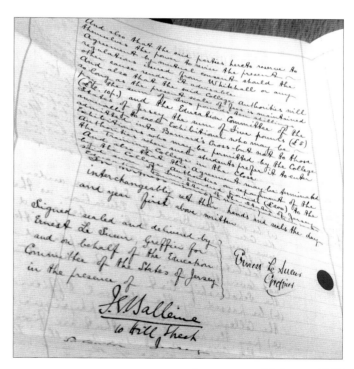

Agreement with Jersey, 1905
Courtesy of Wiltshire and Swindon History Centre

Principal	Revd. Canon Steward, M.A
Lady Superintendent	Miss Hill
Head Governess	Miss Forth
Lecturers	Miss Manning
	Miss Crook
Mathematics	Miss Whatley
Needlework	Miss Newman
Arithmetic	Mr Wheeler
Music	Mr J. M. Hayden
Practising Schools	Miss Bianchi and Miss Fanner

(Taken from Our Training College by Canon Steward)

Miss Sewell.   Miss Whatley.   Dr. Baker.   The Principal.   Miss Gardiner.   Miss Stevenson.
        Miss Allen.   Miss Street.   Miss Forth.   Miss Newman.
Miss Montgomery.   Miss Thorp.   Miss Black.   Miss Hill.   Miss Ellis.   Miss Mitchell.
        Miss Thompson.   Miss Fildes.   Miss Gill.   Miss Grist.

The Staff in 1908

Some Members of Staff and their salaries in 1915/1916:

Miss Forth, Principal	unknown (In 1920 it was £591)
Miss Rodgers, Vice Principal	£110
Miss Newman, Needlework	£100
Miss Grist, Education/ School Practice	£70 plus 1 day paid for by LEA
Miss Stevenson	£90
Miss Allen	£92 and 10 shillings
Miss Evetts	£85
Miss Risley	£80
Miss Story	£75
Miss Alexander	£70
Miss Hellmann, French Lessons	£7
Miss Hall, Cookery	£10 and 9 shillings
Miss Steele, Housecraft	£8
The Revd.S. Baker, Lecturer and Chaplain	£250

The Staff in 1914

Miss Whatley

Miss Mary Whatley LLA was a former student, who headed the Certificate list in 1887. She was appointed to the Staff in 1888 as Third Governess and stayed at College until 1918.

> 'Miss Whatley was utterly content – round, plump, solitary. She supervised our needlework. Each student made a specimen book showing all forms of stitchery and an example in miniature of every garment, all of which was anathema to me'.
>
> *Evelyn Hart*

It was through Miss Whatley's efforts that a branch of the Prisoners Parcels Association was organised and in 1916 it was reported that over 500 parcels of much needed food and clothing had been sent out from the College, packed by the students, who 'gladly carry on this bit of war-work'.

> 'Miss Whatley receives many grateful letters. Scarcely does a parcel fail to be acknowledged. And the men's simple, truthful words reveal a patient, cheerful endurance, a readiness to help others, and a gratitude in pathetic, poverty-stricken and isolated conditions which is eloquent'.

'The Doll Show' at King's House was started by Miss Whatley. Dolls and garments were collected for Christmas presents to 'little ones of the slum districts in London'.

Some of the dolls and clothes were made by children and were examples of techniques that they had learnt in school, such as seaming, hemming and knitting. Garments included 'wonderfully nice knitted jerseys and knickers'.

Many tiny frocks, as well as smaller garments, were made in King's House. This would appear to have been an annual torture that was thoughtfully and perhaps gleefully, perpetuated by former students who supplied dress material and yards of flannelette for the purpose!

Clara Grant's school in Bow in the East End was one of those that received dolls and clothes. Writing in 1934 after Miss Whatley's death, Clara described her as having been like a Fairy Godmother to the children. Her 'love, humility, sympathy and constant care for those in need were marks of a fine character and an inspiration to us all'.

Miss Whatley left College 'after many years of zealous, devoted work to take part in the wonderful scheme of education for our soldiers in France, which the universities had arranged behind the lines of the Army of Occupation. How much the whole College missed her'!

A postcard from a Prisoner of War
Courtesy of Wiltshire and
Swindon History Centre

Courtesy of Wiltshire and
Swindon History Centre

Grist to the Mill

Sarah Agnes Grist was admitted to the College on February 6th 1893 aged seventeen. Sarah had been a pupil teacher in Melksham and when admitted to College she was placed in Class 1 in the examinations. Her College Record shows her placed in the first rank generally, and she also gained first place in Religious Knowledge, Advanced Hygiene Studies and Drawing.

On leaving College she furthered her career by gaining the Cambridge Teachers' Diploma and the 'Lady Literate in Arts' (LLA) qualification. The LLA was held by many of the staff at this time, before women were allowed to graduate from university. Miss Grist took every opportunity to advance her career in Higher Education and returned to College as a lecturer.

The Salisbury Training College staff photograph of 1908 shows her as a young woman aged 32. She remained on the staff as Mistress of Method, and later as a Lecturer in Education until her retirement in 1937, when she was 61 years old. She was a forward-looking member of staff who worked hard at the College, both as a student and as a member of staff.

> 'Her exceptional talent and enthusiasm have been invaluable and she had a special genius for making the too-congested Training College week yield the almost impossible maximum of well-distributed time. We wish her the utmost happiness in her newly gained leisure and in the freedom to pursue her interest beneath the roof of the house she has chosen and equipped with a keen eye to modern methods'.
>
> *STC Magazine, 1938*

Winifred Taylor (1926-1928) had fond memories of Miss Grist:

> 'My loving memory of Miss Grist was on school practice. I remember a drab classroom of senior boys following her with rapt attention. They didn't see an elderly lady in a long tweed skirt, hand knitted stockings and flat shoes prancing around their classroom. They saw young Lochinvar as he swung his fair lady to the saddle and they heard his triumphant shout: "She is won!" What an example of teaching English Literature!'

Miss Fanny Street: a 'High Flyer'

Miss Fanny Street, elder sister of AG Street, the writer and broadcaster, was educated at Wilton Elementary School. She was a pupil teacher there before entering College in 1897. She then moved to Whitelands Training College for a third year. After spending a further two years there as a member of staff, Fanny returned to Salisbury as a History lecturer. She left in 1905 to study at Royal Holloway College, gaining a First Class Honours degree in History in 1907. Salisbury Training College celebrated her success with a half day holiday!

Miss Street subsequently became Senior Governess at Barnard's Cross, but left in 1912 to return to Royal Holloway College as a Lecturer at London University.

Miss Street's illustrious career included founding and being the first Principal of Hillcote College for Working Women in Surbiton, Surrey. She was Acting Principal of Royal Holloway College from 1945-46 and a leading figure in the British Federation of University Women.

A College Romance

Beryl Derham started working at the College as a scullery maid in the mid- to late-1920s. She worked her way up to the position of Cook. Beryl's daughter wrote:

'I know that she was very happy working there, and proud of the fact that she started at the very bottom of the kitchen hierarchy and worked up to the top position of Cook. She used to speak of the 'special' food served to the top table – the dignitaries and lecturers. She retained a keen interest

in cooking throughout her life, always sharing recipes with friends and family.'

Beryl's husband, William Dawkins (known as Bill), worked as a gardener at the College.

The Joy of Learning!

By 1901, teachers had more freedom over the choice of subjects and how to teach them. The expanding school curriculum was reflected at the Training College.

'A new subject every year, or an old subject in a new dress, appears to be one characteristic in modern education! This year, Hygiene and Physical Exercises are more to the fore than they have ever been, and twice these years have Miss Fildes and Miss Holmes brought out their Troops of Students for inspection. The ordeal lasted a whole day at King's House and half a day at Barnard's Cross. The course is that of the new Syllabus of the Board of Education, and every Student has to display both her own drill and her power of teaching it. Vigorous physical exercise is the order of the day, and jumping and skipping have been added to the various Swedish Gymnastics, besides Netball at King's House and Morris Dances at Barnard's Cross'.

Netball has made a good start this season, though at times we have been tempted to give it up in favour of Aquatic Sports! We can, however, still say that our ardour is undamped! It is a first-rate game for physical development, providing plenty of running and vigorous arm movement for everyone, and its positions are both healthful and graceful.

Nature Study was a new elementary school subject in the early 20th century and inspectors were keen to see how training colleges were preparing their students. Salisbury received a glowing accolade. A report that was written in 1902 on the teaching of Nature Study in Training Colleges said that 'Salisbury undoubtedly stands first'.

'The Clay-modelling from Salisbury was among the best work that I have seen. The specimens of fruit and nuts were well modelled and full of character, the form, hardness and texture of the Almond being wonderfully well rendered'.

Salisbury was commended for the fact that the subject was taught on sound lines and in an eminently practical and interesting manner'.

Canon Steward, himself a keen naturalist, welcomed the inclusion of Nature Study. Speaking at a conference, he encouraged teachers to do outdoor work and to make use of the child's innate ability to observe and perceive the world of Nature, which could then be expressed in his own way through modelling, drawing and painting. His words, 'let teachers begin as learners with their children', were forward thinking for 1902!

A Timetable, 1894

A Timetable, 1894   Courtesy of Wiltshire and Swindon History Centre

Dora Hughes (1910-12) remembered the Nature Walks at College:

'There were enthusiasts, plodders, dreamers, oddities, finders of freaks and rarities.

At our head was a supreme enthusiast, who helped, inspired, encouraged and guided each and all of us.

The oddity was never known to set out without a small, disreputable, mouldy school satchel, which always returned to College as empty as it started out. The enthusiasts usually led the way, talking, observing, hunting, poking, pulling up celandine to examine its tubercles, pulling down bryony to note its tendrils.

The calmer spirits plodded along behind, with eyes quick to note the indulgent smiles of passers-by, the frank curiosity of numerous small errand boys, the pitying glance of the Choristers.

The dreamer and the oddity, as a rule, carried out investigations together, but, sad to relate, the results of their labours usually amounted to nothing! Upon one occasion, when told to make a sketch of a patch of undergrowth, the oddity was heard to exclaim, "I say, I can't see the thing I was drawing." "No wonder," replied the dreamer, "You are sitting on it."

Towards the end of the walk, we gathered round our leader and presented for inspection our spoils. For the successful it was a joyful moment, for the remainder depressing.

Climbing hedges and jumping over or into ditches is not conducive to tidiness, and it was a flushed and by no means dignified party which straggled through the welcome gates of the College after a nature-walk'.

Teachers who are in search of help and advice might do worse than join

THE SCHOOL NATURE STUDY UNION

which is steadily making its way in the school world

Nora Curtis Botany Notebook 1908

Barnard's Cross Library

Courtesy of The Salisbury Museum

DOMESTIC ECONOMY

DRAWING

ENGLISH LANGUAGE AND LITERATURE

FRENCH

GARDENING

GENERAL ELEMENTARY SCIENCE

GEOGRAPHY

HANDWORK

HISTORY

HYGIENE

MATHEMATICS

MUSIC

NATURE STUDY

NEEDLEWORK,

PHYSICAL TRAINING

READING AND RECITATION

RELIGIOUS KNOWLEDGE

TEACHING PRACTICE AND THEORY

Barnard's Cross Dining Room

Student Debate

The principles of child development and the growth in the understanding of developmental psychology were slowly having an impact on the style of education offered to children. Ideas from earlier educational innovators were by now beginning to permeate schools and colleges.

It was a time of new ideologies and theories. Students would have debated the theories of Pestalozzi, Froebel, Montessori, Dewey and the McMillan sisters and others. What a challenge for the College to prepare the students to deal with the abundance of systems! One can imagine them enjoying lengthy discussions about the impact of the new ideas on the education of children.

Violet Marjorie Lowe – a student in the 1890s
Courtesy of The Salisbury Museum

More Inspections

There continued to be regular College inspections by HMI, most of which were very positive. In 1900 Mr Scott Howard HMI declared the College to be 'one of the best equipped I know regarding accommodation'.

In 1903 eight inspectors visited the College and in 1905 no less than ten inspectors paid a visit, in addition to the Archbishop's Inspector. Mr Barnett HMI commented:

'The work of this college is earnest and thorough, and its life and tone are admirable. The teachers whom it sends out are hardworking, high minded and intelligent. The additions to the beautiful old buildings, and the Barnard's Cross extension, are all that they should be, and testify to the health and vigour of the institution'.

The next year four inspectors came, and it was reported that the students were working under the best possible influences and they knew of no college with so few rules. The inspectors advised that in winter, lectures should not be held at seven o'clock before breakfast.

Violet Hayward commented:

'This was by no means the unmixed blessing that he intended. We (1908-1910) found that it made life hectic. Breakfast was put forward to 7.45 a.m. and chapel to 8.20 am, the bell ringing for the first lecture as we emerged. Three of these were shortened by 5 minutes and we were told to make up the total one and half hours per week in our own time – but when was that? Every minute of the day from 6.20 am to 8.30 pm was planned for us. We then repaired informally to the dining room for a bowl of soup or beaker of milk. Once a week one was on the early bath list, and this must be completed by 9.20 p.m. when the bed bell rang'.

Violet Hayward, *Our College*

The inspectors gave occasional lectures to students during their visits. Some appear to have been more interesting than others. One of the ones that students enjoyed was in 1897 when a science inspector gave a lantern lecture showing photographs taken by himself during his summer holiday near the Matterhorn.

Inspector Rankine demonstrated his care for the students and their pupils:

'I contend that what young people want is not to be crammed with knowledge, but that they should be well cared for in their bodily health, their food and exercise.

There is another thing that they should have in moderation and that is a little bit of fondling – that is to say, they should be treated with kindness, in order that when they go into a school and become Infant Mistresses, they do not frighten the children with sour looks'.

STC Magazine, 1905

As today, inspections were very much part of school and college life. Records indicate that students remembered the College motto 'In quietness and in confidence shall be your strength'. They prepared well and worked hard.

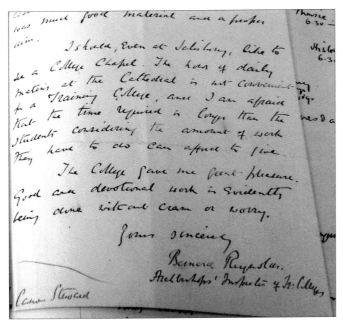

Letter from the Archbishop's Inspector
Courtesy of Wiltshire and Swindon History Centre

Examinations

In 1893 Canon Steward recorded the rise in examination results. However, in the early 1900s there were attacks on the standards of work and achievement in Training Colleges in general, and some were particularly aimed at Church Colleges. There was some general feeling that too much time was given to religious studies, to the detriment of wider education. The examination results from Salisbury Training College indicate the high standards which were gained.

1893   Salisbury ranked with Brighton, Stockwell and Tottenham, holding first place in needlework and reading and third in history.

1902   46 firsts and 2 seconds out of 48 students. In the Archbishop's Examination, Salisbury ranked with Tottenham at the head of all Church Colleges with 47 firsts and 1 second.

'The discipline and tone of the College are excellent, and there is every indication of the care with which the students are treated in all the relations of their academic life. The teaching is the most striking feature of their work. It is strong, educational and sympathetic'.

Inspection Report, 1902

'As we write, the Scholarship Examination is proceeding. An unusually large number of students have presented themselves and the Common Room has been requisitioned to accommodate eleven of them. Some of our readers may doubtless remember the difficulty they had in finding their way about the College. Since Audley has been added, this has so intensified that signposts have been erected at the many four-crossways. The front gate has placards to keep out callers, from butcher-boys upwards, who would otherwise distract the unfortunate occupants of the common room'.

STC Magazine 1901

List Day 1900

'What day so suited to the arrival of the dreaded list as Friday! And yet at breakfast that day there sat the Students as sedate as usual. The earthquake wave proceeded from the contents of that official envelope in the Principal's room to the Mistresses' table, but strange to say it went no further. The most unusual signs of levity in those decorous personages were unheeded by the girls. But when school time came, the secret perforce leaked out… what an age the Principal was taking in making his appearance that morning! He evidently could have taken no short cuts across the Cathedral green on that eventful day. At last he arrived. The poor seniors in the schoolroom realised for once, at least, that time was counted in heart throbs. Only those who have been through a similar experience can imagine the emotions called forth by the reading of the list. But it was over – and afterwards – how the telegraph office was besieged, necessitating a relay of clerks'.

STC Magazine, 1901

What were "Major Days" and "Crits"?

An excellent description was provided in the 1966 College Magazine by Irene Hilditch who was a student from 1917-1919.

'Wednesdays were "Major Days." Each student had to give three lessons during her two years' course under somewhat harassing conditions. A class of children would be brought in from one of the Practising Schools. Every Wednesday at 2 p.m. three such classes would appear, and each of three students would give a Major Criticism Lesson in the presence of a group of fellow-student critics, and a College Lecturer. Oh, misery me, what an ordeal! After the classes had been sent away, there was a half-hour session of critical survey of the content and presentation of the lesson, the teacher's demeanour and degree of class-control, and the children's response or lack of it. Then a teaching mark was awarded by the Lecturer (privately of course) and one was given to understand that this counted considerably in the assessment of one's professional capabilities, made at the end of the course. The immediate reward of this exercise was a large slice of special "Major" cake at tea-time'.

How delicious that cake must have tasted to the students!

Dora Hughes (1910-1912) wrote that 'Majors' were:

'Three events of high importance, and no greater bliss could be imagined than to gain a "VG" or even, though this was almost beyond human dreams, an "Excellent" from the Principal himself.'

More Giving a crit
on the Blackbird

Prize-Giving

For the majority of students 'Prize-Day' was an exciting day to be enjoyed. Important visitors were invited to witness the celebration of the students' hard work. There was usually a special tea and always an address, which was recorded in the Training College Magazines. The Principal made a statement about the students' work during the past twelve months. In addition to academic awards, prizes were presented to the Senior Student and a ballot was held amongst students to decide who would be presented with a prize for 'the hardest worker'.

Each year the event was recorded in the *Salisbury Journal*.

'The pretty grounds of The Salisbury Diocesan Training College were filled on Saturday, June 26th 1915, with those who responded to the invitation by Miss Forth, the Principal, on the occasion of the College Speech day. Before the proceedings began, tea was served on the lawn, and the distribution of the certificates took place under the shade of the trees. The students, under the conductorship of Dr Baker, rendered enjoyable items of music, including national songs such as *The British Grenadiers* and *The Campbells are coming*.'

SPEECH DAY

AT THE

Salisbury Diocesan Training College

ON

SATURDAY, JUNE 24th, 1916.

THE RT. REV. THE LORD BISHOP OF THE DIOCESE

WILL TAKE THE CHAIR AT 5 P.M.

MUSIC :

National Songs :

      "Marching to Candahar"

      "Ye Mariners of England"

      "Cradle Song"

      "Here's a health unto His Majesty"

Part Songs :

      "Night sinks on the wave" - - - - *Smart*

      "Here in cool grot" - - - *Lord Mornington*

      "Oculus non vidit" }
      "Expandi manus" } - - - *Orlando di Lasso*

      "O skylark, for thy wing" - - - - *Smart*

      "Come, fairest nymph" - - - *Lord Mornington*

GOD SAVE THE KING.

School Practice at 'appy arnham'

School Practice consisted of six isolated weeks, and an assignment to Harnham brought sighs of relief. (All the children here were in one room, and taught by the headmistress – the sole staff.)

It was truly 'appy arnham', for the delightful pupils occasioned no dangerous rise in the blood pressure of 'them students', while the staffs' unbounded belief in their capabilities was touching. Just imagine being able to give 'The History of India' in a brief half hour lesson'.
Violet Hayward, *Our College*

(Violet was given a Very Good Mark for the lesson on India!)

Run and Jump!

Cycling became popular after the production of the 'Rover' safety bicycle in 1885 and the pneumatic tyre in 1888. The College Cycling Club was popular and regular excursions were enjoyed in the locality.

In the 1896 Michaelmas edition of the Salisbury Training College magazine there is a delightful description of an outing by coach and cycle. The thrill of cycling and the freedom it gave are very evident. What a day out!

'It is Saturday morning in early June – the glorious June of 1896. Through the latticed window we catch glimpses of a blue sky and hazy atmosphere, which tell of a continuation of intense summer heat. The mid-day sun will be scorching. Yet one ardent cyclist has already proposed the question 'Where shall we go this afternoon?' Another with happy inspiration has suggested a ride to Bishopstone and return by coach.

Half past two arrives and we set out. We realise the leafy shade of The Close only by contrast with the glaring heat of Harnham. Over the uneven chalk road, so well known in class-walk days, we push our machines. Almost breathless we reach the top, and before we descend the slope in our temporary character of pedestrians, we take a well- earned rest. But, as we learnt a hundred times as Salisbury students, if the longest day has an ending so even has Harnham Hill. By the time we have skimmed over one mile of hard-baked road we have forgotten the walk, the heat, and the chalk, and are revelling in the joys of the wheel. We are conscious only of a slight breeze, of exhilarating movement, of green fields and happy talk'.

In 1916 Hilda Noyce recorded a blissful cycle ride whilst having a brief stay in Calne:

'Mabel, Dot Beazley and I cycled to Castle Combe and had a gorgeous day. The ride was ripping, the scenery perfect. We ate sandwiches and drank lemonade (out of bottles) on the bridge. If I ever get married I will honeymoon at Castle Combe'.

In 1904 playing fields were acquired on Harnham Hill, which probably meant Hockey was played there. Croquet and Tennis were played on the College lawns. In 1910 students at Salisbury Training College were enjoying the relatively new sport of Netball. It gained in popularity amongst women as it avoided physical contact and did not involve male participation.

In the 1915 College Magazine, Miss Story reported that Cricket had started:

'Cricket has been started, and the sight of new shiny stumps has filled many a heart with a glowing ideal. "What can not be accomplished?" Alas! When the reality comes in the shape of a particularly hard ball, the dream generally ends in a rude awakening caused by the noise of the ball in some quite mysterious way *hitting the wickets*'.

Drill or PE took place outdoors whenever the weather permitted, with students wearing the correct clothing, of course.

'Black shoes, black tights, navy tunics and white blouses with long sleeves. Tights of black cotton lisle went baggy at the knees after the least exercise, but were a great improvement on the old clumsy bloomers'!

Sport was an increasing part of the College curriculum which most students appear to have enjoyed.

Physical Exercise in the Garden

Courtesy of The Salisbury Museum

At Leisure

The students limited leisure time gradually increased. There were occasional parties, including Fancy Dress Parties and even dancing!

> 'Our breaking up party on December 9th was once more kindly helped by Mrs Steward. She had arranged a unique little concert, which was preceded by tea and followed by supper and dancing. We spent a most enjoyable evening. The schoolroom had been decorated by the Seniors and was prettily arranged'.
>
> *Our Quarterly,* New Year, 1897

Restrictions on going into the city became more relaxed. Students were requested only to venture into the city in pairs, or accompanied by a recognised friend. They were dissuaded from excursions into the city on Market Days or to the fairs. Visits to the City Library were allowed and to the Museum.

From 1896 there were annual outings to places of interest, such as the New Forest or Bournemouth: In 1897 students enjoyed a day out to celebrate the 'brilliant achievement of our Seniors'.

> 'A party of twenty went off by the 9.40 train to the seaside with the Principal, Miss Forth, Miss Whatley, Miss Hayward, and Miss Hinton. In the morning we enjoyed the sea and the cliffs and the pines – and the breeze blew straight off the sea, and the Isle of Wight and the Needles stood out bright and clear'.
>
> STC Magazine, New Year, 1897

Stonehenge – a popular excursion for students

Mission Sales and Bazaars were a regular feature of College life. In 1899 the College held a bazaar to raise further funds for the Chapel. Stalls included needlework, a game stall with fresh hares, and a fishpond. It was a great success.

Many students gave up their spare time to support various charities. The College developed a link with St Winifred's Home, Wolverhampton. Each child living in the home was linked with a college student who would write and send gifts at Christmas and on birthdays. Students made the best use they could of any spare time.

What amusement did the students have during the years of World War One?

The new games field meant more enjoyment of sport:

> 'Canon Sowter has taken a deep interest in the College. It is to his generosity that we owe the provision of our games field on such easy terms, and nothing pleased him better than to see it full of happy, vigorous girls at play any afternoon'.
>
> STC Magazine, 1916

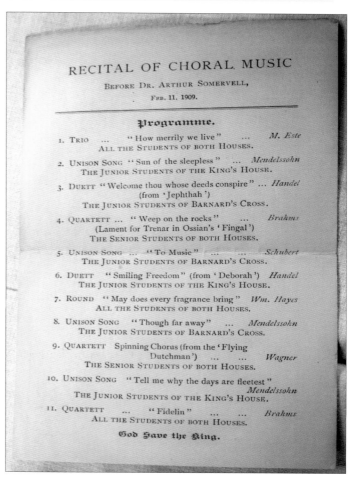

'Midnight Feasts were a feature of College life. There seemed huge pleasure in consuming quantities of acquired eats and drinking tea, cocoa or minerals from a tooth glass in somebody else's cubicle, preferably a long way from your own, all in the dead of night, to the accompaniment of as much subdued hilarity as one dared. If, on creeping back to one's own Dorm through chilly dark passages one was pursued by a "Gov" in dressing gown, carrying aloft a lighted candle, why that only added to the fun and excitement. I never heard of anyone being actually caught, though there were narrow escapes.

The Junior Classroom was cleared on Saturday evenings and became the scene of a 'Saturday Hop' - Polka, Barn Dance, Waltz, Veleta, Lancers and Washington Post were our favourites, and we made what musical accompaniment we could on a rather indifferent piano. But once a month there was held an impromptu entertainment to which the Principal and Staff were invited. They appeared to be enjoying the amusement we aimed to provide, though they may have occasionally been shocked by our antics'.

Irene Hilditch (1917-1919), *College Chronicle*, 1966

Rosemary Edwards (1943-1945) recounted a story handed down by her mother, Rita Potter(1917-1919). There was a scandal in Rita's time when a Theological College student eloped with a Training College student in a boat up the river. They were never heard of again!

Students' Common Room   Courtesy of The Salisbury Museum

College Cycling Club   Courtesy of The Salisbury Museum

Royal Celebrations!

The College shared enthusiastically in two memorable royal celebrations between 1891 and 1918. The first was Queen Victoria's Diamond Jubilee in June 1897:

'Surely of all professions, "Teachers of Elementary Schools" are characteristic of Her Majesty's reign. The whole of the state-work for these schools has been done during the years 1837-1897. Teachers in training bear Her Majesty's name; they are Queen's Scholars'.

'Very glad were we to hear that Jubilee Day was to be a holiday, and where so fitting a place to spend it as in that Royal demesne, the New Forest. What a day of delight it was! Miss Hill always caters well for us, but the veal pies and other wonderful eatables in the hampers were unequalled!' In Salisbury was a transformation scene; the High Street was gaily garlanded and all was prepared for the evening's illuminations … and truly our King's House was turned into a fairy scene. Fairy lights are twinkling down each side of the rose beds and the light streaming through our beautiful mullioned windows …it is not College, but a palace in Fairyland …but by Friday our Jubilee time was over and we had to settle down to hard and steady work for the Certificate examination'.

The Coronation of King George V and Queen Mary took place on June 11th 1911. Once again, King's House…

'blossomed with roses and fairy lamps. Barnard's Cross students decorated their house and entertained guests from the rival establishment.

After singing *God save the King*, our guests went back to King's House, and we retired to our dormitories with mixed feelings. We had had a jolly holiday, we were tired and happy, but the air breathed Certificates …'

The Salisbury Club and the Magazine

Following the Reunion in 1894 the Head Student, Mildred Gill, expressed a hope that 'opportunities could be afforded for the meeting together of ex-Salisbury students, to renew old friendships and to keep strong the link that bound all to their Alma Mater'.

The inaugural meeting of the Salisbury Club was held at the National Society's room in Westminster on July 17th 1897. The object was to 'bring together Mistresses working in London and its neighbourhood, who have much in common from the fact that they were trained at Salisbury'. More than 80 former students attended, the Principal presided and a constitution was drawn up.

By 1899 the Home Branch had been formed, as well as branches in Portsmouth and Southampton. The Guild Service was regularly held and Club programmes included outings, musical entertainments, garden parties and cycling trips. By 1914 there were branches in the Isle of Wight, Birmingham, and Bournemouth.

'A discussion on the best place for our summer outing was much disturbed by the sound of an aeroplane and the meeting moved on to the lawn to watch the flight past the Spire'.

Our Magazine, which had by 1898 become the *Salisbury Training College Magazine*, was produced three times a year and informed past students about life in College, through serious reports and letters, as well as more light-hearted articles.

'We have been refreshed by the humour, moved to tears and laughter by the recollections it called up, inspired by its note of call to service and by its revival of some of the highest and best moments in our lives'.
Christmas 1913, Barbara Forth, the new Editor

In 1916 the Home Branch contributed funds towards the Prisoners' Parcels Scheme. More than 250 prisoners were being provided with regular parcels by ex-Students and their friends. Magazines produced during the First World War reflect the difficulties of getting to Salisbury Club meetings. Railway travel was uncertain and war work made it impossible for many former students to attend. The shortage of paper and the expense of printing militated against the production of the Magazine, but its importance was recognised by Miss Forth in the 1918 issue.

'How great is the need at the moment of a cheering word from Alma Mater – and how the thought of the College motto, In Quietness and in Confidence shall be your Strength' requires reinforcing, so that it shall meet and assuage the heaviness, dread and bitterness which have been the lot of so many during this sad year'.

Setting Chapter 2 in context: A Table of some significant events

Date	Educational	National	Local
1891	Free Education Act provided some state payment of fees	Britain linked by telephone to the continent.	The College celebrated 50 pioneering years of teacher training.
1892		Thomas Hardy writes 'Tess of the D'Urbervilles'	Public swimming pool opens in Salisbury
1893	The School Attendance Act raised the school leaving age to 11	Conan Doyle writes 'The Adventures of Sherlock Holmes'.	
1894	The Bryce Commission was set up to investigate how to establish secondary education		
1895		Marconi invents wireless telegraphy	Coach horses stampede on Salisbury Plain
1896			
1897	The Voluntary School Act provided grants to public elementary schools	Queen Victoria's Diamond Jubilee Womens' suffrage campaign gains momentum	Army buys land on Salisbury Plain
1898	NUT – pension scheme for teachers	Discovery of Radium	
1899	Board of Education Act. It provided for a register of teachers	Outbreak of the 2nd Boer War	
1900		British Labour Party founded	
1901		Death of Queen Victoria	Large fire in Salisbury market place
1902	The Balfour Act – School Boards abolished, LEAs established	Coronation of King Edward V11 Peace with the Boers in S Africa	First train from Salisbury to Amesbury
1903		Powered flight by the Wright brothers	The first 25 students arrive at Barnard's Cross, the 2nd College hostel
1904	Medical Inspections in schools	J M Barrie writes Peter Pan	Official opening of Barnard's Cross
1905		Russo-Japanese War. Theory of Relativity proposed by Einstein	Opening of Salisbury Library
1906	King's Scholarships were abolished	Dreadnought launched at Portsmouth	
1907	Board of Education - every secondary school must offer free places to 25% of its annual entry.		
1908		Suffragette disturbances SOS signal introduced	Record April snowstorm hits Salisbury First Salisbury streets tarred A cinema opens in Salisbury
1909		Bleriot flies over the Channel First Old Age Pension introduced	Salisbury Women's Suffrage Society founded
1910	Start of Boy Scouts & Girl Guides	Death of Edward V11	Excavations at Old Sarum
1911		Coronation of King George V Amundsen reaches the North Pole	The College Diamond Jubilee Death of Bishop Wordsworth
1912		Scott's Antarctic expedition Titanic sinks on maiden voyage	Woolworth's founded
1913	Junior Technical Schools and Junior Art Schools recognised by Board of Education.		Old Sarum Airfield opens
1914		Archduke Franz Ferdinand assassinated – start of WW1 Christmas Truce on Western Front	Archaeologists discover Roman remains at Rockbourne
1915		Lusitania sunk	Stonehenge bought by Cecil Chubb at auction. Floods in South Wiltshire Zeppelin over Southampton
1916	Play Centres started	Battle of the Somme Battle of Jutland	Tom Adlam, one of Salisbury's greatest heroes, subsequently awarded the VC for his courage on the Western Front
1917	Introduction of the School Certificate Examination	America enters WW1 Revolution in Russia British Summer time introduced	Boscombe Down opens as flying training unit
1918	The Fisher Act – school leaving age raised to 14	End of WW1 at 11 a.m. on the 11th November. Rationing introduced. Women over 30 given the vote	Stonehenge given to the nation

Dora Hughes was a student at the College and later became Headteacher at St Edmund's School in Salisbury. In 1952 she retired and in that year she wrote an article in the Training College Chronicle. It provides a warm and fascinating insight into College life.

'Looking Back' by Dora Hughes

My journey (to college) had not been long, for my home was in Salisbury, but this fact did not make the entry into college any less exciting or momentous. It was quiet in the hall, and I stood still for a moment to savour the full realization, that here I was, in college.

On looking back, it seems that life was very simple and unsophisticated for the student of forty years ago, and by present day standards, austere.

It was not long before the pattern of college routine emerged. Eight o'clock lecture was preceded by a cup of tea, and a round flaky biscuit, if you reached the lobby in time. Later, it was not unknown for cups of tea to find their way up to the dormitory, but woe betide the carrier if she met Miss Hill, then growing old in years, but in spirit, alert and watchful as ever, never allowing the slightest deviation from College rules if it could be avoided.

The first Autumn term went quietly on its way. Lecturers, College staff, fellow students and senior students became individuals, and, in some cases, personalities.

There was little specialisation or individual work in those days. Students might drop certain subjects in favour of taking an "Optional Subject", if they wished, and I remember making the weighty decision that I would give up French and take Optional Botany, and though I have often regretted the French that I did not do, I would still rather have the memory of the botany lessons and the nature walks with Miss Stevenson than the French I might have done.

Memories come, too, of our beloved Principal, Canon Edward Steward, at that time gradually withdrawing from his active work in the College, but who still took some English and Divinity with his students, for which we can never be too thankful.

Miss Barbara Forth, now Vice-Principal, was becoming the centre of the everyday life of the students. In her wisdom, during the early days of the first term, she made opportunities to come into direct contact with her first year students. We were required to study and memorise a hundred lines of verse. In due course we went individually to her room, with its deep chintz covered chairs and gleaming oak table, on which it seems there was always a bowl of roses.

I believe I am right in saying that we took our work very seriously. For myself, I know that I enjoyed to the full every moment of work during those two years, and among my

Teaching Practice report from Eastleigh

Courtesy of Wiltshire and Swindon History Centre

Miss Forth with Students   Courtesy of The Salisbury Museum

most precious hours were those spent in the library, rather meagre in those days, but – a library.

Saturday evenings ended joyously with dancing in the Gym.

Sunday was a day apart, beginning with eight o'clock Communion in the Cathedral. Apart from those Sundays when we were permitted to attend town Churches, students went to Matins, and usually Evensong at 3 o'clock in the afternoon in the Cathedral.

School practice then, of course, was in Salisbury schools only, apart from one crowded week teaching at Eastleigh. This was spoken of with bated breath for many a week before it happened, and proved almost as great an ordeal as we feared, tempered though it was by the excellent organization of the school. How well I remember the homely little dining room of the house where we were boarded for the week and where, each evening, we made desperate efforts to prepare apparatus and do some background reading.

So the months slipped away, marked by an ever-growing interest in the work and personnel of the College. Friendships blossomed and sometimes faded; comradeship, one of the best of all good things in communities, flourished, while at the same time, there was

the process of building deeper and more lasting contacts, based on a developing sense of values and understandings.

How swiftly the weeks of the last term fled! Exciting questions and topics were forever rising. There were decisions and indecisions, confidences, promises, sweet idle chatter, summer afternoons by the river, and always the overshadowing of the Cathedral, the perfect beauty of the Close. Against this accompaniment could be sensed the sweetly sad theme of farewell, that made each day's requiem.

Came the examination at last, on which so much depended. A few tense days and that was over "for better or for worse," and then it was really the end. The last parties were held, the books were gathered together, the goodbyes said. The hall door opened and shut many times. The gravel crunched beneath the departing feet. The Cathedral clock chimed the hour. It was time to go. One last look around the hall, quiet and empty again, a belated goodbye to a flying figure anxious to catch her train, and then out into The Close.

The future was what mattered now! Freedom lay ahead and independence, though £72 10s 0d a year was not a princely salary, even by the standards of 1912, but the tremendous thing was you were going out into the world to teach'.

Miss Constance Beatrice Lilian Male, 1888-1969

'All through my growing up in Norton-sub-Hamdon, village politics were very much dominated by the formidable and somewhat eccentric character of Miss Male. Miss Male trained at the College from 1907-1909 and lived in Barnard's Cross. She very soon became a pioneer of social reform at a local level, and later as a district and county councillor in the 1950s. She probably would have felt her greatest achievement was saving the village school from closure at the outbreak of the Second World War. Thanks to her hard work, the village still has a thriving primary school.

She embodied all the special qualities of a past age of duty and service instilled both at school and at college. In "quietness" she went about her daily duties, not looking for praise but to benefit the common good and with "confidence" she achieved fulfilment through education in the broadest sense all through her life. She was a thoroughly good person and a credit to the founding principles of Sarum St Michael.'

Caroline Minchinton (1972-1975)

Miss Male in her Red Cross Uniform

A Christmas Card from Clara Grant (1886-87)

WANTS

Dear Friends! Since first I came down East,
In Wapping to reside,
I find myself quite full of WANTS!
May they be satisfied!

Remnants of ribbon, cretonne, cord,
Odd ends of silk and wool:
Odd ends of silk, for Patchwork. Ah!
That box was ONCE quite full!

Bon-bon boxes, full or empty,
Cast off ancient toys -
Dolls and wardrobes - all are welcomed
by OUR girls and boys.

Now, please to hear my piteous cry,
Send bundle, sack and box:
'Prusom Street Buildings, Number 8
St Peter's London Docks'

by Clara Grant
As printed in the
Salisbury Training College Magazine
New Year, 1897

Clara continued to work tirelessly for the children and families in the East End.

Katharine Annie Baker

Katharine Annie Baker was born in 1898 and was a student at the College from 1916-1918, during the Great War. Her daughter recalled several anecdotes that her mother had related about college life at that time:

'She often talked about the creaking staircase in King's House and the newel post going right up to the top. She mentioned the ghost 'The Grey Lady' said to move around King's House.

Katharine used to have bad nosebleeds and on one occasion had one during Cathedral Evensong. The Verger was asked to collect a key. He brought a very large one from the main door and thrust it down her back. The nosebleed stopped quickly.

On the last day of the final term it was customary to go to the end of the college garden and throw your boater into the river and watch it disappear'.

What happened to all those hats?

Katharine made many firm friends at college as recorded in her autograph book. Entries in the book demonstrate the warmth and affection which students had for each other and also for the College.

Katharine's younger sister Sybil was also a student at the College from 1928-1930.'

Drawn by Pat Jones

The Floods of January 1915

After Christmas, Miss Forth was summoned by telegram to return to Salisbury, as the 'disaster of flood had overtaken our beautiful King's House'.

'As we swung around Exeter Street (in a large motor omnibus) we could see over the Palace walls a whole sea of water enveloping the garden, and leaving the Palace and Cathedral standing as islands in it.

Our destination was the College, and to our surprise we could walk to it, only fording the mill race which poured through the front garden gate from the sea which filled the garden, all the lower rooms and reached right to the front railings, Under guidance we reached the back yard, and after climbing an almost horizontal ladder and a chain of kitchen chairs, climbed the Infirmary fire escape and reached the safety of the first floor.

It was weird to go downstairs and find a brown, still flood lying about 18 inches deep. Carpets, pianos, sofas and other important pieces of furniture had been mounted to table height, or raised in the Wardrobe Room, or on the dais in Miss Forth's sitting room; the tea chest and flour bin and all the stores had been rescued - but alas! The Principal's papers had had to be ruthlessly bundled out of bottom shelves and Altar Frontals were still in part soaking below water level.

It was an experience to go to the Cathedral on Epiphany morning. Can you, my readers, imagine that brown, desolate-looking flood from end to end of our grand Cathedral nave, and the feeling of its chill and darkness behind you?

The Fisher Act 1918

The Fisher Act of 1918 raised the school leaving age from 12 to 14. Young workers between 14 and 18 were given the right of access to day release education and all fees in state elementary schools were abolished. The Act also included the provision of services such as medical inspections, nursery schools and centres for pupils with special needs.

Many of the changes could only be implemented in part, or not at all, as a result of the economy of the country after the First World War.

Courtesy of The Salisbury Museum

College during the First World War

'Rumours of War interrupted the peace of our midsummer holiday and our Principal (Miss Hill) had to hurry from Wales to Salisbury to make sure that the ardour of the Red Cross Society did not lead them to turn the King's House into a Military Hospital, thus hindering the training of 150 of those women teachers, who, by the drafts of schoolmasters and men students to active service, are now more than ever needed'.

'The year of 1915 opened amid terrible circumstances of war and earthquake, of accident and floods, but we hope and pray that it may see the end of this awful war and the re-establishment of a firm and lasting peace. The Scarborough raid and the Zeppelin scares have made the thought of invasion common, and the darkness of our towns at night suggests the same idea.

Extracts from *Our Quarterly*, Whitsun 1915

In the early months of the war the *Salisbury Journal* reported on the worsening situation in Belgium. Students from the College raised money to support Belgian refugees.

Edith Olivier, a local author, wrote of soldiers in uniform crowding into the Cathedral for Sunday services. For off-duty soldiers, town life offered a welcome relief and the streets were described as 'brown with khaki'.

This influx of soldiers into Salisbury had an effect on the lives of students at the College, whose personal freedom was certainly restricted. They were initially banned from the main streets, since it was believed that soldiers had 'brought disease' into the city. Staff therefore carried out the students' personal shopping.

By 1915, however, expeditions on bicycles were permitted for Botany classes and arrangements were made for students to attend concerts at the Assembly Rooms and plays at the Palace Theatre in Endless Street. A selected choir of students from the College was invited to a Patriotic Meeting in the Victoria Hall, which was attended by 'at least 1800 women and girls, some of them of the very poorest in Salisbury. The students sang patriotic songs with excellent effect and the choruses were taken up with great vigour by the audience, led by the whole body of Students in the gallery'.

By 1917, even though the city was still out of bounds on Market Day, the students contrived to escape the claustrophobic restrictions of The Close by offering to undertake errands for the staff rather than vice versa. The concern for students' safety is matched by the kindly

attitudes towards them of Cathedral dignitaries at this time. A student records how Dean Burn would always open the gate to the path up to the West door with a bow, and would allow the 'en bloc' procession of students to precede him to Matins.

The war also brought a precursor for civilians of what was to come in World War Two, especially the effect of Zeppelin raids from 1915. These new weapons had a considerable impact on a vulnerable population. There were no air raids on Salisbury itself, but the Training College reported one night when all lights had to be extinguished as a Zeppelin was reported over Southampton.

The shortages affected other areas of life. By January 1915 the streets of Salisbury were darker, with no lights, but the police provided hurricane lamps. There was a scarcity of gas and coal and the students had not only to black out their windows, but also wrap their red blankets around their legs for lectures. Extra bedrooms in The Close were rented, possibly so that students need not return to their lodgings in the city on winter afternoons or evenings.

The College Chapel remained an essential part of daily life as Irene Hilditch recalled:

'In those war-shadowed days, College Chapel, morning and evening was a "Must". There had to be a very water-tight excuse for an empty place. However, very few of us, if any, questioned this; indeed in those war-shadowed days Chapel attendance gave a real sense of support and fellowship'.

During 1918 the whole of Great Britain was subject to rationing of meat, sugar, butter, margarine and lard. The students frequently referred to food shortages.

The awareness of wartime disasters inevitably brought sadness and low spirits. Students would have felt deep sadness about the loss of Lord Kitchener and many others in the sinking of HMS *Hampshire* in 1916. It was recorded by Hilda Noyce in her diary:

'*Wednesday June 6th*
News of Lord Kitchener's death. The *Hampshire* bound for Russia with Lord Kitchener and staff on board was torpedoed off the Orkneys.'

There were tears after letters and newspapers brought sad news of loved ones. There was always the awareness of wounded servicemen in the hospitals and in the city, or men on leave or preparing for departure. Students sent parcels and letters to soldiers on the Front and in return they received moving and beautifully written letters and cards of thanks.

Students would have rejoiced when they heard that 2nd Lieutenant Tom Edwin Adlam, educated at St Martin's School and later Bishop Wordsworth's School, had been awarded the Victoria Cross for his outstanding courage at Thiepval in September 1916. The St Martin's School log book records:

> 1916   Dec 1st
> 2nd Lieutenant Tom Edwin Adlam VC
> Re announcement in the "London Gazette"
> He having been admitted as a pupil on Nov 1st 1899, and continued till Sept. 19th 1906, a half-holiday was given in honour of his distinction.

The Easter 1918 edition of *Our Quarterly* expressed deep sympathy to Canon Steward on the loss of 'that gallant young officer Capt. Arthur Steward, his second son, and to those members of the College who have been called upon to give of their nearest and dearest to this great cause'.

The years of World War One tested the students' stamina and spirit to the limit.

> 'The war still drags on and it is not easy to say much of it at such a time as this when our hopes grow large with the expectation of victory and peace, and yet our hearts grow sick with hope long deferred'.
>
> Extract from *Our Quarterly*, Easter 1918

When the fighting ended on November 11th, 1918 there was excited rejoicing and thousands of people filled the Cathedral for the Thanksgiving Service, standing tightly packed, students amongst them. Students were free to go out in groups for walks, a concert was hastily arranged in College and now, as one student expressed it, they 'felt free to worry only about Final Practice and Certificate Examinations'.

> 'On Armistice Day 1918, every single individual in the College, from the Principal to the Porter went wild with delight. All study was abandoned after the great news broke at 11 a.m. and in the afternoon we attended a Thanksgiving Service in the Cathedral. So many thousands packed the great building that I remember standing by a pillar not far from the West Door and sitting now and then on a low stone wall. The atmosphere was charged with deep emotion and a sense of relief unspeakable, there as everywhere else in the whole world. In the evening we celebrated by a hurriedly arranged but highly successful concert'.
>
> Irene G. Hilditch, *STC Chronicle*, 1966

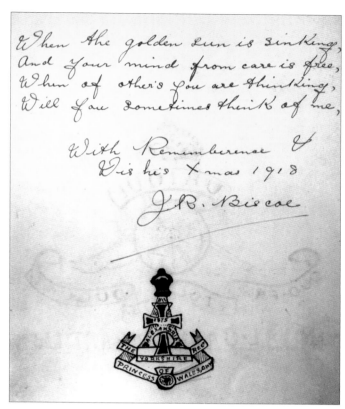

Courtesy of Wiltshire and Swindon History Centre

Courtesy of Wiltshire and Swindon History Centre

WAR WORK AT SALISBURY

'It is doubtful whether any city has been more ready than Salisbury to recognise its responsibility in this war in seeking to share its burden in helping the men and in bearing something of the burden of the war. The College has tried to play some part in these works.

At the Guest House for soldiers, started by members of the Salisbury Women's Suffrage Society, and conducted and worked by Salisbury Women, thousands of men in the Camps around us have found a home in their spare hours, and have enjoyed the rest and refreshment of quiet rooms where they can read and write or play games, of music, of a lounge in the garden, and of well-served, comfortable meals. Here, on some weekdays and on Sundays, Members of the College Staff give up their few spare hours to act as hostesses and helpers, and on Sunday morning, between breakfast and the Morning Service, two of the staff and a little band of Students cut stacks of bread and butter ready for afternoon teas.

The greatest piece of work done at college is owing entirely to Miss Whatley's initiative and organisation and that is the work of sending out prisoners' parcels. The Home Club entrusted her with £10 of its reserve fund; the students undertook to pack parcels as required, one after another of the members and friends adopted prisoners, and now 250 men are in regular receipt of parcels of much needed food and clothing through our College Agency. Miss Whatley keeps in touch with the whole of the work and has received many grateful letters. Scarcely a parcel fails to be acknowledged, and the men's simple, truthful words reveal a patient, cheerful endurance, a readiness to help others, and a gratitude in pathetic, poverty stricken and isolated conditions which is eloquent.

Miss Newman is constantly busy with socks for soldiers, clothes for Belgians and Serbians, and other good works in the needlework department'.

STC Magazine, Easter 1916

Salisbury Market Square 1914

An Extract from Margaret Dudman's Diary 1915-1917

September 3rd 1915 Arrived at King's House in a 'fly' from Salisbury Station. Was given a cubicle in 7 Room on the first floor. Not having had any teaching experience was told I must do 12 weeks of teaching practice instead of the usual 6.

October, 1915 Was admonished for wearing the College straw hat too far back on my head.

May 20th Crit.lesson at St Edmund's on "Belgium the Cockpit of Europe". Dried up before the end of the lesson

April 1916 Crit. lesson at St Edmund's Infants. Told the H.M.I. I did not think the infants understood the prayers they were repeating. Was told I should not be allowed to take a scripture lesson while holding such views.

January 1917 Lord Ord (college doctor) says I have "trench feet". My father asks what would it be called if there was no war on?

March School practice at Eastleigh. Get an A - from Miss Forth who says that College Training should eradicate my Hampshire accent.

March 15th An outbreak of German Measles. The San. is full and those of us not affected are sent home. We write a magazine to cheer up those in isolation.

April Ask Miss Forth if our year can put on an evening entertainment for the J's. She is horrified and asks if I have forgotten it is Holy Week. I had!

Today Summer Time is introduced for the first time. I resent losing one hour of College Life. Three of us cycle to Stonehenge which is tremendously impressive. No other sign of human life but the three of us in that vast landscape.

June Archbishop's Results – I get a 1st, and send a wire home in expectation of a P. Order which duly arrives. The Rev. Newham who marked our Prelim. papers tells me not to abbreviate Timothy into Tim!

June Country Churches. I go to St Thomas' and meet a former VI Form boy from Bishop Wordsworth's School. He walks back to Kings House with me. I have to report this to Miss Forth who asks if my father would approve!

(Students still had a good sense of humour-even during the war years.)

Poppies painted by Kate Sykes

Bishop Wordsworth and Canon Lear

Bishop Wordsworth, speaking at the College in 1901, said that the work done by Training Colleges 'must rank as one of the very highest influences of her late Majesty's reign'. He went on to say that the College had 'taken its part in making education general, in making it religious and in finding a useful and happy career for women'. Bishop Wordsworth died in 1911. He was remembered with gratitude.

'How well he championed us through the time of the College enlargement, the building of the Chapel, the opening of Barnard's Cross, and the existence of the Hostel, giving his sanction and guidance, and overcoming the objections of others by his own strong support'.

Students, former students and staff contributed to the cost of the magnificent recumbent figure of the Bishop that is in the Cathedral, and to the canopies over the choir stalls in his memory.

At Whitsun 1914 the College Magazine mourned the death of Canon Francis Lear, Archdeacon of Sarum, who had been 'guide, philosopher and friend to every Lady Superintendent up to the present time'.

I'll not forget!

Evelyn Hart (1892-1983) was a student at College during 1910-1912. She went on to teach history at South Wilts Grammar School, Salisbury during the Second World War. After Evelyn died her friends published some of her poems in a book called 'Leaves in the Wind,' in aid of Salisbury Cathedral Spire Fund.

KING'S HOUSE

King's House,
Beyond the river the western sky
Crimson and gold where the sun has set
The meadows where the cattle lie
In deep cool grass – could you forget?

The quiet Close, with its old stone wall,
Velvety green, where the moss is wet.
The garden where the cuckoos call
In Spring, in Spring – could you forget?

That finger, poised in the perfect blue,
Or wrapt in grey mist, the Spire that kept
Its silent, changeless guard o'er you
At noon, at night – could you forget?

The colours fade from the afterglow,
Come the sigh of reeds by the water met -
O my heart cries out for the long ago -
Old loves, old hope – I'll not forget!

Evelyn Hart

The Training College, Salisbury.

Chapter 3

The Dawn of a New Era

1918-1938

College at the end of the First World War
'A Crying Need'

Students who entered college immediately after the end of the First World War must have been jubilant that the terrible fighting was over at last. Six million men from Britain had been conscripted to fight: of these, 750,000 were killed and 1.7 million were wounded, many of them young men. Hundreds of thousands of children lost their fathers. Many students may have lost fathers, brothers and other close friends and relations in the war.

View of the Old Deanery
Courtesy of The Salisbury Museum

The optimism of pre-war years had diminished. People mourned their lost loved ones. In towns and villages throughout the land war memorials were erected as a sign of great respect for those who had died.

Living standards were hard. Britain was gripped by enormous debts and there was a growing feeling amongst the public that the Government was extremely wasteful. In 1921 unemployment reached its highest point (11.2%)

since records had begun. Many women, who had enjoyed more independence through work, were forced to give up their jobs to returning soldiers.

Women began to have more of 'a voice' as did the working class. Men over twenty-one and women aged over thirty who owned property had been given the vote. Society was now more democratic and the strict class hierarchy of Edwardian Britain gradually began to disappear.

David Lloyd George, the Prime Minister, appointed Sir Eric Geddes to head a committee on National Expenditure, soon dubbed 'The Geddes Axe.' The Cabinet agreed to cuts of £52 million, which was enormous for the time. It led to a massive reduction in social benefits, including secondary education. At the end of 1921 wage cuts of 8 shillings a week had been imposed on 6 million workers: this is equivalent to a fall of £58 per week today. There was mounting public resentment to the cuts, which culminated in the General Strike of 1926.

What of the College at this time? In 1919 a Church delegation met with Herbert Fisher, President of the Board of Education, and concluded that money should be used to maintain the College so that:

> 'Teachers trained in the milieu of religious dedication would be able to give not only religious instruction but also witness to Christian life in all schools, provided and non-provided'.
>
> LST ibid

At College Speech Day in 1922 the Bishop spoke of teachers as second to the priesthood in value as persons in the nation, but many teachers at the time felt themselves to be undervalued.

Students at College found themselves in a time of educational consolidation. The Revised Handbook for Teachers, issued by the Board of Education in 1918, recommended:

> 'Each teacher shall think for himself and work out such methods of teaching as may use his powers to the best advantage and be best suited to the particular needs and conditions of the school'.

The changes in education, which had been proposed earlier, were only implemented in part, due to the cuts. A lack of resources prevented any significant change until after the Second World War.

Student group

THE KING'S HOUSE TRAINING COLLEGE, SALISBURY.   W.L.Brind

There was growing interest in the works of Dewey and Montessori, and Susan Isaacs' books on the social and intellectual growth of children began to have impact. In her book 'The Children we Teach,' she wrote, 'The children themselves are the living aim and end of our teaching. It is their thought, their character and development which make the purpose of our existence as schools and teachers'.

The impact of the cuts was felt by students who completed their course in summer 1922. Many found employment difficult. On Speech Day that year Miss Forth reported that the 'forty unplaced students of that year were all placed by Christmas'.

Financial economies were urged on every side. In the years 1919-1923 there was great concern about College finances. The College sent a special application to the Board of Education in February 1922, which shows the difficult circumstances of the time.

'The College Library and general equipment were starved during the war and educational loss thereby had never been made good. We had hoped by an additional grant to be able to rent an extra house and so, out of Voluntary Funds, to have equipped a dormitory in King's House as Library. This is a crying need in the College.

At present the library is in the Entrance Hall, Receiving Room and Committee Room and is used for other occasional purposes. It is therefore impossible for it to serve the students for Silent Reading and Study and the work of the College is suffering much for want of such a room'.

The College received a grant in March 1924 from the Board of Education amounting to £10,034, which included allowance for the increase in salaries. Their overdraft was cleared in 1925. The College could once again look ahead with more confidence.

"For lo, the winter is past"

'The long winter of War, which seemed endless, has, please God, passed. May 1921 bring God's own Peace and Blessing to the Church, the World, our Empire, our College – to every loyal member of our Alma Mater. May she and all her children live and grow in this year, and help to bring to our Church and Nation that true inspiration which in these days of Reconstruction is more needed than ever before'.

Miss Forth, STC Magazine, New Year, 1921

Salisbury War Memorial unveiled by Lt. Tom Edwin Adlam VC in 1922

Courtesy of The Salisbury Museum

Miss Barbara Forth	Principal	1913 - 1928
Miss EM Rodgers	Vice-Principal with responsibility for Barnard's Cross (retired 1921)	
Miss OW Sinclair	Vice-Principal	1921
Miss Newman	Needlework	
Miss Lavinia Mary Hardy	Geography (with Miss Allen)	retired in 1929
Miss Vera Lane Edminson	English	
Miss Marjorie Leonarde Story	PE, Games, Hygiene and Physiology	1915
Miss Cecilia Lilian Malcombe	Art	1920
Miss Gladys Fowler	English and French	1925

Miss Thorp, Miss Allen, Miss Grist, Miss Stevenson and the Revd. S Baker continued throughout this period. Miss Newman retired in 1925.

College Staff 1925-1927

Courtesy of The Salisbury Museum

Miss Bertha Dunn	Principal	1928
Miss FJ Woodman	Vice-Principal Education and History	1928
Miss Elliot Smith	Education	
Miss Margaret Smith	Education and Needlework	
Dr Elsie Smith	English	1928
Miss Lock	Geography	
Miss Sylvia Hume	Education and Speech Training	1935
	The Teaching of Scripture in Junior and Infant Schools	
Miss Phyllis Cornwall	Residential Gardener	1935
Dr Emily Daymond	Music	1932
Miss Elsie Barnard	Music	1936
Miss B McRae	Geography	1936

Miss Allen and Miss Thorp retired in 1932. Miss Grist retired in 1938.

Dr Baker retired at Christmas 1933 and the Revd H Carlton Morris took his place.

Comments made by the students illustrate the lasting influence which the lecturers had upon them:

'One of my greatest joys was the choral singing we did with Dr Daymond. No choir I have sung with since has given me so much pleasure'.

'Miss Grist (dear A.G.) was Chief Lecturer, strict disciplinarian and critic on School Practice – but always fair and understanding and, on occasion, sympathetic'.

'Miss Dunn (B.M.D. as we called her) was a true musician who inspired all her classes. In Quietness and Confidence lay her success'.

'I should not have gained the various positions I had without the initial training of such stalwarts as Miss Grist and the Misses Margaret and Elliot Smith'.

'Miss Stevenson instilled in me a lifelong interest in and love of the countryside'.

'Dr Smith would allow nothing but the very best use of English, correctly and intelligibly'.

'Art work was a joy, for Miss Malcombe taught us to be adventurous with colour and line'.

Joan Tapscott (1937 -1939) summed it up well:

'They were all so enthusiastic and eager for their students to excel. Living within College as they did, they gave so much, perhaps more than we realised at the time. In retrospect I feel that the influence of the College, its ancient buildings, lovely garden and, above all, the dedication of the staff, has stayed with me. It seemed almost a sacrilege when the College was closed down'.

Old Deanery
Courtesy of
The Salisbury
Museum

The Old Deanery

In 1923 the College acquired the Old Deanery. In her report of 1922 to the Board of Education Miss Forth, the College Principal, spoke about the need to develop the College accommodation. The Dean was about to move to another house in The Close and suggested that the College could make use of the building. It was adjacent to Audley House and would also make a continuous front to the College. The College Council accepted the offer, which at this time of financial crisis was a brave and far-sighted decision.

In 1960, Miss D. A. Todd, College history lecturer, wrote the following description of the building's origin:

'In 1220, the foundation stones of the Cathedral were laid; and in 1222 the Bishop, Richard Poore, issued a Statute through which eventually Salisbury was to have perhaps the finest Close in England. Houses began to be built on what we now call The Close. In 1277 Robert de Wykehampton was elected as Bishop of Salisbury, and he then gave his canonical house to Walter Scammel, Dean, and his successors in the office of Dean for ever. Thus this house began its long record as the official residence of the Dean of Salisbury, a record which ended in 1923, when the Training College leased what became known as "Old Deanery". One particularly striking feature of the Old Deanery is its size – which shows most clearly the importance Richard Poore attached to a canonical residence, his insistence that the clergy should be properly housed and have sufficient facilities to carry out their duties of hospitality'.

In 1992 H. F. (Francisca) Fellowes visited the Old Deanery. Her father, Andrew Ewbank Burn, was the Dean of Salisbury from 1920 until 1928, and was the last Dean to live in the Old Deanery. It is remarkable that he was the sixtieth Dean to live there. Francisca remembered arriving in 1920:

'I can remember nothing of the journey, just arriving at this huge house with a big garden in front. Behind there was a rose garden with a clipped yew hedge to show off the roses, to the left an orchard, on the right a big kitchen garden and between them rough grass, a legacy of the 1914-1918 war. Best of all was the river with mown grass along its bank and a broad gravel path dividing it from the once lawn. To the south were three fir trees surrounded by a clipped hedge, which was very useful as a dressing room when we bathed. The river was much cleaner then'.

Over time many alterations were made to the Old Deanery and when the College took it over, in many ways it had the misleading appearance of an early Victorian building. An inspection in 1948 failed to disclose its early origin. A later survey undertaken by the Royal Commission on Historic Monuments in 1959 made some extremely important findings which thankfully saved the building from demolition.

Miss Forth made plans for a large Assembly Hall with a movable stage, housing for two lecturers (Miss Grist and Miss Stephenson), bedrooms for 24 students, a Prefects' Room, studies and classrooms. There were attractive grounds with a large expanse of river, a tennis court and netball court. The walled garden between the Old Deanery and the North Canonry provided fresh fruit and vegetables for the kitchen in King's House.

There was now room to develop a larger library in King's House. Miss Forth proudly remarked that the Old Deanery was 'a marked gain to the whole work of the College'.

Student memoirs provide an insight into what it was like to live and work in the Old Deanery:

'In my first year I did most of my study in the Extension Library, but sometimes in the Main Library. The Old Deanery Room was large and spacious and had a lovely big table at which we could do our private study. We had to be careful that the shutters were closed when the light was on as we were under the eagle eye of Miss Grist'.
'In the second year I shared the "Guest Room" in Old Deanery. I was asked to make plans of Old Deanery in connection with fire drill but in spite of careful measuring I could not make the first floor and the ground floor fit together. There was one piece of the first floor, next to Miss Barnard's room, to which I could not get. When I mentioned this I was told that I must have been wrong in my measurement and that such accuracy was not needed for the plan for fire drill. Had I been more insistent the Medieval Hall might have been discovered then!'

A student from 1930-32 recalled:

'After half-term we were moved to a room over the post office just outside the Arch as King's House top was considered unsafe. In spite of certain privileges we hated this but, to compensate, after a few months we were give free choice and finally spent a wonderful College life in the "Chapel Room" of the Old Deanery'.

The Old Deanery was a special place to live and work. Further changes and renovations would be made to the building which has always been a place cherished in the hearts of students.

The Old Deanery at the end of the First World War
Courtesy of The Salisbury Museum

The Old Deanery Opening Ceremony

Miss K. C. C. Flint (1922-1924) described the ceremony:

'March 6th 1923 – what a joyous and thrilling day it was for a First Year Student! Crowds of people flocked into King's House and as the hour of the opening drew near everyone's steps were directed towards the Old Deanery. Students found their way through the gap in the wall leading from King's House garden and foregathered in the Old Deanery front drive through which distinguished visitors were passing into the front hall and up the great hall.

Rehearsals and practices had taken place so that the procession, singing and service should go off without a hitch. Much thought had been given to how the students singing of Psalm 145 in procession through the entrance and up the staircase should be conducted. I must confess that I never sing that very beautiful psalm without waving a smile as I invariably picture Dr Baker leaning perilously out of Deanery hall window, waving a long and ivory baton, as we lifted up our voices chanting "I will magnify thee, O God my King." At stages throughout our slow progress four abreast up the staircase (which creaked ominously with the weight of the traffic) students of the music class were stationed to beat time, taking their cue from one inside the great hall who could see Dr Baker performing his dangerous and difficult task. I think it can be said that we were united in the sentiment if not the singing of the final verse – "Let all flesh give thanks unto his holy name for ever and ever".

So we eventually filed into the already crowded hall and found our places, and the impressive service of Dedication and Opening followed. There was dear Bishop Donaldson (or Sinclair Sarum as we affectionately liked to remember him) in glorious apparel, fully robed in cope and mitre. Somewhere the benign figure of Canon Steward fits into the otherwise misty background; and centre of course, was our beloved Miss Forth (wearing, I am sure, her gorgeous amethyst pendant) whose usual happy, confident and charming presence pervaded the room.

The Bishop prayed for God's blessing on all the work undertaken for the cause of education in this fine addition, and hoped it would enhance the growth and reputation of the College.

The solemn ceremony ended, and we all felt another important era had opened in the College annals. And so I am sure it has proved to be under the incomparable regime of Miss Grist and Miss Stephenson, and I look back with gratitude on the privilege and good fortune afforded to me in spending my second year in Old Deanery East Room, with its unforgettable view of the Cathedral Spire'.

Medieval Hall Mysteries

There are certain mysteries and dramas surrounding the Medieval Hall/Old Deanery.

The Chapter Act Book from the Cathedral records that in 1571 John Farrant was admitted to a year's probation as lay-vicar and Master of the Children of Salisbury Cathedral. He subsequently became the Cathedral Organist. Farrant's wife, Margaret, complained to the Dean about her husband's unkind behaviour towards her. Farrant lost his temper with the Dean and in February 1592 left the Cathedral during a service and made his way to the Old Deanery, where he attempted to murder him. The Dean escaped the murder attempt and Farrant was quickly expelled from all offices of the Cathedral. Immediately after the incident John Farrant fled to Hereford, where he became organist of the Cathedral.

Did Cromwell once stable his horse in the Old Deanery when visiting The Close? It is certainly possible that Cromwell visited Salisbury. There was a plan by the Sealed Knot for a Royalist insurrection to start in March 1655 and one of the cities to be seized was Salisbury.

Lucy Sanderson Taylor described the Old Deanery when she lived there in the 1940s. There was an alcove near a student's room 'reached by walking from the main front door towards the back of the hall, turning left and left again. Turning right one found another door which opened on to a sunken cobbled area where, according to legend Cromwell stabled his horse on his visit to The Close'.

Mary Choules (1939-1941) lived in Audley in her second year. She remembered that the air raid shelters were 'all the way over in Cromwell's Cellars underneath Old Deanery'.

Rosemary Edwards (1943-1945) recalled her student life at College during the war:

'There was a grand staircase in the Old Deanery which was in such a fragile condition that we were told to use it only in an emergency, so we used the servants' stairs instead. Near to these stairs was a large wall hanging. Behind this, we were shown a tiny entrance into a windowless, doorless room, very narrow, which had been discovered by workmen a few years beforehand. The room was divided into two, and beyond it was a crude manger with some hay still in it. I took a strand, which I still have. We were told that considering the artefacts that were found in the room, it was possibly used as a hiding place by the Duke of Monmouth as he fled after the Monmouth Rebellion'.

STC Magazine, 2011

It is well documented that The Duke of Monmouth hid in Malmesbury House in the Close. Were Oliver Cromwell and the Duke of Monmouth once visitors to the Old Deanery? It is exciting to think that they may have been, but the mystery remains.

Medieval Hall (Old Deanery)

Painted by Sue Finniss

Carl Weeks and Salisbury House, Iowa

The Revd Stanley Baker

Salisbury House, Des Moines, Iowa
Courtesy of Salisbury House & Gardens

The Revd Stanley Baker was appointed to the College as Chaplain and Lecturer in Divinity in 1903. He was a key figure in the founding of Barnard's Cross Chapel. Romance was in the air and in 1907 he married Miss Buller, who had been a Governess in Barnard's Cross since 1903. He was described by Margaret Janson-Smith (1930-1932) as 'a rather eccentric and lovable character', as is shown in these reminiscences:

Dr Baker, 1931

In the 1920s Carl Weeks, an American from Iowa, was staying in Salisbury. Carl was a pioneer in womens' cosmetics and had made a fortune. When he saw King's House he liked it so much that he wanted to buy it and transport it back to America. This not being possible, he sent architects from the States to measure it up and, in 1928, a similar house was built in Des Moines, Iowa. The American house, named Salisbury House, has some additions, which include a spire from the Poultry Cross in Salisbury, an angel head from St Thomas's Church and a figure from Old Sarum. Many furnishings came from a Salisbury antique shop. Some of the tiles for the roof came from Trafalgar House, Downton, Salisbury.

The family lived in the house until 1954 when it was bought as the headquarters of the Iowa State Education Association. In 1998 it was purchased by the Salisbury House Foundation as a 'historic house museum for the educational and cultural benefit and enjoyment of the public'.

'Dr Baker, a great influence musically and intellectually, kept chalk up his sleeves and in winter held a small hot water bottle across his waist under his cassock. On meeting one in the High Street, he would throw his arms in the air in welcome and the whole lot would be scattered on the ground'.
Phyllis Gattrell (1929-1931)

'He lived with his wife and daughter in the Hall of the Vicars Choral in The Close and came daily, rain or shine, to take our services. His was dedicated work, performed with care and devotion. He was also responsible for Music, and he had a small room in Barnard's Cross in which he gave free lessons in violin playing or for any other suitable instrument. He was a kindly, bearded and spectacled person who always appeared in cassock and clerical collar. He kept a store of little jokes and anecdotes with which he was always ready to lighten conversation'.
Margaret Logan (1926-1928)

Dr Baker left College in 1933 and became Vicar of Laverstock on the outskirts of Salisbury. He was also asked to open a Mission on the edge of the parish, which he named St Christopher's-at-the-Ford. A local resident has affectionate memories of the somewhat flamboyant black-clad figure, always wearing a cloak and a black hat that had a little rosette on it. 'He would sweep off his hat to greet us'.

Dr Baker and the Cathedral Glass – just a good story?

There is a story in Salisbury about a bearded Canon who wielded a spade and sought permission to dig up peoples' gardens in order to find the medieval Cathedral glass that he was convinced lay buried there. This is certainly a good story, but the truth needs a little unpicking.

The 'glass story' begins at the end of the 18th century when James Wyatt, an eminent architect, was given the task of remodelling and restoring the Cathedral. During this process much of Salisbury Cathedral's medieval glass was swept away into the city ditches, where it lay undisturbed for more than a century. Dr Baker, intrigued by the story and determined to find the glass, consulted old maps and traced the ditches before employing a glass diviner to do a test. A former student remembered him telling them that fragments of glass had been found. Great was the excitement and 'there was no Scripture studied that day'! Dr Baker then set about organising excavations. He described what happened in the 1933 College Magazine:

'The search began nearly eight years ago, when we began with the one slender clue that the glass was thrown 140 years ago into the Town Ditch. Excavations have been carried on upon the site of the ditch commonly called the Town Ditch, which conveyed to the river the waters of the channels until 1853 flowing along the principal streets of the city; and of a ditch just the other side of Harnham Bridge into which for many years the rubbish of the city was cast. On several occasions success has appeared to be imminent, but again and again hopes have been dashed to the ground. At last, about a year ago, we set the digger to excavate a filled-in ditch on the left hand just as you enter the College playing field near De Vaux Place. Here a rich haul was made of 13th century grisaille glass'.

Margaret Simmance (1936-1938) was invited to tea with Dr Baker and his wife and saw 'in the little workroom upstairs, his reassembling of the broken Cathedral glass'. After it had been restored, some was given to St Andrew's Church, Laverstock.. Other pieces were given to Boyton, where Canon Steward, his friend and former Principal of the College, had been Rector. Winchester Cathedral also has a fine window made from the Salisbury glass. There is uncertainty, but it would appear that Dr Baker had offered the glass to Salisbury Cathedral, but that his offer was declined and Winchester became the recipient. Margaret Janson-Smith (1930-1932) wrote that:

'The Salisbury Cathedral authorities treated the poor old boy shabbily. At first they refused to accept the glass, but later allowed a few medallions to be placed in a side window'.

Did any of the glass ever return to Salisbury Cathedral? The matter remains shrouded in mystery, but Dr Baker's exciting 'finds' can still be admired in Winchester Cathedral, in St Andrew's Church, Laverstock and in the east window in the Church of St Mary the Virgin, Boyton.

Dr Baker's attempt on the Spire!

'Another memory is of climbing with Dr Baker to the last row of pinnacles on the Cathedral Spire, where he stuck firmly and could only be freed with much intake of breath and pushing and pulling'. Phyllis Gattrell (1929-1931)

Austin Thorp, a current Tower Guide, made this comment:

'He could have climbed up one of the two pinnacles ringed – the ball flower decoration on the spire and on the pinnacles provides quite good hand and foot holds. If he did manage to get further up and wedge himself between the spire and a pinnacle he might well have needed much pushing and pulling'.

Dr Baker with the Chapel Prefects

Courtesy of The Salisbury Museum

Miss Dunn was an English graduate (Oxford) and for the previous seven years she had been one of HM Inspectors.

Saturday September 21st 1928

'I, Bertha Mary Dunn, begin my Principalship of this College. Arrived 7.30pm, motoring from home (Esher). Miss Cook and the domestic staff already here. In the morning I bought a small bureau and other furniture for my room; the study already contained nearly enough for my needs, and the bedroom everything. I have a 'bare' taste in the appointment of my rooms and prefer space to many fitments; this must be owing to my having done peripatetic work for the last few years. During this week Mr King came to see me, partly to welcome me and partly to discuss the question of four additional students believed to be allocated to this College as a result of the closing of the Home & Colonial Training College. Miss Cook showed me the parts of house where it is proposed to accommodate them. One of these places I vetoed at once, and queried another, as creating too much pressure'.

Extract from Miss Dunn's Diary
Wiltshire and Swindon History Centre

In *College in The Close* Lucy Sanderson Taylor wrote:

'She brought to her task an orderly mind and a love of drama and music, of English and French literature, as well as Christian care. Despite great fluctuations in numbers of students and staff, she led the College successfully through the years of the Depression'.

In the Midsummer 1933 Magazine, Miss Dunn thanked old students for their gift of a 'much appreciated' electric iron. She explained that the effects of the economic recession meant that the Reserve Equipment Fund was very low and the College could not afford furniture and amenities:

'We are badly in need of one or two things, which, considering the present and future reduction in government grants, one is hardly justified in claiming from the Council; for example an up-to-date wireless set, stout garden seats for students to use when studying, a set of pigeon-holes in the Dining Hall in which students can keep their own table-napkins'.

Student reminiscences about Miss Dunn often focus on her musical contributions to College life. Realising the value of the subject in education, she ensured that Music occupied a leading place in the College curriculum.

On a lighter note, Phyllis Gattrell (1929-1931) remembered the occasion when Miss Dunn fell outside the Cathedral. The students rushed to help her, but she protested: 'Please don't bother, the Bishop is coming'.

Everyman Morality Play, 1928

Courtesy of The Salisbury Museum

'Miss Story – a good sport'

Miss Marjorie Leonarde Story joined the College staff in 1915 with responsibility for "Physical Training". She was a Fellow of the British Association of Physical Training. In 1915 her salary was £75 a year.

Miss Story

Miss Story's appointment illustrates the growing importance of Physical Training and sports in the College, although facilities needed improvement. An inspection report of 1927 praised many aspects of the College but noted some shortcomings. The playing fields were poorly drained and there was need of a good hall for Physical Exercises.

Physical Training (PT) in addition to Hygiene, English and Teaching were compulsory subjects for the Certificate examination, but Games were not compulsory beyond what was deemed useful for school work.

Miss Story was kept very busy as she acted as coach for all games. By 1936 two full-sized netball courts with good surfaces were in use on the hockey fields. There were two tennis courts in the Old Deanery Gardens and one at King's House.

Miss Story appears to have been a strong and forceful character, standing no nonsense! Her students were important to her and she cared about their welfare. Fientje Taconis (1939-1941) paid tribute to 'Miss Story, our slightly eccentric and masculine-looking PT teacher'. Two students remembered her cycling around Salisbury, on days when students were allowed in the town, in order to keep an eye out for any unsuitable men who might take advantage of them.

In her first year at College, Eve Ramsey (1925–1927) shared a room close to that occupied by Miss Story ,who was nicknamed 'The Limb.' Eve got on well with her but 'woe betide any student who was not of sporty disposition'.

Phyllis Gattrell (1929-1931) recalled one occasion when she was in the company of two students from the Theological College:

'On a glorious summer day I was rowing with two 'Theos' when one said "Look out – the Story is on the bank" and, just in time, I was pushed to the bottom of the boat and covered with a tarpaulin. Miss Story's reprimands were graded in colour of paper – pale yellow was fairly mild, deep yellow was stern, but "woe betide you" if the paper was orange. But Miss Story was helpful to me, keeping in touch right through my teaching career and spurring me on to higher positions'.

Margaret Simmance (1936-1938) remembered 'our PE lecturer, Miss Story (a bit of a dragon) insisted we always wore hair nets during PE which was often performed barefoot on Deanery lawn'.

Ednor Ball (1937-1939) emphasised how much she and other students learnt from Miss Story, 'Miss Story's Company Sergeant-Major approach, her amazing stamina and enthusiasm allowing no sloppiness, was supported by the reasons she gave'.

Miss Story retired from the College in 1944 after 29 years of devoted work.

INTER-HOUSE MATCHES AND COMPETITIONS

The 'Shield Matches' have just been finished. The weather last term prevented the hockey match being played off, so for the second time one of the summer games has had to decide this year's owners. King's House won the Netball and Barnard's Cross the Rounders. It is high time the Shield changed hands, and Barnard's Cross are to be congratulated on their double victory.

The King's House Jumping competition was won by the Seniors, with a straight jump from the floor of 4ft. 5ins.

SUMMARY OF EXTERNAL MATCHES

Only five of the eight external hockey matches were able to be played. The weather was bad enough to affect other grounds beside our own. Of these five we lost to Trowbridge and Warminster, but won the Young Liberal and Trowbridge High School matches.

SWIMMING

Open-air baths were opened in Salisbury last year, and we were able to make use of them during the last month of the summer term. This year we have been unable to have a special day reserved for us, and the Baths Committee have been short-sighted enough to make no provision for any women's sessions.

B. PULLEN
M. BELBIN, Joint Secs. of House Games Committee
M. L. STORY, Coach

STC Magazine, 1933

COUNTRY DANCING

'We did more Country Dancing than Games because the tennis courts were at the bottom of the garden at King's House and balls were often lost in the river, and the playing field near Harnham Gate was often under water'!

Muriel Hodder (1923-1925)

Hockey Team 1931   Courtesy of The Salisbury Museum

Drill Competition Winners   Courtesy of The Salisbury Museum

Right: Sports Day Bowls

Courtesy of The Salisbury Museum

Guiding was a very popular activity at College under the leadership of Miss Story, who was District Commissioner for The Close.

> 'There are at present 62 members of the two Companies, and sixteen recruits will be enrolled before the end of the Lent Term. The two Companies are, for the present, working on rather different lines than they have done during the past three years. It is more than useful to have our Divisional living at the gates of The Close, and to know she fully understands the difficulties of the Companies as none but an old student can do'.
>
> M. L. Story, District Commissioner for the Close
> *STC Magazine*, 1932

In 1932-1933 a Cadet Ranger Company was formed as the 13th Sarum Cadets. The 8th and 13th were in King's House and the 9th at Barnard's Cross. Numbers fell due to the reduction in students attending College, but the separate groups remained, even when Barnard's Cross students were transferred to King's House. Each month there was a combined meeting where interests were shared and friendships developed. In 1939 the Sarum Cadets attended a Church Parade in the Cathedral and were given the honour of making the standard bearer party for the County Standard at this Parade.

Ruth Watts (1933-1935) recalled:

> 'I joined the College Girl Guide Company and attended all the meetings and a large County Rally and Service in the Cathedral'.

Mary Phelps (1936-1938) remembered:

> 'I joined College Rangers, meeting in the gym once a week. Miss Story was our Captain and a second year student, Elizabeth Golledge, our Patrol Leader. We wore navy gym-slips, black stockings, white blouses and College black and white ties as our uniform'.

College Rangers

The Secret Passage

Florence Rencie Langford (1937-1940) recalled an exciting trip down a secret passage led by the intrepid Miss Story:

"One day Miss Story took some of us through the 'secret passage' in King's House. We went in the entrance, a 'door' in the panelling at the turn of the stairs to the Senior Classroom. The Passage ran along the north wing towards the Cathedral and there was another entrance in the panelling part way along. When some plants had been removed (creepers of some sort) from the outer wall it was possible to see slits which must have been air vents as it was quite fresh in there. The 'main passage' went along under the large front window of the Senior Classroom. The whole room had a false floor and the part inside this window was raised still more and the 'passage' must have gone along in there.

We eventually came out of a trap-door outside the Bursar's room in the South Wing, which was up the stairs from the Milky Way. There was a grating which would also give air, although it was obviously much later in design. I met an earlier student at one Reunion who said that there is another branch of this passage leading up to the North Gable Dormitory and the entrance at the top of the stairs just outside a cupboard which was a priest's hole. In my time this cupboard was used to store surplus crockery from Barnard's Cross. This passage, she said, was used for fire drill."

The mystery remains as to what has become of this passage.

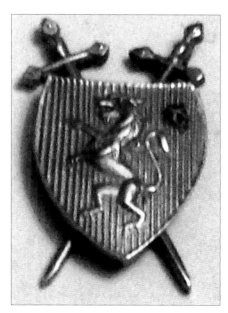

College tie pin

The Second House

In 1924 the Second House of the College, Barnard's Cross, celebrated its 21st year in fine style, as described by a student:

"It was a glorious weekend, from the sacred fellowship of the Sunday Service of Holy Communion in the little chapel to the picnics, meetings and entertainments which filled our days and nights. Our gratitude and love expressed itself in a birthday present of £85, which has been spent, we hope, most profitably and enjoyably on a set of Wireless for our Alma Mater."

Another student, who had returned for this occasion, recorded her memories of the early days:

"Twenty-one years seems an ocean of time to maids who have not yet come of age and who are Students at Barnard's Cross. But one who was there on the opening day can tell them that twenty-one years can become a little rivulet across which a middle-aged teacher can step, and come back to the 'Coming-of-Age Festivities' as though she were a Student numbering but eighteen years of life.

How good those days were when our sole Classroom was the present Library, in which our Class of 25 gathered all day long, to be taught by Canon Steward, Miss Forth, Miss Buller and Miss Allen – and Miss Fitzgerald presided over the Dining-room and cared for our out-of-work hours and our health.

The night to remember was certainly the one when a rushing, violent stream of water came pouring down the staircase and flooded the new Classrooms and the Dining Hall below. In the dark of night, members of the Staff stole out and fetched the Principal from his well-earned retirement. He, armed with his umbrella and accompanied by the Hot-water Engineer, arrived in time to find that though all the new ceilings had been spoilt, the bath tap had now been turned off and the stream stopped at its source.

The countryside must have wondered for days before, and on the railway journey, why staid Headmistresses looked so young and blooming and possessed such overflowing spirits. Had they come into the House and seen the welcome we received and witnessed our pleasure in racing round to see old things and new, they might have understood. At the great Assembly in the Hall on Saturday night all the speakers vied with each other in recording the honour and glory of our octogenarian College and twenty-one years old Barnard's Cross'.

By the mid-1920s about 78 students lived at Barnard's Cross. The top two floors were long dormitories divided by wooden partitions into 'horse-boxes' (cubicles); and a thin piece of matting covered a few floor boards. Winifred Buxton and her friend Winifred Jones spent their first year there, and shared a room in the annexe at St Martin's Rectory in their second year. (This annexe was used when Barnard's Cross was full)

Margaret Logan's vivid description helps us to imagine the horse-boxes:

'In windy weather, with every cubicle window and the end window open at the top, the brown curtains dividing each cubicle from the central passage would blow wildly. Each cubicle was furnished with a single bed, a chest of drawers with mirror and we provided our own white cover on which to lay our toiletries. There was also a washstand with china basin and ewer, and on the floor stood a tall enamel jug for carrying water from the bathroom. We hung our pictures on the dark wooden partitions. I had a water colour of Beachy Head, and a picture of "The Laughing Cavalier", bought complete with frame at Woolworths for 6d'.

Margaret was a Presbyterian and one of the Nonconformist students at Barnard's Cross. They attended the twice daily Chapel services with everyone else. On Sundays students could go to any church of their choice, sometimes walking to George Herbert's church at Bemerton.

Barnard's Cross Tie

Barnard's Cross Hatband

PT Inspection at Barnard's Cross

Barnard's Cross Staircase   Courtesy of The Salisbury Museum

Student life inspired an article called 'The Knock on the Door' in the Barnard's Cross Magazine of 1923:

'Woe betide the student who shall take a lecturer's bathroom, and who, just as she is stepping from the bath hears a gentle knock and a voice saying "Who has my bath, please?"

Knocking on cubicles often causes consternation. The most unwelcome time is in the morning, when to stop the voice and send away the person who is making it, we sleepily declare that we are wide awake.

Last, but by no means least, are the knocks on the lecturer's door. If we go ourselves we knock boldly and firmly, but if sent for we tremble on the brink and quaveringly knock, and await the stern "Come in".

Some of us are even now knocking at a door, which when it has been opened to us will give us a fuller and wider view of life, and its happiness and sorrow'.

Canon Edward Steward, the much loved former Principal of the College and founder of Barnard's Cross, died on April 11th 1930. A memorial tablet was placed in Barnard's Cross Chapel. Other tablets were placed in King's House Chapel and in the Cathedral.

In grateful loving memory of

EDWARD STEWARD Magd. Coll : Oxon. M.A.

Canon of Salisbury Cathedral

Founder of Barnard's Cross 1903 and Principal

Until 1913

At rest 11th April 1930

His Memorial lives in the hearts and lives of his students

As seeing him who is invisible

The Channel Islanders

By the 1920s a steady number of students crossed the sea from the Channel Islands to the College. Many of them lived at Barnard's Cross, but some were at King's House.

A student, identified only as '*Une Jersiaise*', wrote a passionate 'Defence of my Island' for the Barnard's Cross Magazine in 1923:

'According to many of the uninitiated, Jersey consists of a small patch of land on which are found a few inhabitants of doubtful intelligence, speaking a queer language, tethered cows, small, slow trains and many potatoes. Strange to say, there are a few other things here. We are able to rise to the inspiring heights of possessing water works, buses, telephones, a museum and even wireless. We also know what a printing press is, and with wondering eyes we have gazed upon aeroplanes and patent knife cleaners. We are able to dance a little, and sometimes we produce operas. Jersey is beauty. Surrounded by seas of changing blue, she is far lovelier than eastern gardens. Lacking rivers, mountains and forests, she yet has a peculiar charm belonging to jagged cliffs tumbling into rough seas, fields of trembling grasses and meadows of golden buttercups. Skies are often blue, the sun shines for many long hours and the air is fresh and keen. Yes, Jersey certainly is one of the chosen places of this earth'.

Students at Barnard's Cross, 1932-1934

The following 'snapshots' portray a few of the Jersey students, who subsequently returned to the island and gave long and dedicated service to education, right through the difficult years of the Occupation and beyond.

Gladys Gruchy was educated at the Jersey Pupil Teacher Centre before entering College in 1921. Her niece remembers her mentioning the cost of the reference books that she had to buy for College, as well as the expense of travelling to and from the island. Miss Newman, wrote in a reference in 1923 that Gladys had 'considerable skill in Needlework and should prove an efficient teacher'.

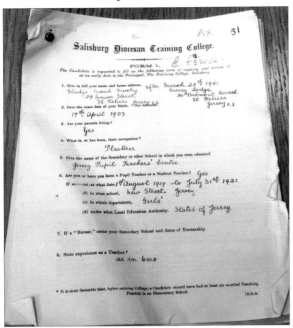

Gladys Gruchy's College Application
Courtesy of Wiltshire and Swindon History Centre

Dr Baker, the College Chaplain also wrote a warm reference:

'I have the greatest pleasure in bearing testimony to Miss Gladys Gruchy. Her work for me has been steady, conscientious and intelligent, and in every way excellent. She is a good sound Churchwoman, and her character is such as to make her influence upon the children of the very best. As regards Music, she has been one of our Chapel organists, and has accompanied the services with great efficiency and good taste. She is excellently fitted to be a successful teacher of singing in school'.

Gladys returned to Jersey after her training and taught there for 42 years until her retirement in 1966.

Florence Mary Renouf was at College from 1927-1929. She attended Jersey Ladies' College before spending time as an Observation Teacher at Trinity Central School in preparation for Teacher Training. She wrote of the link with Salisbury which was forged by Miss Montgomery, former student and lecturer, and by then the much loved and respected Head of the Jersey Pupil Teachers' Centre.

'Maybe she encouraged her girls to train at "her" college, for in 1927 five of us applied and were accepted. We all lived at BX, the States of Jersey having contributed to the cost of the property and two places were reserved for Jersey students each year. As a Junior I slept in a cubicle in D dormitory. My cubicle was furnished with an iron bedstead, a chest of drawers (with a mirror), matching washstand with china jug and basin, a soap dish and a glass water bottle that the maid filled with fresh drinking water. A sliding curtain, green I think, acted as the door of the horse box. The Lecturer's Room was occupied by Miss Thorpe. At the end of term we had a midnight feast and the next day she casually remarked that she had heard mice through the night, but had never seen any!

During my second year I shared a room with two friends at Number 8 The Close. The housekeeper, Margaret, had at one time been a maid at KH. She provided a pot of tea for those who left for early study at BX and sometimes bread and butter. That winter was particularly cold and men were employed scraping and carrying away the snow in St Ann's Street. The water in our jugs at Number 8 froze solid and the jugs cracked and broke. One morning the tank in the attic burst and the water froze on the stairs and formed icicles as it cascaded over the sides. Margaret was very apologetic to her 'dear young ladies' for the discomfort they would have to endure.

For the half term holiday we gathered at KH with others who lived too far away to go home. Rules were somewhat relaxed. We could go into town on market day to see the auction of animals in the market square, we could help ourselves "ad lib" to apples brought in by the old gardener's wife and we could go to see a film, 'Alf's Button'. The Chaplain, Dr Baker, with his wife hired a "charra" and took us for a delightful drive in the New Forest before entertaining us in their home – tea being served in their china cups – such a change!

I was sorry to leave College and still think of those days with nostalgic affection. I did private tuition in Jersey until appointed to a Special School for Barnardo and Jersey Home for Boys, then twenty-five years at St Saviours School. I adapted to a wide range from Infants to 14+ and a Remedial Class'.

Beryl Woodsford was educated at the Jersey Intermediate School, where her headmistress was Miss Montgomery. Beryl entered College in 1932 and she lived at Barnard's Cross. Extracts from her College references in 1934 suggest that she was a promising young teacher:

'I have the highest possible opinion of her personal character, her whole-hearted devotion to duty, and her thorough loyalty. I have no doubt that her teaching and practice of the Christian Faith will be a real and living influence with the children'.

Dr Stanley Baker Emeritus Chaplain and Lecturer of Salisbury Training College

'As a member of the College she is very satisfactory, being a Chapel Prefect and a genuine influence for good, and yet a popular leader among her fellow students. Her kindliness and vivacity endear her to the children whom she teaches'.

B. M. Dunn, Principal

Beryl retired in 1971 after doing 'wonderful work in remedial teaching at the Jersey General Hospital'. Her daughter, Jean Hanning, followed her to College in 1961.

Miss Montgomery

Last, but not least … Miss Montgomery, student and lecturer at Salisbury Training College, taught these three students, as well as many others. She became an important figure in the developing educational world of Jersey. A former pupil of the Pupil Teacher Centre described her as 'something of a pioneer in Jersey educational history and far in advance of her times when she first came here. I know that most of us found ourselves better equipped educationally than other students when we went up to our various Training Colleges.' The Pupil Teacher Centre subsequently developed into the Jersey Intermediate School and Miss Montgomery remained the Principal. Miss Forth, Principal of Salisbury Training College, wrote about her in 1938, describing her 'complete devotion to secondary education in Jersey and the building up of a well-trained Teaching Staff for the schools of the island'.

Friendship, Fun and a little more Freedom

These were the years of 'the two houses' (King's House and Barnard's Cross) and students felt a sense of loyalty and 'belonging' to their house. Miss Forth, the Principal, wrote: 'The life of the College is one, despite its many buildings, and the Students are constantly passing across the Close to and from lectures in one house or another'. Reminiscences reflect enjoyment, fun and laughter, as well as friendly rivalry.

Students seldom went into the city as they had little or no money to spend. Winifred Buxton (1922-1924) remembered afternoon walks, always in pairs, on the downs:

'Larks singing, hurrying clouds over distant vistas which always seemed to beckon us onwards, flowers in the short turf, and always the sight of that lovely spire in the distance'.

In the winter students used to go tobogganing on the downs.

Picnics at Grovely Woods were accompanied by singing and laughter. The annual Stonehenge Picnic continued, with the students travelling in an open charabanc. Expeditions for Advanced Geography were seen as opportunities for enjoyment, as well as learning.

Visits to the cinema took place by permission only. 'Way down East', a 1920s film that involved a child born out of wedlock, was deemed unsuitable. Town was out of bounds on market days and students were only allowed out at night if returning from a lecture, or visiting a member of staff for advice on School Practice.

In Summer 1924 the students went by train to the British Empire Exhibition at Wembley. Miss Forth, having forgotten to tell The Close Gatekeeper that they would be returning late, had to send him a telegram from Wembley. In the 1930s expeditions included visiting Stratford-upon-Avon to see *The Winter's Tale* and to London to see *Othello* at the Old Vic.

Male visitors were not allowed, unless they were relatives. Some students managed to discover a remarkable number of attentive male cousins… At the weekly Saturday night dance at Barnard's Cross, the only male present was Dr Baker, the Chaplain. There was plenty of in-house entertainment and Fancy Dress parties were very popular. Winifred Buxton (1922-1924) describes her year group as

Staff/Student Picnic 1935-1937

Sports Day 1930s

Courtesy of The Salisbury Museum

'bubbly, excitable, possibly at times foolishly irresponsible, but we were also very friendly and happy together'. Nicknames were widely used and Winifred and her friend Winifred Jones were known as 'Froggie and Stilts', their nicknames having been acquired on the hockey field.

Each house had its own Dramatic Society and performed many plays. In 1931, a dramatic version of the *Pilgrim's Progress*, compiled by Miss Dunn, was enacted by 'staff, students and friends of the College'. Moliere's *Malade Imaginaire* was performed on King's House lawns at the June Parents' Day. The annual Nativity Tableaux at Barnard's Cross were seen as a particular highlight. Christmas Parties were held at both Houses and Barnard's Cross sometimes had celebrations that involved fireworks in the garden.

Literary Societies grew and flourished, with students enjoying reading and discussing poetry, watching lantern slides, participating in play readings and debating literary subjects. Many lectures were given, the subjects including topics of historical interest, art, travel and education. There was also a French Circle. The Choral Society was started

in 1928 and by 1930 a small choir was competing in the Wiltshire Music Festival, where it won First Prize, with Miss Dunn as the conductor. At Barnard's Cross a choir sang carols to neighbours to raise money for Dr Barnardo's Homes and the Madagascar Mission.

Norah Hallett was at College in the early 1930s, by which time the students were allowed more freedom at the weekends:

> 'We wandered around the market and our favourite teashop was the House of Steps. I often went with Betty to her mother's house on Saturday and she provided us with a delicious tea, including watercress and other salads that had been bought in the market that morning. A nice change from College teas!'

Janet Tarr (1932-34) remembered that students were encouraged to go to a vantage point to see the Duke and Duchess of York on their visit to the area:

> 'I have never forgotten how radiantly lovely our beloved Queen Mother was – and, of course, is'.

During her second year, Elsie Tiller and her friends lived in the Old Deanery and enjoyed having tea in their rooms at the weekends, with their parents providing delicious cakes.

Friendship has always been a feature of Salisbury Training College. Living together and sharing so many experiences forged friendships that stood the test of time. Margaret Logan (1926-1928) summed it up:

'I have very happy memories of my college years for the standards that were set and the lasting friendships that were made'.

Time off! Courtesy of The Salisbury Museum

College picnic, 1929 Courtesy of The Salisbury Museum

An Exciting Escapade!

Marjorie Ventham (1926 -1928) spent her first year in the "Top Dormitory" at the top of the main staircase in King's House.

'I had the small middle cubicle where there was a small door in one corner which opened on a flight of steps down to the ceiling of the Principal's sitting-room and showed the whole expanse of the roof of King's House. It also provided me with a breath of fresh air when the weather was very warm, and I usually kept the little door open and my curtain at the entrance to my cubicle drawn across for privacy.

The door was a source of great interest to all students and was the means of my greatest scare while at College. A friend persuaded me to climb the roof. We descended the steps to the enormous roof timbers and had no difficulty in walking on the beams over Miss Forth's sitting-room and bedroom, Miss Story's sitting-room, Nurse's sitting-room and South Dormitory as far as the Sanatorium.

King's House Staircase (STC Magazine 1937)

I decided that was far enough and my friend was persuaded to return with great reluctance. I was becoming worried about the time for I had to be back in my cubicle with the door closed before 9.30 p.m. for "quiet time". We safely negotiated our return until we reached the ceiling over Miss Forth's sitting-room, when my friend caught her foot in the electric cables and nearly fell, to my great horror shaking the

ceiling. We rushed up the steps, I shut the door, pulled my curtain and we were just going down the stairs when I heard voices. Miss Forth and the Head Prefect had come up to investigate. I pushed my friend into the wardrobe cupboard at the top of the stairs and we stayed there, covered in dust, for about twenty minutes. When I thought it was safe to come out of the cupboard and we had managed to get rid of the dust and cobwebs, I returned very quickly to my cubicle. In the meantime, Miss Forth had interviewed my dormitory prefect and requested to see me! Needless to say, my apology to Miss Forth was accepted, but all other requests about my door were firmly refused. It was Miss Forth's first experience of her ceiling shaking and probably her only one!'

LTS ibid

One Way to Keep Warm

Jimmy Dunn Courtesy of The Salisbury Museum

The accommodation was often very cold in winter during the Thirties. One student found a good way of keeping warm at night:

'In the first year I was in a temporary cubicle in what was the extension library in King's House. This room had swing doors and James, the Principal's large ginger cat (known affectionately as Jimmy Dunn) was able to push them open. As the cubicles only had curtains in the doorways he would come and settle on any convenient bed. As it was very cold in the winter we could draw an extra red blanket and my dressing gown, on the bottom of the bed, was pink. Jimmy, on the bed also, was not good aesthetically, but very warm'.

LST Ibid

The close connection between the College and the Cathedral was maintained. Students were invited to visit the South Canonry garden on Sunday mornings in the summer, and members of the Art Class were allowed to sketch there any time. Students attended the College Chapels twice a day during the week, but were free to go to the Cathedral, or churches in the town on Sundays.

'A certain Cathedral dignitary sometimes assisted the Chaplain by coming to conduct Evensong. He was very asthmatic and when he recited psalms and prayers quite a gale blew through the little building, so much so that word used to be passed round as we neared the Chapel – "Put your hats on tightly, girls, the Canon's here tonight".'

Irene Hilditch, 1917-1919

Each Sunday evening a group of students formed a nave choir for congregational Evensong at the Cathedral. They were accompanied by a 'squeeze-box,' which was wheeled forward towards the front pews. Miss Dunn was usually present. On one occasion a student arrived late and whispered an apology to her, but she is said to have replied, 'You should apologise to God, not to me'.

College Chapel Interior

Doris Pidgeon (1937-1939) had 'tears falling down my cheeks when I first sang Harvest hymns in the Cathedral and thought of my parents and brother celebrating the Harvest Home in my Devon village'.

Dr Baker was the Chaplain from 1903 until 1933 and he was succeeded by the Revd. H Carlton S Morris. Students were appointed to be Chapel Wardens.

Margaret Simmance (1936-1938) helped to decorate the window sills in the Chapel with buttercups and cow parsley on Ascension Day. Another memory was of tea with the Chaplain and his wife at 24, The Close. The students had enjoyed playing the Moonlight Sonata on the pianola.

Gertrude Miles (1936-1938) described her duties as Chapel Warden:

'My duties were to ring the bell for services, arrange books opened at the appropriate passages on the reading-desk, and conduct the Chaplain (we called him 'Prof') from his sanctum to the Chapel when all was ready'.

At Christmas 1934 the Bishop of Sherborne and Mrs Allen gave a party to the whole College at King's House, with 'hilarious games, dancing and very original competitions. An informal supper was laid in the Dining Hall, with a roaring fire in the dog-grate'.

The Bishop of Salisbury (the Rt.Revd. St Clair Donaldson), the Dean of Salisbury (the Rt. Revd. John Randolph) and the Archdeacon and Precentor of Sarum (the Venerable Harry Carpenter) all died within nine months of each other in 1935 - 1936. These three people had all been in close touch with the life and work of the College and had taken a personal interest in staff and students alike. The Bishop had been given the affectionate name of 'Sinclair Sarum' by the students.

'Prof' Morris

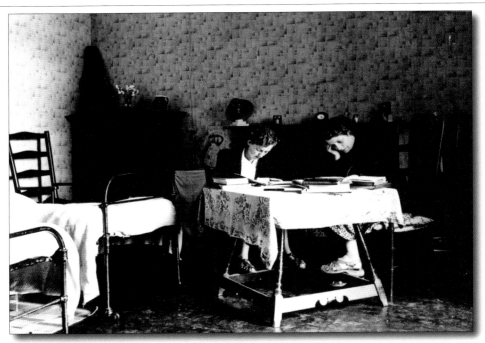

Students studying in the late 1920s (Courtesy of The Salisbury Museum)

In the 1998 College Magazine, Winifred Hedgeman described a typical College Sunday when attendance at all services was compulsory:

8.00 a.m. Holy Communion in the Cathedral – a limited number of seats in the choir were reserved for the college, for which we had to sign on Saturday night. If you missed the service you had to attend 9.00 a.m. prayers in College, taken by the Principal – and tell her why you had missed 8 o'clock.

10.00 a.m. Compulsory choir practice for everyone, a run through for the daily Matins and Evensong held in College Chapel Monday – Friday (attendance compulsory).

11.00 a.m. Cathedral Matins – compulsory unless one had brought to College a letter from the Vicar of our 'home church' to say that we were accustomed to a sung Eucharist as our normal Sunday worship. Although this letter was lodged with the Principal, every Sunday morning we had to go to her study at 9.55 a.m. precisely to ask for permission to go to St Martin's. Periodically she would attempt to dissuade us in favour of Cathedral Matins.

2.00 p.m. - 4.00 p.m. Sunday afternoon was 'quiet time' when we were not allowed to move around College.

6.30 p.m. Evensong in the Cathedral in our allotted places in the South Transept. If there was a vacant seat, Miss Forth demanded an explanation from the absentee.

In this 'compulsory day' Winifred found the sung Mass at St Martin's 'an oasis' and looked back on it with great affection.

'Establishing a Pattern in our Lives'

By the late Thirties the routine was much less rigid. A student from that period, who lived in the 'North Extension', remembered:

'I cannot remember how long it took to establish a pattern in our lives, but by half-term we had done so: - rise at 6.30 a.m. (own choice), get a bath – anywhere (nobody else was having one) – find a cup of tea, do organ practice or help in Chapel, breakfast at 8 .a.m., short service in Chapel (I believe attendance was optional by this time), lectures at 9.30 a.m., milk and biscuits in the Milky Way, more lectures, dinner 1 p.m. games field or visit schools, tea 4.30 p.m., then Rangers, Choir, Drama group and other activities before supper followed by Chapel at 8.30 p.m. We were in bed and lights out by 10 p.m. Saturday and Sunday were comparatively free. When we were second years we went to early service in the Cathedral and came back to Deanery Room for a whole hour of talk with friends while we drank cups of tea'.

LST ibid

Missionary Zeal

The lively interest in Mission work continued, and in 1930 students helped at the 'Salisbury Missionary Exhibition'. The College branch of the UMCA (Universities' Mission to Central Africa) organised evenings that were 'interesting and exhilarating'. Bazaars, sales of work, activities such as hair cutting, making sweets, darning stockings and mending punctures raised money for the school that the College supported at Miesi in the Diocese of Zanzibar. Barnard's Cross supported the Madagascar Mission, but when the House was closed the two missionary societies joined together as 'King's House Missionary Study Circle', sharing activities and dividing income between the two Missions.

Students went abroad for mission work, sometimes because of shortage of teaching posts in England, but also in response to missionary calls. The 1932 Magazine records Violet Hurn as Principal of the Missionary College in Ibadan, S Nigeria, Dorothy Saintsbury working in British Honduras and Georgina Lee as Headmistress of the Girls' High School in Ijebu Ode, Nigeria. In 1931 Dorothy Stubbings went to Nganwa (Eastern Africa) as an educational missionary. Old students also worked in the Mission field in Tanganyika, Uganda, Southern Rhodesia, Basutoland and Jamaica, as well as in many other parts of the developing world. They were welcomed back to College, where they often gave talks to students and visited members of staff.

The Play Centre

In 1935, with the support of the College Managers and Canon Willson, a Play Centre was opened at the George Herbert Infants' School on Friday evenings. The First Year Infant/Junior Group students made this their special project: they visited the parents, made games and toys, and in groups of five were responsible for each meeting. On one occasion when a group was late, two small boys set off for College to fetch them, which indicates how much the evenings were enjoyed!

When the Coronation was celebrated in 1937 a party was held at the school, after which the children came to the College garden to watch a performance of 'Beauty and the Beast' and to enjoy a treasure hunt. They arrived wearing home-made crowns and left cheerfully waving balloons.

When the George Herbert School closed, St Martin's School became available and the Play Centre continued there. Equipment from the first school was restored along with several toys found in the Deanery attic. The toys were scrubbed and cleaned by the students who sought special permission to go out and purchase extra supplies of 'Lux' soap flakes. All was ready on time for the 60 children who arrived for the first session:

'The children were registered as they entered, and it was found that many of those invited had brought the rest of their family and in some cases older children as well. In fact the age range was nine months to ten years. The children usually began to arrive in twos and threes from 4.30 p.m. The girls made a line for the playhouses, the boys for the trucks, barrows, building apparatus or mechanical toys. Play continued for the next hour; trucks loaded with bricks and perambulators with dolls were pushed among a noisy, happy crowd of children. Amidst the noise a voice arose, 'Toys away now, children.' Miraculously, it seems, the collections were gathered into small arms and taken into the adjoining cloakroom. While this was happening the playroom was arranged for story groups. At 5.45 stories were finished, and the session closed with musical games. The children stalked from the room sedately shaking hands with the tired and grubby students'.

STC Magazine, 1939

Christmas 1938 was a special time for the children at St Martin's School, as students presented a performance of *Snow White and the Seven Dwarfs*, *The Three Little Pigs* and *The Old Woman who lived in a Shoe*. They were delighted when Father Christmas arrived with a sack brimming over with treats.

St Mary's House

St Mary's House in St Martin's Church Street was run by an Anglican Order of nuns who had care of several girls. On Friday evenings the students taught the girls some simple country dancing. In July 1928 they entertained some of the girls and two Sisters to tea and a treasure hunt and games in the College Gardens, followed by a performance of *Cinderella* in the Old Deanery Hall. A student recalled, 'that the time for departure came too soon, for both hostesses and guests showed that it had been a really successful party'.

In 2008 Edith Maidment (née Harding) wrote a fascinating account of her life, including her two years at Salisbury Training College. She was born in the village of Semley and in 1918 started at Bishop Wordworth's School, boarding at a hostel in Salisbury. Edith spent a year as a student teacher before starting teacher training:

'At College I elected to study French and Art as my two main subjects. The French group was made up of girls from the Channel Islands and those from Bishop Wordworth's School. The Art Group met at Barnard's Cross and the lecturer was Miss Malcombe.

I found life at College very restricting. Students had lectures in the mornings and evenings, free time in the afternoon. We were not allowed to go to town on Tuesdays and Saturdays, when the market was there. On Saturdays, if you wanted to go for a special outing, you signed to say where you had gone. On winter Saturdays you must be in by 6.30 pm, in the summer by 7 pm. If you went for a country walk it must be in threes.

During the first year at College we did a needlework course: basic stitches had to be mastered, and a darn perfected. I remember cutting a hole in the knee of my gym tights to perform the feat. The darn was given full marks, so the mutilation of my tights was justified. We also had to produce a "thrift" garment. Thriftiness was a big virtue in those days after the First World War: money was scarce and it was a case of "Make do and Mend". I remember unpicking one of my dresses, washing and turning it and making a child's dress from the material'.

Edith recalled the dreaded 'Majors':

'Each week at College, a student had to give a lesson to a class brought from one of the Salisbury Schools in front of the lecturers concerned and students of your year. These lessons were called 'Majors' and we congregated together beforehand to sing the 'Major' song to give us moral courage. I cannot remember all the words but it ended with 'Marching along to Majors – doomed to do or die!'

Edith Maidment, *On Semley Hill: A Memoir*

Freda Brigden (1919-1921) remembered the *Major Song* sung before dinner to cheer up the "victim".

'Major days, major days,
Crits that set you quaking
'Mid the crowded watchers waiting
    In a haze, mem'ry strays,
You forget your notes of lessons
    Aims stray far away'.

Sung to the tune of *College Days*.

The College Staff and Students, 1923-1925

Biology Illustration — Mary Cole. 1926.

Staff and Students 1923-1925

Courtesy of The Salisbury Museum

King's House Regulations

Courtesy of Wiltshire & Swindon
History Centre

Salisbury Training College.
KING'S HOUSE.

Each Incoming Student is expected to note carefully the following Regulations —

Boxes must be of moderate size, and must have the Student's initials painted clearly outside. Two small boxes are preferable to one very large one. On the inside of this circular letter is a list of clothing required for College life.

All articles of clothing must be marked with the owner's initial and surname. Cash's worked tapes are best for this purpose, as marking ink washes out. Students are advised to keep a complete list of their clothing for reference ; as there is but small accommodation, it is wiser to bring only the clothes required for the special term.

Unnecessary books and novels should not be brought, as there is a good Recreation Library in the College. Students may not bring cakes, etc., *with them,* but eatables can be sent afterwards from home, provided that such food is only eaten at meal times as allowed, and kept in the store cupboard.

All medicines are provided by the College ; it is considered undesirable that Students should take any medicine of their own without the knowledge of the House Mistress.

Students must be responsible for the safe keeping of the money and trinkets which they have in their possession at College. *They must bring a small box with a lock for this purpose.*

The College will assemble on ___22 SEP. 1931___

Tea will be provided for those who arrive before 5.30. Students are requested to let the House Mistress know the train by which they will arrive. *This rule applies to each vacation throughout their College life.*

All necessary clothing required for the first night should be packed in a small week-end case, of a size suitable for short holidays.

Signed ___A Cook___
_____ House Mistress.

To Miss ___Norah Hallett___

Each Student must bring this Circular Letter with her for reference.

Freda Brigdon

Whilst living in Audley, Freda (1919-1921) had an unforgettable experience:

> 'One of the sights of College Days I shall never forget was to see from our Audley dormitory window the whole of the great West Front of the Cathedral change to a wonderful lucid green just as the sun was about to set. It is so rare a sight in England and fades so quickly. We were fortunate to see it'.

Was this the Northern Lights over Salisbury?

Sybil Harty Geraldine Baker

Sybil Baker, who was the younger sister of Katharine Annie Baker, trained at the College from 1928-1930. She lived in a room over the North Gate entrance to The Close. She was also an artist and one of her drawings was from inside the gate looking down the High Street.

After teacher training, she undertook further studies at the Trinity College of Music as she was an accomplished pianist. Sybil became very ill with rheumatoid arthritis and she was treated at the Royal Mineral Hospital in Bath with gold injections. Bath was bombed in the blitz, but luckily Sybil escaped unhurt. Her health deteriorated further but her brain remained very active. She became totally blind and sadly died aged just 39. She was a remarkable woman who loved life and was a great loss to her family and friends.

A 'Snapshot' of Mary Uppington

Mary Uppington(1935-1937) arrived at College after spending a year as a pupil teacher at the PNEU School in Southampton. In her first year, she had a room on the third floor in the attics of Old Deanery, but she then moved to Audley with her great friend Elizabeth Golledge for the second year. Mary trained as an Infant/Junior teacher and took English as a main subject. She had happy memories of Botany field trips and of cycling into the countryside at weekends.

One of Mary's School Practices was at Downton School, where she had a class of 35 infants. She divided the children into three different groups for Number work, using 'sum cards' with those who could divide and subtract. Shells were provided for counting. Reading was centred around nursery rhymes, using sentence strips and word and picture matching activities. Games and drama were also used and Mary commented that the children were 'very interested in the rhyme because they had dramatised it the day before'.

A gramophone was used for Music. The class sang nursery rhymes and were also encouraged to move to music. Mary told a little story about 'helping in the house' and suggested various actions such as sweeping the floor, brushing boots and beating eggs that the children could do in time to the music.

Relaxing by the Boathouse

Courtesy of The Salisbury Museum

The Training College,
m The Close,
Salisbury.

Miss Mary Uppington has a poised and courteous manner in dealing with children.

She has a thorough grasp of Education Principles and a good background knowledge, so that she will develop into a valuable teacher with experience.

She shows originality and determination and would always do her best for the children of the school.

She has made a special study of reading and her interest in this fundamental subject makes for scientific and intelligent teaching.

B.

Mary Uppington's reference
Courtesy of Wiltshire and Swindon History Centre

In 1937 Mary took up her first teaching post at Petersfield Infant's School. After the outbreak of war large numbers of children from Portsmouth were evacuated to Petersfield. The school was shared; the Petersfield children had their lessons in the mornings and the Portsmouth children and their teachers took over the premises for the afternoons. Mary's two daughters, Hannah and Sarah Boothman, both followed her to College in the 1960s and 1970s respectively.

What were PNEU schools?

The PNEU movement was started by The Parents' National Educational Union (PNEU) began as a central organisation in 1895. The movement was started by Charlotte Mason in 1885. She wanted education to be a positive extension of home life and for learning to be fun. She also put great emphasis on a broad curriculum, particularly music, art and nature.

NO SMOKING

'Those who smoked were allowed to do so in the Handwork Room on Fridays for one hour. I was not a smoker and do not smoke now, but once I did smoke by the river one dark night with several of my friends, and felt really wicked'.

Student from the Thirties (*LST ibid*)

Two wonderful years at Salisbury Diocesan Training College, 1927–1929

Vera Johns died in 2011 aged 101. She attended College reunions until she was well into her nineties. In 2004 some of her memories were recorded in the College Magazine.

'It was with great anticipation that on a sunny day in September 1927 I first beheld the wonderful King's House, where I was to spend the next two years. This splendid old house, now the museum, was at its best, the flower beds in front still full of blossoming roses. But the outstanding glory was the great Virginia Creeper which covered the whole façade of the building, with its autumn blaze of gold and scarlet. I felt that I was entering a palace.

We newcomers entered a small side door, where Juniors and Seniors were all being sorted out with their new dormitories. We were given a beautiful room in the front, looking straight across to the Cathedral. This had been the Dean's bedroom and still had lovely William Morris wallpaper on the walls.

Our Principal, Miss Forth, was a wonderful lady, small in stature but great in personality, deeply respected and perhaps a little feared by the Junior students.

Sometimes the restraints of our sequestered life did become too much. On one notable occasion, a student who was usually a sensible country girl, charged from the top to the bottom of the King's House curved staircase, swinging round the great newel post and shouting "Aarh…" at the top of her voice! Reaching a group of us at the bottom, she came to herself and appeared to be just as frightened and astonished as we were! Of course the noise was heard in the Principal's study and the perpetrator was duly sent for. A few minutes later she emerged from Miss Forth's study looking so white-faced and dumbfounded that we feared the worst. "What happened?" we asked. In a trembling little voice she replied, "Miss Forth asked me why I did it and I said I didn't know, but I had just felt like it… and she said that we all feel like that at times, but we must learn to control these feelings". Our respect for Miss Forth was much increased.

I loved staying late after evening service in the Cathedral and listening to the outgoing voluntary on the great organ. The lights were all gradually put out or dimmed and it seemed as if our magnificent Cathedral was itself being gently put to sleep.

One early Spring morning two or three of us decided to go up to Old Sarum before breakfast. We dressed quietly and made our way to the High Street Gate. This was still closed for the night, but we climbed through the small opening and ran or walked all the way up to Old Sarum. It was a magical and glorious feeling to breathe the cool air and watch the sun rise over this ancient place, and we did not want to leave. We had to run even faster to be safely back in time for 8 o'clock breakfast and our mild exploit was never known.

My birthday at the beginning of May was during a school practice week at Amesbury village School. Here the Headmaster rejoiced in the wonderful name of Mr Cowmeadow, whilst his wife, Mrs Cowmeadow, was Head of the Infant School. At break she hurried across to the school house to feed baby Cowmeadow. They were both excellent teachers, strict but kind.

Most of my College memories are very happy ones, of friendly and rewarding times leading to the development of a deep and lasting faith, based on our Christian motto'.

"In Quietness and in Confidence
shall be your Strength."

Students in the 1920s

Courtesy of The Salisbury Museum

Courtesy of The Salisbury Museum

'Uniform was white blouses with our College tie, and navy blue skirts. Our beaver hats were black with a college hatband, striped for King's House and zigzag for Barnard's Cross'.

Elsie Tiller, a student in the 1930s, could never quite understand the general dislike of the compulsory hats: 'I was perhaps old fashioned enough to be proud to wear one'.

Many students resented the hats that made them so conspicuous:

'We had to wear ungainly beaver hats in the winter and our silhouette on the chapel wall at the evening service caused much mirth. When we went to Whitelands, we had to wear our boaters and the children used to shout after us "the white 'at brigade"!

The Seniors wore panamas in the summer, but the Juniors only had straw hats and when they got wet the crowns rose to peaks that were difficult to flatten. How thankful we were to get rid of these "donkey's breakfasts" at the end of our first year. It was the secret custom on the last night of the Summer term to make a raft of these straws (first removing the hat bands), take it down to the river and set light to it, before letting it float away into the darkness.

We wore navy blue drill tunics for Physical Training, over which we wore a long coat if we had to cross The Close. On one occasion the Principal met a girl with her coat unbuttoned and her knees visible, and after that we had to wear skirts as well. Imagine what we felt like on a hot summer's day! We wore black tights and black plimsolls for Physical Training. We had small brooches to fasten our ties down, a black shield-shape with Barnard's Cross or King's House in white. The blazers were at first navy with STC in white on the pocket, but as this looked like a tennis club, it was changed to a Tudor Rose'.

The students' 'morals' were well protected. Hanging their tights, worn for PE and Games, out of cubicle windows to dry, met with reproachful prohibition.

In fashionable circles trousers were beginning to be worn by women, but the Training College students were not even allowed to wear trousers in a play, unless they were made of paper, and they must not have been borrowed from men.

Students could get out of their uniforms and don their own dresses on joyous Saturday evenings. Vera Johns remembered that her mother had made her 'a patterned dress with a full circular skirt, the fashion that year. I delighted in secretly running down to the river to the magical pine grove, and in the darkness of the late evening I sang and danced so that my skirt swirled out into its full circle'.

Uniform was abolished in 1935, but hats were still obligatory for Chapel. Gertrude Miles bought a 'daring navy blue fur felt with a scarlet feather slotted through the crown'. Fellow students considered this very bold, but she got away with it. College and the outside world were growing a little closer.

Student Group 1930s   Courtesy of The Salisbury Museum

Students in the late 1930s   Courtesy of The Salisbury Museum

Fire Practices were a regular part of College life. Students in 1901 were aware of a 'large and threatening fire in the town, which burnt out a factory and also made a great gap in the picturesque old Market Place. We fully expected to have a revival of energetic fire drill and shivering plunges down the chute, but Miss Hill mercifully spared us'.

Margaret Logan (1926-28) remembered Fire Drill at Barnard's Cross:

'The ringing of hand bells indicated Fire Drill. A red blanket was thrown down to indicate the "seat" of the fire. We then climbed through a window in the dormitory, down an outdoor iron stairway in our dressing gowns and assembled in the grounds below. This usually happened after bedtime in summer and caused some hilarity'.

The Hadow Reports, which were produced by the government's Consultative Committee, had a significant impact on the development of the Education System.

In 1926 *The Education of the Adolescent* proposed the division of the elementary school system into two stages, Junior and Senior, with a break at eleven for all.

The 1931 Report *The Primary School* and the 1933 Report *Infant and Nursery Schools* showed considerable concern for the welfare and well-being of pupils and contained several forward-looking ideas. The introduction to the 1931 Report stated:

'The root of the matter is, after all, simple. What a wise and good parent would desire for his own children, a nation must desire for all children. Class sizes should take account of 'the experience, the curiosity, and the awakening powers and interests of the children themselves. The curriculum of the primary school is to be thought of in terms of activity and experience rather than knowledge to be acquired and facts to be stored'.

The importance of good Nursery and Infant Education was the key focus of the 1933 report. With regard to teachers: 'Freedom in planning and arranging her work is essential for the teacher if the ever present danger of a lapse into mechanical routine is to be avoided'. (Many current teachers could probably make pertinent comments about this point with regard to education in England today!)

The Plowden Report of 1967 revisited many of the original proposals made by Hadow. The recommendations concerning the structure of education were eventually adopted and implemented, although the complete re-grading of schools into primary and secondary levels did not occur until the 1944 Education Act. In 1936 it was agreed that the school leaving age should be raised to fifteen, but this was postponed owing to the outbreak of war and was not implemented until 1947.

The Hadow Reports must have featured in Education lectures during this period and led to many thoughtful discussions and debates amongst College students. What would they have thought of the progressive and optimistic ideas which were put forward?

BADGE & BAND. SALISBURY TRAINING COLLEGE – THE CLOSE.

Am at School under Miss Scott this week. Lesson to Ett...

A student who entered College in 1931 remembered features of the course for primary teachers:

> 'The teaching of reading was paramount, the sentence method being particularly advocated, although phonics were seen as being very important. One of our holiday tasks was to make a sentence board that was suitable for classroom use. Projects were 'in vogue' and for my final school practice, I did Hiawatha and spent countless hours searching for feathers, hessian, beads and raffia. The children loved it as much as me'!

In 1936 the College accepted a student who had previously been refused a place elsewhere. Rheumatic fever had left her with a heart murmur and she must have been overjoyed that her application to Salisbury was successful.

> 'I opted to teach Upper Junior/Senior and the subjects I chose were English, History, Biology, Art and Music. I still had to do some work in Needlework and Handwork, because almost every teacher needed to teach these at some period of her career. We also had to take courses in Hygiene and P.T, and in Divinity. Theory of Education was also a "must" and my tutor was Miss Grist, whose thorough training stood me in good stead throughout my career. I always enjoyed my Biology lectures and practical work under Miss Stevenson's enthusiastic supervision, but the zoological side was not familiar to me as this had been considered not quite "naice" for schoolgirls. Owing to my heart murmur, I had not been allowed to do any physical exercises at school, but I "got by" under Miss Story's bracing supervision. Art work was a joy, for Miss Malcombe taught us to be adventurous with colour and line'.

Harrowing School Practice?

> 'In my first year I went with Lottie Extance to Twerton Senior Boys' School, Bath, where we were the only two "ladies" among eleven schoolmasters. 'We were in excellent lodgings with a landlady famous for her pancakes'.
>
> Irene Filleul (1926-1928)

Dorothy Touzel (1928-1930) enjoyed her week of School Practice in Parkstone in a well-run school with a friendly atmosphere:

> 'We boarded at a nearby guest house where we were very well treated and the food was particularly good'.

Letitia Grottick (1934-1936) went to Swindon for School Practice:

> 'We were taken by coach. We had been led to believe that Swindon children had never seen a garden, so we all made 'gardens' in boxes, tins, bowls etc. They were all put on the rack in the coach. Several times on the way we were strewn with plants and soil when the coach hit a bumpy or twisting patch of road. In Swindon my friend and I went to the Circus one Saturday afternoon. It was the first time either of us had been to such a place and we felt very guilty about going'!

Gladys Bone (1923-1925) went to Wilton Boys' School for a fortnight's School Practice in her second year. This was the first time that students had been allocated to the school and the experience was new to the Headmaster. Whilst discussing a P.E. lesson that she was going to take with the senior boys, Gladys suddenly realised that the fact that she would be clad in a gymslip and white blouse was an alarming shock to the Headmaster:

'For the boys to see me thus clad was highly dangerous to their morals – a gymslip was OUT. Feeling very silly, I told my troubles to "The Limb" (Miss Story), who was to criticise the lesson. She passed me on to "Aunt Bee", Miss Forth, the Principal. Bravely I explained the situation and awaited her verdict. Obviously she thought it quite ridiculous, but I must courteously do as the Headmaster wished, and give my lesson in a navy skirt and white blouse.

The memorable day dawned. It was a scorcher. Suddenly, in the greatest agitation, "The Limb" rushed up to me (wearing a white blouse and green gymslip for good measure) and whispered: "An HMI has arrived. On no account modify the lesson for the heat, pretend we are in the Arctic". This Inspector believed in physical exertion to the point of collapse for all concerned.

So in the boiling sun, on that asphalt playground, the lesson was given. On its success or failure depended the reliability of "The Limb's" marking and assessment system. Success was ours! The boys, having no option, had responded well to the point of collapse. I felt dizzy but the standard for the College had been justified and all was well'.

Gladys Peach, *A Patchwork Quilt*

Nature Walk on School Practice 1935-1937

Children on School Practice 1935-1937

In the Thirties the ordinary course in Art was transferred to the Morrison Hall which was quite a distance from College. This meant that students often had to carry patty tins full of poster paint through the streets quite quickly in order to be back at King's House for lunch. A student recalled that no paint was ever spilled! She also remembered 'The Piper':

'One day, just after we had started at the Morrison Hall, we heard a piper playing the bagpipes outside. Miss Malcombe dashed out and persuaded him to come in. The planned lesson was scrapped and it became one of sketching the piper. We should have liked him to play while we drew, but he insisted he could only play if he walked around the hall. Joan Mancy subsequently made a lino cut from her drawing and it was printed in the College Magazine'.

IMPRESSIONS OF COLLEGE BY AN INSPECTRESS

'Miss Monkhouse described her impressions of the College and its work from her experience as Inspectress. She said she had known the College for 13 years, and in a way knew it more intimately than anybody there, except perhaps the Students and the Staff, because she had the pleasure of visiting it in almost every capacity. She saw the students in their work and in their play: she heard them sing; she saw them sew; and she could almost feel them think. (Laughter.) She very nearly saw them asleep, because she looked in their bedrooms to see if they kept them tidy. All she saw filled her with admiration, respect and affection. (Applause) First of all it was so thoroughly honest. A great many beautiful things went on at that College. The work of the students, she thought, was directed with a feeling of beauty behind it, and that filled one with love and respect for it. The College was also very alive'.

Miss Monkhouse, HMI Speech Day, 1924
STC Magazine, 1921-1925

The College must have been pleased that someone as helpful and positive as Miss Monkhouse was still inspecting the College in the 1930s:

'In March Miss Monkhouse came with her colleagues to inspect the practical teaching. The students were working in a number of schools in Wiltshire and Dorset, and also in Salisbury and Bournemouth and all these centres were visited by the inspectors. Warm praise was given to the practical training which the students were receiving, and they commended the variety in the types of schools to which they gave access'.

Diocesan Training College Salisbury
Report for the Collegiate Year, 1932-1933

Examinations remained plentiful and difficult. In the 1920s students were examined in: Teaching, English, Hygiene and Physical Training, Geography, Mathematics, Biology, Music, Drawing, Needlework, and Handwork which was combined with Needlework. In 1927 Housecraft and French were added to the list. Staff tried to be as helpful and supportive as possible. Miss Fowler, a Lecturer in French during the 1920s, inspired students in the three-hour French Final examination by placing a red rose on each desk.

In the Salisbury Diocesan Training College Report for 1932-1933, an interesting comment is made about the academic standard of students at this time.

'In the final Examination of the Joint Board of Reading University and Associated Training Colleges, the College sent in 97 students, of whom 85 obtained certificates. One has to be re-examined in two subjects and 11 in one subject. No students failed the whole examination. The number of successes is not so large as usual. It is true, probably for the whole country, that while the recent admissions of numbers to the Training Colleges has implied a lower academic level among the students, the standard of the examination itself has tended to rise in deference to the educational needs of the times'.

The Report commented on the increasing demand from Local Authorities for teachers who are well qualified in 'Scripture.' In 1933 all Salisbury students were presented for the Archbishop's Examination in Religious Knowledge and every student passed.

Students survived the regular inspections and examinations. The College continued to strive to ensure that they were well prepared to teach and to face whatever challenges might lie ahead.

UNIVERSITY OF READING AND ASSOCIATED TRAINING COLLEGES

Certificate Examination for Two-Year Students
1932–34

HYGIENE

MONDAY, JULY 2, 1934, 2–4.30

Please write T. C. 4 at the top of the first page of answers, or on the outside of the cover of your answer-book.

Four questions only to be answered, of which Question 1 is compulsory.

1. 'In no case should one interpret conduct on the part of a pupil as misdemeanour without first attempting an explanation on the ground of physical or organic causes.' Discuss this.

2. Describe the structure and functions of the skin. What knowledge of infectious skin diseases should a teacher have, and how should this knowledge be used?

3. What principles should govern the choice of a diet? How can digestion be helped or hindered?

4. From what points of view is slum clearance essential?

5. (a) What measures should be taken to safeguard the eyesight of children in schools?
   (b) What are the common causes and symptoms of deafness?

6. Write notes on **three** of the following :—
   (a) (i) Jenner,   (ii) Lister.
   (b) 'Safety first.'
   (c) Prevention of deformities of the feet.
   (d) Rickets.
   (e) Dental decay.

4 N 4

Hygiene Examination Paper

Courtesy of Wiltshire & Swindon History Centre

Final Examination Certificate, 1923

Courtesy of Wiltshire & Swindon History Centre

'Life in Training Colleges is very far removed from the steady monotonous round of twenty years ago. The isolation which was said to characterise each College in the old days has been broken up in many ways, but in none more effectively than that which has led two Womens' Colleges to amalgamate for a short time and share each other's life'.

> Report of the Board of Education for
> the Empire Education Museum

Whitelands Training College had opened in 1842, exactly one year after Salisbury Training College. The exchange of students for 'five long summer days' started in 1920.

'The journey is undertaken by char-a-bancs; at seven on Saturday morning the Salisbury Students start for London, and with a stop at Basingstoke for "elevenses", drive straight on through some of the prettiest scenery of Hants and Surrey, approach London through Brentford and reach Whitelands in time for 1.15 lunch. After an hour or two to cool the motors and rest the drivers, the Whitelanders start, and leaving the thronged streets soon reach the open country and speed to Salisbury in time for supper. The green soft freshness of The Close, the spaciousness of the College gardens, the coolness of the river and the rich quaint old-world surroundings rest and delight them'.

Salisbury offered study opportunities for Geography, Botany, History and Art, together with visits to places such as Old Sarum, Groveley Woods, the New Forest and Salisbury Plain. In London, students visited galleries and museums and viewed 'sights' by omnibus. They also visited different types of schools, such as Nursery Classes and Schools for the Deaf.

Florence Renouf (1927-1929) commented that 'the high standard of Needlework and Handwork which we saw at Frogmore Special School for Handicapped Children made a great impression'.

'The College was aware that the exchanges were also providing students with many new experiences and opportunities, 'both educational and otherwise'. Florence, whose home was in Jersey, enjoyed visiting Kew Gardens and the Zoo.'

> Diocesan Training College Report, 1932-1933

Winifred Buxton and Winifred Jones (1922-1924), found that the exchange with Whitelands was a revelation. Shocked by the bugs and lice in the slum schools, they cut their hair short. Perhaps this was in fact a good excuse for them to have the fashionable new 'bob' and 'shingle' hairstyles!

Margaret Simmance (1936-1938) had vivid memories of her time in London:

'We saw some wonderful work being done in slum schools where the long Victorian forms were tiered in some of the classrooms. One teacher said that if you asked a child to bring soil to plant a seedling, she could only collect dust from the gutter – the only soil she knew'.

"That the Governing Body of *the Salisbury Diocesan* Training College, having considered the scheme now submitted for co-operation between the University of Reading and certain Training Colleges, hereby approves the Scheme and authorises application to be made to the University of Reading for the admission of *the Salisbury Diocesan* Training College to membership under the conditions set forth in the Scheme".

Courtesy of Courtesy of Wiltshire & Swindon History Centre

In 1923 the Board of Education set up a Consultative Committee to investigate the examination of students in Training Colleges. This resulted in a recommendation that the Board of Education should withdraw from its function as the examining body for the Teachers' Certificate.

Saturday November 14th 1925: An Important Meeting

The College Council was informed that following the decision of the Board of Education, Training Colleges had two alternatives. They could become affiliated to local universities or they could unite and form a Central Examination Board.

The Bishop of Salisbury felt that it would be 'best to affiliate with a local University', but only on the following conditions:

1 Colleges had the right to choose their own Universities.

2 A 2-year course at a Training College should count towards the period of residence required for a degree.

3 Existing teaching staff should be recognised by the Universities.

4 The Colleges should be allowed to reserve a proportion of the curriculum to provide, for example, proper provision for religious education.

5 There should be no question of this College moving from Salisbury.

The Minutes Book recorded that 'it was unanimously decided to endorse the policy of association with a University, demanding safeguards and avoiding haste'.

Considerable concern about the possibility that the Universities might take over the organisation of courses and syllabuses at the Training Colleges led the College Council to invite the Duchess of Atholl, Parliamentary Secretary of Education, to Speech Day in 1926. In her speech, she provided reassurance that the Board of Education did not wish to change the identity, traditions and character of any colleges. Meanwhile, Miss Forth, the Principal, chose to focus on the academic achievements of students, as well as emphasising 'aspects of education that the College offered, which did not occur in a University, but which were as developmental and cultural as the academic'.

LST ibid

At Speech Day in 1927, the Dean explained that the College had decided to become affiliated to Reading University. He was convinced of the advantages that this affiliation would bring to the College.

Courtesy of Courtesy of Wiltshire & Swindon History Centre

T. C. 201

UNIVERSITY OF READING AND ASSOCIATED TRAINING COLLEGES

Certificate Examination for Two-Year Students
1932-34

Salisbury Diocesan Training College

PRINCIPLES OF TEACHING—SPECIAL COURSE B

WEDNESDAY, JUNE 27, 1934, 9.30–12.30

Please write T. C. 201 *at the top of the first page of answers.*

Five *questions to be answered,* **one** *at least from each section.*

SECTION A

1. 'Writing starts from speech, but gradually develops away from it and acquires a technique of its own.' What is the bearing of this fact on the teaching of composition in school?

2. By what means, in the various stages of school life, would you help pupils 'to understand and enjoy informative literature and creative literature'?

3. How would you try to lead elder pupils to some realization of values in newspapers and periodicals of to-day?

SECTION B

4. Show how you would expect the following problem to be solved by reasonably good pupils (a) of 10, and (b) of 13 years old. Indicate how far the differences are due to differences in knowledge, and how far to differences in mental development :—
'Certain types of stamped envelopes were, till recently, sold in packets of 11 for 1/6; now they are sold in packets of 15 for 2/-. Has the price been raised or lowered? By how much?'

The final examination of June 1931 was the third to be held since the Board of Education had ceased to examine. The work of the Joint Committees of Universities and Training Colleges had passed its initial stages. Members of staff had been welcomed by the Senior Common Room at Reading and Professors from the University visited the College for lectures, as well as for oral and practical exams.

A new era had begun.

Miss Forth, the Duchess of Atholl and the Bishop of Salisbury
Courtesy of The Salisbury Museum

1919 must have been a bumper year for apples. Baked apples were often on the monotonous College menu: 'Oh the clatter of 80 spoons and forks attacking 80 apples on china plates'.

Reminiscences from the 1920s show that the students were usually well filled:

> 'The row of maids in black dresses with white caps and aprons standing ready to bring in food; the favourite steamed raisin pudding was more satisfying than the frequent stewed prunes and custard'.

> 'As the Staff trooped in, we all had to stand behind our chairs and not sit until Grace had been said and the Lecturers were seated. Each Lecturer took the head of a table, and we were supposed to move round so that we all had a turn at talking to one of them. We had lots of suet puddings for dinner and plenty of bread and margarine at tea and supper-time. We had jam one day and cake the next at tea. We could have our own 'tuck' at these meals. Tea was made in an urn at tea-time and the same urn was used for our supper cocoa. We were never quite sure what we were drinking, but we were not very critical. There were also large lumps of cheese at supper.

> Sunday supper was a cold meal, including trifle made with all the week's left-over cake, to be eaten when we liked as we came in from Church.
>
> Muriel Hodder 1923 -1925

Norah Hallett, a vegetarian, was told by the Housemistress that if she was hungry she should tell someone – 'but I never did, I just left out the meat and the fish, and survived'. Perhaps Norah benefitted from the rental in the early 1930s of an additional acre of ground at the back of King's House, in order to provide more home-grown vegetables.

Janet Tarr remembered the food as being of poor quality, but she enjoyed 'bangers' which the students were given for high tea on Saturdays. Doris Pidgeon revelled in the food parcels sent by her mother. 'It was a great joy to receive Devonshire Clotted Cream, which we kept cool in a special container hidden in a secret place by the river in the Deanery garden'.

Muriel Hodder (1923-1925) described the enjoyment and comforting ritual of Sunday Afternoon Tea:

> 'In our Junior year we took it in turns, two at a time, to prepare our Sunday tea. We each paid 3d to the two on duty, who bought salmon for sandwiches, and cakes – usually doughnuts. Bread and margarine were sent down to us so that sandwiches could be prepared. During our Senior year arrangements were quite different. We each brought a tea-set from home. On Sunday mornings we "bagged" a small table by chalking initials on it. In the afternoon we set up our tea parties. We were allowed visitors from outside and members of staff. In summer we often held them on the lawn'.

A former Barnard's Cross student observed the garden from her window:

> 'On the lawn I see a snow-white covered table adorned with tea things round which five stately ladies will soon be reclining in deck chairs and partaking of the "cup that cheers but does not inebriate" – a most pleasant scene'.

King's House Dining Room

Courtesy of The Salisbury Museum

Saturday Tea at King's House

Lunchtime in King's House Garden

Courtesy of The Salisbury Museum

Eve Ramsey, a student between 1925 and 1927, shared a room with Olive, a girl whose family had a history of tuberculosis (TB). Eve remembered Olive waking up one morning and announcing that she had the symptoms of TB. She was sent to a hospital in Bath, but sadly never recovered. Eve was given no medical checks herself and was remarkably lucky not to have contracted the disease.

A College Health Report for 1931-32 recorded the fact that two students were removed to the Isolation Hospital with mumps and scarlet fever. One student was away for two months due to appendicitis and another spent half a term at home, recovering from nervous debility. Two students were laid up for some weeks with knee injuries and another was medically advised to withdraw for a year after an unusually severe asthmatic attack.

Gertrude Miles (1936-1938) reported to the Sanatorium (San) after she had been attacked by mosquitoes along the river bank:

> 'There were no antibiotics then and the treatment was hot fomentations at regular intervals, and sitting with the feet up to relieve the painful swelling'.

Illness was no excuse for missing lectures, unless students were in the San. Marjorie Ventham (1926-1928) had memories of a huge classroom in King's House that was heated by one coal fire. Students who sat close to the fire 'roasted', whilst those further away 'froze'. They were checked in and out of lectures and not allowed to change places. Marjorie, suffering from a dreadful cold, was told by the San Sister to sit close to the fire, so she changed places with a friend. Other students followed suit. On finding out what had happened, Miss Forth was not amused. 'The lady with the physical infirmity may stay in her seat; all other ladies will kindly return to their proper positions'.

Influenza affected thirty students in King's House and fourteen at Barnard's Cross in the Lent term of 1932. In early 1933 an epidemic of influenza affected about fifty students and some of the staff. It was, however, fortunate that the subsequent fine and dry weather was favourable to the students' health. Apart from one case of measles, one (rather more serious) of swollen glands, and some small cases such as sprains, there was very little illness for the next eight months. The sick rooms were empty for most of the Autumn term, which constituted a record!

Report for the Collegiate Year, 1932-33

First Aid Practice

Courtesy of The Salisbury Museum

Down with the 'Flu' 1931

Courtesy of The Salisbury Museum

Old Students, Reunions and the College Magazine

'Yet sometimes through it all one glimpses a grey spire shimmering in the mist, or hears the lap of cool water that glides past limes that dip, and catches the scent of new mown grass in a shady Close...'

In 1922 it was suggested that the summer meeting of the Home Branch should be a joint Club meeting. This subsequently became the Annual Reunion. Muriel Hodder (1923-1925) recorded her memories:

'We were afraid we would miss our first College Reunion at Whitsun 1926 because of the General Strike, but happily disputes were settled and trains began running again. We stayed at the College, and all it cost was a box of chocolates for the student whose bed we had occupied, and a contribution to the Kitchen Staff Box. We had a Communion Service in our own Chapels on Sunday morning and many of us went to the Cathedral at 11 a.m. After lunch at the College we went to tea at KH or BX for tea with the Lecturers in the garden.

What a chattering there was over tea as we recognised, in dignified head mistresses and in mothers of families, the gay slips of students of earlier days.

After breakfast on Monday we were each given a packet of sandwiches and cake and we went out for the day. Over the years, our group went to Stonehenge, Old Sarum, Sandbanks and Bournemouth. We returned to College for supper and chats and left after breakfast the next day'.

In 1933, 350 former students attended and Dr Baker preached at the Guild Service in the Cathedral. The College Magazine for 1935 shows that by then there were eleven branches: London, Portsmouth, Southampton, Bournemouth, Weymouth, Midlands, Jersey, Guernsey, Somerset, Isle of Wight and the Home Branch. Staff and former staff often attended meetings. Miss Montgomery was still the 'untiring President' of the Jersey Branch and the Home Branch had 222 visitors to its summer meeting. The Salisbury Club was flourishing.

Salisbury Training College Magazine

In her first editorial in the College Magazine, which covered the years 1928 to 1932, Miss Dunn, the Principal, conveyed her strong desire to promote unity amongst students and old students. She appreciated the value of the magazine and made her mark on the publication, which was produced yearly until 1939. Poetry, articles and reproductions of drawings all began to appear, as well as a 'Calendar of Events', which showed the variety of lectures and performances, as well as 'occasions of recreative excitement and social jollity' that were on offer to students alongside their curriculum work, school practices and examinations. A League of Nations Union Lecture and a League of Nations Meeting are both in the 1934 - 1935 Calendar. The Meeting was attended by all the students, both events being linked with efforts to maintain peace at a time when there was growing concern about events in Europe.

Whitsun reunion 1930   Courtesy of The Salisbury Museum

Riverside reunion 1930   Courtesy of The Salisbury Museum

The original College garden   Painted by Kate Sykes

'The peonies still flower well, but we have added a number of young Delphiniums, Lupins, Campanulas, Geums and Pyrethrums which can be divided in years to come. Students and friends contributed other plants and cuttings in the autumn and from these we have some healthy looking carnations and several slips of Kerria Japonica, Buddleia and Daphne. A well grown tree of Forsythia Suspensa has also been trained against the wall and sturdy specimens of Azalea Mollis, ready to flower, have found a home near the front of the border… with so much interest in our undertaking, we ought surely to do well in time'.

STC Magazine, 1934

During difficult times the beautiful garden provided a peaceful sanctuary for the students.

'Our England is a garden and such gardens are not made
By singing "Oh how beautiful" and sitting in the shade'.
Rudyard Kipling, *The Glory of the Garden*

By the 1930s some students and staff had begun to take a keen interest in the garden at King's House. They wanted to restore the western border of King's House to something of its former beauty. The Principal gave her permission and the gardening group, including Miss Stevenson, worked regularly to this end. They planted many new shrubs and plants and moved others to new positions, replanted bulbs and sowed seeds.

Miss Grist and companion in the garden
Courtesy of The Salisbury Museum

During the 1930s the grave financial situation of the College led to measures being taken to reduce expenditure. Main meals were served for the whole College at King's House, but more drastic action was needed and it was decided 'most regretfully' to close Barnard's Cross in July 1937. The students transferred to King's House for their second year. Number 38 The Close, which had been opened as a staff house in 1929, was also closed. Barnard's Cross Library was merged with that at King's House and Missionary, Literary and Drama Societies also merged.

The altar cross and candles from the Chapel at Barnard's Cross went to the King's House Chapel, and the ones from there were taken to St Andrew's Church in Laverstock. The stained glass windows went to the King's House Chapel in 1941-1942.

Barnard's Cross was rented by The War Office (Southern Command) for three years, with the possibility of extension.

> 'The students from Barnard's Cross had to be housed at King's House. They complained that there was much less freedom at KH and the crockery was much less interesting – our plates were white with a black band and STC monogram, whilst theirs were cream with a coloured border of fruit'.
>
> Margaret Simmance (1936-1938)

Miss Dunn, whilst aware of the sadness caused by the closure, nevertheless wrote positively in the 1938 Magazine: 'The new blend of College unity which has resulted from this fusion made in obedience to stern necessity will always appear to me as one of our greatest compensations'.

The Library with its reminder, 'Speech is Silver, Silence is Golden'.

The bare scrubbed stairways leading to the dormitories.

The cubicles, 'horseboxes' with portable china wash basins and ewers and curtained doorways.

The end windows of D and E dormitories with their varying aspects on the Cathedral spire.

The maids in black with white aprons lined up in the hall.

The trestle table in the basement with jugs of hot cocoa for those who answered the 6.30 a.m. rising bell summoning to early study.

The mulberry tree at the top of the steps leading from St Ann Street.

The little crooked tree on the lawn, passed morning and evening as we attend Chapel.

The Chapel with its lamp kept continuously burning, to symbolise in Dr Baker's words, … The Spiritual, corporal unity of the College".

Margaret Logan

Barnard's Cross Team
Courtesy of The Salisbury Museum

In October 1929 America was faced with a major financial crisis. This was partly due to too much speculation on the Stock Market. People in America rushed to their banks to try and withdraw their money. 'The Wall Street Crash' had a disastrous economic impact on other countries, including Great Britain. In Britain it was the most serious financial depression of the twentieth century. It had a devastating impact, with unemployment doubling from one million to two and a half million and Britain's world trade falling by half.

What impact did this have on College? In 1932 the number of entrants permitted to the College was reduced from 99 in the previous year to 85. Staff had to accept a reduction in their salaries. By the end of 1932 there were 1,100 unemployed newly qualified teachers.

Times were hard and the College was unable to recruit the permitted quota of students. In 1936 only 59 students entered College. The birth rate in 1918-1919 (18 years before the age of College entry) had dropped significantly. In 1937 Church Training Colleges in Brighton, Peterborough and Truro had closed. It appeared that the number of Salisbury entrants for that year could possibly be only 40. In the College Magazine of 1937 Miss Forth, the retired College Principal, made an appeal for help from Old Students.

'Secondary Schools are not putting Teaching before their pupils as a vocation – a Missionary career. It is that as we well know, and one which can fill and inspire a life and make it beautiful and full. Young people today are no more afraid of effort and adventure than we were, and, if only we take trouble with them, can be set aflame with the right enthusiasm. Will you not try, this year or next, to send at least one extra Student to be trained at your old College?'

Miss Dunn, the College Principal, was determined that the College would remain open and placed an advertisement regarding opportunities at Salisbury in the 1937 Magazine and elsewhere.

A student at College in the thirties recalled that although the students lived in College some were very short of money:

'Miss Grist warned us not to deal with moneylenders but some students regularly pawned their watches for the fare home at the end of term and redeemed them at the beginning of the next term. She also warned us against hire purchase, telling us how, when she was a young teacher, she returned to her lodgings to find that all the furniture in her bedroom had been re-possessed as her landlady had not kept up her payments'.

(LST ibid)

The country's economic situation gradually began to improve. The 1936 Education Act proposed raising the school leaving age to fifteen years. It offered building subsidies for new or enlarged schools and stated that an "agreed syllabus" of religious education should be followed in all schools.

This resulted in an increased College entry in September 1938, when 105 names appeared on the list in the College Magazine. Building plans were made but the outbreak of war in 1939 prevented any development.

Miss Dunn wrote about the difficulties of the accommodation but also the positive side of the situation:

'Looking on the other side of the picture, our surroundings are among the most beautiful and inspiring of all the Training Colleges, and the advantages of our position in this Cathedral City are more easily to be felt than expressed. Strengthened by this atmosphere, and with space and quiet beauty around us, we have been enabled to cope with many internal difficulties. It is not vain-glory but sober truth to say that the College has maintained, to a degree for which we are very thankful, its reputation for training in character and efficiency'.

STC Magazine, 1938

The peace and beauty of their surroundings, the proximity of the Cathedral, the comprehensive training and the fellowship of each other would sustain the students in the difficult years ahead.

Date	Educational	International/National	Local
1919	'Save the Children' was founded, to improve the lives of children	Great Rail Strike Alcock and Brown fly across the Atlantic	First land bought for council houses in Salisbury
1920			700th anniversary of laying of foundation stones of the Cathedral
1921	Education Act raised the school leaving age to 14 and consolidated all previous laws relating to education. Newbolt Report on English Language declared 'every teacher is a teacher of English'	Sir Eric Geddes appointed by the PM, David Lloyd George, to lead a committee to examine national expenditure. Known as the 'Great Axe' 52 million pounds of cuts were agreed.	Weather vane on Cathedral spire removed and replaced with a cross
1922		English archaeologist Howard Carter finds entrance to Tutankhamen's tomb in the Valley of the Kings	City War Memorial unveiled in Market Square by Tom Adlam VC. Steam Laundry gutted by fire.
1923	Hadow Report: 'The Differentiation of the Curriculum'	Wedding of the Duke of York and Lady Elizabeth Bowes-Lyon	Harnham Slope gifted to the city
1924	Hadow Report: 'Psychological Tests of Educable Capacity'	Mallory & Irvine die attempting to climb Everest	Highbury Avenue, the first Council School was built
1925			
1926	Hadow Report: 'The Education of the Adolescent.' Recommendation that pupils should transfer schools at age of 11	General Strike	Tea party for the wives and families of unemployed men in Salisbury
1927		Lindbergh makes first solo non-stop flight across Atlantic	Opening of South Wilts Secondary School for Girls. 700th anniversary of City charter.
1928	Hadow Report: 'Books in Public Elementary Schools'	Voting age for women lowered from 30 to 21	
1929		1929-33 Britain's world trade fell by half	First car parks in Salisbury
1930		2.5 million unemployed National Govt. formed	Hurricane rips through Salisbury
1931	Hadow Report: 'The Primary School.' Forward looking recommendations were made regarding the welfare and well being of pupils	The first Govt. funded unemployment benefit system paid according to need	Salisbury's last toll bridge (Scamell's Bridge) ends toll
1932		BBC World Service begins World Disarmament Conference in Geneva	2,286 people unemployed in Salisbury at height of Depression New open air swimming baths opened off Castle Street
1933	Hadow report: 'Infant and Nursery Schools' recommended separate Infant schools & encouraged Nursery School provision		Newbridge Road opens
1935		30mph speed limit introduced in cities King George Vs Silver Jubilee and Christmas message to the Empire	League of Nations meeting in Salisbury was attended by students from the Training College
1936	Education Act proposed raising school leaving age to 15 RE syllabus to be followed in all schools	Death of George V Edward VIII abdicates	Urgent appeal for £10,000 to repair Cathedral.
1937		Coronation of George VI and his consort Queen Elizabeth	Regal Cinema opens in Endless Street.
1938	Spens Report recommended 3 types of secondary school: grammar, technical , secondary	Neville Chamberlain's 'peace for our time' speech	Edith Olivier becomes Wilton's first woman mayor
1939	There were many educational recommendations during this era but few implementations	Germany declares war on Poland Britain declares war on Germany Start of WW2	754 council houses had been built in Salisbury by 1939. Arrival of 2,500 evacuees from Portsmouth

'Now our College Days are ended
Farewell all our work and fun,
All our resolutions splendid,
Much attempted – little done.

Now we pass and other faces
Gather in the friendly hall.
Here's to those that take our places,
Next years Seniors, Bless them all!

Though we doff the College hatband,
Still we bear the College name,
Ours to keep her colours flying
All our lives to 'play the game'.

Here's to all who've borne our colours,
Years agone or fresh today.
Health to all who love our College,
Health to Sarum, Hip, Hurray!'

Chapter 4

'For Your Tomorrow'

1939 - 1950

Twenty-one years after the end of the First World War, the world was in conflict again. The Second World War started on 3rd September 1939. King George VI addressed the nation:

'The task will be hard. There may be dark days ahead, and war can no longer be confined to the battlefield, but we can only do the right as we see the right, and reverently commit our cause to God. If one and all we keep resolutely faithful to it, ready for whatever service or sacrifice it may demand, then with God's help, we shall prevail'.

Setting the Scene in Salisbury

Salisbury has a strong military connection. Salisbury Plain

lies approximately 12 miles north of the city and much of the land has been owned by the Ministry of Defence since 1898 and used as a military training area. During World War Two Salisbury was often full of servicemen and women, as well as convoys of tanks and lorries that travelled through the city. Aeroplanes were frequently heard overhead at night.

Salisbury was never seen as a target during World War Two and was fortunate to escape much of the bombing. The Luftwaffe used the Cathedral to fix their position when they were heading to targets in the Midlands. On the night of the devastating attack on Coventry in 1940, local people heard the roar of engines as planes came over in their hundreds. Four years later they watched and heard Allied gliders and planes leaving the country as part of the D Day invasion force.

Southampton was a prime target. It had an important dockyard, as well as the Supermarine factory for making Spitfires. When the factory had to be moved out of danger, some parts of Spitfire production came to Salisbury. Southampton suffered badly, especially in 1940 when it came under sustained attack and much of the city was gutted by fire. It was possible to see the glow of the flames in Southampton from parts of Salisbury. Teachers and children were evacuated from coastal locations to safer areas inland and Salisbury received nearly 2500 evacuees from Portsmouth in September 1939. Bishop Wordsworth School pupils attended school in the mornings, whilst students from Portsmouth Junior Technical College used the buildings in the afternoons.

Staff and students at the College were certainly aware of the very real threat of invasion in 1940. News of the anguish and heroism of Dunkirk, the horror of the Blitz and the bombing of Coventry all filtered through to the College in The Close.

What would tomorrow bring?

St Andrew's Screen

The Revd Stanley Baker, College Chaplain, became Vicar of St. Andrew's Church, Laverstock, Salisbury when he left College in 1933. He was much loved by the students who raised the funding for this beautiful screen, which can still be seen in the church today.

This photograph was used as a Christmas Card in 1939

THIS ANCIENT SCREEN WAS RESTORED BY THE GIFT OF STUDENTS OF SALISBURY DIOCESAN TRAINING COLLEGE, 1903 – 1933

WITH ALL WISHES FOR A HAPPY CHRISTMAS, 1939.

College Staff during the Forties

At the beginning of the 1941-1942 session Miss EAM Maxwell, a graduate of Cambridge in Mathematics and a fellow of the Royal Geographical Society, was appointed Principal. She came from St Mary's College, Lancaster Gate, which had been closed at that time.

Staff remained loyally in their posts during the difficult war years. They took on additional roles as Air-Raid Wardens, Fire Fighters and First Aid assistants.

Several staff remained from earlier years:

Miss E I Barnard	Music
Miss Fowler	Education and French
Miss Malcombe	Art
Dr E Smith	English
Miss Woodman	Education and History
Miss DJ Ayling	Physical Education
Miss I Beadle	Arts and Crafts at the Warminster Project
Miss M Denny	Education (in charge of the Warminster Project)
Mrs Dalton-Hill	Infant Education
Miss D Fletcher	English and French
Miss M French	Deputised for Miss Shute
Miss B H N Geary	History and English (assisting the Warminster project)
Miss M J Gibbs	Junior Education
Miss KM Hefford	Education
Miss JH Harris	Art
Miss RE Mayo	Geography and Mathematics
Miss O G Northcott	Biology
Miss S Riley	Horticulture and responsibility for the garden
Miss P Roome	Physical Training and Hygiene (replacing Miss Story)
Miss LS Taylor	Education
Miss D A Todd	History
Miss EC Trinder	Religious Education
Miss ME Truman	Biology (replacing Miss Stevenson)
Miss E M Villard	Needlecraft
Miss K Shute	Physical Education (part-time)

Secretary and Bursar
Miss Keown replaced Miss DC Oakley Hill in 1947

The Chaplaincy
Bishop Carpenter Garnier replaced Canon Baker temporarily in 1943
The Revd Dr. Prideaux replaced him in 1944
The Revd AG Barker replaced him in 1947

Domestic Officers
Miss AL Taylor was Cook-Caterer in 1945
Miss M Taylor became Housekeeper in 1945. This post was later known as Domestic Bursar.
Miss AM Leest was in charge of the Sanatorium from 1945.

Winter 1947: Choristers' Green from the tower of Salisbury Cathedral   Courtesy of The Salisbury Museum

The College Staff and Students, 1944-1946

Miss Moore welcomed students for Speech Training at her Clinic from early 1940. In 1951 she was appointed to a part-time post in College.

The students held fond and affectionate memories of the staff. Nan Grant (1944-1946) remembered several staff with affection:

'The staff were single ladies and most of them lived in, and, to some extent, were responsible for us. Miss Malcombe (Art) lived out, and she could be seen striding across the Close in her 'trilby' hat and tweed cape as soon as lectures were over'.

Miss Barnard encouraged the students' musical ability, which led to an exciting event:

'There was a College orchestra made up of anyone who could play an instrument. I played violin, badly, and finding time to practise was difficult, but somehow Miss Barnard managed to encourage us all and managed to get a not unpleasant sound. The highlight was when her friend, Vaughan Williams, came to conduct and, under his guidance, we gave a concert… my first meeting with a famous musician.'

Pat Prosser (1945-1947) recollected several staff who had made a lasting impression on her:

'I chose History as Advanced Level Subject and enjoyed Miss Geary's scholarship and expertise. We had some memorable excursions in her ancient Ford car to explore prehistoric sites in Wessex. I enjoyed all aspects of Miss Barnard's Music Course. Many students will remember Mr Luxton, the College Caretaker, who helped to carry our trunks, at the beginning and end of term, up and down the narrow stairways'.

'There were three Miss Taylors in College in 1947. Miss Marion Taylor, our kindly housekeeper, her sister Miss Netta Taylor, who kept us well fed as Catering Officer and Miss Lucy Taylor as Education Lecturer. She was a Scottish Lady with a soft accent and lively sense of humour, who gave fresh impetus to our studies in Education with her wide experience and her wise love for children and understanding of the help they needed for learning. So much she passed on to us remained with us throughout our careers. Her scholarship demanded the highest we could reach in theory and practice, but her care for the welfare and well-being of students was equally marked.'

Miss Todd brought History to life: 'Never before or since, have I come across anyone who could breathe life into the subject like she did. I learned such a lot from her'.

Liba Taconis (1941-1943) recalled:

'Under Miss Maxwell's wise and kindly rule the College began to shed the ethos of a strict but kindly girl's boarding school and move into the twentieth century…In my memory, 'the staff' stand out vividly. Here were varied personalities; all held keys to one or another of my 'doors' and all unlocked them with generosity and enthusiasm – occasionally, it must be said, bordering on eccentricity'.

When Liba joined the staff in the early Fifties she was very impressed by the thoughtful and caring attitude which the staff had for the students. 'I realised more and more how painstaking and loving was the nurturing of each individual, and what heart-searching went on over difficult students'.

Through the wartime years and those which followed, the staff maintained the spirit and the ethos for which the College was known and they sustained the high standards of teacher training.

Miss Mary Maxwell: College Principal, 1942–1954

Miss Maxwell   Courtesy of The Salisbury Museum

Miss Maxwell successfully led the College through the final four years of World War Two and the gradual recovery from it. 'Maxwell House,' the new student residence, was built and opened in her time and she was influential in the plans for the new gymnasium and science block. She adapted the pattern of College work to the changes of university affiliation. She was highly regarded by staff and students who valued her thoughtfulness, tact and dedication.

In 1966 the then College Principal, Miss Ashley, described some of Miss Maxwell's achievements:

'When I set to work to find out Miss Maxwell's achievements I was told, "She got the games field in order!" She planned the gymnasium in which a stage was inserted as the prospect of another hall was then very remote. I was told she had the task of improving the Sanatorium accommodation, extending the kitchen premises, and grappling with the problems of heating; that she began to get rid of some of the 'horse-boxes' and she did get rid of College hats; and above all she achieved the extension of the College into the hostel which now bears her name'.

In the 1942 Salisbury Training College Magazine, Miss Maxwell wrote of her appreciation of the warm welcome which she had received.

'My coming was associated with all the beauty of the Close in summer, and that will remain with me as an inspiration for the future. Whatever may come to us, the beauty we have known here will remain. I count myself indeed fortunate to have Miss Forth at hand, always ready to be consulted and to advise me from the mine of information upon every detail of College that she possesses. Miss Dunn too, has paid several visits since I came and has made my taking over as easy as possible'.

In 1952 Miss Maxwell spent three weeks in Germany at the invitation of the Foreign Office 'seeing Training Colleges and Schools, and meeting some of those responsible for them'. In 1954 she accepted the invitation to be Principal of Bingley Training College. In the 1955 College Magazine she wrote to thank the Salisbury students:

'The beautiful lizard-skin bag raises morale each time I use it, and every time it reminds me of you and your kind and good wishes. The cheque is indeed a magnificent gift and I feel most unworthy of such a tribute. I shall enjoy spending it tremendously, and with great pleasure I shall buy things with it for use in the College. Part of it will be used for a worthy addition to the Chapel, and I am waiting to choose that until the plan for the improvement of the Chapel is made.

I am now happily settled in my North Country College, surrounded by beautiful country but on the edge of the Yorkshire industrial experience, but life is made richer by variety in our work and surroundings'.

Miss Maxwell was a positive influence on the lives of Salisbury students, making their lives richer and strengthening their vocation for teaching.

The Organisation of the College during the War Years

'The organisation of the College during the war years was a daunting task. The beautiful buildings, on an incomparable site, were a great responsibility, but more so was the safety of the residents, concentrated in houses never built for anything but private families living when the fear of air raids and even of invasion was unknown.

When I arrived in 1941, the air raids on Bristol, Birmingham and Southampton were almost incessant, and for each of these the planes passed over or near Salisbury. It was said that they used the Cathedral spire as a navigating point, and that was one reason why the town escaped a raid. On most evenings the sirens sounded at about 7pm and the all-clear in the early hours. This meant that all the residents in King's House went to the room with the pillars, which was a naturally insulated and reinforced building, and all the Old Deanery and Audley residents went to the Old Deanery cellar. The overcrowding was intense, no one slept much and on school practice days journeys had to start early. When we realised that the raiders' intention was not to drop bombs on us, but to pass over to the industrial areas, I persuaded the Governors to allow us to leave everyone in their beds during the 'alerts', except for the 'watchers' (members of staff) who would ring the alarm for evacuation of the upper floors if they judged the raiders were approaching. This seemed less of a risk than that of illness caused by exhaustion and infection from the crowded shelters'.

E. A. M. Maxwell, *SDTC Chronicle*, 1965

Staff air raid wardens   Courtesy of The Salisbury Museum

1939 to 1945: A Portrait of the War Years

All applicants to College during the war years had to be under eighteen years of age before the first day of the September term. If this was not observed, they would be liable to be called up for war service at the age of eighteen.

The College Authorities, the staff and the students were determined to overcome all difficulties, to maintain the work of the College and to live life to the full. War-time conditions were seen as a challenge rather than a deterrent, and life continued calmly and cheerfully. Domestic help was in short supply and all students were involved in cleaning, washing up and preparing vegetables. Funds were often scarce, but there were plenty of extra-curricular activities and students made their own entertainment.

'We were grateful for the peaceful atmosphere of The Close, where cricket was played on the green- with W.H.Auden, the poet, joining in – and tennis on College courts each evening until winter came and drove us round the Common Room hot stove'.

Enid Marshall, 1944-46

Music played a prominent part. In December 1939 students enjoyed a recital by Miss Jean Stirling Mackinley, and in 1940 Miss Story arranged a recital by Mr Dennis Noble.

'It was an immense pleasure to listen to the volume and yet striking variety of his vocal tone, his wonderful clearness of diction and his inspiring rhythm'.

Another concert took place in Spring 1941; students could relax and forget the pressures of wartime whilst enjoying the music of Elgar and Handel.

In addition to outside visitors there were many in-house entertainments, as well as parties with 'eatable dainties, somehow conjured up from rations'.

In December 1939, Audley students invited the rest of the College to 'a most merry review' entitled Flashes in the Black-Out. Students in The Old Deanery invited the rest of the College to an At Home at the 'Village of Stevydene:

'Rustics greeted us in genuine dialect and escorted us around the immaculate village, whose sights included Red Hart Inn, The Village Pump, The Air-Raid Shelter, Lover's Lane and The School'.

The evening ended with excellent refreshment at 'The Village Inn'. What fun the students must have had preparing for this event!

The staff gave an impromptu Christmas party in 1940. This included musical and dramatic items and a scene from 'The Chimes," by Dickens, with parts played by Miss Denny and Miss Jordan.

Students sang carols around The Close in the black-out on winter evenings. They also organised parties for evacuee children, providing presents from a Christmas tree.

In 1939 College societies included the Dramatic Society, Music Society, Literary Society and Missionary Society. Rangers and a Country Dance Club also flourished. By 1942 there was a French Circle, and an Entertainment Committee who had oversight of social events. First Year students held a revue 'In Coll To-night' which included community singing, refreshments and dancing. Dances were held in February and May. Students could still enjoy themselves.

They also heard some excellent talks from eminent speakers at the College clubs and sometimes shared in comparable groups in Salisbury. Pat Prosser (1945-1947) remembered:

'I recall one memorable occasion when a distinguished cleric of advanced years, as Chairman of one such meeting, rose to introduce the evening's speaker, a dramatist of national repute, saying, "Mr L has been here before and I know that at the end of this meeting we shall all be hoping that Mr L will soon come again – Ladies and Gentlemen, Mr L." and T. S. Eliot rose to address the gathering'.

A sign of the times was the newly formed 'Society for the Discussion of International Affairs'. Early meetings included talks on 'What is Fascism in Germany?' and a talk about Poland. In March, Col. White, V.C. of Southern Command, spoke on Asia.

Specific war-time needs such as Red Cross lectures in First Aid and fire watching duties also had to be fitted in, and students and staff helped with the war effort in Salisbury:

'Small parties of students are helping at the hospital at weekends; they are used in the children's wards to carry trays and wash up and be generally useful. They entertained members of the local Association for the Blind last term and are helping to equip our Salisbury War Nursery'.

College Magazine, May 1942

Members of staff volunteered as Air Raid Wardens, whilst others were Fire-fighters and First Aid helpers. Miss Maxwell worked in a Forces Canteen in her spare time. War-time conditions had considerable impact on the proposed building programme and on school practices, outings and exchange visits. Books and other resources became increasingly difficult to procure.

Incendiary raids on Cathedral cities such as Coventry and Exeter led to an increase in air raid practices. Mary Choules (1939-1941) remembered hearing the 'planes going for Southampton' in her second year. Nancy Jones (1940-1942) recalled how 'often at night time we took to the PE room with our palliasses. There was silence as we listened to the deep boom of aircraft overhead'.

Miss Denny, who arrived at College in 1939, remembered the nightly struggle of students in the 'Gym-cum-Air Raid Shelter' as they revised and wrote essays, whilst listening to the wailing sirens and worrying about families and friends.

Liba Taconis (1941-1943) and her friends were permitted by Miss Maxwell to sleep out on fine summer nights. They took folding beds from the 'Gym-cum-Air Raid Shelter' and slept on the lawn outside the Chapel. This had to come to an end when it was thought that Cathedral cities were being targeted by the Luftwaffe, but 'how we loved our open-air nights,' commented Liba.

Rosemary Edwards (1943-1945) described how fire-watching was organised:

'Everyone had to take turn at fire-watching. We were divided into three teams and we took turns to be on duty. If the sirens went off we had to be in the Junior Common Room and ready for action in two minutes, and we had to stay there until the ALL CLEAR was sounded. By this stage in the war there were fewer air raids and I was called out about 20 times, but never saw action. People pulled slacks on over pyjamas and came running downstairs as they were, even with curlers in their hair'.

Kathleen Taylor (1941-1943) had memories of the tin hats:

The blackout room was permanently blacked out, as this was where everyone in King's House assembled when the air raid sirens sounded. Leading off it was a peculiar windowless room where tin hats were kept. Miss Geary chided us for carefully choosing a tin hat, instead of grabbing the first one, for as she so frankly told us, "none of us looked fetching in any of them".

Staff filling sandbags for the war effort
Courtesy of The Salisbury Museum

Firewatchers on the Cathedral 1940
Courtesy of The Salisbury Journal

The rustics of Steveydene

In the first years of the war, before trained firemen took over, students did night time fire-watching duties on the Cathedral, together with an ARP Warden.

> 'We crossed the west end of the nave at triforium level and looked out of the little door at the base of the spire, a terrifying experience. Fortunately we never had to extinguish an incendiary'.
>
> Mary Choules (1939-1941)

Supplied with torches and their own warm clothes, students could look down into the nave and chancel and were very anxious about unguarded lights and reflections. Muriel Robson (1942-1944) remembered that students on a fire watching rota were allowed to wear trousers. This was 'quite something' at this time and Muriel felt liberated – but her mother was shocked.

Three students decided to go potato picking in their first term. They sensibly wore slacks, but to their horror saw Miss Maxwell advancing towards them across The Close. They tried, with difficulty, to hitch up their slacks under long coats. Miss Maxwell, however, was 'a sport' and on being told about the potato picking, she continued on her way.

Food rationing was introduced at the beginning of 1940. In College each student received less than the weekly ration of butter (2oz) and margarine (4oz), as some was left for use in the kitchen. A one pound pot of jam or marmalade had to last a student for a term. Food parcels from home were received with gratitude.

> 'Students varied between the disciplined ones who divided their butter into infinitesimal parts and those who had a glorious binge at the weekend and ate plain bread for the rest of the week'.
>
> Mary Choules (1939-1941)

The College diet was adequate but monotonous. Dried milk and dried eggs were plentiful and Marion Vesey remembered 'many rice puddings and scrambled eggs'. Amelia Mears (1943-1945) recalled long loaves of bread that were 'crumbly, brown and not very palatable'. Jean Reynolds (1945-1947) had vivid memories of the weekly Rabbit Stew, when she collected the bones for her friend, Margaret Watkins, who wanted to make a complete skeleton of a rabbit for her special Biology project. Jean also remembered paddling in the river for crayfish.

The large kitchen garden behind Old Deanery provided excellent vegetables and salads. Amelia Mears and her friends sometimes had a meal in the town after a weekend walk. Beans or dried egg on toast cost 8d and pilchards on toast cost 9d. Enid Marshall (1944-1946) received cheese biscuits from her mother, made from the extra cheese ration that her father (an engine driver) was allowed.

Clothes rationing started in June 1941. The coupon system allowed people to buy one set of new clothes a year.

> 'I had one nice, new dress for special occasions, but most of my clothes were school uniform, altered where possible. We each had to have a pair of trousers in case there was an air raid in the night. We were not expected to wear such garments in the town as this was not considered lady-like, but we did wear them in the winter during lectures. We often wore our over-coats and had blankets belted round our waists to cover our legs as it was so cold. Even so, I had the worst chilblains I ever had'.
>
> Amelia Mears (1943-1945)

Coal was strictly rationed and in very short supply.

Pat Prosser (1945-1947) was allocated a cubicle in North 3 on the third floor of King's House. There was an empty fire grate at the end of the room, but fires were not allowed. However, before the end of term, they disobeyed rules, found some logs and coal and enjoyed some comfort huddling around their tiny fire.

Kathleen Taylor (1941-1943) commented that 'cold and cocoa are synonymous with College in mind'. The huge jugs of steaming cocoa that are mentioned so often were certainly appreciated.

Salisbury was full of troops. This was a cause of concern to the staff, and students were restricted in their activities. Visiting pubs was forbidden and the coffee-house in the High Street and an outing to the cinema on Saturday evenings were the usual weekly highlights. Students were allowed one 'late' pass for weekday nights and one for the weekends. They had to be back in their houses by 9.45pm. Some students, however, managed to break the curfew and to meet servicemen.

Muriel Murphy (1944-1946) and Barbara Carpenter returned each evening to their billet with Canon and Mrs Allen. No lights guided them on their way and they could just make out the dim outline of the Cathedral in the obligatory war-time darkness. The Close Constable, however, had a torch that he shone at the legs of cyclists, to check that they were of female gender. The only men who were permitted in The Close after 9.30pm were those that resided there.

Number 38 The Close housed about twenty students. Florence May Miller (1938-1940) spent her first year there. Miss Fowler was the Warden and she referred to Florence and her friend as 'the elephants of 38' as their room was above her sitting room!

Muriel Robson (1942-1944) went straight from a strict Convent school to College and found little difference between them. On one occasion she and her friends lost their key and 'bunked up' a girl to climb in through the downstairs WC window. They had the misfortune to be spotted by a 'Lady of The Close' and were reprimanded by Miss Maxwell for their own unladylike behaviour.

Rosemary Edwards (1943-1945) commented that students rarely had to pay for going to the cinema:

'There was an unwritten agreement that a GI could take a college student to the pictures on the understanding that there was no conversation or anything else between the two parties. If they did try anything else, they were rewarded with a sharp slap on the wrists'.

Barbara Wright (1944-1946) described how meeting young men was a 'time that was tinged with sadness as we never knew if we would see them again'.

Boyfriends who decided to visit students were given an icy reception by staff, and students received stern reprimands.

Miss Woodman addressed the College on the subject of sunbathing:

'Young ladies must not sun-bathe this year. When I was going round the corner by the Chapel I met a young gentleman from the United States of America and I was shocked and horrified to think what he might have seen if the weather had been warmer'.

Amelia Mears, 1943-1945

War did, however, have its brighter side:

'It must have been the number of lonely members of H.M. Forces and the young men who turned up on leave that induced the powers that be to allow us to hold dances in the Junior Common Room. This we felt to be a tremendous step forward in the emancipation of College students'.

Amelia Mears, 1943-1945

On occasions like this the girls wore long evening gowns that were mostly home-made. Clothing coupons were in short supply.

Post was an especially important part of life during the war. Directly after Chapel the students rushed to the Common Room to see if they had received any letters:

'I had met my boyfriend, who later became my husband, before I went to College. He was a soldier and he sent his letters in a "Green Envelope". These envelopes were buff coloured with green writing on them saying that they held only personal information and nothing about the war, so they were seldom censored. Of course everyone knew who had sent the letter and remarked accordingly, but I was not the only one to receive such envelopes'.

Amelia Mears, 1943-1945

The conditions of war were always present. News was not always welcome. Many students had relatives and fiancés in the armed forces who were killed or wounded:

'Sometimes a message went out: 'Miss X, please go to Miss Maxwell's room and take a friend. Everyone knew what that meant - a brother, an uncle, occasionally a father, killed in action'.

Returning home could be difficult. Enid Marshall (1944-1946) lived in the north of England:

'The buzz bombs started soon after our arrival. These were planes without pilots and the journey via London to Salisbury was too risky, so we went home for Christmas via Bristol'.

Despite the privations of the war years, many students remembered with gratitude their time at College, and the outstanding qualities of their lecturers.

When you go home,

Tell them of us and say

For your tomorrow we gave our today.

John Maxwell Edmonds

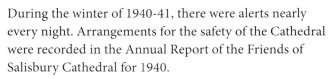

1 May 1940

2 May 1940

During the winter of 1940-41, there were alerts nearly every night. Arrangements for the safety of the Cathedral were recorded in the Annual Report of the Friends of Salisbury Cathedral for 1940.

'One of the anxieties of the past year has been the provision of adequate numbers of fire spotters and fighters to deal with an attack on the building, with its vast extent of roofs and wooden lofts above the vaulting. At present we have, in addition to our own staff of 3 men, a soldier from the Pioneer Corps, 4 senior boys from Bishop Wordsworth's School and a band of students from the Training College'.

By 1942 the responsibility for the safety of the Cathedral had been taken over by the Local Authority. Fifteen men slept on the premises every night, under the direction of trained officers. There was also more in the way of fire-fighting appliances in the building. The Chapter House was used as a billet for people who had been bombed out. Beds and bedding were provided and there was a temporary

cooker plus hot water, lighting and washing facilities. Forty women and children could be accommodated. 'The whole place is tented in with double canvas supported by our own iron scaffolding, to black it out'.

Nan Grant (1944-1946) had vivid memories of these war-shadowed days:

'There were blackout curtains everywhere, and no street lights, but somehow there was a feeling of safety, locked in The Close. We were free to go to the Cathedral or any parish church on Sunday, usually to a morning service. I recall the Dean wishing to have Evensong regularly on Sundays. The Cathedral could not be completely blacked out, so he asked for volunteers...he needed just six. "Bring your blanket," as there was no heating. "Bring your torch," just to see the words, if you didn't know them by heart. He preached his sermon from the pulpit, to a congregation of six, sitting in the dark...memories'.

The Channel Islanders: Evacuation, Occupation and Liberation

Florence May Miller (1938-1940) remembered the plight of the Channel Island students when war was declared in 1939. They were in a quandary as to what to do. Some were under pressure from their parents to return home, whilst others had families who wanted their daughters to be on the mainland. Evelyn Hoyles (1938-1940) managed to get back to Jersey on the last boat. She taught there through the Occupation, returning to the mainland afterwards. In 1974 she was appointed to the Headship of Jersey College for Girls.

Students who were evacuated from the Channel Islands longed to return home. Nancy Jones (1940-1942), paid tribute to them:

> 'They displayed true courage and calmness as all communications with their beloved islands and families were forbidden'.

Jeanne (Jonny) Guille (1944-1946) was a schoolgirl in Guernsey, where her father was the Rector of the Parish of St Peter-in-the-Wood. In June 1940, Jonny's Headmistress assembled the pupils, telling them to go home and tell their parents to read the *Guernsey Evening Press*. Jeanne cycled into town and bought a paper. The headline was 'EVACUATION TOMORROW'.

> 'When I arrived home, the Rectory was full of people asking my parents what they should do. My mother decided to come with us (my brother, my younger sister and myself) and the next day we each went to school with a small suitcase. As we waited and waited, my mother decided that she could not leave her husband alone (he could not leave his parish) and she returned home. Eventually we boarded an empty troop ship that had unloaded troops from Dunkirk. We had to go down into the hold, which was very dirty. After zigzagging across the Channel to avoid U-boats, we arrived at Weymouth, where we were given hot tea and jam sandwiches.

We were then put on a train, together with most of our teachers and a few helpers. When we arrived in Rochdale in Lancashire, it was dark and raining and it sounded to us as though the people spoke another language. Soon, however, we found out how kind everyone was and by the winter we were billeted with local families and were being taught in local schools by our own teachers. During the war I didn't see my parents for five years and only had a very occasional Red Cross message of twenty-five words.

In 1944 I went to College. At first I was billeted in the Archdeacon's house at the end of The Close - just the use of a bedroom. One had to be in by 9.30pm and leave by 8.00 in the morning. Hot water was brought to the bedroom by a maid (dressed in the usual black dress and white pinafore) in a brass can with a lid. By the end of the first term, another student had to leave College for family reasons and I went to see the Principal, Miss Maxwell and asked whether I might move into King's House in her place. To my delight she said 'yes'. I always found Miss Maxwell very approachable and understanding. She looked older than she was as she often wore a woollen shawl to keep warm in a draughty old house.

'I can well remember listening to the wireless in the Junior Common Room on May 9th 1945 and hearing Winston Churchill say, "Our dear Channel Islands are also to be freed today." A few days later, just before we went to Chapel, the post arrived and Dr Smith, my English lecturer, very kindly came and gave me a letter from Guernsey. It was the first real letter from my parents for 5 years. I had only had Red Cross Messages of 25 words every six months or so. Thankfully my parents had both survived the ordeal of the Occupation. I eventually returned home for the summer break on VJ night (Victory over Japan) and as we sailed down the Solent, bonfires could be seen all along the coast. I will never forget that journey'.

A former student, Edith Albiges (1921-1923), was evacuated to Glasgow from Guernsey with her school in 1940, and remained there until the Occupation ended in 1945.

Dorothy and Marjorie Falla, both former students, were remembered with great affection by many people in Guernsey:

> 'Few lives have been more marked by unassuming modesty, quiet fervent love and deep dedication. For many years they had been most popular and successful Head Teachers, and many parents will remember, with gratitude, the devoted care they gave to the island children who were evacuated to Britain in their charge, when Guernsey was occupied by the Germans for those five long years'.
>
> *CSSM Chronicle*, 1965

During the Occupation, the College sent Red Cross messages to the islands:

'From the long- delayed replies, we gather that the schools are open more or less as usual, under the few teachers who remained and 'dugout' teachers. Some of the school buildings are occupied and temporary premises are in use'.

SDTC Chronicle, 1941/1942

('Dugout teachers' refers to teachers who had retired. This included married women who, in returning to teach during the war years, initiated a change. From then on, it became acceptable for married women to continue teaching.)

The Return Home

'The breeze freshens, the dock lights grow dim. Adieu, England, great country of great people. To have lived with you in the shadow has been an inspiration and a privilege. May we never forget your kindness, courage and fortitude, your happy friendly children. May that faith which sustained you in your darkest hour help us to meet the future. Dawn. The mist clears. It is a radiant summer morning, clear blue sky and shimmering blue sea. Impatiently, intently, we stare and stare. Yes, there it is at last! Jersey, the most beautiful island in the whole world! Grosnez, St Ouen's Bay, Corbiere, St Brelade's, Portelet, Noirmont.

We disembark. Our friends welcome us. How good that is! They still have a strained look about the eyes, their cheeks are hollow, their figures slimmer, but they are free and they are happy'.

Jersey during the Occupation

by two former students

School life in Jersey 1940-1945

'On June 20th 1940, chaos and panic reigned. A statement had gone forth that the Germans were practically on our doorstep, and those who wished could evacuate to England. Less than twenty-four hours was given to the Islanders to decide, and eventually nine thousand people got away, whilst the other forty odd thousand looked on in amazement, stayed and awaited events. On June 28th the island was bombed and on July 1st the Germans took possession.

The day after that, a roll-call of staff and scholars was taken, and it was found that roughly half the scholars and a third of the teachers had been evacuated. A re-shuffle had to be made; teachers were sent to other schools and some schools were amalgamated.

The first bombshell was the order for German to be taught in the schools. German was going to be the language of the world and it had to be learnt. Many teachers refused to teach it, but outsiders who had a smattering of German were installed, at a handsome salary, as teachers of German. This was a farce. These people had never taught before and their discipline was nil. They received no help from the permanent staff and were left severely alone. Many gave up the struggle after a few months.

In May 1941 the school leaving age was raised to 15, owing to lack of work and to keep the children off the streets – then the pinch began to be felt very much. The mothers were wonderful! How they kept the children as neat and tidy as they did has always puzzled the teachers. Footwear was the first problem. Beech trees were cut down and made into clogs, with little leather tops. One got accustomed to the noise along the corridors after a while. Clothes came next. One saw a little pink shirt patched with green material, or a blue one patched and sewn in yellow – but patched. Soap was unobtainable – and yet the children came to school clean – washed only in water for the most part. Then one noticed a certain lethargy among the children, and among the teachers too. This was due to lack of food. No fats and no sugar. Bread made from pig-meal, tea made from scraped carrots or beetroots and five pounds of potatoes per week (mostly bad) were the staple diet. Little faces became more and more pinched and little bodies became thinner and thinner. Milk, and soup made from water and vegetables, with an occasional piece of meat thrown in, were issued to the children daily.

School materials diminished weekly – no pens, pencils, writing books, ink or chalk, except in very limited quantities.

The winter of 1944-1945 was, of course, the worst. A wet and cold autumn, resulting in coughs, colds, chilblains and eruptions on the skin compelled the Education Authorities to close the schools. The cheerless and unheated classrooms could be borne no longer, and when, in February 1945, bread ceased to be issued, life became hard and sad indeed.

In March and April 1945, tension became very great among the Germans as well as the civilian population. Those of us who had managed to keep our wirelesses, listened to the news secretly, and knew that great things were happening and hoped that after a long and weary occupation the end was near. It was only the thought that one day the British would liberate us, and the knowledge that their ships had surrounded the island for eleven months, which kept our hearts and courage up.

They came at last and were received with delirious joy by the whole population. The children were then fed and clothed properly.

After the first joy of freedom, the schools are now settling down to normal, and although there is great deal to make up in many ways, yet we all feel that there is now something to work for. We shall never forget the last five humiliating years - but we are trying to think of our life under a hated enemy alien as an evil dream'.

Muriel Le Breton (1915-1917)

1942-1944
Experiences of Political Prisoner No.12184

'In June 1942 our wireless sets were confiscated. This at the time when it seemed that the end of the war would never come, coupled with the removal of this last link with the mainland, had a most depressing effect. Those braver ones who were in possession of small sets, kept and hid them, sometimes in most unexpected places, and listened in.

A friend of mine kept her set. At this time I was sleeping every night at her place, as the school and school house were situated in a rather lonely spot, and the field directly opposite had been turned into a camp for Russian prisoners of war. These prisoners were very badly treated and ill fed. Often, at night, they managed to go foraging for food and clothes, breaking into houses and sometimes acting in a very violent manner and generally frightening one and all. It was not wise to live alone.

Later on, one young Russian prisoner managed to escape from his camp. Half-starved and ill clad, he appeared at my friend's door. Full of pity for him, she took him in. Naturally we all befriended him, finding clothes for him and entertaining him at our homes, although we knew we were running great risks in doing so.   He quickly learnt English sufficiently well to follow the broadcasts. Every night at nine o'clock we would wend our way upstairs, move the duchess table, lift the carpet and then the lino surround to reveal the floor boards. One loose floor board was then lifted, and there, reposing in the cavity underneath the floor, lay the small set. Kneeling down, we all listened-in breathlessly, memorising the news to impart it to trusted friends the next day. How eagerly we heard Churchill's speeches, and the King's at Christmas. In this way we kept up our spirits.

For nearly two years we pursued the even tenor of our days till, in May 1944, someone betrayed us to the German authorities. My friend and her maid were arrested and taken to gaol. The Russian escaped, but after much searching the wireless set was found. We all knew we were in for trouble, but a week elapsed before more people were arrested and it was a further week before another friend and I were ordered to appear at the Gestapo Headquarters for questioning. The three weeks of suspense had been most unnerving. In fear and trepidation, lest I should implicate others, I answered the questions with, "I'm afraid I cannot tell you," or "I do not know" as often as possible. Luckily we all knew exactly what to confess to, as my friend had secretly managed to convey the gist of her first statement to us through someone in the gaol. Needless to say, the Gestapo agent refused to believe me and sent me to gaol. My journey through the town to the local prison was one I shall long remember. See me seated in the front seat of a German car beside the chauffeur, with a fully armed escort in the rear, his rifle with fixed bayonet ready if I should try any ' funny business.' For ten days I was shut up alone in a cell. How hard the prison beds were and how poor and uninteresting the fare - weak substitute coffee, a hunk of bread, soup and potatoes boiled in their jackets.

After ten days we were court-martialled. This awful experience we had dreaded for days. However, we were sentenced to varying terms of imprisonment. My sentence was two months. The others had longer terms and three were sent to France and eventually to concentration camps in Germany. One reached Belsen and was rescued in the nick of time, but my friend, his sister, died in the camp at Ravensbruck.

Many people were being arrested at this time, more than the gaol could hold. Consequently, two of us were allowed to go home after the trial, until the 6th of July.

This time prison life was a little easier. Three of us shared a large, stone-flagged cell with large, barred windows. As political prisoners, we were allowed to bring in our comfortable beds and a sideboard. We kept our food in this and the flowers that were sent to us on top. The German Authorities allowed us a parcel a fortnight and friends, often at great sacrifice to themselves, sent us food. Our windows faced the entrance courtyard and how eagerly we watched the visitors arriving. All that we could do was to wave at them as visits allowed were few and far between. Twice a day we were exercised in a small courtyard surrounded by high walls topped by broken glass. The time in between was spent in eating, sleeping and playing bridge and other card games with prisoners in the next cells. Our cell doors were locked at eight every night and opened the next morning at 7.30. A large, moveable wooden screen ensured a certain amount of privacy, shutting off a corner of the cell. This corner served as hall cum bathroom cum scullery.

Every day we received the "News" which was passed on to us by the men politicals, or smuggled in. Several of the men had managed to fix up a lovely crystal set in their cell and so had the latest news. This was under the noses of the Germans who had actually taken over a third of the gaol.

On August 29th, three days before school began again, I was released from my "Holiday Resort." With mixed feelings of relief at my freedom, regret that the others were not yet free, and grief that those overseas had no friendly faces to greet them, I met those who had come, laden with flowers, to greet me.

Never did grass appear greener or air fresher and sweeter than it did when I walked up the country lane to my home. Here I was welcomed by my very loyal friends, teachers and my faithful dog. How lovely it was to be free'!

Dora J Haquoil, former student, St Ouen's, Jersey

The Chapel of the Holy Angels

The College Chapel was a source of strength during wartime and attendance remained constant in the post-war years. The small building at the heart of the College became imprinted on hearts and minds:

'I was a Chapel Warden in my second year. The most important duty was to see that the lamp never went out during term, as it symbolised the spirit of the College. I can still smell the fragrant oil. We had Compline once a week and I sometimes played the organ, as only a Nunc Dimittis and one hymn were required. Our Chaplain was referred to with affection as 'Proffy' Morris. I loved our Chapel and its services'.

Fjentje Taconis (1939-1941)

'It was in Chapel, surrounded by Christian fellowship and the memorials to our predecessors, that we came to realise that we were part of a precious tradition of Christian-based teaching that had flourished in College for more than a century'.

Pat Prosser (1945-1947)

'The Cathedral at dawn, sunset, noonday, always the Cathedral, rising above us all. All one's thoughts inevitably lead back to the Cathedral and to the College Chapel'.

Dorothy Coffin (1949-1951)

It was decided, following the closure of Barnard's Cross in 1937, that the beautiful stained glass windows from the Chapel of All Saints should be taken to the Chapel at King's House. Miss Maxwell wrote about this in the 1942 *College Magazine*:

'The glass had to be adapted to fit the larger windows, with the result that the figures stand out more clearly and the effect is most pleasing'.

Jonny Guille (1944-1946) attended Chapel services before breakfast on weekdays, and went to St Martin's with her friends on Sundays. She remembered a particularly devout young curate and the fact that they used to say "Praise the Lord for Father Ford".

Above: Angel Corbel in the College Chapel

Left: College Chapel Window

College Chapel

Courtesy of The Salisbury Museum

The Art Studio

The Art Studio, in the old gatehouse behind the Old Deanery, was Miss Malcolmbe's empire. In the late 1940s paper was in short supply, so much newspaper was used and so too were the walls, which were then whitewashed over ready for the next day. Jean Reynolds (1945-1947) described Miss Malcombe:

> 'She was a wonderful character, very tall, impressive, and somewhat angular, with an Eton Crop and wearing glasses. She used to wear a Prince of Wales check suit with a loose jacket over a smart shirt, and brogues for footwear. Her opening words to new classes never changed: "Now let it be understood, I dislike all students". Miss Malcombe, a good artist herself, was a friend of Augustus John, whom she always referred to as "a fine man, whose beard is a home for tired moths"!

Despite Miss Malcombe's formidable appearance, Jean, who enjoyed Art, could spot the twinkle in her eye.

The Vaulting Club

Rangers (Senior Girl Guides)

Florence May Miller, who went to College in 1939, remembered how Miss Story, who was District Commissioner at this time, did her utmost to persuade students to join the Rangers.

In 1942 the College Rangers, wanting to contribute to war service, offered to help on the domestic side of the Salisbury Infirmary. Their offer was accepted gratefully and they put in sixteen hours of work each weekend, working on a rota.

In 1943 Pauline Lucas was chosen from the Salisbury District to be Colour Bearer to the Chief Guide and Kathleen Cope was one of the Colour Party on June 6th.

Fjentje Taconis (1939-1941) belonged to the Rangers. She remembered the song 'Peace I ask of the river – it was very relevant to those of us who found "our river" a place where we sought peace – and, in the company of Miss Stevenson, crayfish'!

Fit as a fiddle!

Puppeteers with
Miss Malcombe ,1941-1943
(Courtesy of The Salisbury Museum)

P.E. 1940s Style

Muriel Robson (1942-1944) remembered the 'very poor P.E. facilities and the dreadful gym in a room with a pillar in it'. She played hockey in the field opposite King's House. Marion Vesey (1942-1944) remembered wearing black shorts and a white blouse for Country Dancing, which was done in bare feet on the grass near the Chapel, accompanied by a piano that had been trundled outside. Pat Prosser (1945-1947) also remembered the uninviting 'icy, murky depths of the town swimming pool'.

Miss Roome founded the College Vaulting Club in 1945 and it was well attended. The 1949 Magazine states that the College representative for vaulting was Eileen Naylor, one of the three students who climbed the Cathedral Spire. Other sports at this time included hockey, netball, tennis and rounders. Ballroom Dancing classes had been very popular in the winter months. It was hoped to re-start the table tennis club, and a fancy dress hockey match raised funds for a new table. In 1948 outside fixtures included playing Sarum Ladies' Hockey Club, Winchester College for hockey and Southampton University for netball.

> At Sarum College in The Close
> Our energy is usefully directed.
> At Sarum College in The Close
> With PT-itus we're infected.
> We get up in the morning and do our PT jerks,
> We all get up at half past five and no-one ever shirks,
> And then we run around The Close in little aertex shirts
> At Sarum College in The Close.
>
> (Extract from song that was sung at the
> College Christmas Dinner in 1947)

Courtesy of Wiltshire &
Swindon History Centre

Memories of a Gardening Student

'When I entered The Close in September 1946, the sun lit up all the buildings. The lawns had been cut that very day, and one's senses were enchanted by the aroma of new mown grass.

It was with great pleasure that I found that I was accepted on the gardening course, to work in the gardens of the Old Deanery, where Queen's House now stands. Our plots were beneath the south wall, on which grew apple and pear cordon trees. We were allowed to eat the fruit! Amongst other work, we were shown how to prune the vines, grown in a greenhouse which stood where Maxwell House now stands.

For me, one of the highlights of 1948 was a visit to the Chelsea Flower Show. This was only the second show to be held after the Second World War. There were also visits to Gullick's Nurseries to learn about dahlia propagation, and to the Seed Merchants near Fisherton Street. School Practice gave me opportunities, as a primary school student, for seed sowing, propagation and cultivation at Charlton Village School in the Spring term.

Miss Riley, the Gardening Lecturer, encouraged us to take the Royal Horticultural Society examination. This has been a valuable asset. I look back with pleasure on my two years in The Close and on all the experiences which I enjoyed as a gardening student.'

Gardening 1940

To the Ends of the Earth

During the war years news came through of former students who were working as teachers and missionaries in different parts of the world.

'Dorothy Stubbings (1924 -1926) has resumed her missionary work and is Head of the Junior School at Achimota College on the Gold Coast. She was unfortunately torpedoed on her way out, but was rescued from a boat, and after some delay arrived at the College. She has now quite recovered from the effects of exposure at sea and is enjoying the work and new experiences'.

STC Magazine, 1941

Other old students who were working in the mission field experienced considerable difficulties with travel:

'Miss Rae and Miss Sainsbury remained in the Honduras and South Africa respectively. Miss Vera Boots, returning to Massai (Kenya) after furlough, had a voyage of over three months'.

LST ibid

College Societies that had a missionary and religious aim flourished during these years. Students continued to support Mtalika Chau School in the Masari Diocese, India. In 1945, £22 was sent to the school as the result of fund raising activities. This was raised to £40 in 1946 by contributions from Old Students, Carol Singers, the Music Club and the Vaulting Club.

An SCM (Student Christian Movement) group was formed in 1944 and met weekly for study, prayer and services in the Chapel. A branch of the Christian Union was established in 1947. This group met for Bible Study, prayer meetings and missionary meetings. The 1948 College Magazine recorded Mabel Jones (1942-1944), who had gone on to do missionary training with the CMS before going to Ruanda.

The Cathedral Branch of the Anglican Young People's Association was also established at this time and College membership grew. Funds raised included money for a school in Gambia and the members were also active in youth work in Salisbury. Students helped to mend Cathedral cassocks during 'work evenings'.

'Although the numbers of these Associations might seem to suggest divisions, or even rivalries, they should be more fairly considered diversity, with the common ground of bringing students into contact with the world beyond College, and relating the Christian ethos of the College to that world'.

LST ibid

School Practice

During the war years it was difficult to find places for School Practices because of evacuation. Schools often shared buildings on a half-time basis in reception areas for evacuees.

'By 1940 all the 102 second year students were billeted in houses or hotels along the coast from Christchurch to Poole, and in inland centres at Ringwood and Eastleigh, so that they might have a full month of Practice. This was before the retreat from Dunkirk, which filled houses, hotels and schools with rescued soldiers. In 1941 all the School Practices had to be arranged in schools in Salisbury and the near area'.

LST ibid

Kathleen Taylor (1941-1943) recalled how 'blackout and travelling difficulties restricted our School Practice itineraries. Only schools in Salisbury and the immediate vicinity could now be used – how tired of students those long suffering teachers must have felt'.

Dora Hughes (1910-1912) was appointed Headmistress of St Edmunds Girls' School in 1942. A member of the College staff commented: ' it is a great comfort to have Miss Hughes in charge of a school upon which we rely so much for the students' training'.

By 1944 schools in a wider area of Wiltshire and Hampshire were used. Students at a school in Eastleigh

An Infant classroom 1940s

Infant Washing Day – School Practice 1945

Students late 1940s

travelled by train. Each student was given 10d to buy tea. Nan Grant (1944-1946) remembered her School Practice in Eastleigh:

'Staff must have had an extra allowance of petrol coupons, as Miss Fowler used her car when visiting students in schools, and sometimes escaping from College. My fondest memory was of Miss Fowler making arrangements for some of us to do a three-week school practice in Eastleigh. There were trains morning and evening and it seemed ideal. Then she discovered that we would need to leave Salisbury station at 7am, as we had to change trains at Romsey, with a fifty-five minute wait. Returning in the evening had the same problem. Winter, freezing, the station master at Romsey got the waiting room fire going and left us fuel to add later. We reached College at about 7pm, late for supper and with preparation to do for the next day. I think that I got about four hours sleep each night, and was so exhausted that the College Nurse took me to sick bay for the last week! She remained a friend for life'.

Pat Prosser entered College in 1945. School Practices in Andover and Gillingham began with an early morning dash up Fisherton Street to the station. The students were given porridge for breakfast on the train.

Ruby Mayoh (1944-1946) recollected that:

'On School Practice we tried to use the theories and advice that we had been given, especially for the compulsory 'Principles and Practice of Education.' We travelled to our schools armed with charts, paints, toys, files and whatever apparatus we had made. Stationery such as writing paper was precious as it was in short supply and we would dash into town whenever we heard that a shop had some. At one of my school practice schools the Head told me that I couldn't have any of her paper as I would only use it! My mother worked for the Agricultural Department and provided me with some packaging and the occasional Hessian bag'.

Jonny Guille (1944-1946) had her first School Practice at St Thomas' School. She had a class of 14 year old boys who were much larger than her and wanted her to go to the pictures with them on Saturday! One of the staff remarked that her name was unusual and that he had been prepared for Confirmation in Eastleigh by a clergyman called Basil Guille. 'That was my father', replied Jonny, and she was invited to Sunday lunch with the teacher and his family.

Her second School Practice was at a little country school at Odstock:

'I remember the Headmistress who insisted that the children called her "Governess", which I thought was rather old fashioned. If the children needed to go across the playground to the lavatory, she would open her desk and tear off exactly two sheets from a toilet roll'.

Gwen Bailey (1948-1950) valued the hard work of the College Staff, who prepared students for what were to be very daunting experiences. Observation days came first:.

'A variety of schools were chosen for us to observe the children at work and play. Town schools, small village schools and one new suburban Primary School showed very clearly how children of the same age varied in behaviour and ability'.

Gwen described her first Teaching Practice of three weeks which was in an industrial area of Poole. She was thrown into the deep end, as due to family illness the class teacher was present only on two days. Another Teaching Practice was in a Victorian stone built Church of England School in Andover.

'My strongest memory of that School Practice was the smell. It came from the large turtle stove that was coal-fired and protected by a large metal fire guard. The smell was a combination of coal fumes and steaming wet coats'.

Benita Brown (1948-1950) recalled cycling to her first School Practice at Bemerton Village School with a card table on her bicycle on which to display books.

In the late 1940s there were few local secondary schools. Students and visiting staff travelled by double decker bus to Eastleigh, by train to Gillingham, Andover and Warminster and by char-a-banc to Bournemouth and Poole.

Rosemary Stone (1949-1951), a secondary student, recalled her experiences:

'Lesson plans read rather like an experiment in chemistry: Aim. Equipment. Method. Result. Conclusion. Feeling that we were wearing a large red letter L front and back, several of us were sent off to Poole. Of course something had been forgotten and one always ran out of material with most of the lesson to go. But slowly, slowly we learnt and did do better next time'.

Gwen Bailey (1948-1950) commented that 'the training we had in Salisbury was second to none. We were encouraged to develop a caring attitude to all children, take responsibility for our actions, and above all to keep our Christian values'.

The McNair Report 1944

The McNair Report addressed the requirements for the supply, recruitment and training of teachers. The recommendations included:

• There should be closer links between Universities and Teacher Training Colleges

• The standard of education and facilities for teacher training should be improved, in order to attract more 'men and women of quality to the profession.'

• Married women should be allowed to continue teaching and should be accepted for training.

• The pledge 'to teach' that was introduced in 1911, should no longer be a requirement for receiving a grant.

• The training course should last for 3 years.

The Butler Education Act 1944

The Butler Education Act aimed to achieve 'free secondary education for all' by raising the school leaving age to 15 and by developing a tripartite system in which pupils were placed in three different types of secondary schools. This had been recommended by the Spens Report in 1938.

Local Education Authorities (LEAs) were to allocate places to children in grammar, secondary modern and technical schools on the basis of the 11+ examination. This was intended to provide equal opportunities for all children.

LEAs were to ensure that there was nursery provision for under 5s and schools for 'children who suffer from disabilities in mind or body.'

The running costs of Church Schools would be met by LEAs. Schools could choose to be Aided or Controlled. Controlled Schools would become the financial responsibility of the LEA but would continue to have denominational worship. Aided Schools would be given a grant towards building costs, and the full costs of teachers' salaries and other maintenance costs. Aided Schools would retain control of Religious Education and could determine the nature of their own acts of worship.

All County schools would provide non-denominational Religious Education and each school day would begin with an act of collective worship 'of a 'broadly Christian nature.'

Children under the age of 18 would be entitled to free school meals and a third of a pint of milk per day.

As a result of the Second World War, the Butler Act was not implemented until 1947.

Examinations

Examination results during the war years indicate that staff and students were determined to overcome difficulties and maintain high standards. The 57 students in the 1939 to 1941 group were particularly successful, despite the stressful first two years of war. The results continued to be very good throughout the war, and in the years immediately afterwards. The examinations for the Archbishop's Certificate continued until 1946.

1949 was the first year in which the Certificate was awarded by the Institute of Education of Bristol University. Awards now differed from previous practice. A student who received Distinction in both Theory and Practice of Education and in her selected subject, would receive a Certificate with Distinction. In 1949 there were 61 Passes, including four which were Certificates with Distinction.

Nan Grant (1944-1946) had vivid memories of receiving the results:

'Each student received through the post four sheets of everyone's results. I recall taking the foolscap envelope from the postman, going into the larder and closing the door, before opening the letter! I had managed to pass everything – whew!'

D-Day: June 6th 1944: The beginning of Operation Overlord

There are many recorded memories of the night before D-Day, when the whole sky appeared to be full of aeroplanes, many pulling gliders. People knew that something special was happening, but they did not know that D-Day had arrived until the following day:

> 'It was the time of our Finals and we wanted to sleep, but heard the noise of planes over and over, all night long for two days and nights – and we didn't know what was happening'.
>
> Muriel Robson (1942-1944)

> 'On the evening before D Day, and on the day itself, the sky seemed to go dark with planes and gliders taking off from Salisbury Plain'.
>
> Amelia Mears (1943-1945)

> 'Never could the symbolism of the serene dignity with which that beloved spire carried its cross on high have struck more poignantly than on D Day, when the College was bemused by the roar of planes, thundering by in their thousands. This perpetual elevation of the Cross, high above all the tumults of the world, is reflected in the unchanging focus of College life, with its morning and evening call to Chapel, where all meet in "caritas" at the foot of the Cross'.
>
> M. B. Denny, 1960

Rosemary Stone (1949-1951) remembered that the homework set on 6th June 1944 was to 'collect and draw six common garden weeds' – and that she was reprimanded for dating her efforts 'D-Day'.

Courtesy of The Salisbury Museum

King's House decorated for VE Day

Channel Island Students on VE Day

VE Day May 8th 1945

Victory in Europe Day officially announced the end of World War Two in Europe. On the following day, May 9th, the Channel Islands were liberated. The students joined in with celebrations in Salisbury. Some of their memories are recorded here. Joan Steggles (1943-1945) and Violet Taylor spent their second year in the flat at 51 High Street:

'One outstanding memory is of Vi climbing on to the window sill to tie red, white and blue ribbon around the neck of the golden ram above the Stonehenge Woollen Shop, as part of the VE celebrations'.

'We were told to take a half day off and help to make the bunting which was put up in all the shops along the High Street to celebrate the end of the war. We had to make paper flags of all the colonies and I was given the task of making an Australian flag'.

Rosemary Edwards (1943-1945)

'In the evening some of us went to the Rose and Crown. None of us had been to a public house before from College, but we felt we should go to celebrate this day. It was quite late when we decided to return. St Ann's Gate would be closed and it was rather far round to the High Street Gate, so we went through the Bishop's Gate and met him admiring his roses in the sunshine. We expected some sort of trouble for taking the short cut, but he must have been feeling really amiable that evening. We had been to a service in the Cathedral earlier when it had been packed tight with people all giving thanks for the end of the war.'

Amelia Mears (1943-1945)

Bishop's Gate

Painting by Jean Watts

Affectionate Memories of the Horse-Boxes

From the late 1890s, dormitory accommodation in King's House was partitioned and divided into cubicles that were known as horse-boxes. Rooms off both staircases, including the attics in the North Wing, were used for sleeping accommodation.

The North Wing

Elsie Tiller (1930-1932) was in Top North, a cubicle room for seven at the very top of King's House, but she and three others were moved out as the room was deemed unsafe.

Seven years later, Fjentje Taconis (1939-1941) lived there:

> 'In Top North I had a tiny cubicle entered through curtains, but its great asset was a door, and stairs beyond that, which were a fire escape leading to a hatch into one of the staff rooms. These stairs had an electric light, and there, after 'Lights Out' – listening for Dr Smith's nightly check that they were out - and in the early morning I would sit studying and writing, for the hours of the day were not enough for me'.

Top North was cleared and painted in 1956, when it became the Upper Lecture Room for the Infant Education Group.

North 3 was on the second floor. It was divided by wooden partitions into three cubicles, with two students in each. Rosemary Edwards (1943-1945) lived there for her first year:

> 'On my first night I heard the Cathedral clock strike every quarter and hour throughout the night, but I got used to it very soon and never noticed it again'.

In the 1940s Dr Elsie Smith was in charge of North Wing. Pat Prosser (1945-1947) remembered that on their 'very first evening, wearing dressing gowns over our night attire, we were invited to meet her and the Second Year students in North over our first drink of NAMCO, a wartime concoction of dried milk and cocoa which was fully available to residential institutions'.

Joyce Burnett, who arrived in 1957, was impressed by the 'grand staircase', but the reality of her accommodation on the second floor was less glamorous:

> The large room was divided into sections by plasterboard partitions that didn't reach the ceiling. They were painted a yellow (straw) colour and resembled stables – hence the name 'horse-boxes'.

Joyce and her friends found empty orange-boxes in the market which, once covered with wallpaper or material

and upended, made good bedside tables. The room was well positioned for reaching lecture rooms and students soon knew every twist of the main staircase:

> 'We had numerous fire drills and were very good at keeping our whistle, torch, coat and shoes near our beds at night. The most circuitous route took us through the roof space to descend into Dr Grubb's study, onto her pink carpet. The ladder was put in place for us to go down to the first floor room, or for them to come up to us if the staircase was too dangerous to traverse'.

At the bottom of the fire escape

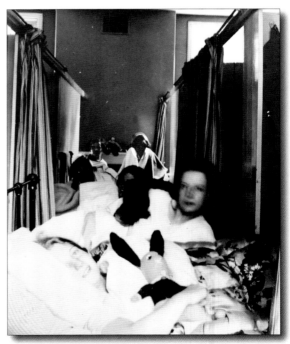

The horseboxes!
Courtesy of Wiltshire & Swindon History Centre

From North 3 to Maxwell …

The last six occupants of North 3 were Jean Hanning, Jean Kitchener, Jennie Down, Carol Snelgrove, Gill Peters and Margaret Southall, who arrived at College in September 1961. Revelling in their new-found independence, there was much noise, fun and laughter. Vivid memories included hanging a smelly Camembert out of a window and dressing up when invited to Dr Grubb's for roasted chestnuts before Christmas. Jean Hanning won a goldfish at the city fair and had to put the goldfish bowl into her drawer on cleaning day, lest it was spotted and reported. Later that year, the students were moved out, so that building work could commence.

The magnificence of Maxwell, the new hostel, was perhaps lost on these girls, who missed the easy companionship of their horse-boxes – but friendships forged in North 3 have lasted more than fifty years.

The South Wing

Long South was a large room at the top of the stairs above the dining room. It was divided into cubicles.

Margaret Hart (1936-1938) roomed in a horse-box in Long South for both years. She felt that she was 'a perfect nuisance to the cleaners, as I kept my apparatus and craft (I was doing the Infant-Junior course) under the bed'.

Ruby Mayoh (1944-1946) and Jean Reynolds (1945-1947) spent their first year there:

> 'There was an iron bedstead, a small chest of drawers, a washstand and a chair. There was no door, but a curtain provided some privacy. We shared large wardrobes at the end of the dormitory and as we did not have many clothes, there was adequate hanging space. We periodically tried our descent by emergency Davy Escape Method to ground level. Kicking away from the red brick with both feet, or risking a scarred nose, exhorted to get on with it from above, and sent around to do it all again, just in case!'

During the 1940s, Miss Story had her bedroom off Long South, and her sitting room was the little room over the King's House porch. Amelia Mears (1943-1945) remembered her with affection:

> 'Miss Story looked after us. She used to ride her bicycle into town to do some shopping, and if she discovered some tasty food like potted meat, she would tell us to hurry along to buy some. College food was adequate, but it could be a little monotonous. Most food was rationed and difficult to obtain'.

How many students fit in a horse-box?

Rosemary Hillhouse and Thelma Cook (both 1956-1958) remembered toasting bread in front of gas fires, having a rota for baths and practising escapes from the building by 'walking their feet down the walls'. Jiving had just become popular, but the students had to be content with hand jiving as anything more energetic was forbidden in their upstairs common room.

Thelma Cook and Jan Thorne (1956-1958) were horrified when they first saw the horse-boxes, but ended up by remembering them with great affection: 'Oh what fun we had – the other stable mates were wonderful company'.

> 'Accommodation for second year students was vastly superior'
>
> Phyllis Gattrell (1929-1931)

Phyllis chose to stay in her horse-box in Old Twenty for her second year:

> 'It was fun and it afforded a good means of exit down the fire escape when one was supposed to be in!'

Gertrude Miles (1936-1938) also remained in her horse-box for her second year, enjoying the privilege of being allowed to study there as she was Dormitory Prefect. Doris Pidgeon (1937-1939) progressed to a room for two students when she was elected Dormitory Prefect in her second year.

King's House was very cold in the winter. Kathleen Taylor (1941–1943) explained that 'the hardy first years in their cubicled dorms were not thought to need such luxuries as heating - or at least only that which was supplied by a very antiquated heating system'. Pat Prosser (1945-1947) remembered that first year students were sometimes allowed to work in their College mothers' rooms when the weather was particularly cold. Most of the students in their second year had gas fires in their rooms.

Glimpses into the immediate post-war years: 1945-1949

'My first impressions of Salisbury Training College were of cold, rainy weather and stark austerity. The war had just ended and rationing was still in force'.

Pat Prosser (1945-1947)

Jean Reynolds (1945-1947) wrote to her parents about an amazing little sweet shop that she and Eileen Jackaman came across in St Ann's Street:

'The selection of Nestles, Cadbury and Bournville brought us to a halt and we went back later with our coupons! Do you remember what Fry's Crunchie looked like? A yellow bubble-cross section with a chocolate covering. I'll send you one. Those with Blue Ration Books have just had their banana quota; two bananas as it happened, so I'll send one as it probably won't keep till next month'.

Jean also remembered spending postal orders from home at The Bay Tree Café:

'Why did the buns and cakes taste so delicious despite reconstituted eggs and shortage of dried fruit?'

Dorothy Coffin (1949-1951) did not eat sugar or sweets:

'I ran a fairly successful black market with my sugar ration and sweet coupons. Oh, the agony when someone's rations disappeared from the locker, and the misery of the 'margarine only' days, as one's butter finished'.

It must have been a tremendous leap for the contingent of Channel Island students who arrived in 1945. The Occupation had just ended and Miss Maxwell considered that they should be made especially welcome after the suffering of the islanders during the war. Cecily Hoyles, Jan Dorey, Fay Arthur and Ruth Le Boutillier all came from Jersey. They soon got to know Pat Prosser, who came from Essex, and Jean Reynolds, who came from Northampton. Jean was very proud of her new parachute silk blouses and real aertex shirts. Friendships began, and some have lasted to this day.

'After six years of war a miscellaneous group of students met in Long South to explore their curtained cubicles and curious attic bathroom up a winding staircase. As we made new friends we quickly realised that the pale, strained group of Channel Islanders (whose entry had been deferred since 1939) had not fared as well as us – from them we learned of tobacco-tin radios and homemade soap. Some of them wanted to talk of those times – others did not'.

Jean Reynolds (1945-1947)

Courtesy of The Salisbury Museum

Anne Spicer (1957-1959), was attending the Reunion in 1975. Whilst scanning the attendance lists she became conscious of someone who was doing the same thing:

'We smiled and introduced ourselves. Ruth explained that she had come to College from the Channel Islands just after the Second World War. Life had been grim. Miss Maxwell, the Principal, had discovered that Ruth did not possess an overcoat and could not really afford one. "Lack of an overcoat is an emergency in an English winter," she said, and funds were made available. Ruth never forgot her kindness'.

Pat Prosser (1945-1947) remembered that two students were secretly engaged. 'They hid their engagement rings as attachments were not encouraged'. Students also felt that 'the atmosphere of Barchester was about in The Close':

'Certain elderly inhabitants complained to the Principal that students were going to the post-box in their bedroom slippers'.

Despite the restrictions and the post-war austerity, many students enjoyed their student years. Valmai Frost (1947-1949) revelled in her time at College:

'Twice weekly visits to the cinema, cream cakes at The House of Steps; dances in town and, oh yes, we even had time to work. On the threshold of our career, to study in the shadow of that wonderful spire, to absorb the beauty of The Close around us - magic, sheer magic'.

Careers and life beyond College were just around the corner and Jean Reynolds (1945-1947) remembered the final packing up:

'Preparations for leaving College are slowly getting under way …the sealing tape you sent me will be grand, thank you. We have acquired several strong boxes labelled Ministry of Food (and smelling of Salmon Grade 2) from the kitchen, and we are busy packing some books to be sent with the trunks'.

Courtesy of The Salisbury Museum

Keep the Flag Flying!
Old Students, Reunions and the College Magazine

The College Magazine continued during the war, but issues sometimes covered two years. Only a small number of Magazines were published between 1942 and 1945, as the paper allowance was very small.

The May 1941 issue shows that as a result of war conditions, few of the Salisbury Club Branches were able to meet. Members were scattered throughout the country, as a result of evacuation. Contributions from teachers told of their different experiences. A student from 1937-1939 was evacuated from Ilford to a tiny village many miles away:

> 'What experiences I am having! There are only nine children, evacuated from different parts of London. I take the Juniors, and very often the whole school, because the Headmistress is so busy with the Canteen. Miss Malcombe would be amused to think of my taking Art with great lads of 12-14 years. But we get on very nicely, doing stencils, pattern work and so on, and the boys are very appreciative'.

Another former student was evacuated from Birmingham to an isolated 'Camp School' in Wales. These were residential schools in rural locations that acted as safe refuges for city children in the war. Winter 1940 was very cold, with bitter winds and hard frosts.

> 'Children and staff had to cross a long, exposed yard to lavatories and washrooms from the dormitories. The staff bedrooms were just cubicles at the ends of long dormitories. Letters are the most welcome thing in my life – never before have I valued letters as much as I do now'.

A teacher who had been working in the Midlands wrote to the Magazine early in 1941. Place names were not always mentioned as the country was at war.

> 'My school has been bombed and I was also bombed out of my lodgings. Very few children came to school, many had no homes and several had lost parents, brothers or sisters. Eventually we were evacuated to …….. (a town in Notts). There were far more teachers than necessary and for a fortnight I did nothing but visit billets and do evacuation clerical work. Now I am living at home and am able to cycle to school. We are, of course, full up with evacuees from London, Felixstowe and Birmingham'.

Miss Dunn commented that many former students were doing magnificent work that involved 'hourly courage and continual patience and sympathy'.

An Old Student revisited her home in Southampton and wrote:

> 'Our lovely St Mary's, where we always held our Guild Service, is a burnt-out shell – no windows, roof or doors – everything a ruin, except the reredos, with the figure of Our Lord intact, and a brave vase of daffodils on the remains of the altar, moving in the breeze'.

It was decided that however difficult the circumstances, an attempt should be made to mark the College Centenary Year. This occasion took place on 29th May 1941. It included a Communion Service in the Chapel, an Open Afternoon for parents and friends and a Service of Thanksgiving in the Cathedral. A College Centenary Fund was set up and all contributions were invested in War Savings for use after the war.

Dr Elsie Smith spoke about the occasion at the 125th Anniversary in June 1966:

> 'I was here for the Centenary Celebration, which was not a celebration at all. We were all eyes on the alert and were more concerned with Air Raid precautions than with celebrations'.

In the 1942 issue, Miss Dunn (Principal) paid sad but proud tribute to former students who had died as a result of enemy action:

The names recorded are:

Eliza Prince (1896-1898), who was killed through enemy action

Marie Moran (1894-1895), who was killed during an air raid on Bath.

Joan Sanders (1932-1934) and Eileen Nodder (1939-1941) who both died as a result of an air raid on Exeter.

Winnie Twist (1916-1918), died as a result of enemy action at night, whilst going to the help of her children.

Once hostilities had ceased, local branches were glad to resume their activities. Eighty members of the London Branch met on 7th July 1945, commenting that 'Our spirits did not match our surroundings, which were still shrouded in war-time gloom'. There was sadness too and many

Coach Trip Ascension Day, 1949

Salisbury Training College Centenary.

Unless war-time conditions make it impossible there will be a CENTENARY CELEBRATION, on **Saturday, May 31st, 1941,** followed by the usual biennial Whitsuntide Week-end Reunion.

12.45   Lunch.
1.45   Coffee and Speeches.
3.0   Thanksgiving Service in Cathedral, with an Address by the Right Reverend The Lord Bishop of Salisbury.
3.45   Tea.

On THURSDAY, MAY 29th, there will be a Centenary Celebration for present students. This will take the form of an Open Day for parents and friends, with a Thanksgiving Service in Cathedral at 3 p.m. The Address will be given by the Very Reverend The Dean of Salisbury. Any old students who wish to come will be welcome.

On WHIT MONDAY, JUNE 2nd, there will be a special Celebration of the Holy Communion in the College Chapel at 8 a.m. The Chapel was dedicated on Whit Monday, 1899.

As has been the custom in recent years the College asks its visitors to contribute towards the cost of the week-end (7/6 for the full week-end till Tuesday morning, or 6/6 if leaving Monday evening).

It has been suggested that the occasion should be marked by raising a Centenary Fund, investing all contributions in War Savings now, and spending the money after the war on one or more College requirements. Suggestions already made for the expenditure of such a fund are :—

(1) A contribution to the existing fund for renewals and additions to the College Chapel.

(2) The provision of amenities for students in College, a hard tennis court being one special suggestion.

(3) A gift towards one or more of the College Benevolent Funds.

(4) A gift towards the U.M.C.A.

Please fill in and return the attached form as soon as possible, in any case not later than MONDAY, MAY 26th, crossing out anything which does not apply.

E. H. STEVENSON,
Hon. Sec.

I hope to be present at Tea on May 29th

I hope to be present at Lunch and Tea on May 31st

I hope to be staying in College for the Whitsun week-end.

I enclose a Contribution of   to the Centenary Fund.

Name

Maiden Name (if married)

Date of Training

Address

Centenary Programme 1941

members, who had suffered during enemy action, are missed from amongst us'.

The Home Branch met in June 1945, soon after VE Day. The Principal gave messages and news from old students in the newly liberated Channel Islands. Telegrams of greeting were sent to the Jersey and Guernsey Branches.

Reports from other local branches reflected the joy of being able to meet again. Members were eager for news of College and of friends. They welcomed staff, both present and former, to their meetings. The 'family feeling' of the College is clearly apparent in these reports.

220 Old Students returned for the 1947 Reunion, which was a particularly happy occasion that was commented on by Jean Reynolds, who was by then in her second year at College:

'Yesterday it was the annual Old Students' Day and crowds of people began arriving on Friday night. It's amazing to see these old stagers, of about 68, coming back in College'.

J. L. Crook was thinking ahead to the time when she too would have left College. Her poem was published in the 1947 issue of the *College Chronicle*:

The Last Term

Soon this well-loved room
Will be no longer mine:
Another's feet will tread its linoed floor
And friendly well-worn rugs,
Strange books will fill those shelves
And unknown faces smile from frames
Upon its mantelpiece and walls.
Some other hands will lift the window wide
To welcome in the fragrant summer air:
Other eyes will see the bluetits as they dart
Into their elm-tree home
And watch the squirrels playing,
Three grey shapes upon the green below.

Will she sit as I have done
Lost in wonder at such beauty,
Books forgotten,
Seeing only green grass, grey walls
And cloudless azure sky?
And at the end of such a day as this
Will she too, with thankful heart
Look up at the star strewn night
And breathe a foolish prayer,
Before she falls asleep,
That this time of peace and beauty
May not end –
This room be hers for ever.

The College Badge

Pat Prosser (1945-1947) recorded the decision to change the College Badge:

'This had hitherto been a single white Tudor rose with the letters S.D.T.C. beneath it. With Miss Maxwell's support we obtained the approval of the Dean and Chapter to use the design of the Cathedral seal, with the College motto round the edge and the date of the Foundation, 1841, and the letters S.D.T.C. incorporated in a new badge'.

The Warminster Annexe at St Boniface College
December 1945 - July 1947

A Potted History of St Boniface College

St Boniface College, Warminster, was founded by the Revd James Erasmus Philipps, whose family were interested in missionary work. The aim was to train young men who had little formal education but were capable of becoming hard workers. The College developed and in 1901 the St Boniface building was completed. Student numbers increased: by 1908 there were 40. By this time one of the clear purposes of the College was to train missionaries. During World War One the College closed and when it reopened a new chapel and lecture rooms were built.

In 1945 The Ministry of Education was urgently seeking to increase the number of teachers. When the Missionary College closed at the outset of World War Two, Salisbury Training College leased it (on a temporary basis) to train another 54 teachers.

After the Second World War, St Boniface Missionary College re-opened in association with King's College, London, as a post-graduate training centre for missionary work. In 1969 the course moved to Canterbury and the College closed. The St Boniface Trust leased the buildings and land to Warminster School.

Salisbury Diocesan Training College at St Boniface

In the 1946 Salisbury Training College Magazine Miss Maxwell, College Principal, wrote about the temporary Warminster extension:

'Many of you will know by now that we have taken, for a temporary extension, St Boniface College Warminster and have fifty-four students there whose course will end in June 1947. All colleges were urged by the Ministry to increase their accommodation to the utmost and this is our contribution.'

Miss Denny was in charge with Miss Geary and Miss Beadle in support. Students respected them all and they were known as 'good sports.' Other lecturers travelled from Salisbury and on Wednesdays students travelled from Warminster to Salisbury by coach for lectures where more space and equipment were needed. Keta Nash who was a St Boniface student recalled:

'Each Wednesday we travelled by coach to Salisbury for lectures including PE (as we had no gymnasium) and music with Miss Barnard. Sandwiches and coffee were served to us in the dining hall and we returned by coach to St Boniface at 4.00 p.m. arriving in time for dinner.'

Past students have extremely warm memories of their days at St Boniface and of Miss Denny.

Joan Williams was the Head Student, 1946-1947:

'We came to St Boniface in December, 1945, without any knowledge whatever of the conditions we should find here. Since then, however, we have built up an active and friendly community, and undoubtedly the experiment at Warminster has been a great success. In many ways we have missed the direct contact with the main College but we hope that will not make us any less loyal members of Salisbury Training College.

We started one term short of schedule, but even so managed to build up gradually a very flourishing social life... The four societies have been very active: the Literary and Debating Society, the Student Christian Movement, the Music Club and the Sports Club have all given much pleasure. We also found time to produce two plays, one of which we took to Salisbury.

The memory of St Boniface will be a long and happy one to those of us who were here, and we all feel very sad about closing down the College at the end of the term.

We wish you all the very best, and thank both staff and students for all the interest you have taken in us.'
SDTC Chronicle, 1947

One year after closing, Joan Williams organised the first reunion:

'We had our own building…and each corner, each sound, each smell made us feel as though we had never been away. The honeysuckle was in bloom, the horse was still in the field and the stones rattled under our feet as we walked to chapel. Just as always! And our chapel was there for us again. It had meant everything to us during our two happy years, and again this time it was the centre and strength of our activities. There the chaplain reminded us of our strong fellowship and we remember our first lesson, Isaiah vi: "Here am I, send me." Again we were sent and scattered, but this time with more confidence, reassured that we were sent by Him.

Farewells were said much more happily in the realisation of the permanence of our fellowship'.
Caroline Bouchholtz, *SDTC Chronicle*, 1948

It is an enormous tribute to St Boniface College that past students still continue to meet annually. In 2014, fourteen past students met in Cardiff with members travelling long distances to be there, including Ireland and Yorkshire. In 2013 someone attended from Canada. Currently the oldest member is aged ninety and the youngest eighty seven.

The past students from St Boniface (see picture below) are a true testimony to the College motto 'In quietness and in confidence shall be your strength'.

> 'At the end of the day when our work is done
> We all join together and don't we have fun!
> If sometimes you hear us say," Well what a place!"
> Ignore us, for really we're proud of St Boniface'.
>
> by The Bard of St Boniface, 1947
> *St Boniface College Magazine*

St. Boniface College Magazine

SALISBURY DIOCESAN TRAINING COLLEGE

DECEMBER 1945—JULY 1947

St Boniface Magazine

Miss Denny wrote this moving letter in the introduction to the magazine:

> 'My Dear Students,
>
> This is both my welcome and my farewell message to you, and it is fitting that the two should be as one, for the solidarity of our life and work and prayer together in this place lies precisely in this, that we have come together here in order to go out from here. We have built a community here for a purpose, but the fulfilment of that purpose lies outside the College, in the years ahead, and now the time has come for us to go into action independently, to strengthen whatever we have gathered here by making our own individual interpretation in life and service in a new setting.

As adventurers we came, and as adventurers we go, not so far afield perhaps as Bonificians of old, but extraordinarily linked to them in the sense of purpose the traditions of their College have given us. St Boniface will always be very dear to our hearts, and for your readiness to share in my perpetual thanksgiving for the privilege of being housed in this dedicated place I shall be forever grateful. The Chapel has in a very real sense been our home.

It has been a big venture to create and disband a College within so short a time, but we have had fun, and despite all the difficulties, your trust and gaiety and helpfulness, and the loyal and strenuous support of the staff have made it for me one of the happiest experiences of a most happy career.

It is with my own enjoyment of teaching behind me that I send you out to enjoy yourselves with children.

You will, of course, know always that my love and good wishes go with you everywhere'.

M Denny

In the magazine a student wrote about life at St Boniface. The first year seemed to be full of 'impromptu entertainments, we talked scandal, explored the neighbourhood and managed generally to have a good time. I now defy anyone to tell me that Wiltshire is monotonous'.

The second year was more serious and all settled down to the job. Three school practices were fun but also very important:

'The St Boniface experience was one that none of the students would have missed. I myself am deeply grateful that I had the chance to come here. The life has been grand and I have formed many friendships which I hope will be lasting. From the Chapel services to the College dances there is not one bit of the life that I would have missed'.

Miss Geary wrote about her life as lecturer at St Boniface. On her first visit in October the interior was 'a wilderness of un-memorable rooms opening off bewildering corridors and erupting out of derelict staircases'. Improvements were soon made in time for the students' arrival in December. She describes how on the first day 'Miss Denny and I had the fun of being mistaken for the cook and char respectively, and in that order'. She describes many happy occasions including a production of *Much Ado about Nothing*:

'Summer mornings at 7 a.m. when the building seemed full of Elizabethan words and music and dance'. She describes a winter when Warminster turned 'into a fairytale setting for an ice ballet' and a final School Practice amid buses that got lost in drifts.

The magazine clearly shows what a happy and full life the students had. In summer children were invited to play on the lawn; in December the Domestic Staff Christmas Party was held in the Junior Common Room. There was a magnificent tea after which Miss Denny distributed presents to the children. Field

Studies were undertaken in the nearby village of Upton Scudamore where several friends were made. A week's camp was held at Bratton in the first week of the summer vacation. Miss Geary wrote 'I shall long remember that week for the intrinsic interest of the survey itself and for the beauty and friendliness of the village – not to speak of the varied humours of camping'.

From the Camp at Bratton, July 1946

BRATTON IN SUMMER

Amid green waves of apple boughs
Red roofs and time-worn stacks appear
Tossed about by greenness.
Beyond, the plain spins far, horizon flat,
Speeding through elms
To faintest, farthest grey infinitude.

Beneath the leaf lie hid
The stream, the mill, the house,
And all the prattle and the shatter
Of human patterning.
The hidden cattle stir and snuffle;
Remotely crows the unseen cock.
Half-glimpsed, the barn roof sags
Upon encrusted timbers.
Sunk deep beneath the earth's green
Rising wave of tousled grass and flower,
The village dreams.

BG (Miss Geary)

Bratton Down   Painting by Kate Sykes

Miss Mabel Denny – 'The wisdom of having lived'

Miss Denny was a much loved and respected lecturer at St Boniface. In the St Boniface magazine a tribute was paid to her by the students:

> We have been fortunate in having a mother at College. Not many students have that; but we have had Miss Denny and she has made all the difference to our College life. It cannot always have been easy to have a big noisy family just at the time when life should be quiet and orderly; but Miss Denny has borne up bravely and laughed with us, and joined in our various moods even to our examination fevers. Above everything she has helped us to remember what home life is amidst the rush of College life, and she has taught us all that growing old is something lovely for in her we have seen the wisdom of having lived. Our College life has been enriched by having her and this Annexe has been something we shall always remember with love'.

When Miss Denny left St Boniface she joined HMI. and was subsequently elected onto the UNESCO Committee, composed of representatives from all over the world. In 1960 after twelve years as a member of HMI and eight months of retirement, Miss Denny returned to take up her 'old job' as a College Lecturer for the Summer Term. Her thoughts and views on this are recorded in the following chapter.

Miss Denny

Miss Denny in Ambrose, 1946

The Beauty of thy Peace... The St Boniface College Chapel

The St Boniface hymn was the much loved *Dear Lord and Father of all Mankind*. Chapel was the background to the communal life at St Boniface with regular daily services. It gave the students a sense of unity and security. Joan Turner, Senior Chapel Warden, wrote:

> 'We have learnt the value of starting each day with prayer and the joy of resting in God each night. The strength and the peace and the sense of unity it has given us will remain with us when we are working in our separate schools'.

A Wedding Gift

Keta Nash was a student at St Boniface College from 1945-1947. Her first teaching post was at St John's School in Frome where she taught a class of 35 reception children. When she left to be married in 1948 the Headteacher asked Keta for a wedding present list. Keta suggested that a piece of 'Pyrex', (the new kitchenware) would be very useful. On her final day a special assembly was held. Every child in the class filed into the school hall, each holding a piece of 'Pyrex', from a pie funnel to a large casserole dish. Keta still uses two of the dishes today!

Keta Moggridge (née Nash) with her remaining Pyrex dish

Drawing by Pat Jones

The Beginning of the Students' Union

'It is with great pleasure that I am able to announce the formation of The Students Union of Salisbury Diocesan Training College. Its function is two-fold … (a) to undertake and be responsible for the organisation of Student life in the College; (b) to give the College unity and to help the students to realise their communal responsibilities.

This year has been more or less experimental and has on the whole worked fairly satisfactorily, although we have made some mistakes and had to face some difficulties; but I hope that the foundations of the Union have been laid, and that our successors will be able to build upon them, remedying our weaknesses, and finally making College life what we all want it be – a strong and corporate unity'.

Dorothy M. Read, President, *SDTC Chronicle*, 1941

How times had changed during one hundred years of College life!

In 1947 a 'delegation' of students from St Boniface, the Warminster Annexe, attended the NUS (National Union of Students) Congress. Their report makes lively reading:

'An enjoyable time was had by all. Amongst many topics, the delegation debated "The Purposes and Problems of Higher Education in Post War Britain". It was moved that examinations be removed and replaced by a report on the progress of each student by his tutor, as in Emergency Colleges. Co-operation was earnestly desired between Training Colleges and Universities; it was felt that there was much snobbery on this point.

The agenda of the week was a big one and many controversial points were raised. We nearly returned fiery Communists, but despite regular doses of *Daily Worker* we emerged unscathed. We would not have missed the Congress for anything'.

St Boniface College Magazine, 1945-1947

Who's for the Spire?

Between the years 1949 and 1951 the upper section of the Cathedral Spire was being rebuilt. The students were captivated by the work of the steeplejacks who emerged from the weather door, forty feet from the top and climbed to the capstone by means of iron rungs placed either side if one of the angles of the spire.

Beryl Bright, a student from 1948-1950 remembered an 'unforgettable experience' which she shared with fellow students Doreen Davies and Eileen Prince. At ground level they chatted with the steeplejacks and were invited to accompany them up to the point where the tower and spire meet. On reaching this point the steeplejacks asked 'Who's for the spire?' The intrepid students accepted the invitation:

'The climb grew more difficult, first up ten wooden ladders placed amongst the timber framework that was the original scaffolding, between the ever diminishing sides of the spire. Then - the leading steeplejack pushed open the weather door and stepped out. I was next, reaching round to clasp the iron rung above with my hand, while feeling below with my foot. So up we went. The first steeplejack twisted to perch himself on the very top of the Cross, while I stood on the capstone, firmly grasping the arms. Doreen and Eileen followed while the other steeplejack waited a few feet below.

Eastwards stretched the river Avon, northwards we could see Old Sarum, and beyond that, Stonehenge. On the grass of the Close rectangular patches of lighter green showed up, clearly indicating sides of graves and, outside, the City was laid out like a model town, its many thousand inhabitants and visitors pursuing their myriad activities, unaware of the elation and exhilaration we were feeling in our exalted vantage point.

Then began the descent. We will not deny our relief at being safely inside the weather door once more. After that the excitement was over – but we had been recognised, even 404 feet up, as I was wearing a bright turquoise-blue skirt, memorable because, as an impecunious student, I had only this one skirt. We were severely reprimanded for our foolhardiness, but by whom and under what circumstances I cannot remember, so great was our pride and joy in being, as far as we knew, the first and only women at that time, to have climbed to the top of Salisbury Cathedral's famous spire'.

Memories are made of this!

'I was late for Miss Room's PE class and the punishment was to teach women in St Mary's Home how to dance every Tuesday evening. I played records and taught them the quickstep, the waltz, the polka and old time waltz. I felt sorry for these girls, who were sleeping in a dormitory and working in a laundry. Miss Room remembered me when I attended a reunion more than ten years later.

While at College I went to a dance at the Guildhall near the market square. It was put on by some germ warfare scientists and at 10 pm Miss Riley, the gardening lecturer, walked in and took me back to The Close. The band was playing ' Only five minutes more in your arms'.

My room mate, Beryl Drysdall and I climbed the Cathedral spire with some steeplejacks. When we came to ground level Miss Barnard met us and she was shaking!

Beryl played the organ in the Cathedral for choir practice when David Willcox had a cold. I met her date and took him to our room because he had a cold too. Miss Maxwell said that I could have two men, but not one.'

Eileen Prince (1948-1950)

Biology Revision on the Roof

Students by river

'Effectively we could have existed in a cloistered world of our own, but Salisbury welcomed us from the start, a number of us being adopted by kindly families who welcomed us into their homes, churches and chapels. The theatre, cinemas, and other facilities were within walking distance, together with Old Sarum, a favourite picnic spot in good weather. The compelling presence of Stonehenge made an indelible impression upon me when a few of us elected to approach it on foot via the "old ways" across the hills one day to see it silhouetted dramatically against a fiery Autumn sky. Salisbury Plain itself was still occupied by a number of wartime military bases, and Saturday night dances in Amesbury and elsewhere offered the opportunity to dance to "Big Band" music on gramophone records and socialise with service men from home and overseas. Winchester and other nearby places were easily accessible by bus, an added bonus being the return hitch by lorry into the market square when funds were low. End of term was usually celebrated with friends, sampling cream cakes at the *House of Steps* just outside the Close.

I left College in 1949 but still recall many familiar faces. Memories and true friendships never die. Happy Days!'

Audrey Booth (2011)

A daring escapade

Coach trip

Extracts from a Report by HM Inspectors
SALISBURY TRAINING COLLEGE
Inspected during the Session 1946-1947

Introduction

The Salisbury Training College for Women is one of the oldest in England, dating back to 1841. It is also one of the most beautifully situated. It has, therefore, all the claims to strength which rest on historical associations, firmly rooted tradition and excellent situation.

The College was last inspected in 1925. In view of the long interval since that date, the present inspection was carried out over a greater period and by a larger number of inspectors than is customary. Mention should be made of the fact that, by courtesy of the College, the Reporting Inspector stayed in the College for two nights and so became acquainted with the normal extra-curricular life of the students.

Nature and Scope

In 1946 there were 201 students on roll, of whom 54 were accommodated at Warminster. It is desirable to say something of the section of the College at Warminster. In 1945 the College Authorities rented St Boniface College. The premises were ill-adapted and the staff of the College could not be expanded sufficiently to meet the needs of an annexe some 22 miles from Salisbury. Consequently, it was only by heroic efforts that the enterprise was carried through. By and large, a very useful piece of work has been done by the College at Warminster and the students there have undoubtedly enjoyed their training and benefited by it.

Premises

Creditable and useful as the efforts to improve the College are, they leave the premises far from satisfactory. Overall there is a shortage of really adequate provision for staff and students in bedrooms, common rooms, lecture rooms and sanitary provision. The full scheme for rebuilding and re-equipping should have high priority as soon as national conditions allow such work to be done.

The College as a Community

The present day student is in some ways more mature than her counterpart twenty years ago. She is prepared for hard work but assumes she will have opportunities for making social contact with either sex, without fuss or subterfuge.

Happily, the College authorities show good sense in their attitude toward the recreation of the students. The existing buildings and facilities at the College are a serious handicap, for they offer little of the privacy and few of the opportunities for care of her person which a girl of 18 or 20 should have. It is difficult to say where in the College, without making a major event of it, a student could entertain a young man!

Within the limitations referred to in various sections of the report, the College gives its students a sound moral and social training; the relations of staff and students are happy, and the students are well-mannered and without doubt conscious of the social responsibility they will carry.

The Health of the Students

There is evidence that the health of the girls is being maintained and that there is not an undue amount of sickness. On the other hand, there appears to be an increased amount of tiredness, possibly due to the strains experienced during the war. The standard of cleanliness and orderliness in the sanatorium and surgery are high. The heating is inadequate. In some cubicles there are no heating facilities. Most serious of all are the heating defects in the sanatorium where recently one girl nearly died due to inadequacy of heating.

Catering Arrangements

The cooking is very satisfactory. An analysis made of the food used in preparing the meals for two weeks, showed that each resident is consuming about 2,300 calories a day. It is strongly recommended that an effort be made to increase the calorie value of the diet. To achieve this, full use could be made of the special allocation of dried milk powder, and perhaps, by careful planning, cooked breakfast could be served every day, and a pudding included in the supper, unless the first course is bulky.

Library

The main part of the College Library is housed in a large and well-lit room, equipped with tables and chairs for study, consisting of 4,500 books. In addition there are some further 500 books at Warminster in the section of the College which is there. Mathematics is not represented at all and the Science section requires to be built up.

Staff

The Principal has made a remarkable contribution to the life of the College in all its facets; more particularly her well-balanced, sensible and cheerful personality has had a valuable effect on the atmosphere prevailing among staff and students. It is due to her that under the very difficult conditions of the existing buildings, staffing shortages and other obstacles, the College has made progress.

The staff are almost without exception loyal, conscientious, and very hard-working, their relations with the students happy. In particular the senior lecturer in Infant Education, the Music lecturer and the Craft lecturer are doing highly creditable work, and the senior English lecturer work of real distinction.

Of recent years, it has been exceedingly difficult to fill posts in Training Colleges with women of high intellectual calibre and suitable experience, and a large number of the present staff have been appointed during that period. This section should not end without tribute being paid to the work of the housekeeper and cook supervisor; the side of the College with which they deal is in a high degree successfully and happily managed.

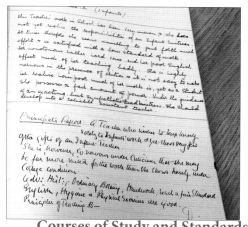

Student report

Courtesy of Wiltshire & Swindon History Centre

Courses of Study and Standards of Work

Taken all in all, the two years' course is a very full one. In the Education lectures the groups were too large and there were too few tutorials and too many lectures. A too full curriculum tends to force the lecturers to do the work which the students should, with more lasting profit, do for themselves. It is also recommended that there should be greater integration of material in each Education course, with more emphasis on the child as the focal point.

The standard reached in English is very high; in Music, some Crafts, Horticulture and Physical Education, apart from the work done in swimming and games, where the facilities are inadequate, good; and in the remaining subjects, with the exception of Art, fair. Suggestions made with regard to the courses offered in Science and Horticulture will no doubt receive the attention of the staff. A good deal of the Students' written work in Divinity was creditable and some of the work of the better students quite first class.

The work of the students in School Practice showed they had received the most careful and painstaking help from the lecturers, and had been given a measure of self-confidence in their ability to prepare a lesson and handle a class. Their sincerity, honesty and readiness to accept advice without resentment made a very good impression on the Inspectors who saw them teach.

Infant play

Doreen Perry

Doreen Perry (Davies) was a student at College from 1948 -1950. She was a remarkable, widely respected woman who left a long lasting legacy to education and to the arts. In 1980 she co-founded the independent classical music record label, *Hyperion*, with her husband, and developed it into an international brand.

She became a Senior HMI before retiring from the profession in 1993. She was then persuaded to join the Governing Body of Sir John Cass Church of England Red Coat Secondary School in Stepney, and was instrumental in turning around the school's fortunes.

Doreen Perry had a clear vision for the school's success and strong beliefs about the right of all children to a good education. She was an inspiration to all members of the school community. Doreen Perry died in 2009, after a full and eventful life.

A Visit to Switzerland: April 1947

Keta Nash, (1945-1947), recalled how fortunate she was to be one of a group of the first students to travel abroad after the war. Miss Mayo led a party of geography students to Wilderswil, near Interlaken. They visited many places and a highlight was the ascent of the Jungfrau by train. The adventure stayed in the memory of many students:

'On 10th April, 1947, a party of geography students and friends, under the care of Miss Mayo, left Victoria Station, London, en route for Switzerland. Weather conditions were excellent, and after an uneventful journey we arrived at our destination, Wilderswil, near Interlaken. For many it was a new experience, and everything came up to their expectations. The weather continued fine and every day was spent out of doors. Amongst the places visited were the Trummelbach Falls, Meiringen, Grindelwald and the glacier and ice grotto, Basle and Berne, where we saw the Houses of Parliament and the Bear Pit.

The shops proved a great attraction. To be able to buy sweets, clothes and food without producing coupons was an almost forgotten experience. After ten very happy days we reluctantly said "Good-bye" to Switzerland and, tanned and refreshed, returned to England … and Finals'.

SDTC Chronicle, 1947

Miss Mayo and students en route to Switzerland, 1947

The Winter of 1947 – one of the worst in living memory

The following poem was written by Kay Drake (1945-1947) and was inspired by memories of The Close during the exceptionally hard winter, when deep, sunlit snow remained for many weeks.

January Snows

No more the gloom – November and December
Passed. And glorious light was seen,
A January to remember.
Deep untrodden snow, blue skies serene
Above us, what joys to treasure -
The sharpening air which took our breath
(Yet never dulled our sense of pleasure)
Spoke to us then. But not of death
Within that lovely hallowed place.
'Twas life eternal, ever near
All filled with peace and love and grace
In memory to be ever dear.
O January of the snows
What beauty came upon The Close.

Light fell on this still scene below
From moon and sparkled stars and sun.
Was this most perfect January snow
Since this fair world was first begun?
The warming walls of house and hall
Stood ancient midst the coldly pristine snow.
There the Cathedral towered over all.
How blessed were we who witnessed it, Although
Our frozen hands and faces daily bore
The signs of January's cold assault, yet still
We gazed and gazed till we could look no more
And still of beauty we'd not had our fill.
O January of long ago
I loved you so ... I loved you so ...

The Salisbury Museum

Setting Chapter 4 in context: A Table of some significant events

Date	Educational	International/National	Local
1940		Food Rationing began. British troops evacuated from Dunkirk Battle of Britain -the Blitz – strategic bombing of London, Coventry, Birmingham, Southampton and other cities.	Church of St Francis consecrated Fire watching parties set up in Salisbury Wilton House and Breamore House were both requisitioned by the army
1941	Green Paper "Education after the War" formed basis of 1944 Education Act	Fall of Singapore. Japanese attack Pearl Harbour. America entered the war	King and Queen inspect troops in Southern Command Workshops in Salisbury started to produce parts for Spitfires
1942		Soap rationing was introduced	American, Australian and Canadian troops arrived in the area Air Raid on Salisbury – gas works was hit. London Philarmonic Orchestra performed concerts in Salisbury
1943	Norwood Report supported 3 types of secondary schools, as suggested by 1938 Spens Report	Dambusters raid on the Ruhr dams	Village of Imber on Salisbury Plain evacuated to provided training area for troops
1944	McNair Report recommended 3 year Teacher Training course. The Butler Act set structure for post-war system of secondary education. Board of Education replaced by Ministry of Education	June 6th: D Day – Allied troops land in Normandy. Start of Operation Overlord V1 and V2 rocket attacks on southern England	Some of the planning for D Day was done at Wilton House
1945	Labour government promoted tripartite system of education: grammar, technical and secondary modern schools	Churchill attended Yalta Conference May 8th: VE Day – end of war in Europe Atom bomb dropped on Hiroshima – surrender of Japan Labour won General Election- Clement Attlee became Prime Minister	VE Day Celebrations! Dancing in the Market Place in Salisbury, street decorations, impromptu parties and the ringing of church bells Departure of soldiers, Civil Defence stood down and the annual October fair in Salisbury returned
1946	Introduction of free school milk Barlow Report recommended more university places for Science students	First meeting of United Nations. Nuremberg war trials Bank of England nationalised	New housing built at Bemerton Heath, Harnham and Amsesbury Salisbury Cathedral School moved into the Bishop's Palace The Common Cold Research Unit opened in Salisbury
1947	School Leaving Age raised to 15. Women admitted to Cambridge University as full students	1946/47 winter one of most severe on record Wedding of Princess Elizabeth to Lt Philip Mountbatten Discovery of Dead Sea Scrolls	20 foot snowdrifts on Salisbury Plain
1948	The 2nd Clarke Report recommended government spending on out of school facilities for children and parents. The Nurseries and Child-Minders Regulation Act provided for the regulation and inspection of nurseries and child-minders.	UK railways nationalised to create British Rail The beginning of the National Health Service Birth of Prince Charles Summer Olympics held in London State of Israel created	One-way traffic in Salisbury introduced Salisbury Infirmary was linked with a hospital at Odstock that had been used as American military hospital. Regional plastic surgery service based here from 1948
1949		Clothes rationing ended Britain signed the North Atlantic Treaty, creating NATO.	
1950		Birth of Princess Anne The end of soap and motor fuel rationing British troops sent to Korea	New Salisbury fire engine commissioned Cathedral Spire Appeal launched, to replace the cross and rebuild the top 30 feet

Towards Unity

'There should be closer links between Universities and Training Colleges'

Bristol University was one of the first to respond to the recommendation (above) of the McNair Report in 1944. The Institute of Education was established in 1947. Salisbury Diocesan Training College, which had been affiliated with Reading University since 1928, now became one of the constituent Colleges of the Institute of Education of Bristol University.

The responsibility for the College syllabus would remain with the individual Colleges.

'The Institute was vigorous in overcoming the isolation of the Colleges. Boards of Studies drew together Lecturers from all the Colleges. Interchange of Lecturers was also to be arranged, to give support in allocating grades and to consult towards comparability between the Colleges'.

(LST ibid)

Miss Maxwell wrote in May 1949 in the *SDTC Chronicle*:

'The College has had a happy year of progress, and now we feel to be fully members of the Institute of Education at Bristol. All of the new external examiners have been to see us, and we look forward to fresh life in our work with their help'.

Student Accommodation in the Forties

Several students including Margaret Frost (1948-1950) were housed in lodgings during this period as accommodation in College was insufficient.

'As "billetees" we asked for the use of the "Quiet Room" in King's House as a base as, during the day, we had nowhere to leave books and belongings and were not allowed to go back to our billets. In some cases the journeys would have been too far anyway. Our request was granted and the room was no longer QUIET'.

The McNair Report in 1944 highlighted the need for better training facilities for teachers to meet the expansion in education. A general HMI Inspection during 1946-1947 urged action to renew College plans for development. The year 1947 was a starting point for the development of the College buildings which would last for nearly twenty-five years. Lecturing space was required in addition to residential accommodation. The Warminster Annexe at St Boniface College provided extra accommodation for two years. In 1948 improvements were made to the existing staff accommodation and to the Sanatorium. The heating system in King's House was renewed. Canon Roland Bailey, Secretary to the STC Governing Body, wrote in a letter to the *Salisbury Journal*:

'It may be of interest to mention that the Governing body is restoring Audley House in Queen Anne style. The house is considered a good example of that period of architecture. At present we are restoring the roof, which requires new timbers, and re-pinning and re-laying the old roof tiles, at very considerable cost'.

Students were frequently startled to hear that they would be going into 'The Wardrobe', or 'Wardrobe' as it is often called. This house originated in the 13th Century, when it was the residence of one of the Canons of the Cathedral. It later belonged to the Bishop of Salisbury and was probably used as a store house and administrative base for his household, hence the name, which was first recorded in 1543. The College rented 'Wardrobe' as a College hostel after the Second World War, to provide extra accommodation for twenty five students and two members of staff. In Autumn 1945 Miss Mayo, who lectured in Geography and Mathematics, the students and the Chaplain and his family all moved in. 'Wardrobe' is synonymous with Miss Mayo, or 'Chloe', as she was affectionately known. She remained the Warden until 1969, when the hostel closed and an era came to an end.

Kay Drake (1945-1947) lived there during the harsh winter of 1946-47:

'One unforgettable memory was the sight of the Cathedral Close under the snowfall of that winter, which remained, in brilliant sunshine, for at least six weeks. It was amazing to view, but had the disadvantage of being exceptionally cold. We were fortunate that Sheila Willing's mother managed to obtain two ex-service duffle coats for us – the genuine articles'.

Honor McWatters (1946-1948) moved from King's House to Wardrobe for her second year:

'I found myself in a small room at the top of the house. It was a long way from a bathroom, but there was a basin and jug for washing purposes. That winter was exceptionally cold, with severe frosts and ice all around, so the cold in my room was intense. For several mornings the water in my jug was frozen and the bedclothes barely kept me warm. As the days went on, the trees, clothed in a covering of ice, were a wonderful sight. Ice-covered twigs tinkled together in the breeze. When the sun came up, little tubes of ice fell off clattering to the ground. It's still all a vivid memory - but despite the beauty of the scene, the thaw, when it came, was more than welcome!'

Wardrobe was a 'special' place to spend one's student years. It left enduring memories and later students will carry on the story.

The Governing Body decided it was necessary to build new accommodation, but plans to build in The Close caused much debate and critical attack. There were plans to demolish the Medieval Hall, as an inspection in 1948 had failed to disclose the early date of the building. Fortunately the Hall was not demolished, as a result of later discoveries. Work on Maxwell House began in late summer 1949. The laying of the Foundation Stone was performed by the Bishop on October 15th 1949:

'The ceremony was not ostentatious, but regarded as one of private deep thankfulness. Students and Old Students, academic and domestic staff, members of Council and interested friends from the City gathered at a service in the Cathedral and, in fine weather, followed the procession of clergy to the site. Workmen and architect had everything in readiness and, with prayer and blessing, the Bishop tapped the stone in place. The "quietness and confidence" in that brief ceremony seemed to symbolise renewed hope after the stresses of wartime'.

LST ibid

King's House Training College, Salisbury. JWS 943

The proposed development

Chapter 5

Let us go Forward Together

1950-1960

Let us go forward together!

What was the background to College life in the 1950s? At the beginning of the decade it seemed as if there would be no end to austerity, but the College, and life in general, gradually began to recover from the tensions and anxieties of the war years. There was the lingering effect of two World Wars, and many towns and cities were pockmarked with the scars of war. In the early Fifties rationing was still in place. In addition to the gradual disintegration of the British Empire, the Korean War (1950-1953), the Suez Canal crisis (1956), and the Cold War all took place during the Fifties. Foreign currency became more expensive and consequently the cost of imports rose. Life did, however, gradually become easier and by the end of the decade the Prime Minister, Harold Macmillan, declared 'You've never had it so good'. It was a rapidly changing and increasingly complex world with many developments in the fields of medicine, science and space exploration. People looked forward with renewed hope.

The Government sought to deal with the demands of education. Every LEA was required to submit plans as to how they would proceed. Five thousand schools needed repairing or replacing. The raising of the school leaving age required 168,000 new places. There was a scheme for quickly constructed and erected huts to provide new classrooms and a great need for more teachers. The higher birth rate from 1948-1949 meant that many more school places would need to be planned for. Fifty-five emergency colleges produced 35,000 extra teachers by 1951.

In 1959 Voluntary-Aided Schools were offered 75% of their building costs and the Voluntary Colleges were offered similar grants. Salisbury Diocesan Training College certainly made the most of these grants.

Throughout the years the College had endeavoured to provide the best possible education and training for its students and in the Fifties it once again rose to the challenge. In the College Chronicle of 1950 Miss Maxwell wrote:

> 'The world is sorely in need of all that is good in our College tradition: let us go on with courage and faith, that the service of our lives may be acceptable to God'.

Miss E. I. Barnard

Countless students over years recalled Miss Barnard with great fondness, remembering her patient and skilful musical tuition and general thoughtfulness and support. In 1951 she succeeded Dr Smith as Vice Principal and became acting Principal for a short time between Miss Maxwell's leaving and Dr Grubb's arrival. With typical humility she wrote:

> 'When one is faced with the full responsibility, one realises more than ever the strength which comes from the loyalty and devotion of staff in all departments, the co-operation of the students and the thoughts and prayers of the large number of old students whose attention is so often brought back to their own College days. I came to Salisbury in 1936 and so my circle of old students known to me personally in College as well as those I have known since is gradually extending further and further'.
>
> *SDTC Chronicle*, 1955

Miss Barnard retired in the early 1960s after 30 years of dedicated and enthusiastic service to the College.

High Street Gate　　　Courtesy of The Salisbury Museum

Setting Chapter 5 in context: A Table of some significant events

Date	Educational	National/International	Local
1950		Birth of Princess Anne The end of soap and motor fuel rationing British troops sent to Korea	New fire engine commissioned in Salisbury Cathedral Spire Appeal launched, to replace the cross and rebuild the top 30 feet.
1951	General Certificate of Education (GCE) introduced, replacing the School Certificate	Winston Churchill PM Festival of Britain held in London Zebra crossings introduced	Cathedral spire restoration completed Salisbury population 32,910
1952		Death of King George VI Opening of Agatha Christie's play 'The Mousetrap' in London.	Bomber crashed on Bemerton Heath Salisbury's Centenary Exhibition, inspired by the 1951 Festival of Britain.
1953	Education Act (Miscellaneous Provisions) extended provision for disabled children to independent schools. LEAs required to provide free dental treatment for all children	Death of Queen Mary Coronation of Queen Elizabeth II Revd Chad Varah started the Samaritans. Everest conquered!	Salisbury Arts Theatre was renamed 'The Playhouse' and re-opened Coronation celebrations.
1954	Opening of Kidbrooke School in Central London, the first custom built comprehensive school	End of Rationing JRR Tolkien's book, 'Lord of the Rings' was published Roger Bannister broke the 4 minute mile record	Stratford-sub-Castle and Westwood become part of Salisbury. 'Lord of the Flies' by William Golding (teacher at Bishop Wordsworth's) was published.
1955	Underwood Report recommended Child Guidance service in every LEA 120 Hospital Schools now in existence. Almost 11,000 new places provided for SEN children and a further 8,000 planned	Winston Churchill retired, aged 80 Anthony Eden now Prime Minister Guinness Book of Records first published	Bishop lays foundation stone of new St Thomas's School Reggie Salberg becomes General Manager of the Playhouse.
1956	Selected Technical and Further Education Colleges upgraded to Colleges of Advanced Technology – most became 'new universities' in the 1960s	Launch of Premium Bonds Introduction of double yellow lines to prevent parking Suez crisis.	First section of new cattle market opened Freedom of the city granted to RAF Old Sarum
1957	School Leaving Age raised to 15 Women admitted to Cambridge University as full students	Jodrell Bank Observatory became operational. Harold McMillan PM. Link found between lung cancer and smoking. Plan to allow women into the House of Lords.	New St Thomas's School opened Church of St Michael and All Angels, Bemerton Heath was consecrated 200 join first Sarum CND march
1958		London Planetarium opened Work on the M1 started Prince Charles became the Prince of Wales 'Blue Peter' was first broadcast Munich air disaster	Opening of Westwood School for Girls. Heavy floods – canoe in Fisherton St. Buddy Holly visited Salisbury Arthur and Molly Maidment Mayor and Mayoress of Salisbury
1959	Crowther Report on the education of 15-18 year olds recommended raising school leaving age to 16.	UK postcodes introduced as an experiment in Norwich First 'mini' car went on sale	First woman minister in S Wilts takes over congregational churches. John Morrison Salisbury MP for 6th time.

Some members of staff in the 1950s

Some members of Staff who had been appointed in the Forties, remained at the College, in addition to new appointments.

Miss Maxwell	Principal	1942-1954
Miss E. I. Barnard	Vice-Principal	
	Music	
	Acting Principal	
Dr V. Grubb	Principal	1955-1962
Miss D. J. Ayling	Physical Education	
Miss M. Babbington	Education	
Miss D. Bell	Art and Craft	
Miss O. M. M. Blackburn	English	
Miss R. A. Bryant	Music	
Miss V. Bunyard	English	
Mrs B. Dalton Hill	Education	
Miss Marie Bishop	Education exchange from Minnesota with Mrs Dalton Hill	
Mrs Fry	French	
Miss M. J. Gibbs	Education	
Miss M. F. Goddard	English, French	
Mrs G. Grainger	Craft	
Miss R. E. Mayo	Geography, Mathematics	
Miss M. Moore	Speech Training	
Miss D. M. Nash	Gardening	

Miss Nash left College in 1957 as the Horticulture and Rural Studies course closed in favour of pure sciences.

Miss O. G. Northcott	Biology
Mr W. Peel	Chemistry
Miss M. F. Rogers	Divinity
Miss D. Saintsbury	Art
Miss L. H. Shawcross	Art and Craft
Miss K. Shute	Physical Education
Miss L. Taconis	Education
Miss L. S. Taylor	Education
Miss D. A. Todd	History
Miss E. C. Trinder	Divinity
Revd A. Osborne	Chaplain
Revd. M. R. Newman	Chaplain
Miss M. K. Luckham	College Bursar
Mr W. B. Gibson	College Bursar
Mrs B. Stockdale	Principal's Secretary
Miss D. Newton	Principal's Secretary
Miss F. A. Taylor	Cook-caterer

In the 1955 *Chronicle* Miss Barnard paid tribute to the seventeen years of loyal service which Miss Netta Taylor had given to the College.

A Return to College

Miss Taconis, who had thoroughly enjoyed her two student years during 1941-1942, returned to College ten years later as a member of staff:

'The ten year interval had of course brought some changes – a small growth in numbers, a transition to treating the students as young adults rather than schoolgirls, though they still did not attain the age of majority until 21. But the beating heart of the College was still in the Chapel, at any rate for me, and to be back with its daily rhythm was a bonus and a joy. There had been many changes of staff and their average age was now much lower, though at 28 I was probably the youngest.

There were new ropes to learn of course, and it felt strange at first to be, so to speak, on the other side of academic procedures of which, as a student, I had hardly been aware. Once again I was surrounded by the camaraderie of friends made through shared experiences and a common purpose.'

King's House, 1953

'Robert Poole'
robert.poole@mac.com

Dr Elsie Smith

Dr Elsie, as she was widely known, came to Salisbury as a young and brilliant lecturer in English Literature in 1928. Nancy Jones (1940-1942) was influenced by her inspirational teaching:

> 'Dr Smith held me enraptured with her total devotion to Wordsworth. Her influence has remained with me as I never tire of reading poetry'.

She established high standards of scholarship and expected excellent written English.

> 'I remember sitting in Audley, looking through the elms to the west door of the Cathedral, sense visually satisfied and intellect stimulated for a lifetime by Dr Elsie Smith. Straight from school, we learned to discriminate, evaluate and appreciate, so that the basis of endless interest was laid.'
>
> Barbara Rees, *College Chronicle*, 1977

Dr Elsie's connection with the Cathedral Library began when it was under the care of Canon Wordsworth, who showed considerable surprise that a woman should seek permission to work there. The Sarum Magna Carta was her particular interest and she gave lectures and wrote a booklet about it. She also helped to repair and restore library manuscripts that had been damaged by damp during war-time storage.

After retiring from College in 1951, Dr Elsie became the Cathedral Librarian. The archives were in great need of care and attention and Magna Carta was precariously housed in an old safe. Her devotion and dedication to her work was such that the following story is likely to be true:

> 'Dr Elsie Smith became so worried about the priceless document that she took matters into her own hands. Each night she would take Magna Carta home with her. And put it for safety under her bed'!
>
> Leslie Thomas, *Almost Heaven*

Robert Key, former Member of Parliament for Salisbury, remembered meeting Dr Smith, 'dressed in black and wearing a black felt hat' on his tenth birthday:

> 'She took me up the stairs to the Cathedral library, and over to an ancient safe, which she unlocked. Onto my outstretched arms she placed a dirty old sheet of vellum with illegible writing on it. "One day you'll remember that you held the Magna Carta in your hands'.
>
> Robert Key, *A Child in The Close*

Dr Elsie died in 1977. Her obituary in the Friends of Salisbury Cathedral Newsletter paints a picture of a formidable custodian of the Cathedral's literary treasures, but also of a popular, gifted and influential College lecturer. Widely respected, she was remembered with admiration and affection.

The Staff Play performed in the early 1950s

Dr V. M. Grubb: Principal, 1955-1962

Courtesy of The Salisbury Museum

Dr Grubb was a graduate of London University, achieving her D.Sc. in 1925. She spent five years as a Science mistress in China and then returned to lecture at London University. Her background in Science was felt to be especially relevant at this time when society and education were becoming much more orientated towards scientific thinking.

During her period as Principal several important changes took place, for example, accommodation improved and student numbers increased:

'The College must continuously change not only in outward aspect but in matters that lie far deeper, yet I hope you will always find it the inspiring, beautiful and friendly place that you have known'.

As Head Student, Anne Spicer had opportunity to get to know Dr Grubb better than other students. On one occasion she heard the fire bell ring. Anne quickly grabbed the "Ticking-in Book" and ran downstairs. After checking that all students were out of the building Anne noticed 'black smoke belching forth from a top storey window in Maxwell'. Fire engines tore into The Close and the firemen duly dealt with the fire.

'I rushed up the staircase and knocked on Dr Grubb's door. "Come in" a voice commanded. There was Dr Grubb calmly sitting at her desk. "Good evening Miss Spicer, what brings you here?" I replied, "Sorry to bother you, but we have a fire in Maxwell and the Fire Brigade is here", "Can't you cope?" she said'. Anne replied that she could cope, but thought that Dr Grubb might like to know that her College was on fire'.

Dr Grubb is perceived as a rather strict and aloof Principal, but she did have a softer side. She retired in 1962:

'This is my last letter to you as Principal of the College. My store of the riches of experience and memory gathered through the years has been greatly added to by my life here in this College'.

STC Chronicle, 1962

'A Special and Wonderful Start'

Geraldine Warrillow (1958-1960) was seriously ill during her last year at school and needed a long convalescence. Her first applications to Training Colleges were turned down, but life began to look brighter when she applied to Salisbury.

'It was September, and term had started when a letter came from Salisbury, inviting me for an interview with Dr Grubb. My parents motored me down; I was accepted and started the next week. I cannot thank Salisbury Training College enough for giving me the chance to be in such a wonderful atmosphere for learning'.

Geraldine taught Art and Biology to children and adults until the late 1970s. She is now a respected Wessex artist (Geraldine Trayhorne) whose work includes paintings and drawings, but she is particularly well known for her hand-decorated pottery. She feels enormous gratitude to Dr Grubb for her kindness and compassion in 'giving her a chance' all those years ago.

Miss Maxwell's Visit to Germany 1952

In 1952 The Foreign Office invited Miss Maxwell to visit some schools and Training Colleges in Germany and meet those responsible for running them. She wrote:

'It was a most interesting time and I am sure I learnt much more than I taught, which was not the primary intention!

It seemed quite an adventure to penetrate into the Russian sector of Berlin, but we were only able to see it from the main roads. The devastation from the raids, and also from the invasion, was too dreadful to describe. I was distressed by much of what I met among the students and teachers. There were splendid people among them, but there seemed to be so much fear and insecurity. Their fear of the loss of personal freedom was intense, and everywhere there seemed to be domination by those in any position of authority, of those under them, even in the non-Communist West.

They would not believe that we in England could make our own syllabuses for teaching, without accepting an imposed syllabus from the Education Authority. They were of course completely incredulous when I described, as I was invited to do, the programme of a modern English Infants' School. Their one test of education appears to be the sum total of facts a child absorbs. The whole experience only made me realise how fortunate we are in our freedom. May we always bring up our children that they will appreciate and maintain it and keep it pure and whole in the light of the Christian ideal'.

SDTC Chronicle, 1952

The Old Deanery Controversy

There had been much ill feeling and concern in Salisbury about the proposal to demolish the Old Deanery. Students continued to live there happily in the 1950s, mostly enjoying its idiosyncrasies and character.

In 1959, the Royal Commission on Historical Monuments was asked to survey the Old Deanery to record details for historical references. Mr Norman Drinkwater and Mr Denys Spittle undertook the survey and found many features which indicated the survival of a thirteenth-century building.

'In the course of this survey by Mr Denys Spittle and myself it became obvious that much of the structure of the thirteenth century Old Deanery survived under later accretions. Demonstration of this fact eventually led to the decision to save the building. As a result of these discoveries the Governors of the Training College decided that the building should not be demolished. There then arose the problem of raising the necessary funds to repair it and fit it for modern college use.

The Ministry of Education, having decided that the various rooms ancillary to the Hall could be used suitably and economically for tutorials etc, was able to help financially'.

Norman Drinkwater F.S.A.,
The Old Deanery, Salisbury, 1964

Sufficient funds and donations were made which eventually produced enough money for the extensive work to be undertaken.

Mr Christopher Green, the architect for the modern college buildings, was appointed architect for the restoration and refitting of the Old Deanery in consultation with the Royal Commission and the Ministry of Public Building and Works. Work was not completed until the Sixties, but an important and beautiful historical building had been saved.

The Old Deanery

Living in the Old Deanery in the 1950s

As the Old Deanery had been saved from demolition, students continued to 'enjoy' the experience of living in such an ancient building. Joan Solomon (1952-1954) recalled her days at College as extremely happy and memorable:

'I was so privileged to be allotted a room in Old Deanery in 1952. I remember walking up the stairs, bearing to the right, then a few more steps to the door into my room. My room mate was Jean Gardiner and we quickly set about arranging the beds and our trunks and belongings. It was rather a shock for me after leaving a sprung mattress and a room of my own at home, to be introduced to sleeping on a straw mattress with the cotton cover meeting in the middle! The walls of the room were of wattle and daub, but we soon found bits of daub were capable of falling on our heads. As time went by we arranged "art works" on the ceiling.

The first night at College was not too restful - what were those scratching noises and squeaks – ghosts or the boiler system?

Just outside our room was an enormous airing cupboard housing the boiler for hot water and radiators. It was very useful for drying personal bits of washing and also keeping us warm during the cold snow of winter. I also enjoyed the luxury of hot baths in an enormous free-standing bath further down the corridor. The floor of the room consisted of wide black boards. We spied through the gaps, hence discovering the original kitchen underneath. On exploring we discovered ancient stone sinks with an open gully for the waste water.

Firmly attached from one of the windows in our room was a rope ladder. Ah! Fire practice! Jean was the first one to be brave enough to have a go and let herself down to the ground outside'.

Happy Days!
Courtesy of The Salisbury Museum

Building Improvements in the 1950s

In addition to the new student accommodation, other improvements were urgently needed. In 1946-1947 HMI had highlighted several shortfalls in the accommodation. A new gymnasium was essential and work began in autumn 1954, which was Miss Maxwell's last term. It was finally completed in 1956, by which time Dr Grubb was the Principal.

'The Gymnasium was a fine, light room of good size, with a well sprung floor, all requisite equipment and access to outdoor area. A joy to students were the showers and changing rooms. And a joy to the member of staff in charge was the provision of a room for her use with adjacent facilities'.

LST ibid

Gwen Williams (1955-1957) recalled:

'The new gym was opened during our time in College – to the delight of P.E. lecturers and athletic students, but to the dismay of the less agile amongst us who could no longer skulk behind the pillars of the old gym when the exercises proved difficult'.

The library was much improved and extended; chairs, armchairs and tables for study were provided. A qualified librarian, Miss Kit Parry, was appointed who had her own study, adjacent to the Library, and supervised cataloguing as well as being responsible for ordering and general management.

The dormitory known as 'Top North' was cleared and decorated to become the Upper Lecture Room for Education lectures in Training for Infant School work. In the year 1956-1957 the rooms on the ground floor of King's House were re-arranged. The old Common Room became a lecture room for Education lectures and general lectures for students planning to teach Junior age pupils. Some lectures, particularly those in 'special subjects' took place in 'The Quiet Room'. Re-organisation ensured that space was found in King's House for a new Common Room, which Miss Taylor described as 'elegantly decorated and furnished'.

New lecture rooms were urgently needed. Strong emphasis was being placed upon the teaching of Science in all stages of education, partly due to the demands of industry. A new 'teaching block' was built in 1957-1958 attached to the Gymnasium entrance corridor. This included two large laboratories on the ground floor and a third laboratory and

The new gymnasium 1956

large Art and Craft room on the upper floor. The teaching block was opened by Sir Lawrence Bragg, an eminent scientist and physicist.

The Principal at this time was Dr Grubb. Anne Spicer (1957-1959) was the head student. She remembered that 'students had been taking bets concerning the naming of the science block, the most popular one being "The Grub House!" Alas, it was always to be known as The Science Block'.

In 1959-1960 a Music Wing was erected on the south side of the gymnasium, containing two Music rooms and ten practice rooms. Space was ample for the teaching of Music as a 'specialist' subject. In earlier years Music had been taught as a general course, aimed at providing a basic background for all teachers and as part of the cultural provision of the College. There was also a small Pottery room on the ground floor.

Maxwell House

Many people opposed the plans to build in The Close. The architecture of the Medieval Hall was not thought to merit the expense and work needed to preserve it. A day's public enquiry was held at Salisbury Guildhall and eventually the Minister of Town and Country Planning finally gave his consent for demolition. The residential places which the Old Deanery provided were still necessary, so fortunately demolition was not immediate.

> 'The essential action at the time was to erect the new building in front of it. A sketch plan was published to assure the public of how the design had been carefully made to adjust the appearance of the new building to its setting among the established buildings, attention being drawn to the height of the roof, the general conformity with features of other buildings, and the fact that the materials to be used would quickly weather to an appearance not incompatible with the rest of The Close.'
>
> *LST ibid*

The authorities commissioned W. Curtis Green, a prestigious and distinguished firm of architects to design the new buildings. They had much experience in designing classically inspired architecture which, although built in the twentieth century, would blend perfectly into buildings such as those of The Cathedral Close. They produced beautiful architectural illustrations of their projects, often quite large pen or pencil drawings, coloured with water colours. The Salisbury Training College Chapel extensions were also designed by this renowned and highly esteemed firm.

In May 1951 the new College building was officially opened by Dame Dorothy Brock. After the OSA service a procession passed through the gateway and open arches in the centre of the building to a marquee erected between the Old Deanery and the new building. After Dame Dorothy Brock had cut the ribbon the Bishop blessed and dedicated the new building which was to be called "North" but very quickly became "Maxwell".

Eighty student study-bedrooms were added, in addition to rooms for three resident lecturers, studies for non-resident lecturers, and two lecture rooms, one of which became the Biology laboratory. The rooms were arranged along each side of a long corridor on three floors, and along wings running west and east. The bathrooms and utility rooms were situated at the north end so that the students' rooms benefited from the sun. The front and rear of the building was laid out to very attractive lawns. The students were ready to move in. How would they enjoy their new accommodation?

The Furnishing of Maxwell

Miss Maxwell wrote about the difficulties of furnishing Maxwell House:

> 'Furnishing the new building was a problem not only of cost, but of being unable to obtain some items. We were well served by our suppliers, many of whom

were local firms with whom we had contacts for many years. It so happened that an Atlantic Liner was at Southampton Docks, where her furnishings were being sold by auction, previous to the ship being broken up.

We were able to obtain some items of furniture of good quality that were suitable for us, and inexpensive. How many miles had Maxwell furniture covered at sea?'

Study bedroom in Maxwell

Maxwell House 1950

Maxwell Memories

Mary Westcott started College in the autumn of 1956 and was given a study in Maxwell. No cost had been spared in the design of the building, but as Mary recalled:

'Built so soon after World War Two, a time of economy meant that certain corners were cut and the most obvious one was very poor acoustics: a pencil dropped on the top floor could be heard in my ground floor room, the telephone, in a box under the stairs was a constant background noise in the evenings, while students in high heels en route to Kings and Audley were not popular. So it was hardly surprising that, on the first evening, Miss Todd (Head of House) called a meeting to emphasise the necessity to think of others and ended by everyone having to pass the "shutting doors" test.

Miss Marion Taylor, the Domestic Bursar, called a meeting for the whole year to set out the main rules:

1   All students must keep their rooms tidy at all times and inspections could be called without warning. The punishment for persistent untidiness would mean that the offender would not be able to choose her room for the following year.

2   Damp towels were NOT to be dried on radiators

3   Laundry – 1 sheet, 2 pillow cases, 1 towel (bath) 1 towel (hand) correctly labelled with name tapes, were to be sent to the laundry once a fortnight in your own laundry bag.

4   All other personal washing to be done (by hand) in the General Purpose (GP) room and dried in the drying room (DR). These initials caused some confusion on day one as we believed them to have a medical connection!

5   All windows on the ground floor were only to be opened two inches. This was because a young soldier had broken in one night after the College Fete, looking for money and Miss Taylor had to chase him round the Close.

6   Food, if kept in rooms, should be in tins with tight fitting lids and consumed as soon as possible. The cupboard for this was above the built-in wardrobe in Maxwell rooms and could only be reached by standing on a chair.

7   Weekly rations of butter to be kept in a lidded dish in the cupboard directly outside the dining room together with table napkins with rings (not silver) which were to be used for lunch, the only formal meal of the day.

8   Used sanitary wear to be dealt with in bathrooms(College mothers would instruct on use of incinerators)

9   Mattresses to be turned daily.

So many rules to follow but hopefully they resulted in student harmony!

A Room with a View

Joan Steele (1953-1955) recollected:

'I loved all the old College buildings, but I lived in the new building, which was named Maxwell House during my time there. The first year I had a ground floor room overlooking the Old Deanery, but if our rooms passed the random weekly checks by the Domestic Bursar for tidiness and turned mattresses etc we could opt for the room of our choice, provided no one else wanted it. I was lucky enough to be given my choice of a top floor room immediately opposite the west front of the Cathedral. I have never had a room with a better view'.

Deluxe study bedroom

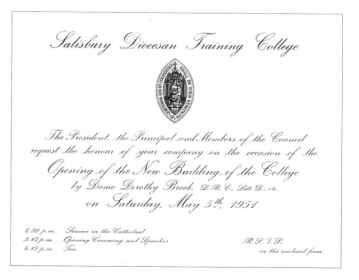

Salisbury Diocesan Training College

The President, the Principal and Members of the Council request the honour of your company on the occasion of the Opening of the New Building of the College by Dame Dorothy Brock, D.B.E., Litt.D., &c. on Saturday, May 5th, 1951

2.30 p.m.   Service in the Cathedral
3.15 p.m.   Opening Ceremony and Speeches   R.S.V.P.
4.15 p.m.   Tea   on the enclosed form.

The Close Rules

Living in the Cathedral Close was idyllic in many ways, but there certainly had to be rules for the students!

1 All students to be in their room by 10.30, having first ticked their name in the book. Second Years to share the duty of checking the list and supporting the lecturer in charge if any student hasn't ticked and can't be found.*

2. Saturday nights. All students are entitled to a late pass until 11.00 pm but all students must walk quietly by removing high-heeled shoes.

3 Two weekends a term are designated for Saturday nights away providing the student leaves details of the address.

*Mary Westcott revealed how it was possible to unofficially let students in by the side door in Audley House by signalling with the lights.

Students with Mr Searle, the Close Constable, 1953

Outside No 38

Settled in Wardrobe

'Survival' is a word that frequently appears in reminiscences of Wardrobe. Those who lived there continued to endure spartan conditions, even in the 1950s:

'We shared study bedrooms. A single bar electric fire was the only form of heating. We sat at a small table to do our studies and if a piece of file paper fell on the floor, it would rise up and down in the draught that came up between the floorboards.

The washroom was on a sort of half landing and was reached by going down a back staircase. There were washbasins fixed side by side around the walls and we stood on bare, unvarnished floorboards. There were no cubicles or curtains to provide privacy, so there was no place for maidenly modesty. In any case, as there was no heating, our ablutions tended to be hasty!

We washed personal clothes ourselves and hung them on wooden driers in the kitchen. On one occasion, students from our brother college, King Alfred's in Winchester, had come over for a dance, or to play in a hockey match. Some of them slipped into the kitchen and removed girls' undies from the driers. They took them back and strung them up on their flagpole'!

Frances Boo-Townsend (1954-1956)

Student with Everest, Miss Mayo's cat. (So named to commemorate the first ascent of Mt Everest)

Courtesy of The Salisbury Museum

Christmas 1958

Courtesy of The Salisbury Museum

Shirley Gray (1959-1961) remembered that hot water bottles were essential, as were dressing gowns and coats on top of the thin blankets that College supplied.

'Near my bed were large French windows which opened on to the lawn, leading down to the river - how much cold they let in on autumn and winter nights! With only an electric fire to heat that huge room, we never seemed to be able to get warm'.

The magnificence of the medieval building was not, however, lost on the students. Jillian Bagley (1949-1951) spent both years in Wardrobe:

'For the first year, four of us shared the large downstairs room with the beautiful eagle in the centre of the ceiling. Having survived our first year, my friend and I decided to move upstairs to a room overlooking the front, which was called "The Retreat." It was a lovely room with sloping floors and ceilings and a floor-level diamond-paned window.'

Fire Practices were a regular feature of life and Jillian remembered 'an adventurous climb across the rafters and through a loft opening that brought us out on to the main staircase – the only time we were allowed to use it'.

Winifred Brown (1951-1953) awoke during the early hours to hear the loud ringing of a bell.

'We closed our windows and ran downstairs and into the garden. Miss Mayo counted us all and then, beaming broadly, apologised for waking us. The practice should have taken place the previous evening, but the alarm had failed. Now it had rung on its own. However, everyone had had a good rehearsal. As we climbed the stairs, there were a few mutterings, "Where was Mrs Dalton-Hill?" Next day we were all invited to sign a card which was inscribed "To the memory of Mrs Dalton Hill who perished in the fire at Wardrobe." This was attached to a bunch of flowers laid outside her room. The joke was well taken, and enjoyed throughout College.

Another memory was Miss Mayo's warning to students about sunbathing in the garden: 'Please remember that we have Canons to the right of us and Canons to the left'.

Students were often reluctant to say farewell:

'We used up reels of black and white film, hanging out of the gallery window to "snap" the Cathedral and posing on the lawns. The craziest thing was persuading Sheila to pose in her swimming costume in the shallows of the river at the bottom of the garden – at about eight o'clock in the morning! Happy, happy days'.
Kay Drake (1945-1947)

Number 38, The Close

Number 38 was known as 'Chappies Place'. The Chaplain, the Revd A Osborne and his wife and young son had a flat in the house. Marjorie Burnett and Penny Roper (1954 -1956) were delighted to move there for their second year:

'It was strategically situated near the High Street gate and the delights of the town … freedom beckoned. However Mr Searle, the Close Constable, kept a fatherly eye on things – and on us'.

The accommodation was spartan; the kitchen and bathroom were basic and could have served as cold storage units. The rota allowed one bath a week, so we never lingered in there. The scullery had a stone flagged floor. A wobbly clothes rack hung from the ceiling, decorated with pants, socks, stockings and little suspender belts– can you remember them?

Our room, however, was a haven of cosiness; new divan beds, fitted bookshelves and a GAS FIRE for which we paid not a penny. When it was exceptionally cold we left it on all night long, turned down low, of course. We also had a little wireless with an indoor aerial draped around the picture rail. *Saturday Night Theatre* on the Home Service was a regular date, with a mug of cocoa and cakes left over from tea'.

The Chaplain sometimes invited students to his flat on Sunday evenings to listen to his 78rpm records of *The Dream of Gerontius*:

'We sat on the floor and Mrs Osborne provided cups of tea and chocolate biscuits. The gramophone was immense and its huge horn took up nearly a quarter of the room. How privileged we were to live in such a beautiful setting'.

The Revd. A Osborne with students & family

No 38 in the snow January 1954

The Mystery of Hayloft

Pamela Smith's description suggests that Hayloft was at the very top of the building, on the floor above the horse-boxes. She arrived at College in 1956:

'I soon discovered that I was to be in a room in King's House, sharing with two others. I was taken up numerous stairs to the very top by Audrey, my College Mother. Hayloft was divided into three rooms, two of which accommodated three students, and there was one single room. My bed was under the window and always seemed to be on a slant as the floor was so uneven. I did fall out several times whilst there. We had great fun up there in this ancient building and often chatted till the early hours. Our washing and bathing was on the ground floor and the toilets just one floor down. If we had to pay a visit in the night, we were in fear and trepidation of meeting The Grey Lady, who was said to haunt the staircase.

Winter in Hayloft, huddled around an old gas fire, blankets wrapped around us, writing essays … these memories are still with me'.

Horse-box inhabitants with Matron, 1957-1958

The Chapel

CHAPEL OF THE HOLY ANGELS

Miss Maxwell, writing in the 1952 *College Chronicle*, expressed the wish for a larger Chapel on the same site. The Chapel could seat only 143 people and with rising numbers there was an urgent need for greater capacity.

In the meantime, daily services continued, with additional ones on major festivals. Services of Preparation for School Practice and Dedication Services for those who were leaving were introduced by the Chaplain, the Revd A. F. Osborne, and were greatly appreciated.

The Revd A. Osborne was remembered for his devoted work in College and Chapel. He was succeeded by the Revd M. Newman in 1956 and from this time the Chaplains became non-resident and also had the charge of the parish of Coombe Bissett. Dr Grubb, who became Principal in 1955, officiated at Sunday morning services and members of staff took the evening prayers. The Cathedral clergy also took occasional services.

Chapel Practice on Saturday mornings was compulsory. The Chapel Wardens took the register to make sure that no one was absent without permission. Former students remembered being 'huddled in top coats and gloves' whilst they practised hymns and psalms.

By 1956 the fulfilment of Miss Maxwell's wish for a larger Chapel was becoming more likely, largely through the generosity of former students who had responded to Dr Grubb's appeal:

> 'The Chapel is a place of hallowed memories and I believe that the old students will wish the best possible workmanship to be put into this and many will want a part in it'.

More than 700 individual donations were received, in addition to two legacies. The new roof was paid for by the Governing Body. The extension of the Chapel was part of the 'prestigious commission' of building and restoration at the College that was taken on by Messrs. W. Curtis Green, R.A, Son & Lloyd, Architects.

Aisles were thrown out on the north and south sides of the building, making it possible to seat 200 people. The work began in January 1957 and the Dedication Service, which was taken by the Bishop of Salisbury, was on September 29th. Governors, members of staff and past and present students made up the large congregation.

Many gifts were presented, including 54 'memorial' chairs. A new Sanctuary Lamp was given by students from 1941-1943. The Sanctuary ceiling was painted in blue and gold and the stone angels were also decorated in these colours

by Miss Saintsbury, who was appointed as Art Lecturer in 1956. The Chapel bell was moved to the west wall.

> 'Canon Steward's vision of the Chapel at the centre of College life, and the source of inspiration for its work, was renewed'.
>
> *LST ibid*

Sunday best for chapel!

Chaplain & Chapel Wardens 1951-1952

An Earlier Escape from Closure

Miss Todd joined the College in 1948 to teach history and remained until the closure of the College. Throughout all this time she was a member of the Governing Body. In 1998 she wrote a lively article about the College's earlier escape from closure:

'After the war, numbers in College rose as far as available accommodation permitted. Both living and teaching accommodation was cramped in the extreme. Biology was then the only science offered, in a makeshift laboratory at the front of King's House, next to the kitchen. Horticulture was offered for a short time, and the only room available for that was contrived from the former coal hole in Old Deanery.

In the 1950s, once things had settled down to some extent after the war, the Government pressed ahead, trying to fill the demand for a large increase in the number of trained teachers. The Government insisted that students should be housed and taught in good accommodation. Salisbury Training College was willing to accept an increase in students, but both the Governing Body and Principal were aware of the inadequate situation in a College which nevertheless had over the years turned out well-trained teachers.

There were three proposals. One was to improve the existing accommodation. The second was to move the College into purpose built accommodation outside The Close. The third alternative was to close. After many meetings, interminable discussions, calculations of finance, it was due to the persistence and hard work of the Principal aided by members of the Governing Body, that the first alternative was chosen; an underlying factor was the strong feeling that the College's position as a Church Training College in such a beautiful setting, with the advantage of some old and restored buildings, would contribute much to students. This extremely important decision saved the College from closure, and set it on the road of building and constantly improving all facilities, so that, ironically, when the later decision was made to close the College, it had reached a total of 450 students, and its property and surroundings were enviable.'

Miss Todd, *College Newsletter,* 1998

Students by the Cathedral

Picking primroses in Grovely Woods

A walk in the snow   'Robert Poole'

College Memories

'Salisbury Training College was my "home from home" from 1949-1951, initially as one of the last of the "billetees" and then as one of the new students in what was then known as the "New Building".

The first year was a bit hectic as we had to cram everything into the daytime and leave for our respective billets in the evening. Arriving there late was not allowed. I always wanted to see the sunrise at Stonehenge on midsummer's day and this seemed to be the golden opportunity to do just that. I obtained permission for those of the "billetees" who were interested and we spent the night in our common room – seriously misnamed "The Quiet Room." We left very early in the morning on bicycles that we had begged or borrowed having made a previous arrangement with the Close 'policeman' to let us out at that early hour and we cycled to Stonehenge arriving well before sunrise. There were only about forty people there including several Druids who carried out their ceremony burning incense and doing various other things. It was a clear morning and we did see the sun rise in the right place and the first rays did fall on the 'Altar Stone'.

The second year was so different. The "New Building" lived up to its name. Everything was bright and clean and everything worked – including I hope, us. Most of our 'billetee' contingent was on the top floor, if I remember correctly, and we did away with all of the required rotas that were supposed to be kept for baths, washing and so on. We found that we could do all these things whenever we wanted without getting in each other's way. The only one that was strictly kept was the signing-in book at night. I was responsible for these rotas so I know that one was in order.

Apart from all the necessary hard work that went into the two years there was time for 'in-house' enjoyment too. Sunday services in the Cathedral; early morning tennis in the summer with the barn owls flying overhead on their way home to roost; impromptu musical nonsense in "The Quiet Room"; sliding along the corridor floors on a cushion – or the back of your skirt! There were off-days too, but don't we all have those – even now? But on the whole, it was a pleasant, happy way to acquire a qualification that would last a lifetime and help future generations of children to further their own careers'.

Joan Keel (1949 -1951)

A Link with Clara Grant

From the 1950s Miss Heath was Sunday School Superintendent at St Barnabas Church, in Bradwell, Newcastle-under-Lyme in Staffordshire. It was there that she influenced Jennifer Knock, whom she encouraged to become a young Sunday School teacher. Jennifer later went on to train at the College of Sarum St Michael from 1965-1969. In the 1920s and 30s, Miss Heath was a Lady Church worker, first in Poplar, then in Bethnal Green. She ran a Women's Fellowship group in Bethnal Green and asked Clara Grant to give a talk.

'At one of our Women's Fellowship meetings, Miss Clara Grant came to speak to us. She gave a thrilling account of the work at the Settlement and of the Farthing Bundles. In the cold weather the boys who had no shoes stood in their caps. There was always a long queue. Miss Grant also spoke about hygiene, strongly advising everyone to keep windows open. She concluded with "after all I have said you will be surprised to hear that I never open my windows". She paused, gave a smile, and then explained that this was because the windows were never closed'.

The paragraph about Clara Grant is from an unpublished booklet of memories by Miss Clare Heath.

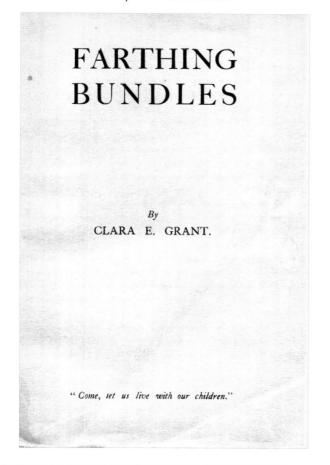

FARTHING BUNDLES

By
CLARA E. GRANT.

" *Come, let us live with our children.* "

Fern Street Settlement

'Many old students, who worked with Miss Whatley for Miss Clara Grant's settlement when in College, will be interested to know that the good work is being carried on by Mrs Way, Miss Grant's assistant.

Miss Grant's "Comforts and Gifts Fund for the Old," and the "Outings and Holiday Funds" are now incorporated into a "Clara Grant Memorial Fund," thus carrying out one of her greatest wishes. To this fund, Her Majesty Queen Mary has given £100, and many of Miss Grant's friends have sent contributions.

Mrs Way pleads for help for the Saturday morning "Bundles" – any odds and ends are welcomed: Beads, shells and match-boxes to hold them, little toys, scraps of material, cotton reels, bits of pencil and crayons, Christmas cards, books and pictures.'

STC Chronicle, 1951

Drawing by Pat Jones

Courses of Study

The College course of study was set out for prospective students in the Training College Prospectus of 1955:

'The College course extends over two academic years and students have the opportunity of choice during their first term of the age range of the children they are preparing to teach.

All students take a course in the principles and practice of education including religious education, health and physical education. They may choose to work either:

1   With infants (children 3-7 years old).

2   With the older classes in a primary school (children 7-11 years old).

Or

3   In a secondary modern school.

In addition students select two or three subjects from the following list: - Divinity, English, History or Geography, Biology, Mathematics (not at present offered) French, Music, Art, Craft (Needlework, Weaving, Puppetry, Book-Binding), Gardening. Selected students may take an additional special course in Physical Education instead of one of the subjects mentioned above.

A Religious Education Course is provided for all students. The College, during its history, has provided and desires to maintain, a succession of students able and willing to teach the Christian Faith'.

Joan Steele (1953-55) recalled:

'Our Education lecturer was Miss Lucy Taylor, a Scottish lady of great intelligence, who taught those of us following the Secondary Modern Course, and gave us the confidence to walk into a classroom and deal firmly with those pupils who, perhaps, would rather have been elsewhere. She insisted that after two days of 'School Practice' we must know the names of every child in the class – in those days about 36. We were devoted to her, and she taught us so much. My main subject was English, taught by Miss Blackburn, another brilliant lecturer. Miss Trinder took us for Divinity, my secondary subject. We were made to choose two Craft Subjects, and I chose Needlework and Bookbinding (in desperation!).

We studied general subjects, and I remember Miss Mayo taking us for Maths. She warned us that if we used any visual aids, such as films, we must check them carefully before showing them to the children. Someone had not done so, and had shown a class a film called 'Right from the Start', which proved to be not about Maths, but about breast feeding (much more risqué in those days!)'.

Student outside SPCK Bookshop

Students wearing dresses made in needlework late 1950s

The Love of Sport

Yvonne May (1950-1952) commented that 'there was no proper hall for vaulting and the old gym ceiling was low'. Anne Salter, who also arrived in 1950, remembered Miss Ayling's Modern Dance sessions. Margaret Frost (1948-1950) had memories of Health Education, including the incubation periods for childish diseases, and how to spot flat feet, ear defects and bad eyesight'.

Stephanie Offer (1954-1956) discovered that the Gym Club still used the old gym with pillars that she remembered from childhood visits with her mother, who had been a student in the 1920s. In the 1956 College Chronicle Stephanie expressed appreciation of the new gymnasium.

> 'The vaulting and other work improved considerably, owing to better and more varied apparatus, and to the increased space'.

The Vaulting Club had a small but enthusiastic membership. Vaulting Displays were a regular part of the College Fetes that raised money for the UMCA.

Dancing was popular, with Old Time evenings, ballroom dancing and country dance parties. Sheila Cole (1957-1959) had particular memories of the Rudolph Laban Music and Movement sessions:

> 'Oh, the embarrassment! Those awful home-made tunics and matching knickers (mine were peach-coloured)'.

Hockey, netball, rounders, tennis and table tennis were well established by 1958. Matches were played against local clubs and teams, including King Alfred's Training College in Winchester and Southampton University. Students also took part in local tennis tournaments and could use the 'very cold open air swimming pool in the town'.

Sport continued to be an important part of College life.

Shorts! Maudella Pattern 2929

'Clothes – Maudella 2929, pattern for shorts. Shorts! Two inches above the knee at kneeling position, not shorts by today's standards. One covered the knees with a dirndl skirt to cycle to the games field – no knees were to be shown by Miss Maxwell's ladies as they cycled to the games field – rightly so! Coupons were still needed for clothes or materials and availability was impeded by low funds. Still – the world was looking brighter and countries were re-developing very quickly. So were fashions – and HOW we tried to keep up on a very modest budget. There was no competition or jealousy; we were just a trifle envious when someone like Mary E flaunted new clothes, including hats (!) at every opportunity'.

Margaret Frost (1948-1950)

Country Dancing, summer, 1950

Above: Secondary students dance display team, 1956

Left: The town swimming pool

Investigating the Expansion of Science

In the mid-1950s students could study Nature Study and Biology, taught by Miss Northcott:

'Week by week we were given a subject on which to make notes and drawings for our Nature Diaries. Subjects ranged from fruits and seeds to winter twigs, mosses and pond dipping, providing a Nature Study lesson every week for three terms. Think of it, a whole year's syllabus ready-made. Added to this, each student had to make a detailed study of a tree of her choice extending over three terms. I know of few students for whom this was a labour of love. It would not be exaggerating to describe it as a labour of compulsion. Over the years, however, feelings have mellowed and a sense of gratitude has replaced earlier emotions'.

Anne Smithson (1950-1952) enjoyed studying Biology in the newly-opened laboratory:

'Part of the course was to make a year-long survey and study of a chosen habitat. Several of us were allocated a coniferous plantation above Odstock Hospital. Many of us had brought our bicycles from home, so after the tedious trudge up Odstock Hill at least we had a magical swoop down, following an afternoon's scramble through the trees and undergrowth. People often remember places by their sights, but my plantation experience is of smells: mainly the ranger's collection of vermin rotting at head-height in a display that lasted through every season, then the autumnal pong from stinkhorn fungus that grew in abundance'.

Mary Westcott (1956-1958) remembered Miss Northcott's afternoon expeditions:

'Hanging over a bridge to pick liverwort, caught trespassing in Lord Radnor's beech wood collecting fungi, bringing home a seven foot giant hogweed - and the joke rebounded on us, as it turned up in our identification exam the next day and we had neglected to identify the thing'.

The growth of Science in schools and the growing national demand for more Science teachers meant that Training Colleges needed to provide courses in both Chemistry and Biology. Salisbury reflected the national picture and Miss Northcott was joined in 1958 by Mr Peel, who had responsibility for Chemistry.

Miss ML Story: Staff 1914 – 1944 and Coach Guide 1957 A Good Sport!

Miss Story was determined to continue to live life in 'retirement' to the full and as a hobby became a courier on Coach Tours. In 1951 she started with local firms but soon became bored with this. In 1954 she was appointed as an official Guide to show overseas visitors something of Britain and, backed by the Welsh Tourist Board, offered her services as a Guide for Mid-Wales. Miss Story revelled in the work and enjoyed regular trips to the Elan Valley, Brecon, Shrewsbury and other interesting locations:

Between March 19th and September 13th 1957, she accompanied 112 tours and met 1,421 people. Just as in her life as a College lecturer, Miss Story always gave her best.

New Biology laboratory, 1951

Hiking, Biking, Boating et al!

Clubs and Societies began to flourish in the 1950s, as students determined to enjoy themselves after the war years. A new club in 1957 was the Hiking, Biking and Boating Club; parties of students sped off for excursions at the weekends, often taking a picnic. When the weather was not suitable they held Country Dances or watched films about Youth Hostelling. In the summer they had an opportunity to go boating with male students from the Theological College in the Close.

In the same year a Jazz Club was formed:

> 'An inspired group of people who were addicts of the new trend in modern jazz music decided that the Organisation of College Clubs was lacking in one respect: that of a jazz club. The new common room provided ample floor space for the antics provoked by the strains of Humphrey Littleton and Chris Barber. But, alas, the polished wood blocks were too precious for such vigorous treatment, even from bare feet, so the group of people decided to transfer their official channels and form a Jazz Club. The first meeting, beginning with a flourish, was attended by a record number of sixty-two members. The members found that these monthly meetings provided a vigorous outlet for all excess energies and pent-up feelings accumulated through College life.
> T. Hatcher, *STC Chronicle*, 1958

There were several sports clubs, and a range of interesting and varied musical events presented by the Music Club. In 1955, The Dramatic Society and Poetry Circle combined to form the Literary and Dramatic Society. A range of well-supported plays was presented over the decade. A drama competition took place in the spring and students also enjoyed weekly play-readings with some of the theological students.

Guide Club was popular, with varied topics at meetings and a summer weekend camp:

> 'The climax of our year came with our summer weekend camp. We walked to Bishopdown Farm with our beds and our food on our backs. Our lightweight camp was set up very quickly and we were soon off for a ramble, following part of the course of the Avon. Miss Mayo, who was a Guider, came to supper in the evening. On our second day in camp the weather was not so kind and those who had decided to sleep under the stars had to beat a hurried retreat into the tents'.
> B. A, Harris, *STC Chronicle*, 1958

A Cappella Group, 1957

Occasional visits were made further afield such as the visit in 1958 to Stratford-upon-Avon to see Romeo and Juliet with Judi Dench playing the part of Juliet! By the kind invitation of Salisbury Film Society, students were able to enjoy a range of films.

Entertainment included College dances – in 1958 there were five during the year – and excellent variety concerts. Many students still recall the pleasure and humour of these often informal concerts which sometimes poked gentle fun at some of the staff. Barbara Jerrett (1956-1958) had the honour of playing the part of Dr Grubb. Trixie Gillingham (1958-1960) was Entertainment Secretary and enjoyed organising several successful concerts.

> 'The dances and entertainments in the past year have been very successful. We have had the added advantage of using the Gymnasium stage. The theme for the entertainment during Christmas dinner was "Modes of travel under petrol shortage during School Practice". This caused much mirth and was greatly appreciated by staff, students and visitors'.
> *STC Chronicle*, 1957

Dances and College Balls were held in the Old Deanery Hall:

> 'If we were there for a dance we were warned not to stand or sit at the sides of the floor, and there was an element of precautionary persuasion not to be too enthusiastic or heavily rhythmic in our movements in case we stressed the structure near to collapse!'
> *Anne Salter (1950-52)*

Mary Westcott remembered special events with fondness:

'At College Balls it was necessary to sign up with the name, address and occupation of a 'male person' you would like to invite. The large room in Old Deanery would be used and the event would be attended by two or three lecturers. All guests should be introduced to them and the gentleman would be expected to invite one of them to dance. No alcohol was allowed. Gentlemen could be invited from King Alfred's College Winchester, the Theological College, and young officers from Larkhill'.

Mary recalled one occasion when, after a Ball, ladies underwear fluttered from the College flagpole. Miss Grubb commented 'What will the Bishop say?'

What excitement there must have been! College dances had more worrying moments as Thelma Cook (1958-1960) recalled: 'We had to introduce our partners to Dr Grubb at the College dances and tell her about their occupations'. It must have been worth it as several lasting relationships were formed.

Occasional tennis matches with the theological students provided a further opportunity for male interaction. Times were changing as the Sixties approached!

Right above: Refreshments in the New Forest (non-alcoholic!)

Right: Tennis with the 'Theos'

Below: College Concert Programme

PROGRAMME

National Anthem

1. College Orchestra: Leader - Miss Edna Moore
   a) 1st Movement Violin Concerto in A minor   Vivaldi
      Soloist: M. Grubb
   b) 3rd Movement Piano Concerto in D   Haydn
      Soloist: C. Cologne

2. Choir: All Second Year students
   a) Strings in the earth and air   C. le Fleming
      Accompanist: J. Langridge
      Conductor: G. Williamson
   b) Balulalow (from Ceremony of Carols)   Benjamin Britten
      Accompanist: B. Chivers

3. Piano Solo:
      Arabesque in A   Debussy
      G. Mansell

4. Duo for two pianos
      The Clockwork Bear
      B. Gillingham & R. Legg

5. Choir of First Year students:
      "Day that I have loved"   C. le Fleming
      Pianists: J. Lowman & J. Carter

6. Piano Solo:
      Jardins sous la pluie   Debussy
      C. Cologne

7. Madrigal Group:
      How merrily we live   Michael East
      My love dwelt in a northern land   Elgar
      The Goslings   F. Bridge
      G. Williamson, M. Grubb, J. Langridge, G. Mansell, S. Morgan, G. Read
      Accompanist: G. Strain

8. Piano Solo:
      Étude in A♭   Chopin
      G. Strain

9. Augmented College Choral Society:
      Hymn to St. Peter   Benjamin Britten
      Cantata: The Four Seasons   J.S. Bach
      Soloists: G. Williamson, J. Langridge, Mrs. Percy Bird
      Piano: Miss Audrey Bryant
      Accompanied by String Quartet

The Gardening Girls

Gardening was not for the faint-hearted, as Dorothy Coffin (1949-1951) remembered:

'Those weary hours in a dark subterranean lecture room in Old Deanery, leaning over evil- smelling bits of this and that, trying to decide if it was fertiliser, seeds or some diseased plant! The freezing mornings trying to "double dig" in the gardens, were offset by the hot sunny days, when we tried to lose ourselves in the shade of a hedge when Miss Riley's back was turned'.

Miss Nash arrived at College in 1951 as Head of the Horticulture Department. At this time there was a large walled-in vegetable garden behind King's House where the lecture rooms, hall and gym were latterly built. There was an orchard at the side of this garden and another walled garden, including a glasshouse with a vine, in front of the Old Deanery. Miss Nash left in 1957 after the introduction of the new Science curriculum and the gradual disappearance of much of her work.

Old Deanery Garden, January 1950

'Gardening was one of my main subjects and it was my turn to read the max/min thermometer and the rain gauge, and it had to be done before breakfast. There was a heavy frost and everything was black or white, whilst a mist from the river blurred outlines. Job done and I was packing up, when suddenly a shaft of sunlight broke through, making everything sparkle. At that moment seven swans flew overhead, had they landed and turned into handsome princes, I would not have been surprised. It was a never-to-be-forgotten moment of sheer magic.'

Rosemary Stone (1949-1951)

Faith and Outreach

'The beauty of The Close, the quietness of the river and the proximity of both city and country. I remember walking along the stream at Harnham, picking snowdrops at Odstock and the Chapel filled with buttercups for Ascension'.

Peta Craven (1950-1952)

Religious societies at College in the early 1950s included the Student Christian Movement, the Christian Union, the Missionary Circle, the Cathedral Branch of the Anglican Young People's Organisation and a UMCA (Universities' Mission to Central Africa) study group.

Students continued to feel called to service in parts of the world that included Africa, India, Pakistan, Brazil and Thailand. Former students who were now working in the mission field sometimes returned to give talks at the College. Dorothy Stubbings (1924-1926) taught in both Uganda and Ghana and was awarded an MBE for her contributions to Education and Guiding.

Between 1953 and 1955 the religious societies, with the exception of the Christian Union, amalgamated in the College Fellowship. Mission meetings, films, visiting speakers and retreats were all part of its programme, and were well attended. The Christian Union recorded a healthy membership of twenty-six in 1958.

The College continued to raise money towards the work of the UMCA, with which it had time-honoured connections.

Training College Fete Revived

'Salisbury Diocesan Training College students revived an old tradition, lapsed for some years, when they held a garden fete in the College Grounds, The Close, Salisbury, on Saturday, in aid of a UMCA school in Africa, of which a former college student is headmistress. These fetes used to be held annually and it is hoped now to do so again. The attractions included puppet shows, a demonstration by the vaulting club and a dancing display by the advanced P.T. group. There was also an exhibition of students' art in the studio, and conducted tours of the new extensions to the College, formally opened in May.'

From the *Salisbury Journal*, 1951

Christian Union, 1950

Fête Publicity Day

Rag Day, 1958

Courtesy of The Salisbury Museum

Student Life-Cycle

'In the summer of 1954 I was summoned for an interview with Miss Maxwell at King's House. I vaguely knew about Salisbury – it had a Cathedral, was in Wiltshire and was quite a long way from Oxford, where I lived. How to get there without any money? I would go on my bike! Into my saddle bag I stowed away a pair of stockings, a coat and skirt, a blouse, summer gloves and my best shoes.

I left my mother a note saying 'Gone to Salisbury' and crept out of the house at crack of dawn. I remember well how beautiful it was as the sun rose over the Newbury downs. I pedalled up hill and down dale, through little villages and towns …Newbury … Andover …There were no bypasses, ring-roads or motorways then. It was a happy ride with just one little nagging fear. "I hope that I don't have a puncture"! This thought lent wings to my feet.

I parked my bike in Salisbury market square, popped into the "Ladies," changed into my finery and went on to King's House, where I tentatively rang the bell.

Miss Maxwell's room was all cosy chintz and the interview was pleasant. I was given afternoon tea, of which I nervously partook. Then Miss Maxwell enquired,

"And what time is your train"?

"I didn't come by train", I answered.

"Oh, perhaps you came by bus"? she suggested.

"Well, no, actually I cycled".

For the moment the Principal was reduced to silence. She gave me a strange look!

The ride home was another new experience. It became very dark and my new worry was whether my lights would work all the way. I was met soon after midnight by a furious mother who told me that I was foolhardy, irresponsible and stupid. And then she made me a cup of cocoa!

Two wonderful years at Salisbury were well worth a long bike ride'.

Marjorie Burnett (1954-1956)

College Mothers

Students found that having a College Mother was very supportive. In 1945 Pat Prosser described arriving at Salisbury Station and being met by her mother, who looked after her for the first two weeks and was 'kindness itself'. Anne Salter (1950 -1952) found it an extremely re-assuring experience:

'The College system of mother student supporting new daughter student ensured that I had an extremely happy and confident first year in College'.

Mothers gave advice and support on so many different aspects of College life. Joan Russett (1949-1951) wrote a helpful, caring letter to her daughter Margaret in 1950:

Dear Margaret,

I expect you are wondering to whom the strange handwriting belongs, so I will not keep you in suspense but tell you that I am your College 'mother.' You may have heard of College 'mothers' before, but in case you haven't I will tell you that I am, at present, a first year student, but when we return in September I shall then become a 'second year' and it is the custom for all 'second years' to have 'daughters.' We look after all the new people like yourself when they first come to college and try to make them feel cheerful, for most people are upset for the first few days after leaving home… It's a wonderful life really, one is part of the large community here at college and one need never feel lonely!

Everyone has been rushing about today. We have all been waiting for the 'Daughter' list so be put up so that we could sign for daughters. Most students sign for girls in or near their hometown. I think by the way that you are the only one from Bournemouth. There are quite a few girls coming from Dorchester, Weymouth, Swanage, Exeter, Taunton, from the Midlands, from Wales and from the Channel Islands so you will be quite a 'mixed bag'. Our year at present numbers 72, but I think your year will be about 98 strong so some people are having two daughters. I decided to have two daughters, that means you will have a 'sister'.

Do write and ask me anything you want to know about College and I will do my best to answer your questions. I shall do my best to give you a happy 1st year at College. I hope to hear from you very soon.

PS Send a photo if possible when you reply. Tell me about yourself.

Love Joan

School Practice in the Fifties

Student group 1952   'Robert Poole'

Miss Taylor praised the students for their hard work, courtesy and poise. However, there were clear rules set out for School Practice.

1   All students must wear hair tied back to avoid catching head lice.

2   Students should wear clean, smart clothes(e.g. No ladders in stockings)

3   No necklaces (they could hurt a child when you bend over him to inspect his work).

4   The Infant group must make a work-book for every child in the class, from kitchen paper joined together with a figure-of-eight stitch. College mothers will teach this method.

5   Most materials for School Practice must be bought from College by the students.(School funds were always limited.)

6   MOST IMPORTANT. When entering a staff-room at breaks, wait to be invited where to sit. Taking a teacher's special chair will not increase your popularity.

Students recalled their School Practice experiences:

'We were encouraged to pin work to walls with dressmaking pins – "not drawing pins dear, they are far too ugly".

Four students   'Robert Poole'

In our first term we had practice in local schools, but in the summer term we were "bussed" to schools in the Poole area. If one owned up to travel sickness one could be placed locally again. Most of us enjoyed the coach journey home, relaxed and singing student songs. In the second year, when we were visiting rural schools, weekly, we used public transport, but one person was allowed to use Mrs Dalton-Hill's sit-up-and-beg bicycle, known as "the camel". The longer final practice in Bournemouth was dreaded, but proved not to be quite as bad as we feared'.

School Practice preparation in the garden

Men in Rooms!

In the mid-fifties, students were only allowed to entertain boyfriends on a Saturday and a room had to be booked, either the Quiet Room in Maxwell or the Parlour Room in King's House. Details had to be given and a chaperone named. No-one seemed to object if two students invited two men and chaperoned each other.

Anne Spicer recollected that there had been agitation to entertain 'Gentlemen Friends' in student rooms for a long time. 'Unrest had rumbled on and at every Student Union meeting the question of "Men in Rooms" was raised'. It was decided that Anne would petition Dr Grubb about the issue.

'A special appointment was made to see Dr Grubb. We were met with a very frosty reception. "Is this necessary?" was the first question. We skilfully argued our case. The Inquisition seemed to go on for hours'.

Dr Grubb agreed to present the petition to the staff for discussion. Several weeks later the answer came that men would be allowed in rooms for a trial period.

'The weekend arrived. Many students had invited their boyfriends to afternoon tea. On Monday morning I was summoned by Dr Grubb. I felt all was not well. She was sitting at her desk looking like thunder. Could I explain myself? Did I know that a student's boyfriend had stayed the night? No, I did not. I must admit I was horrified. Lots of angry words were said while I looked on helplessly. Finally, Dr Grubb stood up and came and sat on the corner of her desk'.

Dr Grubb was very upset and Anne comforted her and apologised again. She asked if they could have another chance. Eventually permission was granted, just before the 1957-1959 students left College.

Mary Westcott remembered students being given a talk regarding sexual matters by a Doctor. Not long after the talk all engaged students were encouraged to attend Family Planning Clinics in the town. Mary commented, 'Things were beginning to change but was it enough for the coming of the Sixties?'

An Initiation Ceremony

The Theological College, founded in 1860 and situated in the Cathedral Close, was a source of eligible young men for student teachers. During the Fifties and onwards several activities were shared between the two Colleges.

Joan Steele (1953-1955) was told about a very surprising initiation ceremony:

'The Theological students had an initiation ceremony in which they had to come into Maxwell House ground floor bathrooms, take a bath, and get away without being found out! (At that time the only man in our College was the Chaplain, and we had to ask permission to entertain men at all, and then only in the Quiet Room in King's House.) One student had nearly been caught, and had taken refuge in the drying room opposite, among all the lines of washing!'

What a very narrow escape!

Men!

College Students as Guinea Pigs

The Common Cold Research Unit opened on Harnham Hill on the outskirts of Salisbury in 1946. Its purpose was to solve the mysteries of the common cold. The offer of a free break that included a little pocket money was of course attractive to students. Ann Borthwick and Alice Jones (1954-1956) bravely took up the offer one half term.

'Apart from twice daily examinations, we were free to enjoy a ten-day holiday in our private flatlet. The flats were tastefully furnished, with central heating and American style fittings. Everything was provided for our comfort and amusement, including books, games, radio and gramophone. We chose our meals from attractive menus and they were delivered three times a day. But there were rules and if we ventured out into the gardens or onto the Plain, we had to maintain a distance of thirty feet from any other person'.

Alice and Ann did not catch colds. Neither did they achieve their study targets, but they improved their table tennis skills, enjoyed lengthy walks and built a lasting friendship.

Fifties Floods   'Robert Poole'

Feeding the Fifties

'College Food was always a problem …'

Mary Westcott (1956-1958) explained that the problem was not that the food was bad, but that it was so much better than school dinners. There was an inevitable consequence:

'We ate far too much and practically everyone was dieting or pretending to do so. The mid-morning cocoa and huge, sticky buns were very hard to resist, especially in the winter. Those ghastly grey flannel 'shorts', which were fitted on arrival by someone from Elliotts the Outfitters, were purposely made inches too large and caused great amusement when first worn, but, alas, we soon grew to fit them.

Dining memories are of plain but satisfying meals, produced under restricted circumstances. We had rhubarb and ginger jam EVERY tea-time for two years – never to be consumed again! The great rhubarb garden was just outside the dining room passageway that was later called the Milky Way'.

Anne Smithson (1950-1952)

'Meal times in College were an interesting tradition in our era. Each student had to collect her own serviette and ring (which must not be made of silver) from a small cupboard near the dining room before lunch. The students then stood behind their chairs and waited for the entrance of Dr Grubb, followed by the rest of the staff. Grace was then said and lunch was served. Friday was always a meat-less day. Sometimes there was fish, but more often it was cauliflower cheese that contained a lot of stump. The only meal that we generally missed was Saturday lunch, a curry that was viewed with great suspicion as it was made from left-overs from the previous week. If we were in funds, we bought egg and chips at the Cadena in Blue Boar Row. Seeing Augustus John, the famous artist, there with his long beard, wide-awake hat and long, flowing cloak made the meal even more interesting. At weekends we were given 'rations' because there was no tea or evening meal provided. Rations consisted of bread, a triangle of processed cheese, an egg and a piece of cake with some fresh fruit. On Sunday mornings we made toast over our gas fire (strictly forbidden) and stewed mushrooms in milk over our gas ring'.

Mary Westcott and Angela Fudge (1956-1958)

Christmas 1959

'Treats' were limited in the austere days of the 1950s. Some food was still rationed when Stephanie Offer (1954-1956) arrived at College, but she enjoyed every minute of College life and fellowship:

'We had ten shillings a week to live on and still managed a gin and orange at the Cathedral Hotel on Saturday nights and the odd cheese scone and coffee at The Red Lion'.

Barbara Jerrett (1956-58) celebrated her 21st birthday at College:

'About six of us each had a teaspoonful of sherry in an egg cup – the limit of our extravagance. Our weekly treat out of two shillings and sixpence pocket money was a 6d bar of Cadbury's Milk Chocolate'.

LST ibid

Freezing but Fashionable!

College buildings were still bitterly cold in the early 1950s, but students learnt to shiver in silence. Any complaint was met by comparing the 'comforts' of the present day with the 'terrible wartime experiences'. The 1950 clothing list stated: 'Clothes must be plain and warm. A warm blazer or short coat to wear in the house is essential for the cold weather'. A waterproof, warm winter coat, wellington boots, hat, bedroom slippers and warm dressing gown were also on the list:

'Who would believe now that when we arrived at College, we had so few clothes? I had one grey skirt which my Mother and I had bought at Colmers in Bath, and several jumpers and blouses to ring the changes. I remember one of the students asking me if my white evening dress was an underskirt! Trousers were banned in The Close'.

Stephanie Offer (1954-1956)

Students also had more frivolous outfits, as Margaret Frost, a 'billetee' (1948-1950) remembered:

'Mrs Bridle's thrill at ironing our long evening dresses for the very few College balls was lovely to see. She fondled the taffeta, satin and silk and once garlanded my mauve taffeta with fine black satin ribbons. I didn't have the heart to tell her that it looked funereal – and had to suffer my partners' annoyance at getting caught up in the lasso of ribbons'.

Margaret hung up her first pair of nylon stockings to dry in the General Purpose Room at King's House, but sadly 'lost them to someone else's legs'.

Students were also expected to bring regulation PE shorts, aertex shirts, gym shoes and a gym dress. By 1956 dance tunics had arrived. Mary Westcott (1956-1958) remembered 'strange, limp cotton, sleeveless dresses that had been carefully made by our mothers, with knickers to match'.

During Mary's first term, wintry weather set in early. This was the time of the Suez crisis; oil and petrol were both rationed and so too were heating and hot water in College. Students were in fear of having to leave College in order to 'join up' in one of the armed services.

Mary was in the Infant Education Group. Their lecture room was in the attics in King's House:

'It was terribly cold, with frost patterns on the inside of the windows. We were allowed the use of one two bar electric fire, which we passed around the room. Mrs Dalton-Hill, our lecturer, encouraged us to bring our hot water bottles'.

Despite their modest budgets, students tried to keep up with fashions, dressing smartly and clattering up and down the stairs in high heeled shoes –and even stilettos! 'Pony tails' were popular at that time, but hair had to be 'put up' for teaching practice.

There were, of course, some memorable students:

'There was Ann - tall, blonde and always elegantly dressed in tailored suits, hand-made shoes, blue mascara on her eyelashes. Fresh from finishing school in Paris, her first appearance on the hockey field delighted us (but not Miss Shute) – full make-up, wearing Victorian drop ear-rings and carrying a shooting stick "in case we had to sit down"'.

Mary Westcott (1956-1958)

'Robert Poole'

Meeting the Queen Mother, 1958

When the Queen Mother visited College in 1962 she referred to an earlier visit which she had made in 1958. Mary Westcott remembered talking to her on that occasion:

'It was the year the Cathedral celebrated its Sept-Centenary with the installation of the first set of flood lights, something very special so soon after the war. We were in our last term at College and had been given a Close Pass in the form of a piece of cardboard about the size of two postage stamps (paper in any form was precious then) for, after dark, people visiting The Close had to pay for entry.

This particular night was a Sunday, so many students were out till the last possible moment, whilst others had their heads down, revising for exams, but somehow the news got out that the "Queen Mum" was in the Close on a private visit. I imagine that this information came from our friend the Close Constable. It was gone 10.30 pm so the doors were locked, but we unlocked them and rushed out of Kings and Audley to stand in an orderly group to watch. I cannot think that we shouted or waved but she came over to us and (I can still hear her saying) "Where are you from?" She talked to us for several minutes before resuming her tour.

Next day we were summoned to a meeting with Dr Grubb, the Principal, who was furious with our behaviour, not because we had unlocked the doors but that some students had appeared in dressing gowns and, worse still, bedroom slippers! It did occur to some of us that we might fail our finals, but legend has it that that chance meeting led to the Queen Mother returning some years later to open the new buildings!'

Students 1950s   'Robert Poole'

Students 1950

'Robert Poole'

Looking towards the Sixties

The extension of the two year training course had been under discussion for much of the 1950s. Miss Taylor was actively involved with the process. She reported that at a conference in June 1957, Dr Grubb had spoken about the value of Science in the Training College Curriculum, whilst others emphasised the need for prospective teachers to be competent in the English language. Further discussion considered the differentiation of courses for Primary and Secondary work and the advanced study of Special Subjects.

Second year students in the College were asked for their views before they left in July 1957. In general, they felt that they needed more time to study more fully the material of their course, and more time for practical experience in schools.

Dr Grubb shared her vision of the development of the College in the 1959 *Chronicle*:

> 'This project will take two years and by then we hope to number 240 students, a fair proportion of whom will spend one of their three years in lodgings'.

The three-year course would start in September 1960.

Keeping in touch

The various local branches of the Old Students' Association (known as the Salisbury Clubs) continued to meet. Guild Services were held, as well as outings and social events. Past and present members of staff attended these meetings. The Weymouth Branch met on May 9th 1953:

> 'Miss Mayo and Miss Taconis were our College visitors. We were shown round the new Wyke Infants' School by the Headmistress, Miss W Briggs, who is one of our members'.

In 1954 the Southampton Branch expressed concern about the diminishing number of members. It was thought that it might be unnecessary to have a club at Southampton when Salisbury was so close. Two years later a reorganisation meeting of the Salisbury Club was held.

> 'As it is so much easier to reach Salisbury from places like Southampton and Bournemouth than it was in former days, we have found that our younger members prefer to join the Home Branch rather than the local branch. In the case of Southampton this has led to the decision, rather reluctantly reached, to close the branch and transfer the membership to the Home Branch. Bournemouth, Portsmouth and Weymouth will probably do the same in the near future'.

In 1959, in addition to the Home Branch, there were branches in London, Somerset, the Midlands, Jersey, Guernsey and Devon. 330 people attended the joint meeting in Salisbury. The Association was alive and well.

Staff and Students, 1952
' Robert Poole'

'Robert Poole'

Farewell to College

It was the last night of our College lives. We had survived our drinks farewell with the lecturers. Then there was the ragging by the first years - and suddenly it was all over. Within two months we would be on the other side of the fence, having a class of our own and being responsible adults. I couldn't sleep, so I crept down Audley stairs into Kings and from there into Maxwell, where I met another restless wanderer. We climbed onto a flat roof and down into the garden. Down by the river we decided to spice things up a little by negotiating the hedge around North Canonry (then the home of Colonel Sir Reginald Kennedy Cox.) We were wearing pyjamas and half hoped that the butler, a notorious student-watcher, might be at one of the windows. Once in The Close we jumped over the newly planted row of horse chestnut trees.

As the Cathedral clock struck one, we found that a small door in the west front was unlocked. I have often wondered whether anyone else has ever walked up the nave, in pyjamas, bare feet silent on the old stones and listened to the creakings of that ancient building. We returned the same way that we had come, having marked the end of our student lives'.

Mary Westcott (1956-1958)

Courtesy of the Salisbury Museum

Courtesy of The Salisbury Museum

Courtesy of The Salisbury Museum

Chapter 6

The Swinging Sixties

1960-1970

The Times They Are-A-Changin'

The Sixties was a decade of tremendous change: capital punishment was abolished, abortion was legalised, racial discrimination was outlawed and the birth control pill was introduced. The Cold War and the fear of conflict were ever present. 1962 was the year of the Cuban Missile Crisis, when nuclear war was narrowly averted. This was an era of protests, including the Aldermaston 'Ban the Bomb' Marches and demonstrations opposing the war in Vietnam. *We Shall Overcome* sang Joan Baez, whilst Bob Dylan sang of *The Times They Are-A-Changin'*. Never was a truer word spoken.

In 1961 Yuri Gagarin was the first man to go into space. In the same year John F. Kennedy became President of the USA and there was optimism for a safer, freer world. In 1963 Martin Luther King called for an end to racism in America. Waves of shock spread across the western world on hearing of President Kennedy's assassination. The first heart transplant took place in 1967. In 1969 Neil Armstrong and Buzz Aldrin took that 'one small step, but a giant leap for mankind' on the moon.

Teenagers began to break free from the conventions and norms of previous generations, and to find a voice. Mary Quant launched the miniskirt in 1965 and 'swinging London' became the centre of the fashion world. High Street shops started to sell affordable fashion for the young, who no longer had to dress like their mothers. (Hooray!) There was 'headiness' in the air – and England's sensational World Cup victory in 1966 added icing to the cake! The 'peace and love' generation was exemplified by the hippies. Beatlemania hit the country, and sixties teenagers will remember 'Top of the Pops' and 'Juke Box Jury'. Television now boasted three channels! Society was multicultural, but people were proud to be British. 'I'm backing Britain!' was the slogan in 1968.

Educational provision was improving, with better resources and facilities. More university places became open to women. There was, however, concern about the inequality of the selection system, and of educational provision and opportunity. Change was in the air.

'Labour's manifesto for the 1964 General Election couldn't have been clearer: Labour will get rid of the segregation of children into separate schools caused by 11-plus selection: secondary education will be reorganised on comprehensive lines'. Education in England, Derek Gillard 2011

In the primary schools, teachers were encouraged to be innovative and creative, and to use a child-centred approach. New 'open plan' schools reflected the decline in whole-class teaching. The 'integrated day' became a by-word in primary education, with classroom activities being structured in such a way that children would 'learn by doing' in small groups. The focus was on how to use and extend the child's innate curiosity about the world, rather than seeing him or her as an empty vessel that needed to be filled.

So many changes in just one decade!

View from West Harnham

Painted by Jean Watts

Three Years as a Student

The Three-Year Course started in 1960, with 210 students in College. The Education Department now had four members of staff. A Transition Group was started for students who were training to teach in either upper primary or lower secondary classes. Following the earlier demand for Science teachers, there was now a demand for teachers of Mathematics. Mr Breakall was appointed to lecture in Mathematics in 1960 and this subject soon became compulsory for all students. The importance of Music, Movement and Dance was increasingly recognised and Miss Amos was appointed to the PE department in 1960.

Rural Studies was dropped, as the focus was now on Biology and Chemistry – and Physics from 1962. The loss of the subject was deeply regretted, as the local area provided great scope.

The Three-Year Course was ready to go!

Members of Photographic Club

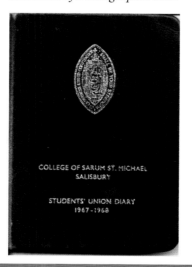

The Visit to Salisbury Training College of Her Majesty, Queen Elizabeth, the Queen Mother

On November 15th, 1962, Her Majesty Queen Elizabeth the Queen Mother visited College to officially open the new buildings.

Jenny Smith recalled:

'The majority of students saw the Queen Mother for the first time as she entered the Assembly Hall for the short service of dedication of the new buildings. The Bishop of Salisbury outlined the buildings and development of the College, and then the Queen Mother declared the buildings open.

Then it was the turn of the Second and First Year Students, who had been waiting patiently in the Gymnasium to see the Queen Mother, as she passed through the Gymnasium on her way to the Music Block. Here Music students sang to her, showing the Music Wing in action.

The Royal Party proceeded to the new residential hostel, and we noticed with delight that the Queen Mother waved to the workmen who had gathered upstairs in the Old Deanery. Having unveiled the plaque on the hostel wall, the Queen Mother was shown round by two students who said afterwards that it was just like showing a parent round, which illustrates perfectly the informal spirit of Her Majesty's visit. Although remaining truly regal, she had the gift of making everyone feel at ease by her real interest in them'.

Excerpts from the Queen Mother's Speech

'I learn that, in this Close, there are not only houses of great beauty and antiquity, but a College which occupies some of these older buildings, unites them with new ones more suited to their present function, and is itself the oldest women's college founded by the Church in this country.

But education, as a matter of learning, is of little value unless it is combined with something deeper. Here, in a Church Training College, where the chapel is the centre of the college, where a ceremony begins with a service of dedication, where you combine in fellowship seeking the interpretation of the Christian faith for the children of today, you have an especial task and an especial privilege. Most of you are students who will presently be both mothers and teachers; you will have much to give to children.

I have been told that shortly after your foundation, the first Chaplain, Canon Hamilton, gave to your college the motto that I see on the crest of my programme – "In quietness and in confidence shall be your strength". This is a text for all time and may I wish you a renewal of that strength.

I have much pleasure in declaring the new buildings open'.

The Salisbury Journal

The Salisbury Journal

The Old Deanery — a Dignified Inheritance

Following the results of the 1959 survey on the building, and the discovery of its true value, the decision was made that the Old Deanery should not be demolished. Eventually, sufficient funds were made for the restoration work to be undertaken.

The Medieval Hall was declared open in 1963 by the Marquis of Salisbury, who was the Chairman of the Royal Commission on Historical Monuments.

> 'Miss Ashley expressed the thanks of all of us that such an historic building had been saved. The Great Hall remains medieval with a unique roof structure, and will be used for educational and dramatic purposes; most of the remaining rooms in the north and south wings are already in use. The Solar, with its beautiful views of the river and The Cathedral, is now used as a library, and it was here that the guests were later given tea.
>
> The story of the discovery of the Old Deanery's architectural worth is dramatic, and so is the result of the restorative work. Most colleges can boast of new, modern buildings, but few also have such a dignified inheritance, which has been beautifully restored at great expense'.

STC Chronicle, 1964

Restoration of Old Deanery   C.J.Watts 1963 from my room in Maxwell House.

In Loco Parentis

In the Sixties there was more freedom, but Miss Ashley's letter shows that as most students were under 21 they were still subject to tight rules and regulations. Students of today would find it incredible that a letter was sent to parents setting out the background to College regulations. In the Sixties most students accepted this as normal and the majority kept to the rules (most of the time).

Let's Celebrate!

SALISBURY TRAINING COLLEGE
65 The Close.

Principal:
Miss A.M.D. Ashley

Telephone:
Salisbury 3316.

10th July 1963.

Dear   Mr.

As your daughter will be under 21 when she comes here as a student I think it is desirable that you should know the background to the College regulations that are being sent to all students.

It is our wish that students should have a similar freedom to that which we find they are allowed in their homes and that the pattern of social life should be similar. They are therefore allowed to entertain friends of either sex in their rooms in College hostels on Saturdays and Sundays until 10.15 p.m. and as their hostesses permit in lodgings. We feel sure that you are in the habit of trusting your daughter to behave according to the standards she has acquired from you.

Students have a maximum number of "nights away" for each term and may use their own discretion in deciding about long or short week-ends. They may request occasional permissions for absence during the week to attend some special occasion such as a family wedding.

We find that many students have already worked or spent holidays away from home so that parents are accustomed to allowing their daughters to stay elsewhere than in their own homes. Students if doing this leave their addresses with their Hostel Wardens or hostesses and they must at all times conform with regulations covering time of return to College and telephone the office in the event of unforeseen delay.

We have in the past asked parents to inform us if they do not allow pillion-riding. Please make it quite clear to your daughter if that is the case. We find it inadvisable to make rules that could only be enforced by an amount of supervision distasteful to students and unsuitable in a large College with a small number of resident staff. We expect students to show a trustworthy and responsible attitude to their work and to the reasonable requirements of community life.

In case of illness your daughter must accept the directions of the College Doctor and Sanatorium Sister.

In any difficulty she will be able to consult her Hostel Warden or her personal tutor or to see the Chaplain or myself.

Yours sincerely,

A.M.D. Ashley

Some members of staff in the Sixties

Some members of Staff who had been appointed in the 40s and 50s remained at the College, in addition to new appointments.

Dr V. Grubb	Principal	1955-62
Miss A. M. D. Ashley	Principal	1963
Miss E. I. Barnard	Vice-Principal	1951-66
Miss M. F. C. Rogers	Vice-Principal	1964-67
Miss D. Roantree	Deputy Principal	1967
Revd M. R. Newman	Chaplain	1956-61
Revd D. Burden	Chaplain	1962-68
Revd B. Coleman	Chaplain	1969

Miss A. D. Amos	Physical Education
Miss D. J. Ayling	Physical Education
Miss E. Baggs	Education
Miss E. I. Barnard	Music
Mr W. Bate	Education
Revd D. Bevan	Education & Divinity
Miss D. Bell	Craft
Mr D. Bindon	Mathematics
Miss M. Binham	Education & Divinity
Miss O. M. M. Blackburn	English
Revd H. Blenkin	Divinity
Mr A. Brinn	Music
Miss R. A. Bryant	Music
Miss V. Bunyard	English
Miss M. Cowan	English
Miss M. Cox	Education
Mr W. Crisp	Education
Miss L. M. Currie	Divinity
Mrs B. Dalton Hill	Education
Miss B. Danielli	Physical Education
Miss M. Davey	Education
Miss M. Dean	Music
Mr J. Dodridge	Mathematics
Miss J. Flarty	Art
Miss C. Game	English
Miss M. J. Gibbs	Education
Mr S. Gibbons	Combined Studies
Miss C. Greene	English
Miss S. Higgins	English
Miss J. Highley	Education
Miss J. Hughes	Education
Mr J. Kaye	Mathematics

Mrs M. Langdon	Education
Mr K. Lockett	Physics
Miss J. Machesney	Art
Miss R. E. Mayo	Geography
Miss Mogford	Education
Miss M. Moore	Speech Training
Mr M. Neville	Pottery
Miss O. G. Northcott	Biology
Mr P Pain	Education
Mr W Peel	Chemistry
Mr R Pick	Physics
Miss M Poole	History
Mr KS Rogers	Geography
Miss M. F. Rogers	Divinity
Mr A. Quest	English
Miss D. Saintsbury	Art
Miss M. Sanders	English
Mr J. Say	English
Miss Sime	Education
Miss P. Snelgar	Art and Craft
Miss L. Sanderson Taylor	Education
Miss D. A. Todd	History
Mr E. Vass	Education
The Revd B. Williams	History
Mr T. A. Wright	Education
Mr W. B. Gibson	College Bursar
Mrs E. Kay	Assistant Bursar
Miss M. Green	College Secretary
Mrs J. Parsons	Assistant Secretary
Miss E. Potter	Catering Officer
Miss M. Taylor	Domestic Bursar
Miss A. Walker	Domestic Bursar
Miss K Parry	Librarian
Mrs James	Education Office Secretary
Mrs W. Gibson	Warden, Barnard's Cross
Mrs P. Young	Lodgings Officer
Miss F. Philips	Sanatorium Sister
Dr Joan Norris	Medical Officer
Miss D. Newton	Principal's Secretary

Reminiscences at every turn

After twelve years as HMI and eight months of retirement, Miss Denny returned to College for the summer term of 1960.

'The splendidly functional new buildings, which are progressively dwarfing the old, can never deprive these of their enduring beauty and worth.

Gone now are the restrictions of 1939: the wearing of hats and stockings in chapel and in the streets, the strictly time-tabled study hours, enforced silences and bed-times, and with them too, the many cramped cubicles and closely-shared bedrooms. A sense of enfranchisement is apparent in the deportment of young women in residence today, in their dress and grooming, as in their social assurance.

I found it difficult to be new in Salisbury! I felt myself to be part of the fabric of the place, woven into its traditions with my contemporaries and all who had gone before. It was my College, run by a new Principal with a largely new staff, and training new Students, but I was old. I belonged and felt happily at home. To all old students and staff I would say SDTC is basically the same, and is enjoying good health and sound growth'.

M. B. Denny, *STC Chronicle*, 1960

Maxwell Corridor

Writing in the 1982 Newsletter, Liba Taconis paid tribute to Miss Denny, 'one of a group of really great people I was privileged to know at SDTC. She looked for the spark in us which she could fan. A sense of fun pervaded her lectures. Her maxim was 'A lesson without laughter is a failure'. In one of her memorable lectures she said "Every child is infinitely precious, and you may be the one to bring out the best in him".

A Breath of Fresh Air!

In the beginning, the members of staff were all women, who were resident at the Training School. It was not until the early 1960s that a significant number of men joined the staff.

Mr Peel was appointed as a lecturer in Chemistry in 1958. His son remembered that his father had been 'quite friendly with Mr Gibson (the Bursar) as they had both started in 1958 and were surrounded by female staff and students'.

When Mr Pain arrived in 1962 to lecture in Geography and History, he found that he was one of only three men on the academic staff. Many of their colleagues were single women who were friendly and kind, but "lived in" and were therefore not concerned about the infrequent pay cheques that made life difficult for men who had families to support. Up to this time, the College had not encountered the needs of non-resident staff with families.

Another area of negotiation was that of expenses. Single, resident members of staff were less concerned about being paid their expenses for things such as travel to and from School Practice visits. It was a different matter for married men, and they had to fight their case.

Mr Pain remembered his first staff meeting, held at 7.30pm on Friday. He left the meeting early, in order to catch the last bus home at 9.30pm. First thing on Monday he was summoned to Dr Grubb to explain himself. Shortly after that the meetings were moved to a more acceptable time.

By 1967 Messrs Bate, Bevan, Bindon, Blenkin, Brinn, Crisp, Dodridge, Kaye, Neville, Pick, Quest, Rogers, Say, Williams and Wright had joined the staff. By 1968, 17 out of the 43 people on the academic staff were men. They made a huge difference to the life of the College.

Staff hockey team, 1966

Infant classroom

Mrs Langdon was as an Education Lecturer who was in charge of Infant/Junior work in 1963. From 1965 she was responsible for the Warminster group and from 1967-1972 had responsibility for the shortened two-year course.

In her book *Let the Children Write*, first published in 1961, she recorded a factual account of an experiment which she conducted during one term of teaching children in Winterslow, a small Wiltshire village school. She believed in 'intensive writing,' which was reaching the pupils' imaginations and teaching them to express themselves in an exciting way. The children were lively but their writing was dull.

> 'I would listen with interest as their young, excited voices clamoured to be heard. Here was no stiffness of expression, dullness of phrase, no stilted, lifeless thought. Here, pouring out, was the very stuff of life, pulsating and vibrating with vigour and individuality'.

How could this translate into their writing? Mrs Langdon decided that the answer was by using poetry and encouraging the pupils to express an emotional experience 'briefly, simply and honestly'. She decided to have one half-hour period a week 'to attempt a new, drastic experiment'.

One day a large spider appeared on the classroom wall. 'Look there's a spider on the wall. Quick – write down the first thing that comes into your head about it'.

The pupils thought she was joking, but did as they were asked. Mrs Langdon stood looking at the spider as they wrote, 'hoping that some miracle would happen to cause the children to write without any words having been given to them'.

> 'Spiders are horrible and ugly, the very thought of them sends shivers down my spine.
> This one has a bloated body, black and brown
> The web is beautiful, dew-spangled delicate,
> But it is a trap'.

The 'experiment' went from strength to strength. The children read widely and wrote freely with expression and joy. Intensive writing had worked!

Mrs Langdon encouraged the same creativity and enthusiasm in her students. Anne Mortimer (1966-1969) recalled an occasion when Mrs Langdon had won an award which included some prize money.

> 'Typically, she treated a party of students to a wonderful picnic at Figsbury Rings; it did, of course, include some exciting role-play, which we later wrote about!'

In her first Education lecture, Diana Potter (1966-1969) remembered Mrs Langdon emphasising that 'Education is an attempt to make sense out of life'. Along with numerous other students, Diana is grateful for the inspiring and stimulating lectures which were firmly focused on the educational needs of children.

During the 1940s an annexe had been opened in Warminster, with great success. In 1965 when the number of students in College had reached 412, an experimental two-year course was provided for 20 married women, whose homes were in that area. St Boniface College was not available, so it was opened in the Warminster Youth Centre. Mrs Langdon was put in charge of Warminster in 1965. The students attended College in Salisbury for two days every week.

The success of this project led to an increased number of enquiries for a two year course for mature students. In September 1966 the College took over a large house, 26 London Road, Salisbury, which was adapted to suit the needs of a day college. In 1967 Mrs Langdon was put in charge of the two year course. Some of the other main subject lecturers worked there intermittently, and the students occasionally came down to the main college to work.

Jane Steeds commented on the 'privilege of studying in the Sarum St Michael buildings in The Close for our main subject studies, and coming in contact with some excellent lecturers.'

Some older students opted for the three year training. Pauline Wilkes (1965-68) was only about three years older than her fellow students, but she was married and therefore classed as a 'mature' student. The mature students brought varied experiences that enriched and enlivened the atmosphere of College.

The shortened course remained popular and included several men. During the late 1960s the former billiard room at the London Road house was transformed into an 'attractive activity area,' that came to be called 'the Coach House'. Groups of students went to work there with children from local schools. Students could ask permission to miss their normal timetable commitments for up to three consecutive days, which they would make up later.

'To many old students, this could seem like the full circle of the wheel, a modern version of the Model School.'

(LST ibid)

The Coach House

The Coach House is an outbuilding of 3 Rougemont Close, Salisbury, which the College purchased for use as an annexe a few years ago. It has been converted into a small but pleasant classroom, and students and lecturers work there with groups of children from local schools.

For the children this means an opportunity to work for a few days in a new environment, and in groups rather smaller than may normally be possible in school. For the College it is a welcome strengthening of links with local teachers and an opportunity for contact with children under almost ideal conditions.

Evelyn Chubb had an unusual route to College. On leaving South Wilts Girls' Grammar School in the late 1940s, she worked at Salisbury Library, but her job came to an end when she announced that she was getting married. Later, in the 1960s, Evelyn worked as a cleaner at the College and it was there that her life changed. Her former headmistress at South Wilts, Miss Moore, was at King's House one day when she recognised Evelyn and expressed her delight that she was training to teach. After Evelyn had explained that she was in fact a cleaner, Miss Moore told her that she ought to enrol at College as a mature student, which is what she did. Evelyn (known as Lynne by her college friends) went on to have a fulfilling teaching career.

The Resurrection of Barnard's Cross

As student numbers rose, it was necessary to seek further accommodation. This was achieved by the re-acquisition and re-opening of Barnard's Cross in September 1965, as a hostel for 50 students. Miss Ashley paid tribute to the 'vision, skill and unremitting hard work of Mr Gibson, the College Bursar. He and Mrs Gibson are now living in Barnard's Cross where Mrs Gibson is Warden of the hostel'.

> 'The years roll back and I am an excited but apprehensive first year. My room-mate, now the godmother of my eldest child, is as yet an unknown quantity. My new trunk sits unopened in the middle of Room 10'.
>
> Jenny Allcock (1965-1969)

> 'A luxury hostel, four-star hotel, or Larkhill mess. These were phrases used by students of Barnard's Cross' 65, within the first few weeks. A Wilton stair carpet and a spin dryer hardly prompted denials of the first two, and the frequent arrival of young army officers only confirmed the third. Queuing for baths was almost unheard of and basins in every room softened the labour of getting up'.
>
> Tamsin Ellis, *College Chronicle*, 1966

'Young army officers' … one such person, now retired, recalls jumping out of his girlfriend's window one evening. The girl friend, who has been his wife for 44 years, remembers being questioned by Mrs Gibson about footsteps in the flower bed!

There were small kitchen areas on each floor and the house had an elegant Common Room with a television. The best part was the Coffee Bar in the old barrel vaulted cellar. It had coloured chairs and tables, a parquet floor with a dolphin mosaic, a piano, a gramophone and a table tennis table. Scandinavian coloured lamps added to the décor, and there was a small kitchen unit. Modern and sophisticated, it had a good 'party' atmosphere and was a place where friends could be entertained on Friday evenings.

Barnard's Cross had a very efficient central heating system.

> 'I had heard that some hostels were rather chilly in winter, and so made myself a thick, red woollen dressing gown. Nothing could have been less appropriate! Only light tropical wear was required indoors'.
>
> Hannah Boothman (1965-1969)

Rooms 40 and 41 at the top of the building were coveted for their magnificent views:

> 'It was Sunday afternoon in late November. The air was still and quiet, smoke drifting lazily upwards from almost every chimney. Looking through the window I could see the Cathedral spire rising mysteriously above the autumnal haze. It seemed to be floating on the mist enshrouded rooftops and back yards'.
>
> Jenny Allcock (1965-1969)

Whilst Barnard's Cross students inevitably 'missed out' on some of College life, the hostel nevertheless had a full and lively life of its own. Many students appreciated being a little apart from College and 'coming home' in the evening. In common with the Barnard's Cross students of earlier years, they made lasting friendships and valued the experience of community life.

Florence of Barnard's

> 'I was fortunate to live in Barnard's Cross for three years. The distance to College meant a walk, which was often necessary two or three times a day. Along the quiet St Ann's Street, through the gateway into The Close, then the serene atmosphere around the Cathedral. What a joy this was. No matter the weather, I considered I was blessed to take this route each day.
>
> I shared a room on the top floor with Claire Lawrence and we looked out over the rooftops of the city, with the magnificent spire taking centre stage.
>
> Mrs Gibson, the Warden, ran her establishment with exacting standards and discipline. Initially, for such a tender soul as I, this was rather intimidating. There were strict rules and occasionally one could slip up and come face to face with the wrath of Mrs G – no running on the stairs, must sign visitors in and out, punctuality at all meals, prompt delivery of items for the laundry and so on.
>
> Mrs Gibson was respected for her values and her regime gave stability and a sense of order. I will always be grateful that I spent those three years under her wing'.
>
> Mary Palmer (1968-1971)

Returning to Barnard's Cross

Barnard's Cross Coffee bar

Setting Chapter 6 in context: A Table of some significant events

Date	Educational	International/National	Local
1960	Teacher Training extended to three years.	Macmillan's 'wind of change speech'. Kennedy elected US President. The first successful kidney transplant carried out.	First Chinese restaurant opens in Salisbury
1961		Yuri Gagarin first man in space.	Cliff Richard at Salisbury Gaumont Stonehenge daubed with 'Ban the Bomb' slogan. First Salisbury Bingo session at Market House.
1962	Education Act. LEAs to provide grants to students for living costs and tuition fees. Parents legally obliged to ensure their children have a suitable education. LEAs responsible for ensuring pupil attendance.	New Coventry Cathedral consecrated Cuban missile crisis E Germany erects Berlin wall First Sunday colour supplement	St Mark's residents protest at proposed city relief road route New Central Health Clinic opened
1963	Newsom Report focused on education of 'average and below average children'. Robbins Report recommended expansion of higher education for all with necessary ability including 4 year B.Ed course for suitable students.	Beeching Report calls for closure of over 2.000 railway stations. Great train robbery in Bedfordshire nets £2.6 million. President Kennedy was assassinated Americans back Civil Rights Campaign	Local railway stations axed City Hall opened The Beatles perform at the City Hall The worst winter since 1947 – heavy snowfall from January to March
1964	Education Act (Boyle Act) permitted transfer of pupils at ages other than 11. LEAs able to dispense with 11+	Nelson Mandela is sentenced to life imprisonment Harold Wilson becomes Prime Minister Channel Tunnel link between England and France Forth Road Bridge opened	St Edmund's School moves to new site in Laverstock Last train from Salisbury to Fordingbridge Fans faint at Rolling Stones Concert in the City Hall Experimental one-way traffic system
1965	Certificate of Secondary Education (CSE) introduced	Capital punishment abolished Post Office Tower opened State funeral of Sir Winston Churchill First Asda supermarket US bombs Vietnam Anti-Vietnam War demonstrations	St Joseph's and Downton Secondary Schools open Work begins on the inner relief road First Traffic Wardens appear
1966	The 1944 Education Act was repealed. Grants provided for employing staff in authorities required to make special provision for educating immigrant children Polytechnics established	Landslide victory for Labour in General Election. Aberfan disaster England win World Cup Mao-Tse-tung announces Cultural Revolution in China First cross-channel hovercraft service Britain's first credit card introduced	Longleat Safari Park opens with "The Lions of Longleat"
1967	Plowden Report on Children and their Primary schools, recommended child centred, individual, non-streaming education and evaluation of children's progress	First heart transplant Sir Francis Chichester sails solo round the world QE2 launched Colour TV begins First automatic bank machine	£250,000 appeal for Cathedral Netherhampton by-pass petition
1968	First Middle School opens in Bradford, Yorkshire	Student riots in Paris President Nixon elected 'I'm backing Britain' campaign set up Martin Luther King murdered M1 motorway completed	Plan for Catherine Street multi-storey car park
1969	Children & Young Person's Act : LEA to be responsible for children not receiving education or in need of care or protection	Concorde's first flight Man lands on the moon Troops sent to Northern Ireland	Old George Mall opens Second stage of inner relief road opens Amesbury by-pass opens ABC cinema becomes Bingo Club

Miss Sanderson Taylor (Lucy) was the Head of the Education Department from 1946 until 1968, when she retired. During this time educational changes included the start of Secondary Modern Schools, the Three Year Course and the B. Ed. degree. Miss Taylor made considerable impact on the College and was held in high esteem by the students. She was very proud of her Scottish ancestry. Miriam Loydell (1949-1951) remembered being in an exceptionally chilly lecture room when the students wore topcoats and Miss Taylor brought two plaids to wrap around herself.

The 150 students in the 1965 intake were divided into Education groups according to which age range they planned to teach. Susan Hill and Elaine Ogg both wanted to teach in secondary schools and were put in Miss Taylor's group. Elaine remembered that Miss Taylor's blue rinse always caused comment on Teaching Practice:

> 'I remember one pupil saying to me during a practical lesson "When is that lady with the blue hair coming again?" She was quite small, but quite a large character. She was very intelligent and always worked hard on behalf of her students'.

Susan's main subject was Mathematics and her subsidiary subjects were Science and Art and Craft. Elaine studied Chemistry with Mr Peel, Biology with Miss Northcott, Physics with Mr Pick and Maths with Mr Bindon. In addition, they both had courses in Divinity, English and P.E. Miss Taylor taught them the Theory and Practice of Education.

Miss Todd, writing in 1998, described Miss Taylor as an 'innovator', whose idea it was to start the practice of students having experience in special schools during the summer holidays. She also worked hard to establish and maintain links with local schools. In the 1978 College Chronicle she explained that links had been strengthened in reciprocal ways. At Highbury Avenue, students did extended periods of teaching practice, but they also spent regular half days at the school, helping children with difficulties. The evidence for this is in the school log books.

Mr Wright was appointed as an Education lecturer in 1967. Diana Harris (1968-1971) was in his Junior/Secondary Education group. Her first School Practice, in a junior school, left her feeling miserable and doubting whether she had chosen the right career. Fortunately for her, she received kindness, understanding and wise counsel from Mr Wright.

'If I promised to persevere with the second week in the junior school, Trevor guaranteed that for my next teaching practice he would place me in a secondary school. He thought that I might enjoy it more. The rest, as they say, is history! I walked into a secondary school and immediately felt at home. All the vibes were positive and I could relate to the teenage pupils. I could actually teach Geography, the subject that I was passionate about. I enjoyed every minute and never looked back'.

Courtesy of Wiltshire & Swindon History Centre

HER FIRST TASK IN RETIREMENT— TO WRITE A BOOK

Miss Lucy Sanderson Taylor receives a record player from Miss R. Earlam (president of the Students' Union) at a lunch at the College of Sarum St. Michael on Friday to mark her retirement after 21 years.

The Salisbury Journal

Courtesy of The Salisbury Museum

Miss Ashley was a shrewd observer of character and was known to admit prospective students who showed potential, even if their formal qualifications were the minimum.

> 'The acceptance by College of students from sources other than grammar schools became not unusual when the necessary minimum academic achievement was accompanied by character which showed potential for teaching'.
>
> *LST ibid*

Miss Hughes, Education Lecturer, commented on her 'compassionate caring nature'. She also wrote about Miss Ashley's lighter side:

> 'Those staff who were in residence during her time can recall the supper times when, in light-hearted mood, she entertained them with marvellous anecdotes and sometimes juggling!'

Miss Ashley cared profoundly about schools and those who worked in them and was a staunch believer in upholding the College motto: 'In quietness and in confidence shall be your strength'.

> 'Miss Ashley also warned us of the dangers of inappropriate dress in the classroom with a story, possibly apocryphal, of a student wearing a low neckline and bending over a class of infants to read. When she asked a small boy why his attention seemed to be riveted on her chest, he is alleged to have replied, "Please Miss, I can see your lungs".
>
> *LST ibid*

In the October following Miss Ashley's appointment the restoration of the Old Deanery was completed. This set the scene for the next ten years of College expansion regarding student numbers and accommodation. In 1963 there were 320 students; this rose to about 460 when she left, and a much larger staff. It was a period of change with many demands, which Miss Ashley handled in a calm and quietly determined manner.

> 'Those ten years were a strenuous period in which to guide a College, involving much in the way of administration and re-organisation.
>
> Probably Miss Ashley's most important and outstanding contribution to the College was her interest in, and concern for people, whoever they were. To her, it was never too much trouble to help people over a wide field of problems, and there are many students who have reason to be grateful for her help. Her interest showed when she interviewed candidates for admission – if they were not suitable she would suggest alternative careers; similarly if a student who embarked upon the course did not seem fitted for teaching, she would go to much trouble to suggest alternatives'.
>
> CSSM Chronicle 1973

The *College Chronicle* for 1965 recorded: 'As many of you will know, the designation "Training College" is no longer used by the Department of Education and Science. The term considered appropriate and now used is "College of Education". This would lead to our becoming "Salisbury College of Eduction", which would have been easily confused with "Salisbury College of Further Education". The Governing Body has therefore agreed to the College adopting a new name, and one that indicates that it was a Church foundation. The College chapel dedication is the Holy Angels and our Patronal Festival is therefore September 29th, the festival of St Michael and All Angels'. Following a Wessex custom and retaining a link with the Diocese, the name and address will now be The College of Sarum St Michael, 65 The Close, Salisbury. *Miss Ashley, CSSM Chronicle, 1965*

Almost from the beginning, the College had a strong link with the 'mission field' and many former students felt called to serve God in their vocation as teachers in far flung places. This continued into the 1960s, by which time an increasing number of students from 'emerging' countries, as they were then known, were being accepted for training at College. Between 1959 and 1961 students arrived from Uganda, Nigeria, Aden and Kenya.

Miss Ashley, who was appointed Principal in 1963, had had experience in training teachers in Southern Rhodesia and was very supportive both of overseas students in College and of former students working overseas. Mr Bate, who was appointed as an Education lecturer in 1965, was assigned the role of tutor to students from the 'emerging' overseas countries.

> 'Mr Bate had a wide ranging interest in education and during several vacations he took off for some remote outpost to take part in summer schools arranged for the benefit of students in third world countries'.
> Trevor Wright (OSA Newsletter 2012)

Miss Hughes (Education) had also had valuable experience training teachers in Uganda. Miss Mayo too was very supportive of work in Uganda, where Miss Gibbs (a former member of staff in Salisbury), was the Principal. The Uganda-Salisbury link was thus cemented. Ugandan students arrived to start their training, and students from Salisbury went to do Voluntary Service Overseas (VSO) at Lady Irene College.

Rosamond Edwards (1965-1969) went to New Guinea on VSO in 1966, and then returned for her third year at College. Rosamond subsequently revealed how the strength of the link between College and Uganda had led staff to assume that this was where she would go. This had made her feel very rebellious. She danced for joy on hearing that New Guinea was to be her destination! In Summer 1967 three students went to do VSO in Malawi, Kenya and the West Indies. Anne Barker (1965-1969) went to Providence Teachers' Training College in Malawi on VSO in 1969 and Hazel Andrews went to Zambia.

Overseas links have continued in later years. One example is that of Roz Jenkins (1965-1969), who continues to do sterling work with her childrens' charity 'Children Alone Trust' in Zimbabwe.

Miss Ashley with two students

Susan Harris

This wonderful Angel Window commemorates an exceptional act of bravery that took place in March 1966. Susan Harris, a student in her second year at the College, courageously attempted to rescue a young boy who had fallen into the river near Harnham Mill. She managed to reach the child and to draw him out of immediate danger. He was then pulled from the water by another person, but Susan tragically lost her life.

The Angel Window, commissioned by the College in memory of Susan, was designed by John Hutton and engraved by his son. It was initially placed in the great west window of the Old Deanery Hall, which became the School Practice Library. It was removed to the Cathedral cloisters in 1982, where it has a prominent position above the door through which visitors enter the Cathedral.

The Angel Window

Jean Watts

Jean Watts and Joan Slade (both 1961-1964) shared a room on the top floor of Maxwell in their first year. It was opposite the West door of the Cathedral and right from the start Jean showed herself to be a good artist. Joan commented on how she made use of her surroundings:

'The stunning view from the window provided a unique opportunity to study The Close throughout the seasons and from first light to dusk'.

In her second year Jean had a ground floor room at the back of Maxwell. This was the time when the Old Deanery was being restored and the work provided first hand material for her to draw. Jean, who now lives in America, is a popular artist:

'She is always busy, her work is keenly sought after and only the thick snow of the Wisconsin winter hinders her production'.

Dance in the Cathedral

Modern Dance

Netball, hockey, rounders, tennis, badminton, judo, keep fit and table tennis were all well supported in the early 1960s. A second playing field was acquired in The Close, as well as three hard tennis courts. Students went to watch English and international matches. A Cricket Club was started by a small group of enthusiasts, but 'many balls were lost in the river whilst playing on the old pitch.'

Elaine Ogg (1965-1968) remembered the PE kit that she had to purchase:

'I had a pale blue sweater with black and white bands around the neckline. I also had the grey PE knickers and virtually knee length divided shorts, and a dance tunic in pastel yellow for the compulsory physical education and dance classes. I remember dancing in Salisbury Cathedral. *The Tower of Babel* was the theme.

Folk dancing was well supported until the mid-1960s. Four dances were held with Theological College students. A noteworthy occasion was when students 'danced on the Theological College terrace, accompanied by live music and fairy lights'.

LST ibid

In the mid-1960s efforts were made to encourage greater participation by arranging tennis, table tennis and badminton matches with the Theological College students. Despite this incentive, interest in sport continued to decline. An attempt was made to change its image:

'Courses in beginners football, keep fit and volley ball, as well as swimming activities and a riding club were added to the usual netball, hockey, tennis and table tennis'.

LST ibid

The College Guide Club

Elaine Ogg joined the College Guide Club when she arrived in 1965. There was a small but enthusiastic membership:

'We had weekends away at "Witans", which were Student Scout and Guide camps. I met my husband, Roger, as a result of one of these events and we have now been married for almost 45 years'.

Elaine made good international friends from different Education groups.

'There was Christine Mugwanga from Uganda, and Aysha and Nagat from the Middle East. When I left College I visited Christine at her teaching post in Bombo, Uganda. Miss Hughes, one of the College lecturers, was often at our Guide events.

Handicrafts, 'sausage sizzles' at the boathouse by the river and international evenings were all part of the Guide Club programme. In 1966 a first year student, Barbara Elkington, designed and made a Club flag for camp. It was described as 'a highly professional piece of work'.

Boyfriends!

In earlier days it would have been unthinkable for boyfriends to have been admitted to College especially to the students' rooms. In the Sixties it was acceptable and many students enjoyed entertaining their boyfriends in College at weekends. Of course they had to be signed in and they had to leave by 10.15 pm.

Jennifer Yarwood (1963 -1966) remembered living in Maxwell House in her second year:

'We would go to the market on a Saturday morning and buy fabric to run up our little shift dresses on our sewing machines to wear to dances the same evening: live groups and invited boys – plastic caps on stiletto heels in a vain attempt to avoid damaging the parquet in the Hall – the anxiety about not being asked to dance.

During the year I met a trainee pilot from the College of Air Training at Hamble, near Southampton. Trainee airline pilots were considered 'good catches' and having one as a boyfriend conferred a certain amount of status.

My College Mother also had a pilot boyfriend and both of us subsequently married them. A number of these trainees would do their flying practice over Salisbury and circle around the Cathedral, waggling the wings of their 'Chipmunks' or 'Piper Apaches' as they did so. It was possible to know whose boyfriend it was if you knew their schedules and could listen out for the engine noise. This seemed to occur quite often during Divinity lectures in my case and was a severe distraction'.

Cherry Greaves made her own dress to wear at a Ball at Culham College:

'I made all my own dresses and one was apricot coloured crystal satin with silver embroidery on the bodice. Culham was our brother college. Until 1967 it was exclusively a male college and the social committee often arranged for a coach to take their students to our college dances. Many of us hoped to be invited to a Ball as their students took a lot of trouble to make it special'.

Cherry later married her College boyfriend.

Ready for the Ball!

View from the Boyfriend's Plane!

Boyfriends of the Sixties – Husbands of Today
Chris Johns and Henry Head

The Boyfriends' Tales

Two boyfriends from the Sixties look back on those heady days of student romance under the Spire!

'I remember my first visit with a feeling of awe at the College set in such beautiful grounds, within the semi-seclusion and somewhat cloistered environment of the Cathedral Close. My other feeling was of pride that my 'girlfriend' was studying in such a wonderful place.

However, her first lodging was in a dark, gloomy Victorian house, where in winter we huddled over a tiny gas fire. At night she was disturbed by many mice scuttling about the room. We tried out every product available to try and get rid of them.

Thankfully, in the next year she shared a room in Queen's with a friend (and future bridesmaid) which had many more comforts and a lovely view.

My visits, often after playing rugby for my then Poly (now University of Portsmouth) gave me insight into College life. No entry before 10 am, observing the "top table" at the scrumptious Sunday lunches, walking, sitting and having a romantic cuddle by the river, and of course building a good relationship with the Close Constable, which was beneficial when the dreaded hour of departure was exceeded! I certainly did not fancy swimming the river or sleeping under the playing field hedge.

I have very fond memories of Sarum St Michael, its setting, and its life and traditions. The facilities were amongst the best. Subsequently, my girlfriend became my wife and the rest is history as they say!'

* * *

'My first link with the College was in 1967 when I was invited by a student, whom I had met at a supper meeting of the Purbeck Arts Club in Swanage, to visit her in Salisbury. No girl had ever given me an invitation like that before, so I was very excited! We had arranged to meet by the Cathedral and, I must confess, she looked much more 'studenty' than she had in her party dress! We walked around Old Sarum, then had tea at the House of Steps, but did not go into the College. On my next visit I was allowed into Barnard's Cross where 'she' resided and even met Mrs Gibson, who was very civil - but she ushered me out at 9.30, holding jangling keys and with her dog on a lead.

One task that I undertook, as a Maths teacher, was to help with a piece of statistics set as a challenging Geography exercise to my girlfriend and her friend, and future bridesmaid. Eventually I worked out that the example in the text book was wrong!

I was invited to the Valedictory Ball on a Friday night. This was a bit of a problem as I was teaching in Rugby and we had Saturday morning lessons. However, having worked out that trains ran through the night, I wrote a test on the blackboard and locked the classroom door. The next morning I opened the door, let the class in, told them to sit down, shut up and get on with the test. I was asked again the following year, and was bold enough to ask permission to miss Saturday morning school.

I stayed the night in a Bed and Breakfast at 100, Love Lane and was disturbed in the morning by the girlfriend, who came up to my room in a very short mini skirt to tell me that she had passed her finals.. Later that day we visited the school where she was to start her teaching career and I was bold enough to say that I thought that the very short mini skirt might not be appropriate!

We got engaged a few weeks later and memories of the engagement year include sleeping on the floor of the flat shared by four recent former students. Lasting friendships with them all have enhanced 44 years of happy married life – so far!'

There was a well-trodden path between Sarum St Michael and the Theological College on the other side of The Close, used not only for meetings of the Christian Union, and country dance evenings that were hosted by the students of Sarum St Michael, but also for more informal liaisons. Some of the younger theological students thought that they were getting close to heaven when they found that they were living in The Close near so many single young women, but equally they were aware that with so many military establishments close to Salisbury there was competition from the army.

Many will recall that The Close gates were locked at 11 p m. A little before this time the Close Constable used to make a tour of inspection, asking the young men politely if they thought that they would be able to be out of The Close by the time the gates closed. One of the theological students is reputed to have replied 'I sincerely hope not'.

As one might expect, several of the informal liaisons subsequently led to marriage, so that many of the Theos, myself included, are pleased to have travelled that well-trodden path across The Close.

Revd. Hedley Ringrose

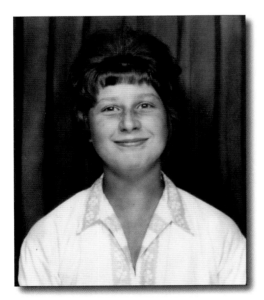

Beehive student

Students of today would be amazed at the much simpler and more innocent pleasures of College days in the 1960s. College Balls and visits by boyfriends have already been mentioned, but what else did students do to amuse themselves?

Diane Baker (1969- 1972) recalled:

'In our first year, in 1969, my friend Cathy Dixon and I used to treat ourselves, very occasionally, to a walk across the fields behind our "digs" to a pub called "The Duck," where we had half a cider and blackcurrant and thought this to be the height of luxury!

We did things like gathering in someone's college room or on the stairs (if one of us was on telephone duty) and playing guitars and singing and drinking coffee. When it snowed heavily one evening we went outside and had a snowball fight'.

Despite the demands of work, students certainly enjoyed themselves. The 'Rag Week' was a highlight of the year. Lavinia Parsons (1963-1966) remembered those happy days:

'The Students' Union organised a "Rag" for charity each year with the College of Further Education. One year, six of us made fancy dresses to represent "Snakes and Ladders," and another year seven of us formed a tableau "Yere be the Moonrakers" on a float'.

There were still numerous clubs and organisations to choose from, in addition to sporting activities and Fellowship (Focus). Musical activities flourished with concerts given by the College Orchestra and Choir. Several students joined the Salisbury Musical Society. Rosemary Palmer (1965-1968) remembered one exciting occasion when they participated in a performance of Britten's War Requiem with the Bournemouth Symphony Orchestra. In the mid-sixties Miss Dean conducted the College choir at the Devizes Eisteddfod. Rosemary recalled:

'Some students were planning to be back in the afternoon in order to prepare for their evening dates, but we unexpectedly won our class and had to stay on to perform in the winners concert. There were some disappointed young men in Salisbury that evening'.

College plays were much enjoyed, for example, in December 1968 "The Critic" by Sheridan was produced by Miss Higgins. A heavy snowstorm did not detract from the entertainment, 'This was a most successful production and gave much enjoyment to all who took part or were in the audience'.

Debates were held and speakers visited College to talk about a range of topics. Clubs often joined together to enjoy lively parties. Several students belonged to the Poetry Circle and many were inspired to write thoughtful poems. A box of equipment, which was found in the loft of the old Art Room, led to the formation of the Art Club.

Miss Taylor shared some happy memories:

> 'The expanse of gardens, the open views to the Cathedral and river, the intimate occasions of social dances, of musical evenings or coffee parties amongst the students'.

She remembered the river 'gleaming in the sunset like a silver sword'. Students appreciated the beauty of the College grounds on balmy summer afternoons, and just being able to relax by the river in the peace and tranquillity below the Spire.

Tea-time visits to The Bay Tree, The Cadena Café and the House of Steps were much enjoyed. Other popular student haunts were The Rose and Crown Inn at Harnham and The New Inn just outside the Close, but more of that to follow in the Seventies!

Snakes and Ladders

COLLEGE OF SARUM ST MICHAEL

VALEDICTORY BALL

AT

the New Alexandra Rooms

ON

Friday 21st June 1968

9PM—2AM

Dance and Beat Groups

| BAR | DRESS FORMAL | BUFFET |

30/- Double Ticket

Cheers for Mateus Rosé! Rag Day 1966

July 1st 1966
Valedictory Ball. Hugh comes to it. Hugh is SO sweet!
July 2nd
Hugh catches 3.50 train to Waterloo. We go round Cathedral and College, second hand bookshop and market. He takes me out to lunch at The House of Steps. He is going to Basutoland for a year on VSO – boo hoo!

Feb 9 1966
Meet John at BX Coffee Bar. He is very nice.
Feb 10
John rings up and we fix lunch on Saturday
Feb 12
Lunch with John at the New Inn. After lunch we go to see 'The Spy who came in from the Cold' at the ABC Cinema. I cook him baked beans later.
Feb 13
John comes round to tell me he cannot take me out tonight.

The Close Constable

The Close Constable (Security Officer) was often very helpful to students and always friendly. Mr Quine, who hailed from the Isle of Man, was the Close Constable in the 1960s. He received a letter of thanks from the then Bishop of Salisbury, The Rt Revd George Reindorp.

'My Dear Guardian-at-the Gate,

One of the nicest things as you come into Salisbury Close is the welcome you get from a refugee from the Isle of Man. Thank-you from all the Reindorps, young or old. If you want a job at Heaven's Gate (to give St Peter a day off) do mention my name as a reference'.

Bill Quine

The Delights of the Dining-Room

Cherry Stansbury (1964-1967) appreciated the College meals.

'The students took their meals in the main refectory and they were very good indeed, with cooked breakfast, hot chocolate and buns at morning break, cooked lunch, afternoon tea and a formal cooked supper'.

Susan Hill (1965-1968) described the formal lunch at 1pm.

'The students took their places and waited for the lecturers to process in, and grace to be said before sitting down'.

Jenni Last (1963-1966) remembered a less agreeable aspect of College lunch.

'Students were obliged to sit in turn at High Table for lunch and this was considered by many to be somewhat of an ordeal. Not only did one have to converse with one's lecturers, but one had to do it in front of everyone else'.

Barnard's Cross had its own dining room and students returned there for meals. Roast chicken and ice cream gateaux were regular favourites on the menu.

Weekend food 'rations' were put out on Saturday mornings in both King's House and Barnard's Cross. They included items such as two slices of bread, two eggs, two slices of bacon, foil triangles of processed cheese, small cans of Heinz baked beans (sometimes curried or with sausages) apples and slices of cake or iced buns. There was no need to starve!

Anne Mortimer (1966-1969) lived in 'digs' in her first year and remembered toasting bread on her two bar gas fire. Endless coffee and tea was made in the small kitchen areas in the hostels, as well as limited cooking, such as making huge omelettes by sharing the weekend 'rations'. Microwaves and 'take-aways' were not yet on the scene. Students in Barnard's Cross incurred the steely eyed wrath of Mrs Gibson if they left a kitchen area uncleaned.

Hannah Boothman and Jenny Allcock (both 1965-1969) shared a tiny house in St Ann Street in their fourth year. 'Survival of the Fittest,' a written record of their meals, shows that eggs, beans, spaghetti, bacon, macaroni cheese and 'tins' were their dietary staples. On October 22nd 1968 they were tempted to eat in College and the comment reads: 'Miss Potter's supper, very good and very filling'. When entertaining fellow students or, occasionally, members of staff, they pushed the boat out and made a cheese and vegetable flan, followed by chocolate mousse served with a tin of Nestles cream, the very height of luxury.

Beans for Tea

Tea with Visiting Bursars

Still Inside The Wardrobe

Wardrobe had changed little since it was taken over by the College in 1945. Spartan conditions remained and some students were shocked when they saw their accommodation. There were so many imperishable memories:

'When I first entered Wardrobe, I didn't think that I would want to live there for three years. Wood panelling made it very dark and the heating system was a stove in the entrance hall that gave out fumes'.
Jane Houillebecq (1962-1965)

Liza Husband (1967-1970), on the other hand, was overjoyed:

'Coming from a modern bungalow in the West Country, to see this home was beyond my wildest dreams'.

'Rumour had it that the baths had been installed during WW2 and from their state I can well believe it. Rusty taps with lime scale and green slime running down from them, gritty bottoms to the baths and a freezing cold room – all this combined to make bathing a rushed event.

After a College dance, woe betide anyone who wanted to say goodnight to their boyfriend in the Wardrobe porch, as the Close Constables came round and shone their torches into every corner until even the most amorous lovers had left'!
Maureen Morris (1967-1970)

'At first our mattresses were horse hair and very old - the sleeping position of the previous occupant was deeply embedded and I had to sleep in that position until new mattresses were eventually bought'.
Jane Houillebecq (1962-1965)

'In some respects we were lucky – there was a telephone to only twenty-five students. And all twenty-five shared in every conversation: why didn't they get that phone-box soundproofed'?

College Chronicle, 1969

The lack of home comforts in Wardrobe was, however, more than compensated for by the friendly relationship between the students and Miss Mayo, the Warden:

'She ruled the house with understanding – and, incidentally, with her own interpretation of the rules'!
College Chronicle, 1969

Cherry Stansbury (1964-1967) shared a large reception room with Suzanne Knight, Bridget Uden and Judy Robson in her first year:

'In the centre of the room was a large table and we each had a bed, bedside cabinet, wardrobe and chair. Double doors led out on to a lawn. The grounds, with a kitchen garden and tennis court, led down to the river. In my second year, I shared an attic bedroom with Lorna Outrim and was kept fit running up and down the steep back stairs. In my final year I graduated to a single room, which overlooked the front lawn and afforded a view of the Cathedral.

A friend was delighted with her eyrie in the eaves – until it came to Fire Practice and she had to use a Bosun's Chair to escape to the ground. She was petrified of heights and only managed it by closing her eyes, which is possibly why she put her foot through a 12th Century window!

One night, Sue Hunt (1966-1969) was awoken by Sylvia, whose face was as white as a sheet. 'She had seen a woman dressed in green and wearing a wimple hat. The woman was very short and was standing at the end of my bed looking at me! She then turned, walked towards the corner of the room and went straight through the wall. Robbie and I were equally as scared as Sylvia, so we pushed the beds together and tried to sleep. Three nights later, the apparition returned and again slipped through the wall towards the long corridor, with the window overlooking the Cathedral'.

The largest room on the ground floor was, to Miss Mayo's delight, converted into a common room in 1960:

'Its Adam fireplace, pargetted ceiling, polished oak floors and crimson curtains made it greatly in demand for social events. Hallowe'en parties, Christmas festivities, 21st birthday parties, wine and cheese events in Rag Weeks and even small dances often took place there'.

1969 was the final year that Wardrobe was used by the College. There was inevitable sadness for Miss Mayo, whose long years as Warden of this remarkable building had come to an end. Wardrobe stood sadly empty for some time, reopening in the 1970s as the home of The Rifles (Berkshire and Wiltshire) Regimental Museum. Miss Mayo retired in July 1971 after 26 years of service to the College.

Mice, spiders, woodlice, cockroaches and other forms of insect life occupied the nooks and crannies of Wardrobe:
'Thus there came to dwell:
Pangur Ban – hunting mice was his delight
Little Grey Moses – a refugee, born in a student's cupboard
Everest – born on the day that Everest was climbed and distinguished by the white tip to his tail
Moses 2 – black, gentle and affectionate, a garden lover and friend
To all of you who were at one time at The Wardobe – Good Hunting!'

R. E. Mayo

Living in 'Digs'

Several students lived out in 'digs' especially in their first year. Isabel Hebdon (1962-1965) explained:

'It was a time of great expansion. For the first time there were three years of students in College. Also, there was a great need for more teachers. Hence, many of us were in 'digs'. Whether it was right to have the first year out I have never really been sure – it was the first time away from home for any length of time for most of us and we did not get the full feel of College life, certainly not at the beginning.

I was in Radnor Road in my first year. I shared a double room. We had breakfast there and an allowance of milk for a cup of coffee at night. Instant coffee was then becoming popular and we drank lots of it. All other meals were taken in College. I cycled in, except in the worst winter weather.

Anne Mortimer (1966-1969) was in 'digs' during her first year.

'I remember arriving in a dark and gloomy hall and seeing a mounted stag's head peering down from the wall. I went up the creaking stairs with trepidation and was shown my room. It felt cold and unwelcoming and had a musty smell. I turned on the two bar gas fire and tried to feel cheerful. Fortunately, not long after, Diana Potter arrived and immediately everything looked brighter and felt better. We were even able to share a joke about our lodgings. I did not find it funny at night when mice would creep out from the gap below the skirting board and scurry around the room. Eventually, unknown to our landlady, Diana kindly let me share her room. I still hate mice, but Diana became a good friend and was a bridesmaid at my wedding'.

Ann Harding (1965-1969) suspected that her parents were not surprised by their daughter's decision to study Geography at College. 'She's chosen that because it will involve visits and trips', was her father's explanation to anyone who enquired!

'Those who were fortunate enough to be involved with Miss Mayo and the Geography Department will remember that the courses were stimulating, with considerable emphasis on practical work. Miss Mayo broadened our horizons with field studies based in Aberystwyth, Guernsey and the Netherlands; my first overseas trip'.

Jersey and Switzerland were also amongst the chosen venues in the 1960s.

'We enjoyed a field trip to Jersey, where we looked at land use and visited a farm belonging to an old student who had married a local farmer. Switzerland was chosen for our second trip. Two mature students came with us to make up the numbers, but they moved to another hotel as they found the accommodation very basic. Our hotel had previously been a TB Sanatorium and still retained hospital beds and polished linoleum floors. However, the view of the mountains from our dining room more than made up for this'.

Cherry Stansbury (1964-1967)

Miss Mayo's Field Studies were successful. Enthusiastic and knowledgeable, she expected high standards, and the students needed a lot of stamina – but enjoyed themselves as well. A beach survey on Herm, sharing bicycles (one rode pillion) in Holland, and reaching the summit of Snowdon are memories that have survived the test of time.

'With truncated and interlocking spurs, captured rivers, misfit streams all the way, wide U shaped valleys, glaciated mountains, corries, screes and ROCK.'

Refrain to a song composed for a variety concert after the 1966 Aberystwyth Field Study.

Geography lecturers Miss Mayo and Mr Rogers in 1978

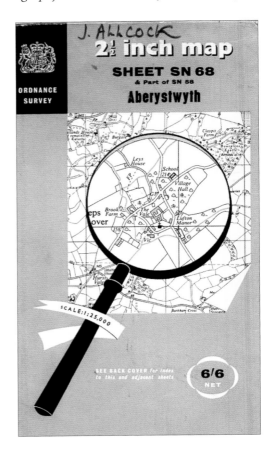

The Hardy Tours

Students who elected to study English as their main subject, remember with great fondness the excellent Thomas Hardy tours of Wessex. These were organised by Miss Higgins and Mr Say, who imparted their knowledge and expertise to the students with enthusiasm and energy. Miss Higgins joined the English department in 1965 and Mr Say in 1966.

The visits brought the poems and novels of Thomas Hardy to life in a landscape which was little changed since they were written. At Stinsford Church we imagined young Hardy enjoying the hymns, and the Mellstock Band playing on Christmas Eve; mysterious Egdon Heath was captivating and we expected the Reddle Man to appear at any moment; the thatched cottage where the Hardy family lived at Higher Bockhampton remained much the same as in Hardy's lifetime. Thomas's sisters, Mary and Kate, also lived here until leaving home to train as teachers in Salisbury.

The visits were inspiring and fostered an enjoyment of the works of Hardy and the world in which he lived.

Hardy's Cottage

My Nature Table

My love affair with my Nature Table all started in Salisbury. During School Practice, many Sunday afternoons were spent with like-minded friends, walking into Laverstock or along the Town Path, or cycling out to Stratford sub Castle to collect old man's beard, conkers, pussy willow, catkins and acorns. Triumphantly, we returned with our finds and then had to write labels for them. This was indeed onerous for in our first year, which was before felt tipped pens were really established, the printing had to be done using dip in pens and Indian ink. What a sight we must have been as we climbed on the School Practice coaches, laden with assorted twigs, frogs' spawn, hips and haws and empty birds' eggs, to name but a few. Yellow and black striped cinnabar caterpillars, sea shells, my precious ammonite and sea urchin fossils, stick insects and the occasional cocoon also found their way on to my Nature Table at different times.

The store cupboard in my classroom (a former Nissen hut) was a veritable treasure trove of dusty jam jars that were ideal for the sticky buds, bluebells, primroses and dandelion clocks that my pupils regularly brought to school. Many of the children came from farms and would rush in, excitedly clutching an old bird's nest, a dead stag beetle, a snail or even, once, a long dead hedgehog that required immediate burial. Small faces shone with pride as they talked about their discoveries in morning 'news' time. I still have a vivid, shuddering memory of a small boy who pulled out a long snakeskin from his pocket. Now my love of nature sadly doesn't extend to things that wriggle, but I managed to control myself and the much admired and exquisitely beautiful snakeskin became the subject of the creative writing that primary teachers loved so much.

Poetry about the natural world wings back to me over the years: 'All along the backwaters, through the rushes tall', 'Now the day is over', 'Old Mr Pricklepin', 'Mrs Peck Pigeon' and many many more.

I wonder if any of my first pupils remember their class Nature Table?

Jenny Allcock (1965-1969)

The Chapel

'As the first group of three-year students, we have had longer in which to appreciate the part played in College life by the Chapel. It is our hope that it will continue to meet and fulfil the spiritual needs of future generations'.

Jenny Smith & Carolyn Taylor (1960-1963)

The Revd Michael Newman resigned in 1961. He was remembered as 'a beloved member of staff and a most helpful spiritual advisor and friend.' In 1962 the Revd Derek Burden was appointed as Chaplain.

During the 1960s there were daily Chapel services, as well as retreats and Quiet Days. College services were held in the Cathedral at the beginning and end of term. The Chapel Choir accompanied services, and sang carols at the Christmas service in St Thomas's Church.

In 1969 the Revd Brian Coleman succeeded the Revd Derek Burden as Chaplain.

The Chapel continued to sustain and enrich College life. Flower arrangements owed much to the expertise and love of Miss Blackburn, Head of the English department, who sits here very neatly, (impeccably dressed), and between the Chapel and Queen's House, both of which were dear to her heart. She retired in 1970, having inspired, encouraged and led so many students into a love of English literature and poetry. Her deep faith strengthened all that she did and her nineteen years at College encompassed drama productions, the Chapel and Queen's House, where she was the resident Warden.

'We regarded Miss Blackburn not only as an upholder of the law (modified if necessary!), but even more important, as a friend, not to mention "The glass of fashion" (Hamlet Act 3, Scene 1). We never knew which outfit would appear next on the stairs; we only knew that it would, of course, be accompanied by matching spectacle frames'!

Elizabeth Fenner (1965-1969)

From Fellowship to Focus

By the mid-1960s College Fellowship meetings were increasingly focusing on social concerns, as well as ecumenical topics. The varied programme included a talk on Youth Club work and a talk given by the Chaplain of a mental hospital. Ruth Wigram, a former student, spoke about her work in the Skopje Earthquake Centre. The "Dare to Think" weekend in 1966 was a stimulating time in which to explore faith. In 1968 Anglican-Methodist Unity was discussed, and other discussions focused on Quakerism and The Church Army. 'Project Unity', the junior section of the local Council of Churches, was publicised by the College Fellowship.

In 1967 Fellowship was renamed 'Focus'. The 1968 College Chronicle recorded that Focus had held talks on the Church and its activities, Trade Unions, Witchcraft, Playgroups in Deprived Areas, Humanism, Youth in Politics and Buddhism. The Student Christian Movement, the Christian Union and Focus continued to thrive in the late Sixties. The inclusion of more light-hearted activities, including playing tiddlywinks with the Theological College students, reflected the informality of the era.

Miss Blackburn

Miss Higgins, 1967

Mr Philip Pain, 1965

The Plowden Report, 1967

In 1967, a major report entitled 'Children and their Primary Schools' was produced by the Central Advisory Council for Education, (CACE) chaired by Lady Plowden. Dr Grubb, College Principal 1955-1962, was also a member of this committee. The Plowden Report was a focus for many College lectures and most students owned a copy.

The Minister of Education, asked CACE 'to consider primary education in all its aspects and the transition to secondary education'. There was an air of optimism about education at the time and the winds of change were blowing in the air. There was an increasingly liberal view of education and of society as a whole. Selection for secondary education was being abolished (although not in Salisbury) and streaming was gradually dying out. Comprehensive Schools and Middle Schools were being established and teachers had more freedom to plan their curriculum.

The famous quotation from the Plowden Report – 'at the heart of the educational process lies the child' – sets the essence of the whole report: each child should be viewed as an individual.

'Individual differences between children of the same age are so great that any class, however homogeneous it seems, must always be treated as a body of children needing individual and different attention'.

Plowden, 1967, 1:25

Some of the main recommendations were:

- Primary schools should be used as much as possible out of school hours.
- A policy of 'positive discrimination' should favour schools in 'deprived' areas.
- Training Colleges should increase provision for teachers wishing to train in teaching English to immigrants.
- Nursery Education should be available for children after the age of three.
- A three-tier system of first, middle and secondary education with transfer at eight and twelve.
- Authorities maintaining selection should not rely on intelligence/attainment tests.
- Corporal punishment should be forbidden.
- The maximum size of primary classes should be reduced.
- More male teachers were needed in primary schools.

Implementation

The implementation of the recommendations made by the Plowden Report was piecemeal. However, it was a major influence on educational theory and policy. College students felt excited and optimistic about the future of education, of which they were to be a part.

The Newsom Report (1963)
Half Our Future

The Newsom Report focused on the education of 'average and below average children'. It argued that the future of the country depended on better education for these children.

The main recommendations included raising the school leaving age to 16; schools should provide a broader range of courses; sex education was viewed as essential; Local Education Authorities (LEAs) should review their provision for religious education; in the final year of school the syllabus should reflect the adult world of work and leisure.

The report stated that Teacher Training should be reviewed to ensure that all colleges were sufficiently staffed and equipped, so that students could teach a main subject and at least one other. It recommended that a Teacher Training requirement for graduates should be introduced as soon as possible.

Middle Schools

During the 1960s many LEAs decided to change from a two-tier system of education(primary and secondary) to three-tier(first or lower schools, middle schools, upper schools). During the 1940s and 1950s, following the recommendations of the Spens and Norwood reports, several relatively small schools had been built. When the trend towards comprehensive education began, many of these schools were too small and some authorities decided on split-sites or dividing schools on the basis of age.

Sir Alec Clegg was the Chief Education Officer for the West Riding of Yorkshire. He believed that the interests, needs and ways of learning of children in the middle age group would be better catered for if they were taught in one school. In 1963 he proposed that schools should be organised into three tiers with age ranges 5-9, 9-13 and 13-18. This proposal required a change of law. The 1964 Education Act made arrangements to allow schools to cross the traditional primary-secondary divide at the age of 11 and experimental status was granted to middle schools.

The Plowden Report encouraged the development of middle schools for 8-12 year old pupils, developing from existing junior schools. Rapid development of these schools then followed. In 1968 the first opened in Bradford, and by 1980 there were more than 1,400. However, middle schools gradually decreased in number and in September 2013 there were only 171 remaining in England. The majority of schools reverted to the two-tier system in order to be in line with the requirements of the National Curriculum.

The Real Thing (almost) – School Practice in the Sixties

Many organisational changes took place in the Sixties. The number of students increased markedly with the start of the three-year course in 1961. Adjustments of the areas of school practice had to be made, so that schools should not be overburdened.

Miss Taylor commented:

> 'The major change was the opportunity for a much longer period of School Practice when the three-year course was established in 1960, and even then variations in timing occurred. The reassuring factor was the way in which students met School Practice with youthful vigour (or, perhaps, with resourceful resignation), wherever they were placed'.

Education group tutors visited each school area to decide on the number of teachers to be allocated and the type of work to be done. Schools were sent confirmation of arrangements and requests made for forecasts of the work expected of the students. A short time before the School Practice, students made preliminary visits to their schools. 'All lecturers took part in supervision of School Practice. Each lecturer in education visited every member of his/her group to obtain a total picture of the School Practice'.

Miss Hughes was an Education lecturer (1965-1978). She used her own experience of teaching in this country, and in Uganda, to promote the values of respect and equal worth for all. She firmly believed in child-centred education. Students may have been slightly nervous about her visits on School Practice but the children were delighted to see her.

Students were expected to prepare thoroughly and have schemes of work to show their tutors. An enormous amount of careful planning and organisation took place to ensure that students, pupils and schools gained as much benefit as possible from School Practice.

'During my years at College (1966-1969) I was very fortunate to experience School Practice in three very different schools. I thoroughly enjoyed each experience and believe they provided me with an excellent grounding for my future career.'

First School Practice (November 1966)

Urchfont was a small three-class school in those days. The rooms were heated by coal stoves next to which bottles of milk were warmed. It was a very cold spell and on one occasion the outside toilets were frozen. The Headmaster and staff were very welcoming, doing all they could to make us at ease. I couldn't have had a better introduction to School Practice.

The School Practice File was very important as a record for the students, and also for the visiting lecturer. The file recorded lesson plans and included a 'Daily Diary' which set out what worked and what didn't. I had eighteen children in my class. A highlight was setting up the 'Nature Table,' which was something new for them. I recorded their great excitement when I took in some stick insects. Luckily, felt tip pens were appearing on the scene, which made making work-cards easier.

Reading was viewed as very important. The Janet and John reading scheme was used with each group at a different stage. The older children had their own Ladybird books and read about one page a day to the class teacher.

Dance and PE all revolved around a 'Firework' theme, with the children making firework shapes and noises - something new for them!

This was a wonderful introduction to teaching and having eighteen children in a class was ideal; although I was only at Urchfont for two weeks I felt that I knew each child quite well. In such a small class, and small school, the relationship between pupil and teacher was very good and the teachers really seemed to know and be concerned for each child individually. I was perhaps a little too friendly with the children, but I tried to be firm.

ITA Reading Book

Second School Practice (February/March 1968)

My second school practice, which was for four weeks, was at Verwood CE Infants' School in Dorset. It was another very happy experience with helpful and thoughtful staff.

In this school, the "integrated day" was in operation. This was a method in which each child may follow his or her own devices, may visit other children in other class rooms, and may plan his or her own day. The teacher should provide constant stimuli and see that the following instructions are carried out:

1. Each child should do a certain amount of number work in the course of the day.
2. Each child should read to the teacher each day.
3. Each child should do some form of written work.

There was a place for informal "together" lessons – such as singing, story-telling, P.E. and for small informal groups for work in things such as flash cards for reading and specific teaching of mathematical points as they arose. Groups for this kind of work would sometimes be organised by the teacher, other groups arose naturally, through the children's own interests.

My topic here was 'People who help us'. All subjects were linked to this one theme and there was much less class teaching. At the beginning of the day there was a class discussion and explanation of the various linked activities which would take place. I had the extra challenge of having to pack everything up at the end of every day as the classroom doubled as the Church Hall and Scout Hut and was used for village activities in the evenings.

The 'Initial Teaching Alphabet' was used in the school, which provided another challenge. This was intended to be a simpler writing system, which could be used to make it easier for English-speaking children to read. Children seemed to cope quite well with it, once they had mastered the alphabet, although some children seemed to find the transition to traditional orthography (T.O.) quite difficult. Although popular at the time, it is rarely used today.

I remember Miss Highley visiting me and, finding that the children were all involved in a wide range of activities, asking if she could kindly observe some class teaching.

Thankfully I had my guitar handy, so I clapped my hands for attention, gathered the children and we all settled down for some impromptu class singing.

I concluded that the teaching practice had been an excellent learning experience all round. The system of teaching was far removed from that of today, but the children were very interested and were keen independent learners.

Final School Practice (May/June 1969)

My final School Practice was at Courthill Infant School in Parkstone, Poole. Once again I was welcomed with enthusiasm and given full support. The class had forty-three 'top infants', which was a challenge. Nineteen children read and wrote in T.O., eight were at the transition stage and sixteen used I.T.A. An assortment of reading schemes was used: Ladybird, Janet and John, Through the Rainbow and Happy Venture. The children were usually heard to read about three times a week. How did the teacher manage that? The College had, though, devised an easier method for students to organise their Teaching Practice File, which I much appreciated.

My theme was 'The Sea', and all subjects were linked to this theme. The children were keen and enthusiastic. But the main problem was one of space as the classroom was extremely cramped. 'Basic Skills' took place in the mornings, and ended with thirty minutes of 'Scripture.' Afternoons were given over to 'Activities', which took a lot of careful planning considering the numbers of children. Drama or P.E. took place each day. My planning was not as expected in 2015, but the children enjoyed what they did and they learned and remembered.

During the practice we had to make a special study about one child, which included observations and notes. I asked the child to write about what made him happy and he wrote, 'Miss Motamer – I love her!'

I have such varied, vivid and happy memories and I am indebted to the hardworking College staff for the excellent training and experiences, which I was so fortunate to have.'

Anne Mortimer (1966-1969)

The College Ethos

The College ethos, combined with plenty of School Practice provided students with an excellent grounding for their future careers. Teachers trained at the College had a positive impact on the children they taught, as illustrated by comments from former pupils who were at school in Salisbury:

'Teachers identified strengths and weaknesses and adjusted the learning to ensure the work was achievable but still challenging. I was taught that if I put my mind to something then I could achieve it'. Pupils were encouraged to have self-esteem, confidence in their own ability and respect for others.

First School Practice

I had avidly read *Village School* by Miss Read and the village school at Donhead St Andrew was the perfect beginning for me. The school had two classes, both of which were 'family grouped,' which meant that children from several different year groups were taught in the same class. Mrs Potter taught the Infants, aged between four and seven and Miss Snelgar (the Head) had the Junior class, aged between seven and eleven.

Many children came from local farms and walked to school, so there were always wellies drying around the big stove in the Junior room. School children were then entitled to free milk and the small bottles were also put by the stove, to take the chill off them. Junk modelling, Flash Cards and the 'Janet and John' reading scheme all spring to mind. I put into practice what I had just been taught by Miss Cox, my Education lecturer, telling stories and reciting poetry, rather than reading them, so as to capture the children's attention. I remember preparing sorting activities, seeing the school lunch arriving in big cans, singing with the children 'Jesus, tender shepherd hear me, bless your little lambs tonight' before home time, taking PE in the playground and spotting from the window the arrival of a grey suited lecturer who had come to visit me, but seemed more interested in talking to the children.

I particularly remember Rebecca, a four year old who had just started at the school. Five years later, in 1970, my father sent me a newspaper cutting with a photograph of Rebecca, then aged nine, running into school on the day that it closed. I remember how sad I felt about the closure, but I still count myself fortunate to have had this gentle introduction to the world of teaching.

Jenny Allcock (1965-69)

On the School Practice Coach

The Voice of College

The *College Chronicle* was described as the 'voice' of the College in 1960. Former students and staff were encouraged to send in their news. A two-day reunion was attended by 338 former students. Branch reports in 1960 included one from the Midland Branch who had a 'perfect day for our coach ride to Llandrindod Wells to see Miss Story'.

In 1965 Branches were still flourishing in Guernsey, Jersey, the Isle of Wight, London, Somerset and the Midlands, as well as the Home Branch in Salisbury. Miss Ashley and other members of staff continued to visit them. During the next few years, membership began to decrease and by the end of the 1960s the London and Midland Branches had both closed.

At the reunion in 1967 good wishes were expressed to Miss Rogers on her retirement. She had been Head of the Divinity department for eleven years and Vice Principal for four years

'Miss Rogers will be remembered as a most stimulating teacher who made Theology come alive, and set high standards of work. As Warden of Audley House she was ready to give time and an understanding ear to all her resident students'.

College Chronicle, 1967

Janet and John Reading Book

Skylark Coaches

During the late Fifties, Sixties, and Seventies students travelled by coach to their many different schools for Teaching Practice.

Skylark coaches, with their colourful livery, were a common sight in the Cathedral Close. The length of teaching practices varied, but Skylark could be relied upon to transport the students to their schools, often leaving at 7.30 am and returning them to The Close by 5.30 pm.

'[The coaches] transferred students to many schools in the Bournemouth, Christchurch and Poole areas, west to places such as Mere and Wincanton, north to Westbury, Marlborough and surrounding villages and east in the direction of Winchester and many villages along the way, including Downton, Morgan's Vale and Hale. At one time as many as ten coaches lined up in the Close'.

Gerald Shergold (Skylark Motor Services)

Anne Mortimer (1966-1969) remembered climbing into a coach bound for Urchfont, one of the schools furthest away, very early on a cold winter's morning, clutching materials for junk modelling, children's books, a home-made weather chart and other equipment. The journeys often took a long time, as there were so many stops at different schools on route, but we were all young and cheerful. One of the coach's registration numbers was HOT 852. This was very appropriate considering the hot and often noisy passengers! Thank you, Skylark, for getting us there and bringing us back safe and sound – in time for our evening meal!

Painting by Kate Sykes

In 1960 a decision was made that the Chapel Wardens and Servers at Holy Communion should wear gowns to add to the sense of dignity in the Chapel. The colour that was chosen was blue, which toned in with the hassocks and psalters.

Gowns were clearly the order of the day and the 1961 *College Chronicle* recorded the report of the Students' Union.

'The Students' Union initiated and carried through a scheme that students be asked to wear gowns at lectures and on all formal occasions. Each student now orders a black gown from a Bristol gown-maker before arrival. The garments were felt to give dignity to the wearer'.

At the beginning of the 1960s students dressed quite conventionally. Cherry Stansbury (1964-1967) remembered her interview outfit.

'Hoping to make a good impression, my mother and I had chosen an expensive coat of turquoise wool with a black curly lamb collar, and I was rather disappointed when I was invited to leave it in the cloakroom when I arrived at King's House. However, I had made myself a very "up to the minute" pink crimplene dress.'

Times they are a-changing!   Drawing by Pat Jones

As the 1960s progressed, hair grew longer and clothes became less formal, although students who arrived in 1965 remember wearing suits for their interviews. Duffle coats, long boots, Scholl sandals, heeled 'court' shoes, miniskirts and shift dresses appear in photographs. Trousers were worn for leisure wear. Most students wore the pale blue, black and white striped college scarves, with the College badges sewn on them.

At the end of the 1960s there was a fashion for 'midi' and 'maxi' skirts:

'I am sure the 1960s fashion for maxi skirts was invented by the inmates of Wardrobe - a yard and a half of material from the market, some thread and some elastic - the skirt took a matter of an hour or so to complete and stopped all those nasty draughts around our ankles.'

Maureen Morris (1967-1969)

Outside Queens House, 1963

The Introduction of the B.Ed. degree

The University of Bristol B.Ed. degree course started in Autumn 1968. It entailed a fourth year of study and was open to students who had reached a required standard at the end of their second year of the Certificate course. The nine students, whose main subjects were Geography, Theology, English and History found it a demanding but fulfilling year. Jennifer Knock (1965-1969) commented:

> 'The work seemed more intense and academic and was assessed by long examinations, as well as course work. We also had to fit in weekly journeys to Bristol and Bath for lectures'.

Relationships between staff and students were more informal and lectures felt more like tutorials:

> 'There was a strong bond between students and lecturers, as we were all at the start of a new venture'.
> Hannah Boothman (1965-1969)

Mr Pain, Head of the Education Department, lectured on the History, Psychology and Philosophy of Education. Ann Harding (1965-1969) valued his 'calm and approachable manner'. Jennifer Knock expressed the gratitude of the group:

'Mr Pain encouraged us to keep our feet on the ground and to see the relevance of what we were studying. He was incredibly caring and his determination to help us to do our best carried us all successfully through the experience'.

Jenny Allcock (1965-1969) was especially gripped by the History of Education component:

> 'Perhaps it was this that lit the spark that eventually led me into researching the history of our College'.

All nine students graduated with Honours in 1969. The following year the College became affiliated with the University of Southampton Institute of Education.

Red Lion Hotel, Salisbury

DINNER

COLLEGE OF SARUM ST. MICHAEL
DINNER TO CELEBRATE
THE FIRST BACHELOR OF EDUCATION DEGREES
9th. JULY 1969

Cream of Watercress Soup
• • •
Christchurch Salmon Mayonnaise
Salad
New Potatoes
• • • •
Orange Sorbet
or
Strawberry Mousse
• • • •
The Cheese Board
• • •
Coffee
• • •

B.Ed. group at the graduation in 1969

'The resurgence of activity by the Union Committee was a feature of 1967-1968. While the system of College Mothers continued to function well, the Union Committee sought to integrate the new students with the College by arranging coffee evenings between new students, staff and the officers of the Union. A new Gestetner soon had copies of the Union Constitution in the hands of the students. A Staff/Student Council was established. A Salisbury Students' Association encompassed students in the Theological College, the Art College and Sarum St Michael'.

LST (ibid)

The Student Union report for those years concluded:

'The great difficulty of College life at the moment is that the ever increasing numbers makes College life more impersonal. The Union has tried to bind its students in a bond of friendship and it has been a very happy year'.

Students were given keys to their rooms: an issue which had been debated for a long time. The small diaries were replaced by larger desk diaries with the College name on the front in silver gilt.

'The last year has seen many innovations in both our academic studies and way of life within the College, but "65, The Close" has not lost its air of serenity and peacefulness.

CCSM Chronicle, 1969

End of Term Service

'To everything – turn, turn, turn,
There is a season – turn, turn, turn,
And a time for every purpose under Heaven'.

Words adapted from the
Book of Ecclesiastes by Pete Seeger

College view from Cathedral Spire

In
quietness
and in confidence
shall be your strength

Chapter 7

The Final Chapter

1970-1978

A State of Flux

'In 1969 the College was a humming, lively community: a mixture of resident students, day students, 'once a week students' and students in lodgings. The number of staff was increasing, and students were getting jobs as soon as they left the College'.

Joan Hughes, *The Last Ten Years*

Sadly, this was not to last. In the 1970s, Britain entered a time of social and economic uncertainty. Northern Ireland was a major concern with much bloodshed and unrest, and Britain was trying to establish its place in Europe.

Youth culture was becoming increasingly fragmented. Flower power, flares and long hair were gradually replaced by hot pants, maxi skirts and Afghan coats. Punk music and fashion appeared in 1974 and discos became popular with some young people.

The changeover to decimal currency took place in 1971 and in 1973 Britain joined the Common Market. Inflation was high and political unrest widespread; strikes, power cuts, and the introduction of the three-day-week in 1972, were exacerbated in the winter of 1973 by the Arab-Israeli war. This led to a worldwide shortage of oil, resulting in high petrol prices. The situation in Northern Ireland deteriorated and in 1972, the IRA (Irish Republican Army) bombing campaign spread to the British mainland. Successive governments struggled with many issues. By the end of 1978, the country was plunged into the 'Winter of Discontent' with widespread strikes.

The summer of 1976 was one of sunshine when temperatures rose and a drought continued until September. In 1977 the nation celebrated the Queen's Silver Jubilee, making the most of this opportunity to forget the gloom and strife. The use of the microchip was developing, with the introduction of the first mass-produced personal computers. Concorde was flying high. At the end of the decade, some people who were not unemployed or on strike, began to feel that, possibly, a better life was within their grasp. In May 1979 Britain's first female Prime Minister, Margaret Thatcher, came to power.

What was the situation at College? The state of teacher training was unsettled in the early 1970s. College lecturers, Mr Wright and Mr Say, researched the College records:

'Change was in the air. If you were a small, single sex college, dedicated to one outcome, the production of teachers, the future was highly unpredictable. The birth rate was falling, there was an over-production of teachers and there was keen competition for the few jobs that were available in teaching. Added to this, the Department of Education and Science was embarking on a crude exercise in manpower aimed at rationalising a system in which the Church of England had played a pioneering role and had continued over the years to provide a distinctive form of teacher education'.

CSSM OSA Newsletter, 2009

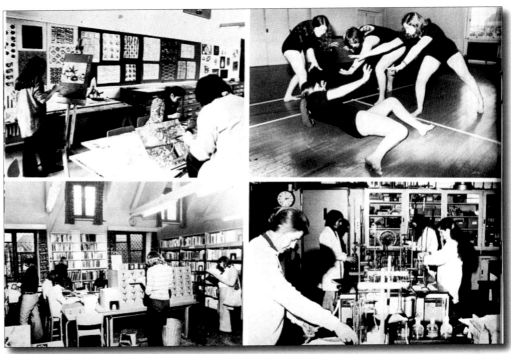

Snapshots of College Life

Eighteen: The New Twenty-One

In the late 1960s, the report of the Latey Committee concluded that the fixing of 21 years as the age of majority was 'no longer relevant to contemporary society'. From January 1st 1970, 18 year olds could vote.

This brought about considerable changes at College. Students were now to be treated as adults and the College was no longer *in loco parentis*. A former student whose younger sister entered College in 1970, commented on the differences:

> 'The restrictions on nights away had gone; gowns were no longer worn for lectures and college life seemed to have become more informal and relaxed'.

Keys to the High Street gate became readily available, reducing the problems of getting back into The Close in the evening. 'Ticking in' books were still needed in case of fire, as well as visitors' books for names and car numbers. 'Weekend Leave' books recorded addresses where students might be found. Whilst rejoicing in their new-found freedom, some students regarded these measures as intrusions into their privacy.

The lowering of the age of majority affected community life. There were now no restrictions on hours or nights out of College and students could spend every weekend away. Sports Reports reflected the difficulty of making up teams for matches at weekends.

The culture in Colleges of Education was changing, becoming more outward looking and increasingly in touch with the 1970s world. Miss Hughes, writing in 'The Last Ten Years', commented that 'The President of the Students' Union, elected by the student body, seemed a very different person from the Senior Student, chosen by staff'.

College authorities began to consult student opinion to a far greater degree than ever before. At the College of Sarum St Michael three students, elected by the Students' Union, became members of the Academic Board.

Return to College

Dr Ian Smith

Dr Ian Smith

Some Members of the College Staff in the Seventies

Some members of Staff who had been appointed in the 1940s, 1950s and 1960s remained at the College, in addition to new appointments.

Miss A. M. D. Ashley	Principal	1963-73
Mr C. J. R. Wilson	Principal	1973-78
Miss D. Roantree	Deputy Principal	1967-71
Miss A. M. Davies	Deputy Principal	1971-78
Revd B. Coleman	Chaplain	1969-77
Revd H. Blenkin	Chaplain	1977-78

Mr R. Alexander	Mathematics
Miss A. D. Amos	Physical Education
Mrs S. Barker	Geography
Mr W. Bate	Education
Revd D. Bevan	Education & Divinity
Mr D. Bindon	Mathematics
Miss M. Binham	Education & Divinity
Miss O. M. M. Blackburn	English
Revd H. Blenkin	Divinity
Mr A. Brinn	Music
Miss R. A. Bryant	Music
Mr R. Bury	Education
Mrs Porter	Geography
Mrs S. Conrad	Art and Craft
Miss M. Cowan	English
Mr W. Crisp	Education
Miss L.M. Currie	Divinity
Miss M. Dean	Music
Mr J. Dodridge	Mathematics
Mrs E. Farringdon	English
Miss J. Flarty	Art
Mr Foster	Music
Miss C. Game	English
Mr S. Gibbons	Combined Studies
Mr G. F. Harvey	Music
Mr R. Head	Art and Craft
Miss J. Highley	Education
Miss S. Higgins	English
Miss E. Hornby	History
Miss J. Hughes	Education
Mr A. Hutchison	English
Miss B. Jackson	Education
Miss L. Jones	Education
Mr J. Kaye	Mathematics
Mrs S. M. Kearney	Art and Craft
Mrs M. Langdon	Education
Dr M. Jones	English
Miss R. E. Mayo	Geography
Miss Mogford	Education
Miss M. Moore	Speech Training

Mr M. Neville	Art &Craft
Miss O. G. Northcott	Biology
Miss Overy	Physical Education
Mr P. Pain	Education
Mr W. Peel	Chemistry
Mr R. Pick	Physics
Miss E. Pointon	Geography
Mrs Porter	Geography
Miss D. Robinson	Education
Mr K. S. Rogers	Geography
Mr J. Roseaman	English and Combined Studies
Miss M. Sanders	English
Mr J. Say	English
Miss P. Snelgar	Art (2 year course)
Mr D. Thomas	Geography
Miss D. A. Todd	History
Mr R. Turner	Education
Miss A. Williams	Education
The Revd B. Williams	History
Mrs M. Paisey	Geography
Mr T. A. Wright	Education

Mr W. B. Gibson	College Bursar
Mr A. G. Evans	College Bursar
Mrs E. Kay	Assistant Bursar
Mrs Hitchnam	Principal's PA
Miss M. Green	College Secretary
Mrs J. Parsons	Assistant Secretary
Miss E. Potter	Catering Officer
Mrs Punter	Housekeeper
Miss Roberts	Catering Officer
Miss Rodden	Domestic Bursar
Miss A. Walker	Domestic Bursar
Miss K. Tunnard	Domestic Bursar
Miss K. Parry	Librarian
Mrs James	Education Office Secretary
Miss Stanbury	Education Office Secretary
Mrs W. Gibson	Warden, Barnard's Cross
Miss Hargreaves	Warden, Barnard's Cross
Mrs Foster	Warden, Barnard's Cross
Miss E. Pointon	Warden, Barnard's Cross
Mrs P. Young	Lodgings Officer
Mrs E. Evans	Lodgings Officer
Miss F. Philip	Sanatorium Sister
Mrs Baker	Sanatorium Sister
Mrs J. Fowles	Sanatorium Sister
Dr Joan Norris	Medical Officer

Setting Chapter 7 in context: A Table of some significant events

Date	Educational	National/International	Local
1970	Dennison Report proposed Direct Grant schools should go comprehensive or fully private The majority subsequently went private	Conservatives win General Election- Edward Heath becomes Prime Minister Britain's voting age is lowered to 18 The Beatles split up	Prince of Wales visits Mere
1971	Education (Milk) Act abolished free milk in schools Margaret Thatcher is Education Minister	OU (Open University) broadcasts begin UK and Ireland switch to decimal currency Spaghetti Junction motorway interchange opens north of Birmingham Postal workers strike Ibrox stadium disaster Riots in Northern Ireland	Closure of RAF Old Sarum Market House site agreed for new Salisbury Library
1972	Children Act ensured minimum age for employment of children would not be affected by changes to school leaving age	Miners' strike for seven weeks Edward Heath declares State of emergency. Power cuts & 3 day week On 'Bloody Sunday' 13 protest marchers are killed by troops in Londonderry Idi Amin expels all Asians from Uganda Olympic Games - Arab guerrillas shoot hostages	The Stonehenge Free Music Festival was held in June for the first time
1973	School leaving age raised to 16 OU awards first degrees Education Act allowed LEAs to arrange for children below school leaving age to have work experience	Britain joins the Common Market Women allowed into London Stock Exchange for the first time VAT comes into effect The British Library is established New London Bridge opens Oil prices rise by 70 per cent IRA start mainland bombings	First Salisbury Festival Altar cross stolen from the Cathedral St Thomas's and Westwood schools merge
1974	Assessment of Performance Unit (APU) formed to assess and monitor pupils' achievement Public enquiry following serious disruption at William Tynedale School Five all-male Oxford Colleges admit women for the first time	Watergate Scandal - President Nixon resigns	Queen visits Salisbury Highbury School moves to Laverstock
1975	The Bullock Report focused on the teaching of English	Margaret Thatcher elected as new Tory leader	Redundant St Edmund's Church becomes Arts Centre New Salisbury library opens Salisbury Diocese 900th anniversary
1976	James Callaghan begins 'Great Debate' on Education with a speech at Ruskin College, Oxford	Summer heat wave-worst drought in England for 200 years James Callaghan new Labour Prime Minister Jimmy Carter elected US President First commercial Concorde flight	Westwood St Thomas's first comprehensive intake St Paul's roundabout completed Salisbury indoor swimming pool opens New Salisbury Playhouse opened by Sir Alec Guinness
1977	Taylor Report recommended major changes in school management Black Paper called for improved parental choice in secondary schools	IRA bomb London The Queen's Silver Jubilee	750th anniversary of granting city charter Cross Keys Chequer first store opens
1978	The Warnock Report focused on 'Special Educational Needs' LEAs required to publish curriculum policies Government plans for new exam to replace O levels and CSEs.	May Day becomes a public holiday for the first time	The College of Sarum St Michael closed after 127 years of teacher training

Education, Education, Education ... Being a Teacher

'How often does a Primary teacher say "I wish that I knew what had happened to the children that I used to teach"?

In 1952 I was teaching a Reception class in Bournemouth. The father of one small boy wrote a letter in which he thanked me for making his little son, Alan, happy in his first year at school. I treasured this letter and showed it to many people over the years. Recently, my cousin used his computer to find this boy, who is now in his sixties. He told him about the letter and Alan wrote to me, telling me details of his life – and what's more, he became a teacher too! Imagine my pleasure to have this news.

This coincidence made me think of the many children and students that I have been privileged to teach over the years. How important our work is; not just in imparting school subjects, but in giving young people a view of the social side of life. What a responsibility is ours and what a pleasure. I am so thankful for having been a teacher.'

Joan Hughes, CSSM OSA Newsletter, 2009

Miss Hughes (Education) and Miss Flarty (Craft) – great pals!

Miss Hughes made an important contribution to Miss Taylor's book about the College, and wrote an interesting account of *The Last Ten Years.*

As Warden of Maxwell House, she was always available to listen to students if they needed advice or reassurance. Students were very fond of her and she became affectionately known as 'Aunty Joan,' although always

respectfully known as Miss Hughes to her face. She always returned for the annual reunion of Old Students, when she sat in regal splendour in a particular part of the Medieval Hall, where a queue of students greeted her.

Miss Hughes is remembered with much affection by many students. The College was a major part of her life and she devoted several years to inspiring students to become the best teachers that they could.

Miss Highley said farewell to the College in 1976, after ten years on the staff:

'She will be remembered not only as a skilful tutor in the Education Department, where she was so adept at conveying to successive groups of students her enthusiasm, knowledge and skill in First School work and in History of Education. She was also chatelaine of 38, The Close and a sympathetic and helpful warden'.

CSSM Chronicle, 1977

During the 1970s, in addition to the students who were following the three year Certificate course, there were those in their final (fourth) year of the B Ed degree course, as well as mature students doing the Two Year Shortened Course at London Road. In-service teachers were also there, doing the new, three year part-time B. Ed degree course.

'The Bachelor of Education Degree

Students are given the opportunity at the end of their first year of registering for the B.Ed degree of Southampton University. For such students the second and final years of the three-year course are extended into a fourth year when the work divides into three elements: Education; Main Subject; Middle Component.

The Middle Component is designed as an experience at university level of the integrated type of study now regarded by educationalists as a sound approach to learning. A small group of students select a theme, probably of topical concern, to which all can contribute in accordance with their particular knowledge and interests. The work is largely independent, although under the guidance of a special tutor'.

College Prospectus (early 1970s)

John Roseaman was a member of the College staff between 1974 -1976 He worked with Steve Gibbons and gave the students enormous encouragement in their independent research for the Middle Component of the degree. He was later awarded the MBE for his excellent work in education and in other areas.

Mr Wright and Mr Roseaman (both Education)

Diana Harris (1968-1971) explained that she was probably rather an unusual student of the College of Sarum St Michael, as she had studied there for SIX years:

'I spent the initial three years at College from 1968 until 1971, was awarded my Certificate in Education and began my secondary school teaching career. However, it soon became apparent that teaching was fast becoming a graduate profession and that a degree would be an advantage to my career. So, whilst still teaching, I returned to College to do the part-time BEd course from 1975 – 1978'.

London Road/Rougemont Close and the Coach House continued to be used during the 1970s.

Aileen Hayfield, (1969-1971) reflected:

'The first day at London Road dispelled a lot of those fears for I met a person who by her friendly welcome and encouragement, made me feel at ease and helped me to look forward to the days ahead. Mrs Langdon was a source of inspiration to the students that she helped to become teachers. Her love and concern for all is something that I will always remember, and be grateful for'.

CSSM Chronicle 1972

Mrs Langdon retired in 1972 and was succeeded by Miss Jackson. London Road closed in the summer of 1976.

'The 41 mature students who were awarded the two-year Certificate gained 2 Distinctions and 43 Credits. This year there were no candidates for the in-service B Ed (Hons) degree, but some 17 serving teachers are expected to sit the final examination in 1978'.

CSSM Chronicle, 1977

Despite the trials and worries of the years, the College remained a hardworking, lively centre of learning, and high standards were maintained to the last.

A College Timetable

Caroline Minchinton (1972-1976) recalled her days at College and the timetabling of subjects:

'Every moment was timetabled. We had a personal tutor (rather like a form mistress), subject tutors and weekly tutorials with either our main study tutors or education tutor.

In Year One, the timetable was divided between our main subject, Education, the integrated day (planning the timetable, core subjects and humanities in topics for the primary school) and the middle component. This consisted of selecting a topic with a group of other students. I remember one of mine was entitled "Buttons"; one then researched the material and worked towards a final presentation. The idea was to select a group leader and allocate jobs to the rest of the group; a much scaled-down version of 'The Young Apprentice'. It was a team building exercise which one then had to analyse, in terms of conflict, what worked within the group and what didn't.

At the end of my first year we were given the chance to be interviewed for the degree course. Providing one had the necessary qualifications for a degree course one was able to opt for a fourth year. Many of us did this and took on extra lessons in Years 2 and 3, culminating in degree work and a dissertation in both Education and our main subject in Year 4.

It was a magical four years and stood us all in good stead, for in quietness and in confidence we were taught to teach, and with an energy and enthusiasm which has lasted more than four decades'.

Special School Practice

Special School Practice was introduced by Miss Taylor during the 1960s. Students were expected to spend some time working at a special school near to their homes in the summer vacation at the end of their first year. There was no compulsion, but many students chose to do this.

Susan Bowser (1969-1972) spent a week at Queen Mary's Hospital for Children in Carshalton. The hospital looked after 300 children aged between 2 and 16 years. There were 30 qualified teachers who were supported by assistants. Teachers had to adapt to an elastic routine that was interrupted by visits from parents and medical requirements. Despite this, she was impressed by the huge variety of teaching going on in the different units that included children with spina bifida, cerebral palsy and muscular dystrophy. Children who were then described as 'severely sub normal' were taught in their own school.

At this time there were many different types of Special Schools and (using the names that were in use at the time) students visited schools for maladjusted children, for ESN (educationally sub-normal) children and schools for those with physical handicaps. Open Air schools for delicate children, schools for the deaf and for the blind were also visited, as well as Special Classes at Junior schools. These Special Classes were something of an innovation, and perhaps a forerunner of the more integrated education system that we have today.

In many cases, this was a worthwhile and maturing experience. Susan Bowser found that her eyes were opened to a type of teaching that she had not encountered before. Some students chose to work in Special Schools after leaving College.

Rag Week

Rag Weeks in the Seventies

Rag Weeks during the 1970s were different from those of earlier days. Students from Sarum St Michael joined those from the Theological College, the College of Art and the College of Technology. In 1972 the Rag Week supported the Mayor's Appeal, helping to raise money for a swimming pool at Odstock Hospital. Events included a Treasure Hunt, a Mile of Pennies in Blue Boar Row, a Monopoly Marathon, Tiddlywinks in the George Mall and the Rag Ball in the City Hall. The College provided many of the venues: a Dance and a Revue took place in the Assembly Hall, a Disco was held at Barnard's Cross and a Cultural Evening in the Old Deanery Hall. 'It's a Knock-Out' took place on the hockey pitch and the traditional Rag Procession still started in The Close.

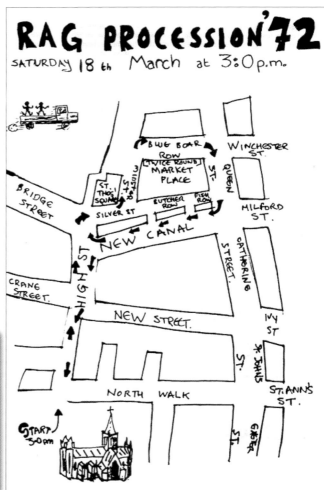

Map of Rag Procession

As the 1970s ticked away, students continued to enjoy a range of social activities. In the early seventies they were unaware of the dramatic events which were about to unfold. Students had much more freedom and independence than those of earlier generations.

Eric Hart was a student at Salisbury College of Art and worked part-time as a barman at the New Inn, in New Street, just around the corner from the Cathedral Close.

'It was a favourite haunt of a good number of ladies from the College and I got to know and socialise with many of them. I had a house in Pennyfarthing Street in the early seventies and on many occasions I provided a roof for the night for waifs and strays from the College who had stayed out later than they should have done and found themselves locked out of the Close. The house was often full!'

Students in the Common Room   Dr Ian Smith

Eric somehow acquired a key to the Close Gate. 'Borrowing a key was a standard practice for the ladies at the time if they knew they were going to stay out beyond curfew!' How shocked the staff and students from previous years would have been!

A Salisbury resident recalled how exciting it was to be a young man in Salisbury at the time. 'We had a reservoir of hundreds of young students at the College-many very attractive'. After an evening at the New Inn, on the way home, along with other young men, they would sometimes have an illicit swim in Salisbury's open-air swimming pool to cool off.

Christmas   Dr Ian Smith

Another way of getting back into College was to wade across the river. Susan Bowser (1969-1972) recalled warily wading across the river late one night, having been warned to watch out for leeches getting between her toes.

Caroline Minchinton (1972-1976) lived in Queens' House:

'Of course there was the bother of the High Street Gate being locked at midnight. Many a girl waded across the river to gain access and no one would know. By the end of our third year we had the excitement of numerous 21st birthday parties happening everywhere. One celebration at the end of the third year featured making tea on the lawn in a huge urn at 4 am, and dancing through the Close to decorate the Constable's box'.

Party in the Quiet Room

Students made the most of their free time:

'Membership of Salisbury Music Society was fun and we also enjoyed plenty of contact with friends from the Theological College, including playing hockey and putting on musical shows. We had dances at College quite often too'.

An annual event, during some of the 1970s, was the 'Stone-Rolling Competition' held against other Salisbury Colleges. Each College would roll a large boulder down a hill to the finishing line. One year, students from Salisbury tricked their competitors by making a large boulder from papier mâché. Escapades and enjoyment were still a firm part of student education in the 1970s!

Donna Curtis (1974-1978) shared her memories of the final College Years. It was a strange time with a much smaller number of students and an eerie sense of finality. In the final year there were only 12 fourth-year B. Ed students. Silence hung over many areas of the College. The library was audited and there was a sense of things gradually being dismantled.

She has happier memories too: students showed a stoical spirit, still living out the College motto. They enjoyed sharing gateaux at The Bay Tree café, when their grants came through, and visiting The New Inn.

Donna was a history student and remembers the monthly get-togethers at the kind invitation of Miss Todd, in her study after her lectures. These became weekly events after the sad announcement of the College closure. A glass or two of sherry was the norm and much enjoyed by all!

Miss Todd had been at the College since 1947. She was the 'austere and outwardly formidable' Head of History. A colleague in the Sixties remembered Miss Todd's expression of disdain when a young member of staff had the temerity to address her by her Christian name (Dorothy) in the staffroom. Despite this, Miss Todd had a wonderful sense of humour and her wise counsel and inspired teaching was long remembered, as was her much loved dog, Bundle, who had his own chair in her study.

Student Protests

The 1970s was a time of general unrest in the country with many demonstrations. Some students showed their strong feelings by joining in a protest, as recalled by Barbara Mansfield:

'During my second year I was elected President of the Students' Union. As well as attending national NUS (National Union of Students) events, we went up to London to join the demonstrations against Margaret Thatcher stopping free school milk'.

Miss Hughes recalled a student protest in 1976:

'In June 1976 the students supported the NUS day of action to protest at education cuts. They withdrew from lectures for the day and took to the streets with sandwich boards and leaflets, but at the same time they showed a responsible contribution to the day by clearing the streets of litter. The Principal, Mr Wilson, was proud that the students had protested in that way, rather than engaging in disruptive action'.

Joan Hughes, *The Last Ten Years*

Visit to Sudan 1976

In 1976, five students, accompanied by Miss Betty Pointon (an Education lecturer) visited Sudan as representatives of the Diocese of Salisbury. Miss Pointon had worked in Uganda for the CMS (Church Missionary Society) prior to coming to College. She was a person who had 'boundless enthusiasm for life, for education and for her belief.' CSSM Newsletter 1998

At this time the Diocesan Link with Sudan was in its infancy:

'There were no photographs of Sudan on the mission board in the Cathedral and in a mad moment one of the students suggested that we should go there and take some photographs to help bring the link to life. We asked Betty to come with us; she said "yes" and so began two years of preparation'.

Carolyn Murray, 1974-77

The group was supported by many people in the Salisbury Diocese. On returning to Salisbury, full of their experiences and laden with photographs, they spent many hours raising awareness of the situation in the link diocese. This visit must have been instrumental in helping to establish the strong link that the Diocese of Salisbury has today with the Episcopal Church of Sudan.

Students always found the library such a calm, tranquil place in which to be. Kit Parry, the College Librarian, wrote about the hive of activity, which really existed:

> 'Monday morning break is over, most of my desk work done, many a note written, many a note read, garnered from the largest pigeon-hole in College. The issue and shelving, book requests and book renewals will take until 3 pm to clear, but already students are working at book strewn tables and making their familiar requests.
>
> By 4.45 three letters and a pile of catalogue cards have been typed. I've started cataloguing and classifying nine books. One of us has fitted in a visit to the School Practice Library, spined twenty books, and finally said "I'll have to go now if this parcel is to catch the post". Only one of us is still on duty. The library is empty again – of COURSE, everyone's at supper'.
>
> *CSSM Chronicle*, 1978

Joy Warman, a student who attended College in the 1960s, recalled her affection for the library:

> 'My favourite place in College was an armchair in the small bay window of the Upper Library. An hour or two there, with a book to read, in sight of the copper beech outside the dining room, was my idea of bliss. English Literature as my main course made a wonderful excuse.
>
> Miss Higgins once set us to write "Thoughts on College" during our General English period. I sat in the library chair and wrote mine: "The lines are fallen unto me in pleasant places" I wrote, quoting the Psalmist. I still think that'.

A Common Room

The Students' Union

The College has its own Students' Union, which is affiliated to the National Union of Students. The College Union is financed, basically, by the Department of Education and Science, but these funds are supplemented by an additional Union fee, payable at the beginning of the academic year. The amount of this additional fee is decided by a General Meeting of the Union.

The Union is a student organisation, the aim of which is to provide, where possible, for all aspects of student life. Most important of all, it requires the involvement of *all* students if it is to run successfully.

Students are now represented on the College Council and the Academic Board, the two bodies which control College procedure, and therefore the students have an opportunity to voice student opinion on any matters that may arise.

All clubs and societies are run through the Union, and we try to cater for all tastes: Folk, Sports, Music, Drama, Student Christian Movement, Christian Union, Guides and Photographic Society, to name but a few. Other interests can be catered for if there is a demand for them. There are dances and balls held in College, and transport can be arranged to social events at Southampton University and other colleges.

There is also a society called *Focus* which provides a common focus for students and staff on matters of social and religious importance. Amongst other activities it affords opportunities to participate in a flourishing Youth Community Service operating in Salisbury.

MAIN LIBRARY DOORS

Music – an Integral Part of College life

The College Orchestra

Music always played an important part in College life. Back in 1841 Martha Gibson, the first student, aged sixteen, wrote about how much the singing instruction, which was provided by Mr Biddlecombe, Lay Vicar of the Cathedral, had been enjoyed.

> 'Since those days, under successive Music Directors, the musical life of the College has enlarged and, up to the closure of the College, various activities and courses were available for singers and players, whether students were taking music as a main subject or not, with opportunities for individual and vocal lessons. The facilities for practice also improved and finally resulted in the construction of the Music Wing'.
>
> Audrey Bryant, *CSSM Chronicle*, 1978

Miss Bryant, a keen cellist, was appointed in 1954 and remained until the College closed. She took over leadership of the Music department in 1964. The team was much-respected, and in the final decades included Miss Dean, Mr Brinn, Mr Foster, and Mr Harvey. All were gifted and enthusiastic musicians. Mr Brinn sadly died after playing a piano solo at a College concert.

> 'Gifted musician as Alan Brinn was, he gave himself wholeheartedly to his work of teaching. His strong humility made him an appreciative and discerning critic of music, but in his criticisms no words were ever heard of unkindness. Serenity and kindness flowed from him to all of us'.
>
> Miss Ashley, *CSSM Chronicle*, 1978

During the 1970s there were quizzes, visits to London to operas and concerts and lively College performances. Saturday Music Schools were organised when eminent musicians from Wiltshire and beyond shared their expertise with students. The choir continued to be a popular part of College life, occasionally accompanying the Cathedral services. Music students played a full part in Chapel services, playing the organ and singing in the Choir. Main Music students had opportunities to play the Cathedral organ.

Carol Bishop (1974-1978) chose Salisbury because she knew that it had a good musical reputation. Choral and orchestral music filled her student years and at the weekend, in the true 70s style, she drove home to play in a local band. Carol, a class teacher in a Wiltshire primary school, continues to share her own love of music with her young pupils.

The musical legacy of the College continues. Sarah Shakespeare (1972-1975) studied Music as a main subject and valued the stimulating course, which even included making an instrument. Still teaching today, she inspires children to appreciate and enjoy music. Sarah has written several wonderful musical plays and composed a Liturgy for Sung Eucharist at St Andrew's Church, Laverstock.

In 1862 a student commented, 'Who could be merrier than we on singing nights?' At the Annual OSA reunions the Cathedral roof is lifted, as past students sing 'Angel Voices ever Singing,' and the music lives on!

There was plenty of sport on offer during the 1970s. Tennis, rounders, table-tennis and volleyball were all played, as well as badminton. There was also a yoga club. Students went ice-skating and swimming in Southampton, and 'Keep Fit' was a winter activity.

The Sports Report in the *College Chronicle* for 1973 makes puzzling reading:

'The year began with a football match during Fresher's Week in September, and a little badminton. Netball was not popular and fixtures had to be cancelled because of lack of support. In November the team met King Alfred's College and suffered an appalling defeat. However, a match was subsequently played against Salisbury Young Men's Team and although "rough going", Sarum St Michael was only just defeated. Owing to the difficulty of getting team members to play at weekends, it was decided to play only local teams. The College played the Salisbury Young Wives and this game was unfortunately marred by the somewhat less than sporting behaviour of the Young Wives. The Salisbury Young Men were played twice more and this time Sarum St Michael beat them in two very good matches'.

Fun at Barnard's Cross

Were these netball matches or football matches? Perhaps Sarum St Michael fielded a feisty football team that eventually vanquished male opposition. Alternatively, maybe the game was netball and the men were nifty on their feet and good at scoring goals. The intrigue remains, as does the nature of that unsportsmanlike behaviour of the Salisbury Young Wives!

Traditional team sports struggled for survival. Frozen or flooded pitches had always been a problem, but the lifting of the requirement to be in College over the weekend almost certainly hastened the demise of competitive sport.

Miss Ayling with PE students

Dr Ian Smith

Dance in the Chapel

Caroline Minchinton(1972-1975) recalled her College days:

'Each week at College, sport and dance was part of the timetable. We had uniform for sport: blue jumper, white aertex polo shirt, hockey skirt and grey knickers. The black tight teaching trousers became even tighter after our daily sticky buns at coffee time and three cooked meals also daily! We also had a leotard and footless tights for our dance classes. Dance was a real passion for some and was included for worship in Chapel services, expressing poetry and prose as well as in Drama and PE. We were delighted to offer dance when on school practice because few schools had included these lessons and the children were very responsive and enthusiastic for something different'.

In the 1978 Chronicle another student fondly remembered Dance at College:

'I am sure all recent students must be very grateful to Miss Amos and Miss Overy for all their hard work and patience as they worked at the unenviable task of persuading stiff and uncooperative bodies to attempt some movement.

I remember the day we struggled into super-tight leotards and headed towards the gymnasium for our first practical lecture in Dance. Our self-consciousness and embarrassment were acute as we began to glide and creep and bounce around the floor! As the weeks went by we forgot our self-consciousness and actually began to enjoy ourselves in the new-found realisation that we could dance'.

Dance productions were much enjoyed:

'The dances that grew out of weeks of argument and work were as perfect as we could make them and, as we finished them, we realised that our enjoyment came not only from presenting a well finished piece of work, but also from sharing the experience of the presentation.

1977 saw the end of dance and gym lectures but we continued to dance. We discovered it not only belonged in the gym, but also in other parts of College life. Enthusiastically, we took Dance into the Chapel for morning worship and down to the river as part of a riverside Eucharist.

All this, a year after our course on Dance had ended, shows how permanent were the seeds planted in our minds, that people can and should dance. No longer will we bewail the fact that we "can't dance" for we know – if you can breathe and walk, if you can raise your head and move your hands, then you can surely dance!'

The Literary and Dramatic Society

College Drama Production

The society remained active during the 1970s. In co-operation with the English department and members of staff, a highly successful Victorian Evening was produced. It was a lively occasion, when all were dressed in 'elegant attire' and enjoyed Madeira and seed cake and claret cup for refreshment. There was dancing, strolls on the lawn, recitations and the singing of ballads and excerpts from *The Importance of Being Earnest*.

> 'The account of this lifts the heart with the realisation that here was an echo of College plays in the gardens, visits to the Assembly Rooms, and Fancy Dress Parties of previous generations of students, and that students were still as full of intelligent, adventurous, innocent and elegant fun as their predecessors'.
>
> *LST ibid*

Three plays were produced during 1974 -1975:

> 'Maria Marten and the Red Barn' was the first of three plays produced in a very dramatically active year for the College. The spirit of drama was captured by the audience who quickly participated in the contemporary fashion, spontaneously hissing the villain and sympathising with the heroine in her plight'.
>
> Mr Say, *CSSM Chronicle*, 1975

Miss Higgins fulfilled a long-standing ambition by producing Christopher Fry's *A Sleep of Prisoners* in the College Chapel:

> 'Under the self-effacing direction of Miss Higgins, many people worked together as a team in the production. As the play gathered momentum, Fry's masterly use of imagery and poetic language opened up to the imagination of the audience something of the great fundamental truths that lie behind the ordinary and the everyday. It was a most moving experience'.
>
> *CSSM Chronicle*, 1975

It was a resounding success, as were so many College productions over the years.

Mr Wright and Mr Say

Projects and Field Study Weeks

The Geography Field Trips that had been so dear to Miss Mayo's heart continued, but with a difference. After all, this was the 1970s. Mrs Paisey, who joined the Geography department in 1971 brought warmth and vivacity to her lectures and a vigorous approach to the Field Weeks that she too loved:

> 'Her particular interest led students into the mysteries of farming in the wilds of Cornwall and in the rural retreats of Suffolk. Those visits are still remembered in remote spots of England that were unaccustomed to Mary's pace'.
>
> *CSSM Chronicle*, 1976

Mr Rogers, Head of the Geography Department, felt that many Wiltshire Primary Schools would have affectionate memories of Mrs Paisey's school-based projects:

> 'The mothers at Westbury still trying to wash cement from their children's clothes, the children from Odstock who flew over the Isle of Wight ("to give them a bird's eye view of where they lived", said Mary), the local headmaster who was shot by an arrow in the New Forest and really did want tomato juice poured all over his shirt: all will remember Mrs Paisey, our colleague'.

The project work about the New Forest finished with students and children cooking venison sausages in the garden at London Road. Lucky children and fortunate students - those were the days!

Outdoor Study   Dr Ian Smith

Mature students at London Road

Judith Nicholls and Sarum St Michael

'I joined Sarum St. Michael in September 1973 as a 'mature' student – at the grand old age of 31. To my shame, I had no real thoughts of becoming a teacher at that point, I was just desperate to study – anything; to my credit, I did (maybe unwisely!) admit this at my interview. My interviewers were clearly very tolerant and took me on.

The College was brilliantly accommodating to its mature students. The timetable meant I was normally able to be home (26 miles away) not long after our children had been brought from school and during school half-term breaks we were allowed to bring our children in to college with us. My three sat patiently (mainly) at the back of the group with a variety of arts and crafts materials I had taken in for them, whilst lectures on the metaphysical poets or various theories of education gently drifted over their heads.

Notably I rediscovered poetry here: Marlowe, the mediaeval mystery plays, Dylan Thomas, TS Eliot, DH Lawrence … I loved it all. After teaching practices in small village primary schools the real 'baptism of fire' came with my first position teaching – first mainly 9th stream children – in a large comprehensive.

It was perhaps the poetry I'd gone back to at Sarum St. Michael that really stuck though. After a few years' teaching, I returned to part-time studying and drifted into writing. Ironically, after 'escaping' from teaching, I was to visit over 500 different schools to run poetry performances and workshops with teachers and pupils of all ages; thank goodness for those early experiences in education!'

(Judith's first book was published by Faber & Faber in 1985 and she went on to write some 50 more.)

VILLAGE SCHOOL

A stile, a field,
some dozen cows and then the church.
A muddy dyke,
some silver roach
and just below the bridge
a sharp-toothed pike
which lurks alone
for small unwary stragglers, whispering doom.

The school, one room.
Beneath high-windowed stone
fixed smiling in her chair
the kindly Mrs Mullins,
large in blue and black
with neatly-curlered hair.
From nine to twelve
and later on till three
she calls our fate
and welcomes all
on ample knee.
A scratch of slate,
a shuffle here or there,
a child in late:
chalk-dusted autumn
clouds the air.

At last a break. Wait
unwillingly for bottled milk,
cool in its rattling crate,
then under teacher's watchful eye
lace-up for play.
Scarves, coats and hopscotch
when the weather's dry
and crying at the gate for home
under a grey Lincolnshire sky.

© Judith Nicholls 1987 from *Midnight Forest*
by Judith, pub. Faber & Faber; reprinted by
permission of the author.

Judith commented: 'I started school
around 1947 in a Lincolnshire village.
The school really was in one room, with
a curtain down the middle to separate
infants and juniors.'

LATE

You're late, said miss.
The bell has gone,
dinner numbers done
and work begun

What have you got to say for yourself?

Well, it's like this, miss.
Me mum was sick, me dad fell down the stairs,
the wheel fell off me bike
and then we lost our Billy's snake
behind our kitchen chairs. Earache
struck down me grampy, me gran
took quite a funny turn.
Then on the way I met this man
whose dog attacked me shin –
look, miss, you can see the blood,
it doesn't look too good,
does it?

Yes, yes, sit down –
and next time say you're sorry
for disturbing all the class.
Now get on with your story,
fast!

Please miss, I've nothing to write about.

©Judith Nicholls 1985, from *Magic Mirror* by Judith Nicholls, pub.
Faber & Faber. Reprinted by permission of the author

Nature Walk

Keeping in Touch

The 'Island' Clubs (Isle of Wight, Jersey and Guernsey) continued into the 1970s and were visited by Miss Ashley, Mr Wilson, Miss Mayo and Mrs Dalton-Hill. Guernsey had 17 members in 1974. The Somerset Club, after almost closing in the late 60s, revived for a few more years.

The College Reunion in 1975 was especially well attended, and notable for the 22 Old Students who were celebrating their Golden Jubilee, having left College in 1925.

College Chronicles in the 1970s included articles, reports and accounts of teaching experiences, with contributions from current and former students. Photographs were included, as well as information about what people were doing. The Chronicles for the last few years included information about what leaving staff were going on to do, and paid tribute to their valuable contributions to College life and work.

A Family Century

An illustration of the fondness which students had for the College is demonstrated by the number of sisters who attended it. There are also examples of daughters following in their mother's footsteps. In 1871, Eleanora Holder was in College followed by two daughters: Eleanora May in 1902-1904 and Gertrude Hope in 1912-1914. From 1935 -1937 Eleanora Holder's grand-daughter, Edith Barbara Hayes was a student. Mary Uppington was at College from 1935-1937 and was followed by her daughters, Hannah Boothman 1965-1969 and Sarah Boothman 1970-1974.

Surely the record must be held by the eight members of yet another family during 1871-1963.

Agnes Amelia Gilbert née Symes	1871-1873
May Pope (née Gilbert – daughter of Agnes)	1901-1904
Alice Pope	1902-1904
Nellie Pope (sister of Alice)	1918-1920
Ivy Pope (*née* Wright – sister-in-law of Alice and Nellie)	1918-1920
Emily Pope (*née* Brooks)	1918-1920
Beatrice Mary Day (*née* Slade – niece to May, Alice, Nellie, Ivy and Emily)	1940-1942
Diana Mary Chillcott (*née* Blake – great-grand-daughter of Agnes Amelia Symes)	1960-1963

What an awe-inspiring family record of College Students!
Diana Chillcott, *CSSM Chronicle*, 1972

Comings and Goings

'College continued to welcome students from overseas. They mainly came from African countries and the last to come was Miss Sophie Mughal from Uganda, after Idi Amin had expelled Asians from the country in 1972'.

The 1972 issue of the College Chronicle mentions 14 former students who were working in Africa at that time. Several were teaching in Uganda at Lady Irene College, one was training in-service mature students to become teachers and another was working with Uganda Broadcasting Services. Yunia Oboa-Otoa (1959-62) was a member of Uganda Ministry of Education Inspectorate and one of her first jobs had been to inspect Lady Irene College. Other former students were working in Malawi, Nairobi and Rhodesia.

During the last three years, when it was difficult to find teaching posts in this country, a 'long list of students went to work overseas and also did Voluntary Service Overseas. Some went between the second and third years of their course, and others soon after they had qualified'.

Miss Hughes, *The Last 10 Years*

The Chapel

June 1974 was the 75th anniversary of the founding of the College Chapel. An outdoor Eucharist had also been planned, but due to bad weather it was held in the Assembly Hall. Even so, a special atmosphere was engendered, perhaps by the informality of the occasion.

> 'The Revd H Blenkin celebrated, using home-made bread and wine with the hand-made chalice and patten. A group of first year students led the singing with guitars and recorder.'
>
> *CSSM Chronicle* 1974

Daily worship continued to be well attended by students and staff. Harvest Festival, Candlemas, Ascension Day and the Carol Service remained valued traditions. In 1975 the Christmas Eucharist was so well attended that some students had to sit on the floor. 'The playing of the orchestra added much to the celebration'.

CSSM Chronicle 1975

Revd B Williams – student tutorial Dr Ian Smith

Dance, which was very popular in the 1970s, was sometimes used in worship. Modern hymns were introduced. 'Chapel is ALIVE'! reported Susan Wear in the 1975 *College Chronicle*.

College was increasingly outward looking and in 1976 the first year Religious Studies students spent three days in Southampton, looking at the role of the Church in the inner city. They were accompanied by the Revd Brian

Coleman (the Chaplain), the Revd Hugh Blenkin, Miss Binham and Miss Currie.

A Chapel Service   Dr Ian Smith

In 1977 the Chaplain, the Revd Brian Coleman, left College to return to parish ministry. In thanking him for his ministry at College, mention was made of his 'thoughtful and stimulating addresses, his sound teaching and notable contribution to the Religious Studies department. He has been a good and wise friend to staff and students alike'.

The Revd Hugh Blenkin, who had succeeded Miss Rogers as Principal Lecturer in Religious Studies, also became Chaplain. Numbers in College continued to diminish. Buildings emptied and closed. The Chapel, in Hugh's caring hands, remained a constant presence at the heart of the College and continued to offer peace to all who entered its doors.

> 'The Chapel was an oasis of calm during the final year. With a small group of students and staff attending daily services, the thread of prayer and praise continued. It was with mixed emotions that we celebrated each festival for the last time, yet in some ways the familiar pattern of the seasons was a comfort.'
>
> *CSSM Chronicle*, 1978

Valedictory: Down but not Out!

Diminishing numbers in the College were first felt in Autumn 1976, when there were about 250 students, with no first years. Lodgings were no longer needed, hostels began to close and other buildings felt empty. Barnard's Cross closed in Summer 1977. Less than 100 students returned for the final year (1977-78) and they were all accommodated in Queen's House.

Staff numbers also diminished as people left for other posts. Others anxiously struggled to understand their position and to ascertain what compensation they would receive, should no suitable posts be offered to them. In October 1977 just over 20 teaching staff remained. .

Teaching jobs were difficult to find due to the falling birth rate, and many students could not find posts when they left College. In 1976, out of 100 third and fourth year students, only eight managed to secure teaching jobs. One student sent 147 applications and received one reply. Students wanting to take the B.Ed degree transferred to other colleges.

Despite the depressing and challenging circumstances, College life went on as usual. Members of staff maintained high standards and the students themselves remained cheerful and full of youthful resilience, keeping up their spirits in true Sarum fashion. The College still held its head high and would go down with flying colours.

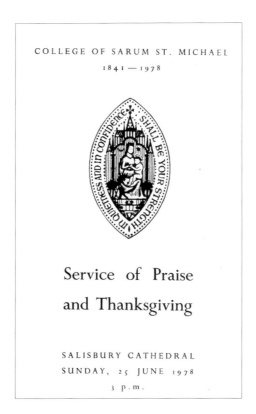

COLLEGE OF SARUM ST. MICHAEL
1841 — 1978

Service of Praise
and Thanksgiving

SALISBURY CATHEDRAL
SUNDAY, 25 JUNE 1978
3 p.m.

The Principal's Residence

In 1970 the new block at the front of the College was completed; this included the first designated accommodation for the Principal. Prior to this, several rooms in King's House had been allocated for the Principal's use. The two upper floors of the new building were to be used for this purpose, with Miss Ashley as the first occupant.

The block was carefully designed to fit in with its neighbours of Audley and Maxwell Houses. The view of the Cathedral and Close was stunningly beautiful. Miss Ashley described the additional accommodation:

'The ground floor of this block will contain a new large lecture room for mathematics, and a new 'dark room' for which several departments have been clamouring. The Principal's room in King's House will continue to be my office. I should be sorry to part with its remarkable ceiling and the coat-of-arms of Prince Henry, son of King James'.

CSSM Chronicle

The Principal's House

Relaxing outside Queens

Miss Ashley's Retirement

Miss Ashley retired in 1973, after 10 years as a much respected College Principal:

'It will be understood that 1973 has not been the easiest year for clear forward planning. So I feel even more enthusiastic about retirement than I felt when I wrote my *Chronicle* letter last year. Many people ask me sympathetically whether I shall miss the College, and my answer is that I am not sorry to hand this over to someone as experienced as Mr Christian Wilson'.

CSSM Chronicle, 1973

Miss Todd wrote an obituary after Miss Ashley's death in 1994:

'Miss Ashley was a person of much kindness, who quietly gave practical help and advice to many. She would pursue her objectives with tenacity and shrewdness and at a time of much change in teacher training, she set herself high standards for what she hoped for the College'.

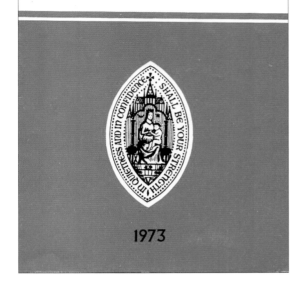

Chronicle
College of Sarum St. Michael

1973

'That this merger will certainly not now take place gives some idea of the very sudden change of direction which we had to take. So, with the decision that the College would be permitted to remain open only so long as was necessary to complete the courses of the remaining students, we shall close completely in 1978'.

Mr Wilson paid tribute to staff and students and their magnificent response to the challenges of the situation. He spoke frankly, ending on a note of determination, and the need to look beyond the present adversity. It is a tribute to Mr Wilson's leadership that, during the final years, students carried on receiving a thorough training and enjoying a range of social and cultural activities, however difficult the circumstances. He did his utmost to maintain the standards for which the College had always been known.

'I believe that we have come through the agonies of nearly three years of the run-down of the College in a way that reflects credit on the dwindling number of students and particularly on the staff, both academic and non-academic. Inevitably, we were all faced with a great number of social and psychological problems in addition to those which, overall, had to be dealt with administratively. Through it all a splendid spirit of co-operation has prevailed'.

CSSM Chronicle 1978

Mr Christian Wilson – College Principal 1973–1978

Who was to succeed Miss Ashley?

'Mr Christian Wilson was chosen. A brilliant organist, he came to us from the College of St Mark and St John, Plymouth. It was a shame for him that although he came to a flourishing College, he had to lead us though the traumas and the final act of closure'.

Joan Hughes, *The Last Ten Years*

His first year at College was a positive one:

'My early impressions – of a College which knows what its aims are and sets about achieving them in a purposeful way – have been confirmed through my experiences at first-hand. Its atmosphere depends not only on its splendid situation but also, and even more importantly, on all those who serve it; and it seems to me that we are indeed well-served'.

CSSM Chronicle 1974

Uncertain times lay ahead and in 1975 Mr Wilson reported on the discussions regarding the future of the College and the difficulty of planning anything with certainty. At that time a possible merger with King Alfred's College, Winchester was being planned. One year later he reported:

Mr Wilson   Dr Ian Smith

Teacher Training in the early 1970s was unsettled. The birth rate was falling, there were too many teachers and less competition for jobs. Added to this, the DES (Department of Education and Science) was planning to rationalise the system of teacher training; one in which the Church of England had played a pioneering role and continued to provide a distinctive form of teacher education. Looking back, the vulnerability of small, single-sex teacher training colleges can now be clearly seen.

It was The James Report (Teacher Training and Education) in 1972 that set the scene for wide-ranging changes. The recommendations included:

- Teacher training should be seen as falling into three consecutive stages; personal education, pre-service training and in-service education and training.

- New three-year degrees should be introduced into Colleges of Education. A new two-year qualification, the Diploma in Higher Education, should be introduced into the polytechnic departments of education.

- Opportunities for in-service training should be increased.

The Report agreed with student comments that 'Many courses place too much emphasis on educational theory at the expense of adequate preparation for students' responsibilities in their first professional assignments'.

In retrospect, the ground was beginning to tremble beneath the foundation of the Anglican colleges, and an alarming, warning statement followed in the White Paper 'Framework for Expansion' at the end of 1972.

'Some colleges may face the possibility that in due course they will have to be converted to new purposes; some may need to close. If Colleges of Education are to find a fuller and firmer place in the higher education family, their staff must face major changes'.

'Diversification' was the buzz word. If you could not fill up your college with intending teachers, you had to think up other courses that might attract students.

Staff at the College of Sarum St Michael were not unduly concerned. This was the only College of Education in Wiltshire, and it was in good standing with the LEA and the university. The need for 'diversification' was understood and confident plans went ahead:

'We planned for expansion, discussed validation, and the change from the concurrent course to 'modules' or unit courses, and plans for new building and new courses went ahead. The planning for a new Nursery course was proposed, and Miss Hughes represented the College on the Institute working party and prepared details for the work'.

LST ibid

Events, however, moved quickly. The Governing Body was informed in Autumn 1973 that the College's future could not be taken for granted. Later that year, it became known that the number of places for intending teachers in colleges would be reduced. Unfilled places would be offered to students wishing to do degree courses in various subjects, as well as those wishing to do the new 2 year Diploma of Education.

Smaller colleges would be expected to amalgamate, or to link themselves appropriately with other institutions. The College of Sarum St Michael had barely 500 students at this time. The 'writing was on the wall' but there was still hope that it would survive.

In March 1974, the Principals of the 27 Church Colleges were informed that by 1981 ten colleges would have closed. (In fact there were 12 closures, whilst others amalgamated. Eight colleges survived)

Two months later, Wiltshire Education Authority received a letter from the Department of Education and Science (DES), saying that 'consideration should be given to the possibility of the College merging with King Alfred's College of Education, Winchester'.

A Possible Merger

The Church of England Board of Education supported the idea of amalgamation. During 1975 negotiations took place between the two colleges. Mr Wright and Mr Say, former lecturers at the College of Sarum St Michael, were able to access archives many years later, and look at documents that help to explain why this merger never went ahead. There would appear to have been three main issues that led to the breakdown of negotiations.

- The first issue concerned ownership of the College of Sarum St Michael buildings. If the colleges merged, but the Sarum campus subsequently closed, would the buildings then be lost to Salisbury for ever?

- °The second issue concerned representation on

The Staff Common Room
Dr Ian Smith

A typical student's room in the 1970s

the joint governing body of the merged institution. Winchester, the larger college, argued for a ratio of three to two in favour of King Alfred's.

• The third 'sticking point' was the question of senior appointments. It had been agreed that the Principal of King Alfred's should be Principal of the joint college. Both parties would have agreed to a Vice Principal on each campus, but this was not sanctioned by the DES. King Alfred's then proposed that at Salisbury there should be the posts of Warden and Deputy Warden. The Vice Principal would have been at King Alfred's, thus making the post of Warden at Salisbury third in the hierarchy.

At this point, negotiations broke down. The Governing Body was not convinced that the merger would do other than see the College absorbed into King Alfred's. Gloomy predictions from the DES forecast a sharp reduction in

the number of places to be offered to Church Colleges. Closures were inevitable. On October 30th 1975, the Church of England Board of Education recommended the closure of the College of Sarum St Michael.

Would Salisbury have had a viable future in a merged institution? There were certainly grounds to think that a merger might have simply been a staging post on the way to eventual closure. Mr Pain, Head of Education at this time, thought that Salisbury would have always been the poor relation. He remarked wryly that 'Death was better than strangulation'.

Mr Wright and Mr Say finished by saying that there was still much that remained a puzzling dilemma. The article, 'The Merger Revisited', concluded with L. P. Hartley's sapient comment: 'The past is another country: they do things differently there'. (CSSM Newsletter, 2009)

Save Our College!

Miss Hughes wrote in *The Last Ten Years* that 'the bombshell that dropped in 1975 was a terrible blow to staff as well as students'.

No-one could believe that College would really be closed down, and there were numerous attempts to change the decision.

'The Governors first asked the Church Board of Education to reconsider the decision and then appealed to the Secretary of State. A deputation, led by the Bishop of Salisbury, together with Governors and four MPs met the Minister to state the case of the College.

'The students organised a silent protest march through Salisbury to meet the Mayor on the steps of the Guildhall and to hand him a letter of protest. The march was organised by the President of the Students' Union, Enid Howie, and was a most moving protest. The students, mostly wearing their College scarves and navy and white College sweaters, walked in complete silence. Two men students carried the carved wooden board bearing the College motto – 'In Quietness and in Confidence shall be your Strength'. They met the Mayor and appealed for his support. If anything could have shown the quality of the College, it was this dignified action by the students'

LST ibid.

Student Protest in the Market Square
Courtesy of The Salisbury Museum

Many letters were written to the Department of Education, the Local Education Authority, the local Member of Parliament and the Church of England Board of Education. There were several desperate efforts to explore other possible intakes of students; for adult education, nursing training or from overseas. One suggestion was to open 'a prestigious language and cultural centre for students from Kuwait'. Approaches were also made to colleges and universities in the USA and Canada.

'Despite these efforts, on February 24th 1976 the Principal announced to the Academic Board of the Governing Body that he had received a letter from the DES stating that the College would receive no further intake of students. This was final.

LST ibid

When the College closed in 1978, the furnishings, books and equipment were sold in a three day sale. The money was invested in the Sarum St Michael Educational Charity, which aims to support and promote the work that was originally done by the College. 'Its object is the advancement of education in accordance with the principles and doctrines of the Church of England'.

What happened to the staff when the College closed in 1978?

The closure of the College was an extremely anxious and challenging time for everyone who was employed by the College. Teachers who had assumed that they were in safe jobs for their working lives were confronted by another side of life.

'A modest proportion of academic staff got other jobs. Those over the age of 55 were granted relatively generous redundancy terms under the Crombie Code, and took early retirement. Those aged under 55 received less generous terms and were thrown onto a job market where few comparable posts were available. Some never worked again in full-time employment'.   CSSM Newsletter 2009

Several members of staff took courses of study and retraining just before or after the closure, and subsequently entered different fields of work.

Staff Procession at the final Service of Thanksgiving

The College of Sarum St Michael

Dr Ian Smith

June 25th 1978

'Oh, the pity of it'

'July 1978 rang down the curtain on 137 years of work in Sarum St Michael, the oldest residential teacher training college for women in the country. Protest marches, letters to the press, a meeting with the local MP, a visit by the Dean and the Bishop to the Department of Education and Science were all completely unavailing: the College must close.

The staff were never given any reason why it had to close, but when asked for explanation, were merely told that there were 'complicated legal reasons' why the merger with Winchester could not go forward, though we never learned what the reasons were. The closure was purely an administrative decision. Officials of the DES were not the least interested in our traditions, the excellence of our work in training so many generations of teachers, and our superb site, probably the best and most beautiful of all training college sites in the country.

We can be proud that our standards, both academic and professional, remained high to the end: many old students from different eras have testified to the fine teaching which they received at Salisbury. Ironically, there were more 'first choice' applications for Sarum St Michael than ever before for 1976, but, because of DES policy, these students never came.

The overwhelming sadness that the ending of nearly a century and a half of life, work and culture engendered can only be imagined. Rather than dwell on this I will sum up in the pithy assessment of Dr Martial Rose, Principal of King Alfred's, Winchester in his book on the history of that College, 'Oh, the pity of it'.

John Say

Reflection and Thanksgiving

'It was with mixed emotions that some two thousand people from all over the country, including the Channel Islands, and even from Canada, gathered in Salisbury on June 25th 1978 to celebrate the life of The College of Sarum St Michael. The Chapel bell rang out for the last time, but the final toll was not one of sadness, for it was a summons to us all – students and staff, past and present, to gather in the Cathedral for the wonderful Service of Thanksgiving for the life and work of a Christian college'.

CSSM Chronicle, 1978

A long academic procession, including present and former members of staff, the College Council, representatives from Southampton University and the Department of Education and Science made an impressive sight as they processed from the Old Deanery to the West Door of the Cathedral in brilliant sunshine.

Mozart's anthem, *Ave Verum corpus natum de Maria Virgine* was sung at the service, recalling the Dedication of the Cathedral. The privilege of living and working in the shadow of the Cathedral was recognised by staff and students alike. Amidst the ever changing scenes and fortunes of life, The College in The Close had lived out its days in a place that was filled with a sense of deep spirituality and historical permanence. There were tears and there was sadness, but, in the words of Miss Sanderson-Taylor, 'there was also great dignity, as became a Church College which had trained teachers for 137 years. It came to an end without losing the identity which was so important to all those connected with it'.

The Rt Revd George Reindorp, Bishop of Salisbury, reflected in his sermon on the history of the College and on the importance of Christian education. He ended with reference to Pilgrim's Progress by John Bunyan, using the conversation between the Evangelist and Christian to encourage those saddened by what had happened to look ahead to the future.

'Dost thou see yonder shining light'?
'I think I do'.
'Keep yonder shining light in thine eye and approach directly thereto …'
'And I saw in my dream that the man began to run'.

Later in the weekend four former students met in the quiet of the evening at Old Sarum for a supper picnic. One of them later recalled:

It was almost deserted as we walked around the ramparts and remembered sitting there on hot Saturday afternoons, watching the gliders take off from the airfield. We remembered too the Shakespeare productions in the Castle on summer evenings – how the mosquitoes had bitten! As we walked, the Infant teacher among us gathered wild flowers for her Nature Table on Monday, and was teased by the rest of us. After sharing supper in the long June twilight, we went to have a final look at the view. As the first one reached the top she called, "Oh look, the Cathedral is floodlit!" and as the rest of us scrambled up the bank behind her to see, the words quoted by the Bishop that afternoon came back, "Do you not see yonder light?"

The College Lives On

'The presence of The College in The Close is but an episode in the long history of the spiritual character of the Cathedral precincts. However, the College carried the spiritual character far into the nation and the world through the teachers trained there'.

Lucy Sanderson Taylor, *The College in The Close*

What made this College so special? Why do hundreds of former students return every year? The Old Students' Association continues to thrive in 2015, 37 years after the College closed. The Cathedral is packed for the annual reunion service. What a powerful testimony to the quality of experience and teacher education that was provided in Salisbury!

Frances Boo Townsend (1954-1956) commented on the annual service: 'It is a moving experience to participate in a service where several generations of students are represented, all remaining faithful to a college that no longer exists except in their memories, but whose influence has been carried all over the world'.

The pioneering community work that was started by Clara Grant (1886-1888) over a hundred years ago, still carries on today at the Fern Street Settlement in Bow. The Settlement recently received Lottery funding and a Nursery School is due to open.

Former students and staff remain committed to their chosen vocation and contribute to education in its widest sense all over the world. They work as teachers, advisors and governors in schools and colleges, as well as with children and adults in churches, clubs, museums, prisons, hospitals, missions and charities. Three current teachers reflected on how the College ethos still underlies their work:

'I frequently look back to my own time as a pupil to guide me. I have always valued the support and recognition given to me and I was incredibly lucky to be part of a community which was a living legacy of the College'.

'The College beliefs and ethos still drive us forward and the resounding message of our 1970 education lectures that 'every child is unique; every child has the talent to succeed' is something that I try to keep at the heart of all we do'.

'The College motto, "In Quietness and in Confidence shall be your Strength", remains as relevant to me now as it was 35 years ago'.

College buildings are still in use today. King's House maintains a fine tradition of education and outreach in the Salisbury Museum. Young voices fill the air. Sounds of chatter and laughter buzz around 'The Quiet Room', now the King's House Café. The Medieval Hall continues the musical tradition with regular concerts. The former College Chapel is used for lectures, but remains a place of peace, memories and quiet reflection.

Writing and producing this story has been a fascinating journey. Following the lives of staff and students against a background of ever changing educational ideas and practice, and setting their story in the context of local history has been a privilege, a reward and an inspiration to us both.

'In Quietness and in Confidence shall be your Strength'.

Index